y.ya out
v/c

THE CHRISTIAN MINISTER
AND HIS DUTIES

THE
CHRISTIAN MINISTER
AND HIS DUTIES

BY

J. OSWALD DYKES, M.A., D.D.

PRINCIPAL EMERITUS OF WESTMINSTER COLLEGE, CAMBRIDGE

EDINBURGH: T. & T. CLARK, 38 GEORGE STREET

1908

Printed by
MORRISON & GIBB LIMITED

FOR

T. & T. CLARK, EDINBURGH

LONDON: SIMPKIN, MARSHALL, HAMILTON, KENT, AND CO. LIMITED
NEW YORK: CHARLES SCRIBNER'S SONS

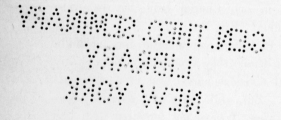

PREFACE

IF a ministry of close on fifty years, during about a score of which it was my duty to lecture to Students of Divinity on their future work, do not plead an apology for the following pages, I fear I have no better one to offer. They would never have seen the light but for the repeatedly expressed desire of former students.

In their preparation for the press I have aimed less at the formal completeness of a scientific treatise than at practical utility. I have tried to keep in mind the actual requirements of candidates for sacred office and of the junior clergy, not in one Church only, but in every evangelical communion. For the duties of a Christian Minister are in all Protestant communities fundamentally the same. Even in details they approximate more closely than our superficial divisions might lead us, on a casual survey, to perceive. But, while keeping present-day conditions steadily in view, I have not forgotten that, like every other theological discipline, Practical Theology must draw its guiding principles from the New Testament, and derive illustration from its own past in the Christian centuries.

Without curtailing the two departments of a Minister's office which, under the names of Homiletics and Pastoral Theology, occupy the bulk of most text-books on the subject, it will be found that more space than is usual in English works of this class has been given to the conduct of public worship—a duty which in every non-liturgical service lays such a heavy demand on the officiating Minister.

The function of a Church Ruler has been omitted, because the Minister's share in the administration of ecclesiastical affairs and in the exercise of discipline varies so much with each separate Church organisation that no treatment of it could find general application.

I owe cordial thanks to the Rev. Dr. John Kelman of Edinburgh for kindly revising these sheets in MS., and favouring me with suggestions of which I have frequently availed myself.

CONTENTS

PART I

THE MODERN MINISTER

CHAP.   PAGE

I. OFFICIAL AND NON-OFFICIAL MINISTRY . . . 1

II. THE MINISTRY NOT A PRIESTHOOD . . . 10

III. LESSONS FROM THE NEW TESTAMENT . . . 20

IV. THE CALL TO THE MINISTRY 30

V. THE MINISTER'S DEVOTIONAL LIFE . . . 43

VI. MINISTERIAL CHARACTER 51

VII. MINISTERIAL MANNERS 57

VIII. HOME LIFE 66

IX. CITIZENSHIP 77

PART II

THE MINISTER AS LEADER IN WORSHIP

X. THEORY OF CHRISTIAN WORSHIP 88

XI. WORSHIP IN THE CHURCH OF THE FIRST CENTURY . 101

XII. SIXTEENTH CENTURY REFORMS IN WORSHIP . . 114

XIII. ORDER OF WEEKLY WORSHIP 126

XIV. SACRAMENTAL SERVICES 149

XV. WEEK-DAY SERVICES 171

PART III

THE MINISTER AS PREACHER

XVI. WHAT IS PREACHING? 180

XVII. PASTORAL PREACHING : I. 188

CONTENTS

CHAP.		PAGE
XVIII.	Pastoral Preaching : II.	204
XIX.	Evangelistic Preaching	216
XX.	Preparing to Preach : Choice of a Text	228
XXI.	Preparing to Preach : Plan of the Sermon	239
XXII.	Diction and Delivery	264
XXIII.	Preparation of the Preacher	282

PART IV

THE MINISTER AS PASTOR

XXIV.	The Care of Souls	300
XXV.	Household Visitation	310
XXVI.	The Sick and the Bereaved	321
XXVII.	The Care of the Young	333
XXVIII.	Cases of Spiritual Trouble	351

INDEX 367

PART I

THE MODERN MINISTER

CHAPTER I

OFFICIAL AND NON-OFFICIAL MINISTRY

THE official familiar to the modern Churches under a variety
of titles, as pastor, priest, clergyman, parson or minister, is
a functionary who had no exact equivalent in the age of
the apostles. It is true that we know little of the arrangements which obtained in many of those groups of converts,
Hebrew or Greek, which were gathered by the labours of
apostolic missionaries in the first century. We are dependent on casual allusions in the few extant letters
addressed to them by their founders, or in the Book of
Acts. But the ordained officers mentioned there differed
in a number of important respects from the modern
ministry. Leaving out of view those younger officers
called " deacons," our knowledge of whose functions is too
slight to found conclusions upon, the closest analogue to a
modern minister must be found in the presbyter-bishop—a
class of officials selected from the membership of a church
or congregation for their age, gravity or experience, to
whom was entrusted a general superintendence of the
religious welfare of the brotherhood. The earliest mention of them is in the Mother Church of Jerusalem, under
the Jewish title of Presbyters or "Elders." [1] The only

[1] Acts 11[30].

I

Churches on Greek soil in which we learn from our sources
that under the missionary ministry of St. Paul presbyter-
bishops were ordained, are the newly-founded communities
in Southern Galatia (*circa* 49), the Church at Ephesus
(*c*. 58), and that of Philippi (*c*. 62 or 63). At a later
date Titus was instructed to appoint them also in Crete.[1]
But they are not named in Paul's letters to Thessalonica,
or to Corinth, or to Rome ; that is, not in any letter of his
of earlier date than his Roman imprisonment. Are we to
infer, as Baur did in the case of Corinth particularly, that
no such office then existed in those great Churches ? Such
an inference *e silentio* would be a precarious one. Nevertheless, it is a mistake to assume, as disputants on Church
polity used commonly to do, that there was a uniform
organisation in the apostolic Churches, which prevailed
over the whole field as well as over the whole half century
covered by our New Testament documents. It seems
pretty clear, on the contrary, not only that a certain
development in Church organisation must be recognised
within the apostolic period, but also that different arrangements obtained simultaneously in different places. But
even if presbyter-bishops were everywhere appointed, they
were far from monopolising every form of congregational
ministry as they practically do to-day. The earlier letters
of St. Paul speak much of freewill services rendered by
groups of exceptionally gifted members, who were not set
apart as permanent officials. They are found not only in
Churches where, as in Corinth, we hear nothing of presbyters,
but also, as at Ephesus, where we are sure presbyters
existed. No fewer than nine forms of such "charismatic"
ministration are named in a single passage of St. Paul's
First Letter to Corinth as exercised alongside each other,
and exercised by different persons variously gifted.[2] Four
or five on the list must have ceased with the cessation of
supernatural powers. Such as survive, with others as well,
have now fallen, mainly, if not exclusively, into the hands

[1] Acts 14²³, 20¹⁷, Phil. 1¹, 1 Tim. 3¹, Tit. 1⁵.   [2] 1 Cor. 12⁸⁻¹¹.

of the regular ordained ministry. It may be that the modern minister is now the nearest representative of the primitive presbyter, otherwise called "bishop." He may even be the historical descendant, by unbroken succession, of that order. But his office covers at least a much wider range of duties. There is no evidence that either the conduct of public worship or the delivery of religious discourses formed at first any part of the official duty of a presbyter-bishop. Their function, wherever found, is described as one of oversight or superintendence : and they may very well have acted as a moderating force on the excesses of enthusiasm. For no great religion ever bursts, new and aggressive, upon the world, to win rapid success, that is not inspired with enthusiastic ardour for the faith it preaches. And in the primitive fervour of Christianity, it was by apostles and prophets that the faith was preached. In the first age, as in every age, conspicuous gifts of impressive speech secured for their possessors an influence both wide and deep; and in the first age, more than in subsequent ones, all might speak, provided only they possessed the gift.

The arrangement, one sees, was of a temporary character, suited to the formative age of the new society. Fairly soon it passed away ; but it is no longer possible to trace the steps by which the services of these gifted volunteers were superseded, until every function needed for the life of a Christian community came to be lodged in official hands. We probably detect some of the earliest signs of change in the Pastoral Epistles ; for example, in the special "honour" bestowed on elders who were also competent to "labour in the Word and in teaching,"[1] and generally in the increased importance attached by these late documents to ordained officers. Whatever be their date, a stage had by that time been reached when the Church could trust less than at first to impromptu enthusiasm, and when the need for a "form of sound

[1] 1 Tim. 5[17].

doctrine" was more keenly felt. It is possible, I think, that in places where the Greek element preponderated and the Greek democratic spirit was strong, some Churches may have retained for a longer period than elsewhere a preference for free and spontaneous services by private members. And the *Didache* is evidence that in a very different part of Christendom, among obscure country churches of Hebrew origin where presbyters were ordinarily in charge, itinerant preachers, "prophets and apostles," still enjoyed exceptional privileges. At the same time, it shows, by precautions taken against the abuse of these high titles, that the palmy days of the "charismatic" ministry were over.[1] The process of transition must have stretched over more than a single generation; and the Montanist movement in the second century, while it meant much more, probably indicates that the primitive system died hard. It was part of the Montanist reaction against change to "reassert," in Hatch's words, "the place of spiritual gifts as contrasted with official rule."[2] The very failure of that reaction no doubt helped to consolidate the power of the official classes in the Church; but probably a more effective cause was the rapid spread of sacramentarian and sacerdotal ideas. By investing the clergy with the mysterious prerogatives of a priestly caste, and making them indispensable channels of saving grace, this secured to them a monopoly of spiritual functions and fastened on the Ancient Catholic Church the yoke of clerical ascendency.

But although, in some later periods of her history, the ministration of non-official members of the Church almost ceased, they have been again and again in various forms revived. The Roman Church itself has known how to utilise such freewill services outside her regular priesthood, by enrolling many groups of devoted servants of Christ, both male and female, who, to the vast enrichment of

---

[1] *Didache*, c. xi. ; cf. Hermas, *Sim.* ix. 25 ; *Mand.* xi.
[2] *Organisation of Early Christian Churches*, 1881, p. 120.

her life, have given themselves to specific forms of
Christian work, philanthropic or educational. The recent
growth in Protestant lands of similar "charismatic"
agencies has begun to force upon our own Churches a
similar problem. The days are past when every detail
in the ecclesiastical life of a parish, every part of the
Church's ministry to the poor or the irreligious, could
be left to the ordained clergy. Lay readers, evangelists,
Bible-women, and city missionaries are doing the Church's
work, though as yet they receive for the most part no
ordination nor possess any defined standing among her
ministers. Already the visitation of the sick poor by
Christian women has been formally recognised in sister-
hoods of Deaconesses; the Church Army, like the Salvation Army, marks an effort to organise aggressive
home-mission operations; and it may not be very long
before the vast array of Sunday-school teachers in England
and America will claim, or, if they do not claim, will
receive, a quasi-official status. In fact, the present
tendency of Church life runs towards the multiplication
of what are called "lay agencies." Should these be kept,
as it is desirable to keep them, in close association with
the Church, the result must be to make the "Minister"
more and more, what he already is in many places, the
organising and inspiring Head of a staff of active, though
unpaid and unofficial, workers for the Kingdom of God.
In the meantime, the ordained Ministry has long ago
annexed, and seems likely long to retain, as its exclusive
sphere, certain other essential departments of Church work,
especially in connection with public worship, which were
originally distributed amongst private members gifted
for their discharge.

Nor is this widening of his official duties the only
thing which distinguishes a modern minister of religion
from any officer known to the apostolic Churches. The
primitive "presbyter" was selected in mature life from
the ranks of the local congregation over whose interests

he was appointed to watch. He received no special training to fit him for so responsible a post; nor did his office in all likelihood entail the abandonment of his ordinary secular avocation. In these respects he closely resembled a Presbyterian " elder " of the present day, or the " deacon " in a Congregational church. It is very different with the modern " minister." In nearly every communion, certainly in the older and the national Churches, he has devoted himself, usually in early manhood, to the service of the larger body, of which the local congregation where his work lies forms only a small part. He has been, as a rule, required to prepare himself for his life-work by a long, expensive, and scholarly education. In most cases he is ineligible for the care of a parish or of a congregation until the entire Church which he aspires to serve has satisfied itself of his qualifications by repeated examination of his gifts or attainments, spiritual and intellectual, and has put upon him its own *imprimatur*. None of these things could have been said of any official mentioned in the New Testament. Practically, therefore, our present-day ministry, Protestant and Catholic alike, represent a type to which the apostolic Church offered no very close parallel.

It is, of course, a perfectly fair question, on which opinions may reasonably differ, whether this concentration of functions in the same official hands has not gone too far for the best interests of the Christian Brotherhood. Two modern forms of ecclesiastical life in this country have answered the question by reverting to primitive usage, leaving free room, especially in worship, for voluntary ministrations by private members. The Society of Friends bases its freedom in worship, as is well known, upon the worshipper's dependence on an immediate inspiration from the Holy Spirit, which is supposed to render every form of *cultus* or prearranged channel for the Spirit's action superfluous or worse.[1] This, however,

[1] Cf. Barclay, *Apology*, x. and xi.

does not exclude officialism in every shape. "Elders,"
whose duty it is to watch over the young and care for
the poor, have long been in existence in the Society.
And although no one is educated for the office of preacher
or ordained to such a ministry, yet such members as have
long proved their possession of gifts for edification may
receive from their brethren some sort of recognition or
approval.[1] It is one thing to widen in this way to the
utmost the liberty of private members in the exercise
of their gifts, or, in other words, to reduce the number
of functions reserved for officials, at the risk even of
exaggerating the fortuitous or incalculable element in the
Holy Spirit's action to the neglect of His ordinary methods.
It is a different thing to object on principle to the existence of office-bearers in the Christian Society altogether.
Where such an extreme position, is taken up, as it is
supposed to be by the "Brethren,"[2] the defender of
ecclesiastical office has two lines of defence open to him.

The one is to show that from the nature of the case,
specialisation of functions in the hands of a special class of
Church members is necessary, if not for the preservation,
at least for the order and effectiveness of the body. As a
mere protest against certain types of hard and fast officialism, repressing free activity in Church life, the reaction of
"Plymouthism" in last century was intelligible and may
have been useful. But all life tends to organise itself.
Every community needs to perform certain common
acts through organs set apart for such service. And the
Christian Society, being subject to the same conditions as

---

[1] "We do believe and affirm that some are more particularly called to
the work of the ministry, and therefore are fitted of the Lord for that
purpose ; whose work is more constantly and particularly to instruct,
exhort, admonish, oversee, and watch over their brethren" (*Apology*, x. § 26).
What Barclay chiefly objects to is the limitation of the ministry to such
as have been expressly educated for it in languages and philosophy.

[2] I am not sure that in some churches of the "Brethren," an informal
ministry is not conceded, as among the "Friends," to certain qualified
members.

other societies, could not do otherwise. It may be going too far to say with Hüffell [1] that, without a ministry of the Word, Christian life would have expired within a couple of centuries. At least the unequal distribution of gifts constituted from the first what Nitzsch [2] calls a " natural or native clergy." And even if our Lord and His Apostles had launched the Church into existence quite amorphous or inorganic, as a loose aggregate of individuals, with none to lead and none to be led, it is quite certain that it would have early addressed itself to the task of self-organisation.

But it is easy to show, in the next place, that it was not so launched into being. From its first day, it had its leaders in the Twelve. One of the earliest acts of the Mother Church taken on their initiative was the ordination of " the Seven " to serve tables : a special organ developed to do a special function. In the same Mother Church under the eye of the Twelve we soon read of " Elders." And the first missionary to the Gentiles on his first mission tour " appointed elders in every Church." If the question be put : Did Jesus institute a permanent office in His Church ? the answer must be : By immediate personal appointment—no ; for in that way what He instituted was the Apostolate, which was not permanent. But, through indirect utterance of His will—yes ; and that in various ways. First, by the bestowal of gifted servants fitted for office ; next, through the Apostles as His plenipotentiaries, when they ordained such persons to an office designed to be permanent ; and, lastly, by the results which have ever since sealed the institution. Hence St. Paul does not scruple to speak of the original office-bearers at Ephesus as given and appointed by the Lord Himself.[3] If it be further asked : Has the modern office of the Ministry been in this sense instituted by Christ ? I conceive the answer must be : In its present form, not, in so far as the precise shape it has assumed in different communities is due to the

[1] *Wesen und Beruf des Evang. Geistlichen* (4 Aufl. 1843).
[2] *Praktische Theologie*, 1847–1867, i. 16.   [3] Eph. 4[11], Acts 20[28].

exigencies of modern need met by the discretion of the Church herself. But, in respect of its essence—yes; inasmuch as the place and functions of the Ministry among us do not essentially differ, though they differ in details, from those of the overseers whom Paul in Christ's name set up at Iconium, Ephesus, Philippi and Crete. Fresh duties have been imposed, particularly the conduct of congregational worship. Special care has been taken to secure a steady supply of qualified men. They are become the agents of a larger body than the Christians of a single city. And they receive a salary, that they may devote themselves entirely to their work. But none of these changes, though important, touches the essence of office. That remains what it began by being amongst the earliest converts :—the oversight of the flock of God. They tend, they feed, they watch for, they rule, the charge allotted to them, and are examples to their brethren, exactly like those faithful men of the first Christian generation to whom St. Paul wrote, or St. Peter, or the author of the Epistle to the Hebrews.[1]

[1] Cf. 1 Pet. 5[2, 3], Acts 20[28-31], 1 Tim. 5[17], Heb. 13[17].

CHAPTER II

THE MINISTRY NOT A PRIESTHOOD

OUR conception of office in the Christian Church will be determined by the view we take of the nature of the Church itself; so that, as two very different theories of the Church obtain in Christendom, there have arisen two contrasted ways of regarding ecclesiastical officers.

Those who accept the Catholic doctrine of the Church as an institution endowed by its Head with power to convey to men His saving grace through the administration of sacramental rites, necessarily regard the clergy, by whose hands alone those rites can be administered, as invested by Christ Himself with this ministry of mediation. On this theory, the ministry becomes a mediating priesthood, occupying, as the indispensable channels of salvation, an intermediate place between the laity and their Lord. And the act which ordains to office, when legitimately performed, is supposed to convey this exclusive right and power to mediate grace, by an unbroken transmission of it from Christ Himself through His Apostles and their episcopal successors.

Against this idea of a mediating priesthood, every Protestant communion, Lutheran and Reformed alike, is in vehement protest; the best of the Anglican High Churchmen as emphatically as any.[1] In that sense, we are all agreed that there is but one unique and perfect Mediator

---

[1] Cf. Moberly, *Ministerial Priesthood*; Gore, *The Church and its Ministry*; Liddon, *University Sermons* (2nd Series); *Different Conceptions of Priesthood and Sacrifice*: *Report of a Conference*, edited by Sanday.

and High Priest, who, having by Himself purged our sins and passed through the heavens, presents for ever before the throne His one atoning sacrifice, and by His intercession procures for all His people the saving grace of the Holy Spirit. This leaves neither need nor room for any other to stand between the soul and God, or to open for any man the way to peace. For through His effectual mediation, we all enjoy the same free access into the Holy Presence, and for our persons and our offerings the same gracious acceptance.

The conception of the Church to which this leads, and which we believe to be both scriptural and primitive, is that of a priestly Brotherhood of spiritual equals. It makes every believer a priest, not in the Levitical sense of one who has an exclusive privilege of access to God and therefore can offer sacrifices on behalf of others, but in the wider meaning of one who has for himself direct access as a worshipper to the Divine Presence. The united Church is at once a community of such priests and a priestly community. But, of course, it is so solely in virtue of its union with Christ, brought near to God in Him, and privileged to share His access to the Holy Place.

The emphasis, it is obvious, is laid by Protestantism no longer on the ministry, as distinguished from the laity, but on the entire membership of the Church. As a visible society, the Church has been by the will of its Founder organised to be His instrument for a double purpose : for self-edification through the development of Christ-like character in its members, and for self-propagation throughout the world. To this whole Body there have been given for the attainment of both these ends, the Word of God and the sacramental means of grace. These are the specific means by which the Spirit of Christ operates age after age in the work of the Kingdom of God.

It is the common belief of the Protestant Churches that Christ has likewise conferred upon His Church a permanent ministry to be her stated organ for the effective proclamation of His Word and the valid administration of His sacraments. But if certain functions, expressive of the common life of the Church and required for her common work, come in this way to be ordinarily restricted to such official members, that is merely for the sake of their more orderly, constant, and efficient discharge. The motive for office is that the ends of the Church's existence may be the better secured. The qualification for office is exceptional ability to secure these ends, conferred by Christ upon certain chosen members. But essentially and fundamentally, the work remains that of the whole Society. For its prosecution the entire membership is jointly and severally responsible : each Christian being under law to Christ to exercise in His service and for His ends such gifts as he has received from the Divine Head.

What we reach along this line as the Protestant theory of Church office is that ministers are representative organs of the Brotherhood, through whom its public and organised activities can be carried on. The fact that certain functions have been so strictly assigned to officers set apart for their more orderly and effective performance, that ordinarily they are never discharged by any private member, is to be explained simply on the principle that when any community engages in common acts, someone must act for it, in its name, and authorised by its mandate. This lays on him no doubt a special responsibility. It even confers on him a certain privilege. But it does not mean in every case, perhaps need not in any case, that all the other members in the body are excluded from exercising in more private and occasional ways services of a similar character for which they too are qualified by their gifts.

For example : we have seen that a general oversight of the flock resident in a given locality was very early entrusted, at least in some cases, to local officers set apart for the purpose under the title of " seniors," or " overseers " ; but it still remained the right and even the duty of a private Christian to watch over the religious well-being of his brother, and, upon occasion, to counsel, or to admonish, him.[1] In the same way, the modern restriction of preaching in congregational worship to men trained and appointed to that office, by no means implies, either that other Christian men are not also taught of God by the "anointing from the Holy One"; or that they have not liberty, if qualified, to proclaim at fit seasons the way of salvation; or that room and opportunity ought not to be made for what is termed "lay-preaching," so that much ampler use may be made than at present of all the ability which God giveth.   Of all Church acts, the administration of a sacrament is that which for obvious reasons has most need to be, and has been, limited to authorised persons.   Yet so far does the inherent right of private members extend, to fulfil in case of urgency the most jealously guarded offices of religion, and so widely has it been by implication recognised, that a right to baptize *in articulo mortis*, and where no priest is available, is conceded by the most ritualistic of all Churches not only to laymen, but even to women.   Were it conceivable that at any time the succession of duly ordained ministers could be wholly interrupted and fail, it follows from the Reformed doctrine of the Church that the duty of providing for the discharge of every indispensable function of Church life would devolve on the united membership. The Church lives on, officers or none.   The King's work must be done; and men gifted by Him for the doing of it can never fail.

At first sight it might appear as if the change at the Reformation from Catholic priests to Protestant pastors had been for the Ministry a serious descent in influence or in dignity.   In proportion as the laity recovered spiritual independence and religious privilege, in that proportion did the clergy seem to suffer loss of position.   They lost their sacrosanct character.   They ceased to be indispensable to the very being of the Church.   They no longer occupied an elevation above the flock and nearer God.   They came

---

[1] Cf. 1 Thess. 5[11, 14], 2 Thess. 3[15], Rom. 15[14], Col. 3[16].

to stand on the level of the people as their spiritual equals. And their office exhausted itself in ministering to the people's wants.

I question, however, if, as a matter of history, the Protestant ministry has suffered either in usefulness or in esteem. For one thing, it still retains in the belief of the faithful the weight which attaches to a Divine sanction. Christ's original gift of ministers to His Church is felt by us to cover the office of a present-day presbyter—not to say, the bishop in Episcopal communions—quite as truly at least as it has ever applied to Roman priests; all the more truly in so far as they more closely reproduce the apostolic " elder " or " bishop." Not only so : there has not even occurred any material breach in the transmission of office from one generation to the next. Such an unbroken succession is hard to prove in detail, and does not possess in the eyes of most Protestants the consequence which High Churchmen assign to it. But at least it is a valuable witness to the continuity of the Church's life. It serves for all of us as a precious link with the apostolic age ; and it transmits to each new generation of ministers the inheritance of a long and honourable ancestry. At the Reformation no sudden or widespread hiatus occurred. There was on the whole a transmission of office. Many of the first presbyters and bishops in the Reformed Churches had been in orders before the change. They took part in the ordination of their successors. And whatever be the value of transmission of orders, continuity has ever since been maintained with as much security in Presbyterian as in Episcopal communions.

But what gave to the post-Reformation ministry its real power and dignity was this, that it was a ministry of the Word of God. It has been usual to say that under the new era the pulpit took the central place previously assigned to the altar. No doubt, preaching did become the chief method employed by the Reformed for bringing the Word of God to bear on the consciences and hearts of

men. But, in truth, every part of the ministerial calling,
not the pulpit alone, was regarded as an application of the
Word of God, and as deriving from that Gospel Word its
value and its efficacy. As a pastor of souls, the minister's
instrument was still the same. If he catechised, the
religious instruction of the young was instruction in
revealed truth. Even the sacraments held an ancillary
position as signs to set forth, and seals to confirm to faith,
the Gospel Word of promise.

It is this prominence assigned to the Word of God,
spoken as well as written, as the one great instrument
given to the Church for the begetting and for the training
of Christian life in the soul, which enables us to appreciate
the position ever since accorded to Ministers in the
Churches of the Reformation. This, and this alone,
accounts for the note of authority which has characterised
their utterances. As authorised exponents and proclaimers
of the Divine Word, they have been clothed with something of its own authority. Not with the authority of the
Church merely, as holding a mandate from it, but with
the authority of God whose Word is on their lips. In
Calvinistic Churches, the usual title of their officers has
been neither pastor nor priest, but "Minister of the Word."
And their traditional arrangements for ministerial education
have been modelled on the same conception of office. A
careful training in the original languages of Holy Scripture
and in the theology of the Confessions, is designed to fit
the future minister before everything else for the exposition,
both in the pulpit and out of it, of the Bible and of the
truths which it is believed to contain. The very omissions
to be noted in the usual divinity curriculum of these
Churches find the same explanation. For instance : that
the minister is to be a pastor of souls has been constantly
recognised ; yet it has not been customary to subject him
to much separate training for that portion of his task.
Still less has it been deemed necessary to familiarise him
in his student days with questions of Christian ethics, or

with cases of conscience, as in a Roman seminary for priests. Still more noticeable is the neglect of any proper preparation of future ministers for the conduct of divine service. In Churches of the Protestant faith where forms of prayer are prescribed, some previous instruction in the use of the prayer-book is usual, although here it might more easily be dispensed with. But where everything is left, as in Congregational or modern Presbyterian worship, to the minister as sole leader, his training for this high function has been notoriously and unaccountably neglected. Nor has even catechetics, or the art of teaching the young, entered into the education of a Presbyterian minister as it does into that of a Lutheran *Pfarrer*; in spite of the fact that the Reformed have never been behind their Lutheran brethren in providing catechisms as aids for the instruction of their children. It may be that too much attention has not been devoted by the Reformed Churches to theology and the sacred languages, but at least it has been a too exclusive attention; and I can only account for the omission of other subjects by supposing that one who fully knew and could rightly teach the Word of God was presumed to be sufficiently equipped by that alone for an office, all whose varied functions centred in the interpretation and enforcement of that Word.

The legitimate authority with which ministers have been accustomed to speak as interpreters of the sacred text and stewards of Divine mysteries was for a long time, and to some extent still is, strengthened by the wide interval which for generations elevated the scholarly and expert minister above his untrained flock. Sometimes, it must be confessed, ministerial authority has been claimed, and has been conceded, too much on such personal grounds. It has rested more than is meet either on the minister's scholarship as a learned student whose dicta the illiterate are not qualified to question, or on his piety as one exceptionally taught of God. Hence it has not always been sufficiently remembered, either by the pastoral preacher or by his congregation, that however superior his gifts for edifying address may be, he is here also an organ and representative of the Christian society, bearing its testimony, as well as his own, to the common Christian faith, as that which is taught by the anointing Spirit to the humblest believer. For the better instruction of the people, to increase their knowledge of Scripture, to correct mistakes and clarify their conceptions of the Gospel, and to enforce the admitted duties of their Christian profession —for such ends has he been raised above his hearers in sacred learning. But that personal experience of the Gospel which alone can make his word living and powerful, is their experience as well; and the testimony which he bears to Christ is the united testimony of the witnessing Church in which dwells the Spirit of illumination.

If I mistake not, it is not in the sermon only, but likewise in other parts of Divine service where their representative character is more evident, that some ministers are apt to overlook it. When the collective Church assembles in one place to draw near to God, each worshipper makes approach for himself and has his own spiritual offering to present. Only a leader is required, a spokesman to voice the common acts of all. This is the minister, who is thereby made a representative, to whose words they all make response, if not audibly, yet, surely, in their hearts.

It is at this point that the question arises whether the leader in worship ought not to be, or at least may not legitimately be, described as a priest—not a mediating, but a representative, priest. For, of course, the universal priesthood of all believers as one with Christ, in the New Testament sense of the word, is to be fully recognised. Their acts of common worship are the " spiritual sacrifices " of what St. Peter calls a $\iota\epsilon\rho\acute{a}\tau\epsilon\upsilon\mu a$ $\acute{a}\gamma\iota o\nu$, a $\beta a\sigma\acute{\iota}\lambda\epsilon\iota o\nu$ $\iota\epsilon\rho\acute{a}\tau\epsilon\upsilon\mu a$.[1] " The sacrifices of God are a broken spirit," and this each penitent brings with him. The whole

[1] 1 Pet. 2⁴⁻¹⁰.

2

congregation join to "offer up a sacrifice of praise to God continually, that is, the fruit of lips which make confession to His name."[1]   Nor is it in the eucharist alone, but throughout the service, that they "present their bodies—themselves—a living sacrifice, holy and acceptable to God."[2]   But I do not think all this requires us to term the leader a priest in any exceptional sense.   For the sacrificial character inherent in the worship of Christian men pertains no more to the minister than to any other worshipper.   He is a priest, but not in virtue of his ministry.   When Anglican Churchmen, if Evangelicals, excuse, or, if High Churchmen, warmly applaud, the use in the rubrics of the Prayer Book of both terms as alternatives—"Minister" and "Priest"—they do it on the ground that he who represents and acts for a priestly community in its priestly acts may be styled in a certain eminent sense a priest.   As an apology this may be allowed to pass, but I cannot join in the applause.   Canon Moberly's definition: "ministerial organs of the Church's priesthood,"[3] we may accept without accepting his conclusions.   When regard is had to the history of the word "priest," and to its employment over the greater part of Christendom, the risk of confusion between the two senses in which it is taken—its Levitical and Roman use on the one hand, its New Testament connotation on the other—is so serious that those Churches of the Reformation have surely done more wisely which have dropped the misleading title altogether.   In this judgment, as Canon Moberly himself has told us,[4] some of the most judicious of Anglican divines have concurred.   Richard Hooker's words are well known: "To pass by the name, let them use what dialects they will, whether we call it a Priesthood, a Presbytership, or a Ministry, it skilleth not; although in truth the word Presbyter doth seem more fit, and

---

[1] Heb. 13[15].   [2] Rom. 12[1].
[3] *Report of Conference, ut supra*, p. 142.
[4] *Minist. Priesthood*, p. 238-239, footnotes.

in propriety of speech more agreeable than Priest with the
drift of the whole Gospel of Jesus Christ." [1]   And with
this the more recent language of the late Bishop Lightfoot is in accord : " It might have been better if the later
Christian vocabulary had conformed to the silence of the
Apostolic writers, so that the possibility of confusion would
have been avoided." [2]

[1] *Eccl. Polity*, Bk. v. lxxviii. 3.
[2] *Diss. on the Apostolic Age*, p. 235.

CHAPTER III

LESSONS FROM THE NEW TESTAMENT

THE fundamental ideas which govern service in the
kingdom of God, and even more the spirit in which it
is to be rendered, remain substantially the same at all
periods. The wise office-bearer of to-day will therefore
draw largely for direction, warning, or stimulus upon the
experience of the past. Biographies of eminent servants
of Christ in every age may serve as models; but in
especial the records preserved in Sacred Scripture were
written for his admonition. The example even of Old
Testament prophets, in spite of obvious differences, can
be made in many ways instructive. Their surrender
to a divine call, their public spirit, their watchman-like
vigilance, their courage, their loyalty to the truth as they
received it from God—have all been put to use by ingenious authors for the profit of the Christian minister.
But naturally the New Testament is richer both in lessons
and in examples apposite to his case. From the charge
which Jesus gave to the first messengers whom He sent
out into the villages of Galilee, down to St. Paul's
directions for the choice of elders at Ephesus or Crete,
its pages abound in material which has been worked out
by a host of writers on this subject, but which the
conscientious minister can best study for himself in its
original setting. Supreme over all is, of course, the
ministry of our blessed Lord Himself, who, both as a
religious teacher and as the Chief Shepherd and Bishop
of souls, set once for all the pattern which His servants

have to copy till the end of time. Next to this in value, though *longo intervallo*, must be put the autobiographic passages in the letters of His foremost follower, St. Paul. From these sources mainly, but indeed from the whole New Testament, endless guidance as well as inspiration comes to the minister who knows how to use it.[1]

That the present-day minister, by whatever title he is known, is virtually the only acting official in many of our Churches, and in all of them the one most in evidence, who unites in his single person almost every form of official activity, is the fact which justifies us in transferring to his work, under one or other of its departments, nearly every significant title or picturesque metaphor applied by sacred writers to Christian ministers of their own generation.[2] He combines the duties of an ambassador on Christ's behalf, of a steward over the house of God, of a bishop and shepherd of the flock, of a presiding elder and ruler, of a leader to animate, and of a pattern to be imitated.

In this collection of expressive terms, the foremost thought (as might be expected) is responsibility for the oversight of souls; although with that is blent, so that the two can hardly be kept apart, the further task of religious instruction. The idea of oversight comes out

[1] On the lessons to be learned from the example and directions both of our Lord and of His apostles, the student may consult Beck's *Pastoral Theology of the N. T.* (T. & T. Clark, 1885). On our Lord as an example, see Blaikie, *Public Ministry and Pastoral Methods of our Lord* (Lond. 1883); and cf. Bruce's *Training of the Twelve*, and Latham's *Pastor Pastorum*. Of St. Paul as a model, an old book is *The Portrait of St. Paul a true Model for Christians and Pastors* (1806), translated from a French MS. of Fletcher of Madingley. The more recent work of Canon Newbolt, *Speculum Sacerdotum* (1894), is based on 2 Cor. 6[4-10]. Dr. Stalker's Yale Lectures for 1891, *The Preacher and his Models*, draw lessons from Hebrew prophets and (in the last four lectures) from St. Paul. See also Fairbairn on *The Pastoral Epistles* (1874); Stirm, "Die Pastoral-theologischen Winke der Pastoral-briefe," in *Jahrb. f. deut. Theol.* B. 17; and Chadwick, *The Pastoral Teaching of St. Paul* (Lond. 1907).

[2] This was done long ago by Gilbert Burnet, bishop of Sarum, in his *Discourse of the Pastoral Care*; whom Vinet follows in his *Théologie Pastorale*.

best perhaps in the Greek ἐπίσκοπος, an officer whose
vigilance cannot be accused of meddlesomeness, because
it has been laid upon him to watch over, superintend,
and act for the community.   The same idea is suggested
by the historical associations of the Jewish title
"Presbyter" or "Elder"; but with this added suggestion,
that the authority of the official ought to be sustained
by such natural influence or power to lead as comes from
gravity, experience, and the wisdom of years.

Of wider compass is that lovely metaphor of Shepherd
or "Pastor"; for it embraces also instruction, or the
nurture of old and young on the pasture of the Word.
But its primary sense is still surveillance or tendance of the
flock, recovery of the strayed, defence in danger; before all
else, personal and self-sacrificing devotion to its safety,
with a peculiar tender flavour of belonging each to the
other—flock to shepherd, and shepherd to flock.   No other
word sends us so straight to Jesus as the model of our
office, or so dignifies our relation to His people by associat-
ing it with His own, or is steeped in more touching and
poetic associations.   We are the under-shepherds of the
one great and good Chief Shepherd.[1]

Next to shepherd comes Steward.   Rooted in Jesus'
own use of the word in this connection, it finds illustration
both from St. Paul and St. Peter.[2]   Like shepherd, it too
carries the same idea of responsible oversight; but its
special reference is probably to the provision of the household of God with supplies of divine truth out of the
storehouse of the Word.   Responsibility for what is taught
in God's house; for its abundance, variety, suitableness,
and purity :—this is what the modern minister of the Word
has to be for ever learning from this image.

---

[1] The full compass of this image is to be studied in Ps. 23 and the great
chapter in Ezek. 34 : next in our Lord's own exposition of it in John 10 ;
then in the restoration of St. Peter to office, John 21, which is illustrated
finally by Peter's own pathetic reference to the subject, 1 Pet. 5[1-4].

[2] See Luke 12[41-48], 1 Cor. 4[1-5], 1 Pet. 4[10].

It is less in his relation to those within the Church than to the world without that a minister, but especially an evangelist or missionary, inherits St. Paul's bold metaphor for himself and his brother missionaries : "Herald" or Ambassador of Peace, bearing abroad to men the divine Word of reconciliation.[1] But however much the pastoral side of one's office may under modern conditions preponderate in the field allotted to many of the clergy, there is no minister of Christ who will not find manifold occasion, as well as opportunity, to become a preacher of God's peace to the conscience ill at ease, or a herald of His grace to sinners yet unreconciled to God.

Each of these titles brings a contribution of its own towards a complete conception of ministerial work. When the variety no less than the difficulty of all these solemn duties is suffered to make its due impression on the mind, no one, I should think, can escape the feeling that too much has surely been laid by our modern system on the shoulders of one man. Where ecclesiastical arrangements permit of a division of functions, one is inclined to say, it must be easier to find agents gifted, one for this, and another for that department. Nor is there anything in Scripture to forbid such distribution of the parts of ministerial duty. That in our ordinary congregations and parishes, where a single servant of Christ carries the whole load, things are not worse than they are, may be an indication that after all the various functions of the office stand closer to one another than is at first sight apparent. Between one department of his work and another, however dissimilar on the surface, there may be found in practice such an inward unity or affinity that the same gifts of mind and heart—the same training by observation and experience—which qualify a man for one part of his office, go far at least to qualify him also for the rest.

---

[1] Only the verbal form πρεσβεύω is found (2 Cor. 5[20] and Eph. 6[20]). But cf. the closely allied κῆρυξ in 1 Tim. 2[7] and 2 Tim. 1[11], which yields the very frequent verb so characteristic of the Gospel—κηρύσσειν.

One thing at least does lend unity to the manifold duties of the ministerial office; one supreme gift there is which is called for by all of them alike. It is the Christ-like spirit—the temper of lowly and loving service to the brotherhood — in which all ministry within Christ's kingdom ought to be discharged.

The New Testament word which we render by "service" or "ministry" (διακονία), while it has yielded a title to the deacon as the humblest officer in the society, describes an attitude which is characteristic of them all from the lowest to the very highest. It is the attitude of the Lord Himself. " I am in the midst of you as he that serveth," said Jesus.[1] St. Paul in one place calls his Master a "minister (that is, servant) of the circumcision."[2] To the Apostolate the term is frequently applied.[3] Indeed, every gifted member bestowed on His Church by Christ is given " unto the work of ministering."[4]

What is to be noted about this New Testament use of the word is not that church officers are servants of Christ. That goes without saying: " Ye call Me Master, and Lord : and ye say well; for so I am."[5] The Christian minister is one whose obedience is due to an unseen Lord, whose discharge of official duty must bear ceaseless reference to Christ's future judgment, and whose reward will lie in the King's ultimate verdict of approval.[6] This primary and indefeasible relationship underlies and governs every other. In particular, it has a most important bearing on the minister's relation to his brethren both as their commissioned representative and as their minister. Yet the exceptional feature about Christian office is not that it is service paid to a Master,—all service is that,—but that it is a serving of one's fellow-servants for the Master's sake. It is a fundamental law of the

---

[1] Luke 22[27].   [2] Rom. 15[8].
[3] See Acts 1[17. 25] 20[24] 21[19], Rom. 11[13], 1 Cor. 3[5], 2 Cor. 3[6-9] 6[4] 11[23].
[4] Eph. 4[12].   [5] John 13[13], cf. Matt. 23[10].
[6] Cf. Matt. 24[46] 25[21], Luke 19[17], 1 Cor. 4[1-5].

new kingdom, that whoever will serve Christ is set by Him to minister to Christ's brethren; and to the officer in His household this law applies with peculiar force. " If any man would be first," said our Lord, "he shall be last of all, and minister of all." [1]   Nay, St. Paul does not scruple to accept for himself a much stronger word : " We preach not ourselves," he writes, " but Christ Jesus as Lord, and ourselves as your bond-servants (δούλους) for Jesus' sake." [2]

Such language, standing alone, might easily lend itself to an interpretation offensive to the instincts of the Christian brotherhood; as if our ministry lay in a servile subjection to our fellow-Christians, or in the humouring and flattering of others.   From this it is saved, partly by its voluntary character,[3] but much more by that supreme responsibility to the common Master of us all, of which I have just spoken.   That forbids obsequiousness to men. It frees the minister from any temptation to serve their mere pleasure, to be the slave of their whims, to live upon their favour, to covet their applause, or to cringe for their approval.   " If I were still pleasing men, I should not be a servant of Christ." [4]

This danger of men-pleasing is not less excluded by the ends which the ministry is designed to effect.   The whole work of the Church on earth, and in particular of its officials, is not rightly apprehended until it is viewed as a co-operation with Christ for securing the results of His own mission into the world.   Of that mission the design, as we well know, was primarily the salvation of individuals from sin, but ultimately the formation and perfecting upon earth of the kingdom——the reign——of God. To that aim was His personal ministry in life and death consecrated.   Toward that aim He continues to work on

---

[1] Mark 9[35].   [2] 2 Cor. 4[5].

[3] Cf. 1 Cor. 9[19] : "Though I was free from all men, I brought myself under bondage to all, that I might gain the more."

[4] Gal. 1[10].

through the ages, using now as His chief earthly instrument the Church which is His body. For the outward
and visible society into which He has been pleased to
organise His followers has this for its chief use and *raison
d'être*, not to be, but to bring about, the realm of God
among mankind. So long as we still need to pray, " Thy
kingdom come ! " so long has the Church as an organised
society its work to do. It has to perpetuate itself from
one generation to another through the Christian training
of its own immature members ; to edify itself by cultivating
a devout and holy life ; to keep itself pure, and therefore
effective for its purpose, through internal discipline ; to
bear witness, by worship and proclamation of the Gospel,
to its Lord and His truth ; and to propagate itself in
missionary evangelism to the ends of the earth. All these
things it has to do as a fellow-worker with Christ ; and it
does them largely through its official members. Strictly
speaking, these things are not ends in themselves. They
are means which the King, the Lord of the enterprise,
employs toward His ultimate end, namely, the perfect
realisation at last of the divine kingdom. Nevertheless,
while subordinate in view of that supreme and final end,
these activities of the Church's life are the immediate
ends for which the ministry exists. As a practical guide,
therefore, in the duties entrusted to him, no minister need
set before himself any higher aim than the growth and
perfecting of the Church as Christ's own living organ or
instrument for the saving of the world ; nor dare he set
himself any lower. The test which St. Paul applied to
public worship at Corinth applies to every detail of a
minister's work : " Let all things be done unto edifying." [1]

If this canon be duly pondered to regulate the several
functions of his office, it is obvious that it must deliver
him from unbecoming subjection to the people's likes and
dislikes. A ministry that seeks the very same result
which Christ seeks cannot be an obsequious man-pleasing

[1] 1 Cor. 14[26].

ministry. It is not the pleasure of his fellow-members that the minister has to consult, but their profit; not what they wish, but what will do them good.

But the same canon, while it guards his legitimate independence, equally forbids him to prostitute his office into an instrument of self-assertion or self-aggrandisement. The spiritual interests of the Church (which in the case of a pastor must mean primarily those of his own congregation) are to be his first consideration, to which private interests must give way. The minister's comfort or ease, his personal feelings even, and reputation, are secondary when they come, as may sometimes happen, into competition with the spiritual welfare of the people entrusted to his care. He exists, he labours, for their sake; not they for his. Still less, of course, dare he permit himself to trade upon his sacred office as a means of worldly advantage, profit, or dignity. To treat the clerical calling simply as a profession of emolument and of some social importance, in which a cultured gentleman, by a decent attention to his duties, may pass creditably and comfortably through life, is an abuse common enough at certain periods, from which I think our Churches are to-day comparatively free. But temptations abound from which aspirants to the office or holders of it can never hope entirely to escape: temptations to seek the " priest's office " for " a piece of bread," to be ambitious of preferment, to grow self-important over the influence which office confers or the respect in which it is held. Especially must danger always lurk for proud or wilful natures in those parts of his work which lift the minister in some respects above the ordinary Christian, as a teacher, for instance, a counsellor, or a ruler. Churchmen in all ages have been prone to " magnify " their office in a sense of which St. Paul would not have approved; forgetting what that stout assertor of his own position tells us, that even Apostolic authority was given him for no other use than to build up the Church.[1] That this tempta-

[1] 2 Cor. 13[10].

tion to a lordly temper was to prove during the history of
His Church one of its most inverterate and serious dangers
was early foreseen by its divine Founder. So much, I
think, we may with reverence infer from the exceptional
pains He was at to guard against it, and the frequency
with which He enforced the duty of humility.[1] Not only
did He again and again define with precision the moral
contrast which His servants were to exhibit in this respect
with secular rulers, He pointedly proposed Himself as
their typical example of humility in service.

Two classical passages in the Gospels deserve here
especial attention. The one is that curious incident when
the mother of a pair of brothers solicited on their behalf
the two most favoured seats in Messiah's future kingdom.[2]
Of this opportunity everyone remembers how Jesus took
advantage to warn against the ambition and lust of
pre-eminence which inspire the intrigues of earthly courts,
and to teach from His own example the novel lesson
that a lowly temper, stooping with unselfish devotion to
minister to others, is in His spiritual realm the one
pathway to distinction. With this should be compared
that strange pathetic scene of the feet-washing in the
Fourth Gospel.[3] Again was the same much-needed lesson
enforced; this time not by word only, but also by
symbolic action. The sole relation betwixt brethren
which is absolutely prohibited is lordship; competing for
priority, the one forbidden attitude. The services we
are called on to render to one another—so the Master
teaches—can never be too obscure or menial or distasteful
for a humility and a love that have taken Him for their
model. Nay, just in proportion as they are lowly, are
they to be accounted precious or honourable. Certainly
there is a "pride that apes humility." Imitations even
of the feet-washing have been known to degenerate into

---

[1] Besides passages cited below, cf. Matt. 23$^{8-12}$, Mark 9$^{33-37}$, Matt. 18$^{1-4}$,
and Luke 9$^{46-48}$.

[2] Matt. 20$^{20-28}$, Mark 10$^{35-45}$.   [3] 13$^{1-17}$, cf. Luke 22$^{24-27}$.

caricature. We escape such risks to the quality of our ministry just in the degree in which it is our Master's own aim that we pursue, and the spirit, not the form, of His great ministry that we copy. " Whosoever would be first among you shall be your bond-servant ; even as the Son of Man came not to be ministered unto, but to minister, and to give His life a ransom for many."

CHAPTER IV

THE CALL TO THE MINISTRY

LIKE the priesthood of which the writer to the Hebrews speaks, the holy ministry is an honour which no man taketh to himself, but when he is called of God.[1] Yet this is not a distinction marking it off sharply from ordinary secular avocations. It is only the highest instance of a general rule. When St. Paul counselled his converts to abide each man in the calling wherein he had been called to be a Christian, he taught by implication the important truth that every man's position in society—even a slave's—was that appointed for him by Divine Providence.[2] In the humbler pursuits of life, where little turns on the selection of a trade or craft, small causes commonly serve to fix a youth's choice. A fortuitous circumstance, a slight fancy, the calling of his father or his mere pleasure, a hopeful opening at the right moment, may be enough to determine one's whole career. In proportion as the services which a man is to render to society are more distinguished, or require an exceptional combination of gifts, do we find him marked out for his vocation by a more decided natural fitness, or by strong predilection or some unusual train of events. Artistic or literary genius, for example, indicates to a few the line of life which is to prove their path to fame. An irresistible hunger for adventure urges others into the career of a pioneer or discoverer. From such cases that of a minister does not essentially

[1] Heb. 5⁴.   [2] 1 Cor. 7¹⁷⁻²⁴.

differ. Nor does his "calling" always disclose itself so strongly, or so early in life, as these. Only because it is a call to the most solemn and sacred form of service to God and man, where the consequences of mistake are more fatal and lasting than anywhere else, is it reasonable to take the utmost pains to discover the will of God, not only correctly, but with a sufficient degree of certainty.

The ways in which a young Christian's thoughts are first directed towards the holy ministry, or his desire for it awakened, are manifold. Parents' wishes, or their early dedication of their son; a studious and quiet disposition; a marked crisis in religious experience; or some facility in public address: such things may have given rise to the idea. No sensible person will permit himself to drift under influences so casual as these into a permanent office, or conclude without much closer investigation that because motives of that sort, legitimate as they may be, have bent his mind in this direction, therefore he has a divine vocation to be a minister. If for his future success it is essential that Christ's minister be truly chosen and sent by his heavenly Master,—as truly, though not so supernaturally or unmistakably as Jeremiah under the Old, or Paul under the New, Testament,—it is no less requisite for his own comfort that he should become well assured of his vocation; able at every season of discouragement or disappointment or hardship to stay himself upon this, that a stewardship has been entrusted to him.[1]

In order to reach a rational and fairly confident persuasion on this point, it is needful to receive a two-fold "call": one inward, which is personal and private; the other exterior, public and official. Not the one without the other, but the one to sustain and confirm the other. What makes this double call requisite is, of course, the twofold relation which he who holds ecclesiastical

[1] 1 Cor. 9[17].

office sustains, at once to the unseen Master to whom his whole life-work is due, and to the society whose agent and minister he is to be. For other kinds of religious work, it is immaterial whether a Christian's fitness be recognised by the society or not. It is enough that the man has heard in his own heart a personal summons to this form of service. Still, as in primitive days, we are constantly seeing laymen led through circumstances and their own pronounced gifts to initiate or carry forward valuable enterprises of Christian activity; and neither they themselves nor anyone else questions that for such a task they have been really equipped and designated by a divine hand, although no hands of bishop or presbyter have been laid upon their heads. But for functions which are to be discharged in the name of the Church or under her authority, it is obvious that no supposed inward call can suffice. Into her ministry may no man intrude himself on the allegation that he is conscious of a call from Christ. Through whatever organ any particular branch of the Church is accustomed to express its will, some valid act of "ordination" must testify to the satisfaction of the Church body with the fitness of a candidate for office and set him apart for definite services. On the other hand, the ecclesiastical presupposes a personal vocation. The importance attached to this act differs in different communions; but no body of Christians, I think, professes to substitute it for an inward call of Christ, expressed to the conscience and heart of the man himself—a secret and personal conviction, antecedent to anything the Church may do, that it is the Lord's will he should serve, if permitted, in this and in no other vocation.

I. How then shall a man perceive and judge of this private call from the Lord? The question is one which not seldom occasions prolonged and severe searchings of heart in serious-minded young men; and, in so far as a matter so intimate and personal, lying between the soul and God, admits of general rules at all, it deserves to be carefully answered.

Let it be said, then, to begin with, that, like all similar questions regarding God's will for individuals, it can only be determined with greater or less probability after weighing well a variety of concurrent considerations. We have no right to look for such extraordinary and compelling signs as would silence all misgiving or render superfluous the exercise of the reason in the balancing of opposed considerations. This is not said merely of outward signs. Few are likely to attach much value to external messages from the unseen, such as dreams or voices or visions. But it sometimes happens that an inward impression on the mind is suffered to overmaster cool judgment, and is taken by an enthusiastic young person for a quite dominant and irresistible command from God. Now, unquestionably, a powerful and settled desire to enter upon the holy ministry is in every case a most important element, and one that can hardly be dispensed with in any case. Yet it is not to be taken simply by itself for conclusive proof that God means him who has it to be a minister. Few things, indeed, require more to be cross-examined than just this strong desire, especially when it is of sudden origin, or when it occurs in early life, or immediately after conversion to God. No wish more natural or honourable can spring up in the bosom of an ardent young believer. But it may have many sources, some of them anything but Divine. If the desire be of God, it will be attended with great tenderness of conscience, fear to be found unworthy or presumptuous, and a trembling solicitude lest one mistake the path of duty. To be genuine, moreover, it needs to be a longing, not for the sweets or honours of office, but for its spiritual successes, with a willingness to face for their sake sacrifices and toils. It must therefore be able to stand the test of delay and difficulty in the attainment of its object, and not shrink from strenuous labour in acquiring through years

3

of training the requisite preparation for the right discharge of ministerial duty.

Where the inclination for the ministry has thus proved itself a genuine and enduring outcome from the deepest religious experiences of the soul, and not a passing breath of enthusiasm, though it is not yet conclusive evidence of a "call," it does constitute the most important fact to start from as a basis. It not only entitles, it requires, the man to go on to search with prayerful conscientiousness for other indications that will confirm it.

1. High on the list of "gifts," the possession of which is an indication of fitness for the ministry, I am disposed to place the specific quality of a man's piety. I do not mean merely that his piety be deep and strong. There is much strong deep piety of a too cloistered type, immured in the interior life, expressing itself in quiet meditation or secret prayer, which feels little need and betrays little desire to throw its energies out upon the evil world. The piety which finds in ministerial work its congenial sphere is of another type. Keenly alive to the religious needs of the society around, it is marked by profound sympathy with the Saviour in His saving work, an active compassion for the sinful, and an impulse to engage in whatever efforts for the kingdom of God lie to its hand. Where such features of the religious life are lacking, even a very devout person may prove ill-adapted for the winning and the upbuilding of souls. Where they are present in conspicuous strength, they are so valuable that they make up for much else. A passion for saving others is to the Church what "public spirit" is to the citizen in the State. It qualifies the citizen of the kingdom of God for official life. It stands high, therefore, among those gifts which mark out followers of Christ as fitted to "become fishers of men."

2. Next come, I think, certain combinations of moral and intellectual aptitudes, not often found united, but much in demand as promising ministerial success. A

combination, for instance, of intellectual sobriety and good sense, with a capacity for being kindled into enthusiasm over great moral issues or high moral enterprises. A combination of prudence and self-control, with a frank, familiar, and winsome disposition which lays itself readily alongside of other people and gains their confidence. A combination of the studious temperament, delighting in close study and severe thinking, with tact in dealing with men, and a fair amount of talent for practical affairs. Given such qualities as these, in rare but precious combination, you have a reasonable likelihood that such a man will make a useful minister, and a corresponding probability that his desire for the work is inspired of God. Of his possession of such qualities no man is himself the best judge. One's early advisers and those who know one most intimately are counsellors whom on these matters one does well to consult, since there is no doubt that it is here mistakes are most often made. Probably few ministers turn out badly through want of piety; but who has not known instances in plenty in which some defect of character, even some fault in manner, or idiosyncracy of temperament, perfectly obvious to his companions, yet discovered too late, if discovered at all, by the man himself, has neutralised far more imposing qualities of mind and heart, or even wrecked in the end ministerial usefulness?

3. Last come, what it seems scarce needful to name, since of these the Church as well as the candidate has to take account, a past life free from flagrant vice,[1] the absence of incapacitating physical defects, sound health with a good voice; and, of course, adequate scholarship, or at least means and ability to acquire it.

Not one of all the matters I have named, greater or smaller, can be safely left out of reckoning when a man would settle with himself, *foro conscientiæ*, the grave issue of his call to the ministry. It is not meant that every

---

[1] This is, as a rule, desirable; though, in view of a few famous instances to the contrary, it cannot be called indispensable.

qualification must be possessed in the highest, or in an exceptional, degree; for then no man would be called. Some things can be better dispensed with than others. Some shortcomings can be compensated for by other advantages. What is meant is that a man's religious life, his natural aptitudes, his physical state, and his theological education need to be, each of them singly, and all of them together, fairly satisfactory. They are all matters in which any marked deficiency ought to be viewed as a grave disqualification, casting doubt on his fitness for office, and doubt by consequence on his vocation to enter upon office.

Every student contemplating the ministry should be encouraged, at one stage of his preparation for it after another, to review his conclusion on this momentous question of a " call " ere it be too late. For, as he advances, the favourable indications on which his judgment is built ought to emerge into greater clearness and to become more, not less, constraining. Absolute certainty it is scarcely reasonable to expect until actual trial of the ministry shall have put the seal of success in after years upon the judgment both of the man himself and of the Church. Yet a high and growing probability inferred, by calm and prayerful reflection, from many signs which multiply as step after step is taken on the path which leads to office—this a student of divinity may reasonably ask for and ought steadily to seek after. He who strives humbly and with earnestness to ascertain the mind of Christ in a matter which touches so closely the welfare of His kingdom, shall not always be left at a loss, but may count on secure guidance in the way the Master would have him go.[1]

II. The action of the Church in conferring office constitutes a second " call " : an outward one, of which the result is to test and to confirm the conviction already

[1] Consult Vinet, *Théologie Pastorale*, Introd. § 7 ; Blaikie, *For the Work of the Ministry*, chap. 2 ; and Fairbairn, *Pastoral Theology*, chap. 2. Dr. Howard Crosby's Yale Lecture for 1879–80, entitled *The Christian Preacher*, is devoted to the qualifications for the ministry.

reached by the man himself in the secrecy of his own soul, that he has been qualified and called by Christ.

It consists of two parts : first, an " examination " or inquiry to ascertain whether the conditions for ordination laid down by the particular Church are in this case satisfied ; and, next, the act of ordination itself. Each of these has an interest for us here, chiefly as it affects the confidence with which a young minister enters on his duties, or the success with which he is likely to discharge them.

The points upon which it has always been and still is usual for the Church to satisfy itself before conferring office, are such as these :—

1. Age and physical health. The canonical age for a presbyter, originally fixed at thirty years,[1] was in 1314 reduced to five and twenty ; and this was retained by most Reformed Churches,[2] although in this country at least I do not think any age limit is now strictly enforced. The absence of disabling defects, mental as well as physical, has always been insisted on.

2. Previous character and repute for Christian conduct, as testified by those who know him—usually his own minister or parish priest, and the head of his school or college. It has also been customary, immediately before ordination, publicly to call for objections to the candidate's life and conduct, and sometimes this step has also been taken in the parish to which he belongs.

3. The purity of his motives in desiring office is a matter variously inquired into ; often at a private interview, but usually by demanding in public, if nothing more, at least a solemn disclaimer of simonaical practices or mercenary aims.

4. His orthodoxy : whether his beliefs are in sufficient accord with the creed of the Church. In many modern

---

[1] By the Council of Neo-Cæsarea in 314, and sanctioned by later councils and by the civil law, cf. Edwin Hatch's art. " Holy Orders " in Smith and Cheetham's *Dict. of Christ. Antiquities.*

[2] In the Dutch Church it is twenty-three (Van Oosterzee, *Praktische Theologie,* i. 50) ; and practically that may be regarded as the minimum acted on by the majority of British communions.

communions this test has been attenuated to a minimum ; but, unless where a Church has no professed creed at all, it cannot be omitted.

5. His scholarship, general and theological. Whatever evidence on this head a Church requires, has, of course, been furnished at an earlier stage than the ordaining act : although a final examination in divinity may still (as with the Calvinistic Methodists of Wales) form part of the ordination services. Bodies which, like the State Churches of Germany, England, and Scotland, draw their students from national universities, can, of course, accept an academic degree as evidence of general scholarship.

6. Any proof the candidate may have already given of capacity for religious work, such as preaching, or of success in it. So far as I know, the Methodist Churches are those which have been led by their traditions to give to this last point the greatest attention.

Naturally, details vary considerably in different communions ; but such diversities in practice are of minor consequence. The important thing for the individual minister is that the Church shares with him the responsibility of decision as to his fitness, and, consequently, to some extent as to his " call." I am far from saying that this task has always been discharged with thoroughness, or in the best way. Nevertheless, it can have no design but to safeguard the Church from unsuitable officials ; and, wherever it is gone about with care, the ordinand is entitled to accept the judgment of his Church as a weighty confirmation of his own—in respect at least to qualifications upon which the Church is competent to pronounce. It is not only the latest, it is one of the best pieces of evidence available, that he has not misread the will of God. Coming when it does at the critical moment of his career, it supplies a welcome support in his final act of self-dedication to the holy ministry.

On this examination and testimony to fitness there has always followed in the ordinals of East and West a declara-

tion of appointment, constituting the Church's own formal
and solemn "call" to office. Originally this was probably
the one essential part of admission to orders, succeeded at
once by the ordinand's discharge of some characteristic
duty of his office.[1] But, of course, it was always befitting
that at some stage in the ritual of ordination, the assembled
Church should unite in a great act of intercession for the
brother whom it was setting apart to sacred responsibilities,
and this was almost invariably accompanied by the imposition of the hands of the ordaining bishop. Respecting
the spiritual value of this part of the rite, there has grown
up a serious divergence of opinion; especially how far its
virtue depends on the Church's prayers, how far on
manual contact by episcopal hands.

To lay hands on the head of one who is being appointed to office was a Hebrew ceremony, of which two
instances occur in the Book of Numbers.[2] The ancient
practice seems to have been in use among the Jews of
later times at the installation of their judges,[3] and thence
to have passed naturally into the Apostolic Church. But
the New Testament cases of its occurrence fall apparently
into two distinct classes. When the Seven were set apart
to serve tables, when Barnabas and Saul were designated
as missionaries to the Greeks by the Church of Antioch,
when presbyters were ordained by Timothy at Ephesus [4]—
it is possible to regard the gesture which accompanied
intercession as simply meant to designate the person
prayed for, and by a significant action to express his
setting apart for a special work. This is probably what
Augustine meant by his often-cited words: "Quid aliud
est manuum impositio, quam oratio super hominem?"[5] By
his time, however, a different interpretation of the act was

---

[1] See Hatch, art. "Ordination" in Smith and Cheetham.
[2] When the Levites were set apart for service, Num. 8[10], and when
Joshua was appointed as Moses' successor, *ib.* 27[18-23], cf. Deut. 34[9].
[3] See Schürer, *Gesh. d. jud. Volkes*, ii. 152.
[4] Acts 6[6] 13[3], 1 Tim. 5[22].   [5] *De Bapt. c. Donat.* iii. 16.

being introduced, based on the other class of Apostolic
precedents.   When the Apostles prayed over their converts
that they might receive the Holy Ghost, they also laid
their hands on them, as St. Paul, for example, did to
Timothy to qualify him as his missionary delegate.[1]   Here
the act has been taken to express a conveyance in some
measure of that spiritual power which the Apostles
possessed.   So soon, therefore, as the idea entered that
bishops were successors of the Apostles, it was inevitable
to transfer to them this ability to convey the special gifts
of the Spirit which qualify for office, and to connect with
that the laying on of their hands in ordaining priests, as
well as in confirming the baptized.   This theory of ordination is as old as the time of Cyprian, and had therefore
been very long current before the awful words " Accipe
Spiritum Sanctum " found their way into any ordinal.
That did not happen in the West before the twelfth
century.   The Church of England has retained these words
in her " Ordering of Priests " ; and this fact lends support
to the claim of High Churchmen that admission to
Anglican orders, though not a sacrament, as the Church
of Rome teaches,[2] does nevertheless convey through the
bishop a χαρίσμα or grace of office.   This effect ascribed
to the rite was stated by Hooker in these terms : " When
we take ordination, we also receive the presence of the
Holy Ghost, partly to guide, direct, and strengthen us in
all our ways, and partly to assume unto Itself for the
more authority those actions that appertain to our place
and calling."   That is to say, as he futher explains it :
" Whether we preach, pray, baptize, communicate, condemn, give absolution, or whatsoever, as disposers of God's
mysteries, our words, judgments, acts and deeds are not
ours, but the Holy Ghost's." [3]

There is no need to take this widely accepted view of
ordination in a crass materialistic fashion, as if manual

---

[1] Acts 8[14-19], 2 Tim. 1[6].   [2] Canons of Trent, Sess. vii. c. 9.
[3] *Eccl. Pol.* Bk. v. 77–78.

contact could be, or were imagined to be, a vehicle or medium by which spiritual grace is conveyed. Indeed, apart from the direct address: "Receive the Holy Ghost," there is nothing even to suggest that the divine gift is bestowed by the bishop, of and from himself. No doubt he is supposed to effect what in the first age the Apostles effected. But it is open to say with St. Augustine, that the Apostles prayed for the Spirit to come upon those on whom they laid hands, did not themselves bestow Him, and that the Church in the person of its leaders observes still the same custom.[1] It is therefore quite possible for a High Churchman to hold, as evangelical Churchmen do, that the effective portion of the rite is the bishop's intercession, and not the imposition of his hands. But, of course, he will still hold that the gift invoked by a successor of the Apostles, and by him alone, is as certainly bestowed and as abiding, as when the Apostles conferred the Spirit on the Christians of the first century.

Nor does the Reformed view, on the other hand, overlook the value of the Church's intercession, or reduce that to a bare form. It rejects the theory of episcopal succession with the consequent limitation to bishops of the power to ordain. It does not suppose that under all circumstances the mere act of ordination secures to the ordained the abiding inward presence of the Spirit, although it does qualify him to administer the sacraments. Nevertheless the Reformed Church has retained what seems to me to be of spiritual value in the rite; that is to say, the solemn intercession of the Church as the Body of Christ in which His Spirit dwells. When the Reformed Church, with or without the expressive and venerable usage of imposition of presbyters' hands, invokes from her living Head in heaven the gift of the Holy Ghost to equip His servant, at his entrance upon office, for every

[1] "Orabant [apostoli] ut venirat in eos quibus manus imponebant, non ipsi eum dabant; quem morem in suis præpositis etiam nunc servat ecclesia" (*De Trin.* xv. 26).

official duty, it asks for the very same blessing which
episcopal ordination is believed to confer. The difference
seems to be, that the divine answer to that prayer, as to
all prayers, is here acknowledged to depend upon moral
conditions of faith and obedience. More turns than on
the Catholic theory upon the spiritual condition of the
man who is being ordained. If the Church, when it sets
apart to office, possesses unconditional power to qualify for
office by a supernatural " donation," irrespective of the
man's religious receptivity, then it matters less whether
he has been beforehand qualified by the secret and inward
grace of Christ or not. Whereas, on the evangelical
theory, ordination proceeds upon and recognises an existing
fact. It presumes the man to be already prepared and
equipped by the possession of spiritual gifts ; in particular,
by such a living fellowship with Christ through faith,
as will enable him hereafter to receive from day to day,
as the need arises, every grace-gift ($\chi\alpha\rho\iota\sigma\mu\alpha$) which is
called for by the sacred duties of his office. On this
assumption, it asks for him as his constant endowment the
abiding presence of the Spirit. The minister knows he has
still his personal part to take in stirring up the gift of God
which is in him.[1] Upon his own fidelity and prayerful-
ness, he knows, will largely depend the daily assistance
of the Holy Ghost in every detail of His work. Nevertheless, the ordination prayer is no empty word ; nor is it
by any means the last, though it is the earliest, solemn
act of intercession on his behalf in which the Church of
God engages. Every conscientious minister who carries
on his ministry in the spirit of that united prayer,—praying for himself the while without ceasing,—feels that he
can rely on the unceasing intercession on his behalf of the
faithful upon earth, as well as of their High Priest above.
Reassured by this, he labours in confident expectation of
an ample and a gracious answer. Nor can his hope be
disappointed. He does receive the $\chi\alpha\rho\iota\sigma\mu\alpha$ of his office.

[1] 2 Tim. 1[6].

CHAPTER V

THE MINISTER'S DEVOTIONAL LIFE

To maintain and to perfect his personal fitness for the work of ministry, so that his official functions shall become more and more the natural expression of his real life—this has now become for the young minister the first of duties.

He has been approved and set apart to office simply on the ground that both he himself and the Church have judged him to be suited for it. By natural temperament, by inward graces of the Spirit, and by intellectual attainments, he is believed to have already reached, not completely, yet to a promising degree, such adaptation to this calling that person and office answer to one another. In other words: he is what an official Christian needs to be; on the other hand, the functions of the ministerial office are precisely such forms of activity as his life will most naturally run into of its own accord. For the supreme instance, ever-to-be-studied, of what this means,—the person and the official work quadrating or fitting into one another,—let him look to his blessed Lord Himself. Of the opposite, sad examples have been plentiful enough: ecclesiastics who mistook their calling; men of quite alien tastes and aptitudes, on whom the clerical profession hung like an ill-fitting dress—something outside their real self and out of harmony with it. Cases of that sort give rise to " officialism." There is no " officialism," in the sinister sense which clings to that word, where the duties of a man's office are just what he loves best to do, that into which the deepest tides of his nature run spontaneously, and in the doing of which all that is best in him finds both satisfaction and reward.[1]

Such a correspondence between the man and his office can never be complete at the outset, that is, at his ordination. Whatever general sympathy may already exist between his inner life and the service to which he is set apart, there must be a crowd of details about official life, its engagements and its methods, which are still strange to him. No one can quite know what his duties are to be or how he is to address himself to their performance, till he actually begins to do them. This is nothing peculiar to the ministry. In every calling the workman's hand has to get subdued, like the dyer's, to the stuff he works in. In every calling, moreover, the first enthusiasm of a young practitioner needs to be slowly replaced by conscientious habits of duty. More often perhaps than in other professions does it happen that a young minister sets out with exaggerated or rose-coloured anticipations, or in a mood of exalted feeling which dies down as the commonplace realities of ministerial experience grow familiar to him. He will have to train himself always to obey the call of duty, even when it is unwelcome, and always to do his best, whether he be in a mood for it or not.[2]

About a process like this there are risks to be escaped or to be overcome, not without labour and self-discipline. It must not be taken for granted that the mere discharge of sacred offices for a certain length of time will of itself and without more ado bring about that perfect stage at which a minister's whole being is subdued to his work, and his work has become the spontaneous expression of himself. It is true that there is no better means of grace nor any finer training for the ministry, than just to do the work of it : provided always that it be done in the very spirit of it,

[1] Cf. Schweizer, *Pastoraltheorie* (1875), p. 223 ff.
[2] For a realistic sketch of a minister's work, showing how unlike it is to the ideal with which one sets out, see Dr. Watson's *Cure of Souls* (Yale Lectures, 1896), pp. 227–234.

not as a function, perfunctorily, but as the utterance of a
soul in fellowship with Christ.   But then that is precisely
the condition which it is so excessively hard to secure and
to maintain.   For of all plagues in ministerial life this is
the most common, the most inveterate, and the sorest—
that its duties tend to become perfunctory, professional
and nothing more; done correctly to the public eye, but
without heart in the sight of God.   For when a sacred
duty becomes customary, it ceases to be so sacred to us.
The sense of responsibility weakens by repetition.   Holy
awe at the solemn issues of one's work rubs off the soul
with long practice, like bloom from the peach when it is
handled.   With this melancholy result in innumerable
cases, that, in proportion as a minister gets used to the
conventional way of conducting divine service and discharging other functions in his daily routine, does he
find it difficult to do them in the old spirit, with a
tender solemn fear, and a scrupulous care not to profane them, and a humbling of his soul because of
unworthiness.

Now the only cure for perfunctory service is the
cultivation of the interior life of devotion.   This includes
a sharpening of the conscience to perceive one's hidden
faults; a deepening of contrition for them when discovered;
a more abiding sense of the divine presence; a firmer and
less unstable reliance on the aid of the Holy Spirit :—everything, in short, which goes to make a holy man of God.   In
particular, I think that feature in personal religion is to
be cultivated which we signalised as the first to be asked
after when one begins to contemplate the ministry at all :
I mean, sympathy with the heart of Jesus in His Saviourhood; in His zeal for the Father's honour; His pity for
the lost; His seeking till He find; His lowly service of
meanest needs; His surrender of all things, even of life,
for the salvation of others.   To maintain this spirit of his
Master, so far as he has it, and to deepen it, and to perfect
it, ought to be, as I think, the first care of a true minister;

for none of his qualifications is so apt to be lost, and of none is the loss so disastrous.

The means to be used for the cultivation of the inner life are so simple and well-known that they hardly need to be named. It is much to be wished, indeed, that the whole surroundings of a minister's life, his daily habits, his companionships, and his domestic arrangements, should as far as possible be of a kind to favour, and not repress, religious ardour, especially ardour in his Master's cause. Mainly, however, like every other Christian, he has to be dependent on seasons set apart for devotional reading, meditation, and prayer. The difficulty in the experience of most lies less in lack of will than in lack of leisure. Present-day ministers stand at a disadvantage, compared with their brethren of an older generation. The days are past when a clergyman's life could be described as a quiet one, with stated, but not too frequent, public appearances, separated by considerable intervals free from interruption, which could be devoted to other pursuits, to study, or to devotion. Survivals of this state of things may still be found in rural parsonages or in Highland parishes; but in the industrial town or large city, the pressure on every minister's time, due to a whirl of public engagements, has crowded out the leisure which was once enjoyed for retirement, reflection, and prayer. His days are spent in public. His hours are claimed by ceaseless demands, arising in part from the organisation of the modern congregation, and in part from the so-called "religious world" outside.

It has come to be a serious problem with many of us how far one is justified in surrendering to the social, philanthropic or semi-political "causes" for which a minister's active co-operation is expected, indeed, is all but demanded, hours which are required for higher things. Even the machinery of committees and societies by which ecclesiastical affairs have come to be carried on exacts from not a few active and willing men a waste of time against which they are beginning to rebel. Our modern methods of doing

Christian work of all kinds need, it seems to me, to be overhauled and simplified. Endless wheels revolve with small result. There is room for a better distribution of responsibility for what is every Christian's affair, a lightening of the load that is laid by tacit consent upon the shoulders of the clergy, with possibly an enlistment of larger aid from such of the laity as have leisure. At all events, no busy pastor ought to be suspected either of laziness or of lack of proper interest, who ventures firmly to decline outside engagements on the plea that his closet or his study is being starved.

Another modern burden under which the minister, like other men in public office, sometimes groans, is his correspondence. His daily post-bag may be counted by dozens, yet courtesy requires a prompt return to every correspondent, who, writing on his own affairs, has forgotten, nevertheless, to enclose a stamp for reply. Even the harmless post-card is hardly accepted as a substitute for a letter. Nor does professional etiquette sanction as yet the cutting down of epistolary style to the curtness of a city office, and periphrastic politeness costs trouble. It is a ceaseless drain upon time and temper, as well as on the purse; but it is one which a busy minister must tutor himself to accept as simply a part of his daily task.

What makes the matter worse is that much of all this daily business is really of a secular character, only in name religious work at all. Therefore it not only squanders one's scanty leisure, it absorbs one's spiritual energies. By its multiplicity and pettiness, it conceals the sacredness of the minister's vocation. It renders more needful than ever that quiet brooding over divine themes which happier generations enjoyed, till in the stillness of devout musing a holy fire burned. If it never was so difficult, it has rarely been more necessary, for the minister to be a man of much private devotion.

It is of no use to quarrel with the conditions of one's age. Granted that there are drawbacks in the din and stress of modern society, there are doubtless compensations also.   Let the sensible minister take stock of his situation and make the most of it; note its perils, and set himself to escape them.   Let him cultivate intimacy with like-minded brethren.   Let him seek inspiration from the most fervid evangelists or missionaries he comes across.   Let him be careful not to lose touch with the actual needs of the world—its sin and its suffering.   Let him learn to utilise for self-recollection the few spare moments that are intercalated between the engagements of the busiest day, and cultivate the habit of ejaculatory prayer.   All these things help.   Above all, let him jealously guard such private hours as he can compass, remembering that times for devotion, if not likely to be found, have at any cost to be made.

Among the High Church clergy, as in the best circles of the Catholic priesthood, a good deal of value is put upon "retreats": prearranged seasons, that is, of deliberate withdrawal from ordinary ways for the discipline of the devout life through exercises which are partly social, but largely solitary.   Such methods do not suit Protestant taste so well.   Yet small fraternal conventions for similar purposes have been tried in other sections of the Church and found useful.   These things may supplement, they cannot replace, daily and weekly periods of lonely devotion in the closet.   Each man must arrange these as he best can.   The morning half-hour, or hour, ere the day begins, before letters or newspapers have distracted one's thoughts; a longer season once a week, preferably on Saturday evening as the Lord's Day approaches: these, with, of course, as I have just suggested, an occasional summons to oneself in the course of the day to recall the presence of God, and silent petitions shot up to Heaven at moments of conscious need:—these may be all that a busy pastor can afford.   At rarer intervals, a whole day spared from holiday recreation for prolonged self-scrutiny and meditation is advisable.   Many a minister, I am afraid, would confess

here to a record of failure—plans formed again and again,
only to be broken.   But he must never give in.   This is
the key of the position.   For such hours of solitude with
God he must fight as for the breath of his life.   To let
engagements, no matter how clamant, rob him of such
hours, and to acquiesce in the loss of them, means failure.
There is no sorer battle in ministerial life ; but defeat here
is fatal.

How the precious moments redeemed for secret
worship can be best used, or what aids to devotion he shall
employ, must be left to each man's own experience.
Many will confine their reading at such times to Holy
Scripture ; but it needs to be read meditatively and with
self-application, not for scholarly study or to find material
for sermons.   Devotional books of the best class are not
too numerous, but they are to be had.   Some have found
stimulus in the lives and diaries or letters of saintly men
like Rutherford, Brainerd, Henry Martyn, or M'Cheyne.
To others these memoirs do not appeal.   One of the most
searching and widely helpful books in English literature is
Baxter's *Reformed Pastor*, which one American writer
counsels the minister to read through once a year.[1]   Others
find they can use with benefit a few choice manuals of
Catholic devotion.   Every man must be guided by what
he finds most helpful.   But such helps, however valuable,
are not for everyday use, nor at any time of the first
consequence.   The great thing to aim at surely must be to
come into the closest and most living contact with the
Father of our spirits through His Son, reviewing in His
presence one's work and the spirit in which it is done, that,
having confessed with contrition its defects, one may catch
afresh a holy enthusiasm from the altar of Jesus' Passion.
For this must lead every earnest servant of Christ to
register fresh vows of fidelity and to re-dedicate himself to
his ministry with revived ardour.   How it is done matters
little.   But the minister's communion with his Lord needs to

---

[1] Shedd, *Homiletics and Pastoral Theology* (Edin. 1869), p. 281.

4

be intimate and unreserved. May we not fitly regard the hour of prayer as a workman's confidential interview with Him whose work he is doing, at which everything is talked over, with infinite reverence, yet frankly, with the generous Master, and instructions and assistance are received in view of fresh labours now to be attempted?

CHAPTER VI

MINISTERIAL CHARACTER

BETWIXT the interior life with its secret exercises, through which the minister strives to bring himself into ever closer accord with the spirit of his ministry, and the public functions of his office, there lies a wide intermediate region of action common to him with other men.

It does not enter into the Protestant conception of a presbyter or clergyman that, like a Catholic priest, he should be separated as far as possible from ordinary life, social or domestic. Ever since the idea entered the Church at an early period in her history, that Jesus had counselled for certain of His followers a superior grade of virtue and of merit, which is optional, not obligatory upon all, the order of the priesthood has come to lead a removed or isolated existence, aiming at this more perfect type of saintship. Freedom from family ties, segregation in separate dwellings, ascetic self-discipline, virginal purity, a daily routine ordered by artificial rules, and a life wholly devoted to religious exercises: all these were steps in a historical process which has ended in denaturalising the presbyter into the priest, and concealing him behind a halo of unearthly sanctity, genuine or imaginary.

Neither the seclusion of a celibate nor the asceticism of a monk attaches to the ideal of an evangelical minister. For one reason, because he is simply the first in a brotherhood of saints, all of whom are his spiritual equals, sharing and sustaining his responsibilities. Also, because it contributes to his legitimate influence as a leader, counsellor, and exemplar, that he should mingle with little reserve in those social relationships which bind men to one another; be husband and father, friend and neighbour, subject and citizen, like the rest. Above all, because true Christianity does not know of two ethical standards of conduct—two codes of moral duty: a lower level which is all that a man can reach who has to lead the secular life, and a higher to which he only may attain who abjures marriage, flees worldly society, and observes a peculiar style of living. That the holiness which suffices for a layman is too poor a degree of virtue to become the ecclesiastic who handles sacred things, is not a notion confined to persons trained in Catholic teaching. It has been found to creep in wherever an exalted reverence for clerical office has possessed the popular mind. Nor is there any security against artificial or unreal distinctions in morals, save by holding firmly to the principle that there can be but one standard of character for all alike—one perfect Christian walk in the Holy Spirit, obligatory on the humblest believer as much as on the bishop of souls.

At the root of this exaggerated demand for ministerial sanctity, there is nevertheless a truth which it is of consequence for the minister to bear in mind. It is not unreasonable for the common people to expect their spiritual guides to be on the whole better men and better Christians than themselves. For although the same principles of conduct bind the pastor and the flock, yet they bind the pastor even more than his flock. All Christians alike ought to aim at the perfection of Christ, for we dare measure ourselves by no inferior model. But to approach that standard is popularly believed, not without reason, to be easier for the man whose days are screened in some measure from the usual temptations which beset life in the world, and are spent so largely in the things of religion. To fall below the standard, on the other hand, is worse and more discreditable in one who is set before the eyes of other men as a selected representative

of how a Christian ought to act. According to one explanation of the word " parson," it means the *persona* who
represents the Church, in whom its ideal is embodied or
its character illustrated.[1] The reason assigned for this
derivation, as Dr. Skeat remarks, " may well be doubted
without affecting the etymology." [2] But the idea is a just
one nevertheless. For, beyond doubt, every minister of
Christ is, in Vinet's phrase, " l'homme symbole." [3] He
stands before the Church and before the public as an
embodiment of the Christian ideal, a specimen Christian,
from whom men may learn what a Christian ought to be.
His life, as Philip Henry put it, " should be the book of
the ignorant." No doubt, the public voice pushes this too
far. Too much is popularly expected from ministers; and
religion is reproached for their defects to an extent which
is excessive and unfair. That is true, I think, even where
the inconsistencies of " the cloth " are not made by the
profane a mere pretext for hostile attacks upon religion
itself. Yet, however it may serve the purpose of irreligious
critics to hold the Gospel responsible for the faults of its
public servants, it remains true, and is to be seriously
pondered by every minister, that he who has undertaken
to be Christ's assistant in the task of showing others the
way to heaven, has need himself to walk very closely in
the Good Shepherd's footsteps. To say that he ought to
be a follower of his Master is to say too little. He is
called to be " an ensample to them that believe "; [4] one
who, with whatever modest misgiving or reserve, may yet
borrow without flagrant presumption the bold exhortation
of St. Paul: " Be ye imitators of me, even as I also am
of Christ." [5] If we who hold office in the Church do not
lay to heart as we ought this more urgent reason for
blameless conduct which lies upon us, other people do not
forget it. The world never does. The Church rarely does.

[1] Shedd, *ut supra*, p. 282.   [2] *Etymological Dict.*, *sub voce.*
[3] *Théol. Pastorale*, 2me ed., Paris, 1854, p. 140.
[4] 1 Tim. 4^{12}, cf. Tit. 2^7.   [5] 1 Cor. 11^1, cf. 4^{16}.

So that, while the very highest type of honourable and irreproachable character is never deemed anything to boast of in a minister of Christ, very slight faults call down severe censure from all but the most charitably-minded persons.

Nor is it without good cause that by some modern German authorities this subject of clerical morality is handled in connection with pastoral duty, as at once the prime condition for its right discharge, and the chief source of the pastor's influence.[1]   But, in truth, it is not his pastoral usefulness alone, it is the success of his ministry as a whole, which requires the minister to be an exceptionally good man.   No doubt ministerial success of the highest kind is conditioned on the superhuman power of the Spirit of God.   In so far, however, as it is affected by the human instrument at all, it is far more affected by his goodness than by intellectual ability.   The most useful ministers are by no means always the ablest, still less the most eloquent.   The influence which a minister wields is moral influence, built on the confidence, respect, and affection which men always give to one whose life recommends his message and puts detractors to shame. Words have little weight unless backed by a consistent example ; private dealing in such a case only provokes contempt ; ministrations without heart are instinctively detected and leave no blessing.   The whole value of our work, in short, is put in hazard when it is not penetrated by that indefinable sense of moral authority which belongs to character and to nothing else.   Says Baxter : " One proud, surly, lordly word, one needless contention, one covetous action, may cut the throat of many a sermon, and blast the fruit of all you have been doing."

To name all that a minister ought to be would be to rehearse the complete circle of Christian graces.   But within the ideal of the all-round Christlike character, incumbent

---

[1] *e.g.* Schweizer, *op. cit.*, Dritter Theil ; Palmer, *Pastoraltheologie* (1863), pp. 143–209 ; Achelis, *Praktische Theol.* (1890) p. 467 ff.

on him as on every Christian, there is a specialised type, determined by the conditions of his calling, which it is usual to speak of as the ministerial character; just as there certainly are faults which deform it more than others do, and which more quickly dissipate his official influence. For both of these we cannot do better than study the indications scattered through the New Testament as to what a church officer is expected to be; especially the directions given in the Pastoral Epistles for the selection of presbyters, as well as for the guidance of Timothy and Titus themselves.[1] To some extent, it is true, these are coloured by local conditions and by the habits of the time. Yet in the main they are applicable everywhere and in every age of the Church. Guided by these inspired directories, we reach the following as leading features in ministerial character :—

1. The groundwork of the character described seems to consist in that grave or serious frame of mind which goes with habitual self-command.[2] Obviously this befits the sacred and responsible position of a minister. It is not inconsistent with constitutional cheerfulness or even with playfulness on occasion. But it excludes uncontrolled outbreaks of temper; it requires all indulgence of the senses to be severely temperate; and it suggests sobriety or moderation in one's judgments on men and things, as well as a gravity of deportment which is neither austere nor sour. The passionateness of a hasty nature and the frivolity of a shallow one are equally out of place.

2. Close on the heels of this follows the gentle or pacific temperament, tutored to meet opposition with patience, and to bear contumely or wrong without undue resentment. " The Lord's servant must not strive, but be

---

[1] Fully treated by Fairbairn in his work on *The Pastoral Epistles*; cf. also Vilmar, *Lehrbuch d. Pastoraltheologie* (1872), pp. 39–56.

[2] The student should examine the precise force of σώφρων, ὅσιος, ἐπιεικής, κόσμιος, and the like words used in N.T. to describe the moral attitude of the presbyter.

gentle towards all, apt to teach, forbearing, in meekness correcting them that oppose themselves." [1] This characteristic Christian attitude, in contrast to the self-assertion and contentious insistence on one's supposed rights which is the usual temper of society, finds scope for its exercise even in the quietest times, when a minister has nothing worse to encounter than the wilfulness or touchiness of good people. In days of rebuke and strife and persecution, it can rise to a heroic height, and discover the strength of a divine patience that knows how to "endure all things for the Gospel's sake."

3. It sounds like an anti-climax to add that the minister is not to be a greedy man nor a lover of money. But no one will feel surprise at the emphasis laid on this [2] who recollects with what sharp eyes the public looks for signs of self-interest in those who profess devotion to higher aims. Money is so completely the god of the vulgar, that they instinctively test our religion by this—is money not our god too? And there is no point where a minister's failure to rise above the world's own level will sooner undermine the respect which society entertains for him. To preach only for a fee, to covet promotion for a bigger salary, to marry for a fortune, to court the well-to-do and neglect the poor, to be stingy to dependants, and so on: by ways like those an ill name is easily brought upon the ministry and the Church.

From these with similar directions it is not hard to gather a fairly exact conception of the sort of Christian whom the New Testament would have an official Churchman to be. And the man who answers to this conception, who is temperate and sober-minded, gentle, not soon angry nor contentious, and no lover of money, is just the man likely to be "without reproach," having, as he needs to have, "a good testimony from them that are without." [3]

---

[1] 2 Tim. 2[24, 25].   [2] 1 Tim. 3[3], Tit. 1[7].
[3] Cf. 1 Tim. 3[2-7] and Tit. 1[5-9].

CHAPTER VII

MINISTERIAL MANNERS

WHEN we pass from moral character to "manners," we
enter a wide and miscellaneous department of conduct,
conversant with the minor ethics of life, with its pro-
prieties and outward details. Here each one's idiosyncrasies play a large part. So much so, that a man's
demeanour, conversation, and bearing, especially during his
unbent hours, are on the whole perhaps the sincerest
utterance of what is distinctive about him—that from
which he is most surely known by his fellows. Yet
nobody but a "character" or an oddity acts on the
principle of abandoning himself to do just what he likes.
Each of us, to a greater or less degree, abstains from the
free indulgence of personal tastes, likings, or whims; because he keeps these things under subjection to some
ruling aim or more general principle of conduct. Thus
one man orders his exterior life wholly in compliance with
social convention or the traditions of his class. Another
tries to fashion himself by his own ideas of what is proper
or becoming to a person in his position. With many it is
the wish to get on in the world or to make a fortune
which forms the determining consideration. Now, for the
minister of religion such a restraining rule is found in his
desire to "give no occasion of stumbling in anything, that
his ministration be not blamed." [1] He is entrusted with
an office, noble and holy, with which the honour and the
cause of Jesus Christ are wrapt up, and it must not suffer

[1] 2 Cor. 6³.

57

at his hands.   It is not his personal reputation as a
man he has chiefly to care for; it is his reputation as a
servant of Christ and an officer in His house.   Love for
the souls he is set to save, which must ever be his highest
motive, prescribes as the normal rule to be observed in
every detail of behaviour, the small as well as the greater:
" Take thought for things honourable, not only in the sight
of the Lord, but also in the sight of men." [1]

Youth is impatient of restraint; and (in spite of the
text-books of his craft which speak here with one voice)
many a young minister, fresh from the freedom of student
years, begins by resenting as unreasonable, if not unmanly,
such deference to what people will think or say of him.
St. Paul was by nature a man of marked individuality,
in whom the love of liberty was exceptionally strong.   In
reading his correspondence, one feels that he sometimes
frets under the necessity of vindicating his actions, or of
adjusting his movements to the prejudices of friend and
foe.   Yet it is he who by precept and example is here the
Church's foremost legislator.   To him more than to any
other do we owe the rule that Christ's servant, though he
be free from all men, must bring himself under bondage to
all, that he may gain the more, becoming all things to all
men that he may by all means save some.[2]   Longer
experience in the ministry brings most of us back to Paul's
rule as our safest guide.

1. The obligation of this canon is most apparent when
it is applied to the borderland of morals, the debatable
ground where dwell what are known as *adiaphora*—
questions of conduct which change their moral complexion
with changing circumstances, or on which conscientious
men may easily differ as to the limits of the permissible.
The great passages in which the Apostle has worked out
with care the Christian duty of the strong-minded to
respect the scruples of weaker brethren, and to abstain from
what will put an occasion of falling in their way, deserve

[1] 2 Cor. 8[21].   [2] 1 Cor. 9[18-23].

to be specially studied by every young minister.[1] The duty is indeed incumbent on all Christians, for it springs out of brotherly love. But for more reasons than one it is peculiarly binding on the minister. His behaviour is more widely known and narrowly observed than that of private Christians. More is looked for from him than from a layman. When he is blamed, religion is blamed. Above all, he is a guide and pattern whom others think it safe to imitate, whose example, therefore, may easily mislead the immature, the ill-informed, or the weak, into doing what is safe for him, yet perilous for them.

One cannot bluntly lay it down as a rule that he is never to do anything which can possibly be ill-taken or uncharitably construed, or for which some persons might blame him. That would be to make him a slave to popular opinion. To his own Master he stands or falls; and so long as he is clear in his own conscience, it is comparatively a small matter for him how society thinks of him. But then it is to Christ Himself, as Master and Saviour of weak and strong alike, that this care for the effect of his example is due. He must "cause no hindrance to the Gospel." He must beware lest through his knowledge he that is weak perish, "the brother for whose sake Christ died." It is not men he has to please, else he would not be a servant of Christ. But for Christ's sake, and for Christ's work's sake, and for the sake of Christ's redeemed, he must not allow himself to do any doubtful act, which he thinks he can do with a good conscience, till he has weighed beforehand its probable effects upon others as well as upon his own ministerial influence.

I have hinted at one limit of danger to be observed in practising this prudential regard to men's opinions. It is when it degenerates into mere prudence or a slavish fear for the judgment of others: asking not, what in view of all the circumstances Christ would have me to do, but

[1] Rom. 14, 1 Cor. 8-10.

what will the religious public say, or my congregation, or the newspapers! This extreme demoralises conscience, robbing it of independence and virility. There is another limit of danger: when by sacrificing to others our own judgment of what is permissible, we help to create, or, by accepting, sanction, a false standard of right and wrong. Some things, for example, a layman may do without giving offence which would be held improper for a clergyman. This may be carried so far that the same act appears, not unbecoming merely, but positively sinful in the clergyman, though quite lawful for other people. We have no right to give way to popular prejudice to the effect of thus erecting Protestant " counsels of perfection." It must ever be made clear that when a minister abdicates his liberty to do what others are doing without committing sin, it is a freewill abdication of his moral freedom, not a betrayal of it. The same danger of yielding unwisely, or too far, will arise as often as a false morality is growing up inside any community. Thus, should an act of self-denial, say, be pressed, not as a voluntary sacrifice of one's rights, but as a duty absolutely binding on every Christian's conscience, or as a term of office, or even of Church membership, then it may become for a time more needful to assert liberty in things indifferent than to surrender it, to correct the sentiment of the community than to respect it.

Subject to these limits, however, the canon for such matters stands: " Give no occasion of stumbling, either to Jews, or to Greeks, or to the Church of God." [1]

2. On similar lines may the minister usually guide himself in less important particulars of ordinary life: his costume and public deportment, for example, or his social intercourse. He can never divest himself of his official character, even when not occupied with the duties of office. Hence his whole behaviour is to be informed by the spirit of his ministry, and influenced by a genuine concern for its highest ends.

[1] 1 Cor. 10³².

As to such outward matters as appearance and bearing, there is a happy mean to be struck between such a demeanour as obtrudes upon the bystander the thought of one's sacred calling and such as would require people to forget it.

At the one extreme there is a peculiar clerical or semi-priestly air—be it hauteur, or primness, or an unctuous affectation of sanctity, or professional stand-offishness—which produces a painful impression on the spectator. It is as if the minister not only could never forget that he is different from other men, but wished them never to overlook the difference. This overdone consciousness of his position is fatal to any frank and purely human fellowship with laymen. At all costs it is to be avoided. Beginning at first in the youthful clergyman as a mere affectation, it grows to be an unconscious habit in the elderly. Whether it appear in a demure look or a self-important one, in a patronising manner or a preternaturally solemn face, or in a professional trick of the voice, it is quite contemptible and often ridiculous. Whatever he is, let the minister be a man, simple and unaffected.

On the other hand, there is an opposite extreme : when the minister of Christ affects the layman, permits himself such an *abandon* of manner, eccentricities of gait, unclerical attire, loud bold speech, effusive demonstrativeness, unseasonable or excessive jocosity, and the like, as to betray, if not forgetfulness of his calling, at least indifference to its sacredness. By thus ignoring any distinction between his own position and that of others, he provokes onlookers to ignore it likewise ; or, if they remember it, as all serious persons must do, then they will be vexed and ashamed at the incongruity between his calling and his deportment.

Somewhere between the two extremes lies the demeanour that is becoming. It is difficult to define in words. Vinet, with a Frenchman's neatness in phrasing, puts it thus: "Il faut . . . sinon qu'on le reconnaisse pasteur, du moins qu'on ne s'étonne pas d'apprendre qu'il est pasteur."[1] Compare Schweizer's clumsier way of saying the same thing: "Man nimmt das Amt nicht überall hin mit sich, sondern nur das Bewusstsein in anderen Stunden vor denen, mit welchen man jetzt gesellig frei umgeht, amtlich aufzutreten."[2]

It is certainly to be desired that a sense of the sacredness of his official duties be never so utterly absent from a clergyman as to exert no sobering influence upon even his lightest or most unguarded hours. But this will not come by effort, or deliberate thinking about the matter. It comes by his being such a man as becomes his office. When the spirit of the holy ministry, grave, simple, sweet and peaceful as it is, becomes the ruling spirit of the man, possesses and informs his inmost being, then will he unaffectedly and unconsciously be everywhere and always the minister. He will need to put on no airs, to check no natural outflow, to study no prim or solemn paces. Being what he is, he will be what he ought to be. So it is best. But since we cannot all be thus ideal ministers, nor be it all at once, there is need for cautions and rules. Hence the text-books on the subject usually give detailed advice. For instance: in dress the pastor is told not to be singular or attract observation, but to wear what good society expects to be worn by men of his profession; following, not preceding, the prevalent mode. In conversation, he is counselled to speak little rather than too much; quietly rather than loudly; to argue seldom and wrangle never; to be sparing of slang; to jest playfully, not bitterly; and never to point his jests with Scripture or subjects connected with his calling. As to demeanour; gravity tempered with habitual affability or accessibility, and relieved upon occasion by innocent playfulness, is what the authorities recommend. Such counsels are not amiss. Only each man has so completely a manner proper to himself that

[1] *Op. cit.* p. 139.   [2] *Op. cit.* p. 265.

wide variations must be allowed if one is not to be pressed
into a Procrustean bed of professionalism. Enough that
each set himself from the outset to train himself into the
most perfect sympathy with the work to which he is
devoted, then let that inner self have free play to mould
by degrees his outward manner; eschewing only with
deliberate endeavour whatever he knows ought to lower
him in the eyes of others.

3. Much casuistry has been expended on the subject of
clerical recreations. But few are likely to go far wrong
here. A conventional understanding seems to have been
reached, rather more liberal than was accepted a generation
back; and amusements still held questionable by the
circle in which a minister moves fall into the class of
adiaphora, and are to be treated accordingly. On the
general question how he shall take his recreation, each man
must be left to decide : two rules only, as it seems to me,
being always kept in view : First, that diversions which
are not found in practice to refresh him, physically or
mentally, for his work, but rather to unfit him for it,
ought, on personal grounds, to be avoided; and second,
that wherever the sentiment of the best members in his
own flock would be shocked by any form of amusement,
the presumption is in favour of abstaining, unless a cogent
reason can be pled on the other side.

4. I imagine the minister will find the same rule of
doing all things for the Gospel's sake, avoiding whatever
would lessen his legitimate influence, to be a safe guide
in social intercourse.

It is in intercourse with his own parishioners or
members of his own flock that mistakes are most likely
to be made. Friendly relations of a purely social character
with suitable families or single persons in the congregation
cannot, of course, be interdicted; and he will indulge in
these with the more freedom as he finds friends of kindred
tastes and culture to his own. The difficulty is, not to
give offence or awaken jealousy by his selection of

intimates. So long as a man is everyone's pastor, he is bound to be everyone's friend. He must " do nothing by partiality " ; [1] that is, in every more intimate friendship which he contracts inside the congregation, he ought strictly to respect this limit, that his kindly pastoral relations with the rest shall in no wise suffer. So narrow and petty is sometimes the tone of society among the lower middle classes from which many congregations are drawn, so divided is it into coteries, so addicted to gossip, and so touchy about its dignity, that not a few promising pastorates are spoilt in this way. A little indiscretion when a young minister begins work in a strange town, a little error due to ignorance of local feeling, is occasionally enough to hamper his usefulness or his comfort for years. It is safer to err on the side of reserve or over-caution, at least till he has felt his ground. Better to risk the imputation for a time of being unsociable, than to let himself be entangled in old feuds, or compromised ere he is aware as a partisan in some local squabble. To the close of his ministry the minister should attach himself to no clique or social set. He will be wise if he suffer no intimacy to become over-familiar, or to monopolise his attentions, or to assume a purely secular complexion. In the unreserve of his most familiar hours, it is well to recollect that he is the minister of God to all his flock, and to all of them alike.

It is expected of a newly-inducted minister, especially when he happens to be the sole representative in the town of his own branch of the Church, that he do a good deal of work not strictly belonging to his own parish or congregation. It is a simple duty of Christian brotherhood to be on the best terms with all the other clergy and ministers of the place, so far as they will let him ; and he owes it to his position to take his fair share, when called upon, in public movements in which Christian men combine. This semi-professional occupation with outside affairs may

[1] 1 Tim. 5[21].

mean a serious drain upon both time and strength, so that (as I have hinted in a previous chapter) it often becomes a question with a conscientious public-spirited minister how far it should be kept up, at least after due homage has been paid to the claims of sister Churches or of the local public. A careful study of the situation may be requisite before he decides; but the principles by which he is to be guided appear to me simple :—

(*a*) No outside work ought to be suffered to infringe upon the duties of his proper pastorate. He is the minister, in the first instance, of a congregation that has called him or of the parish of which he is the incumbent, not of the town or of the public; and it deserves his first care.

(*b*) Those forms of wider service have most claim upon his spare energy which are most directly in the line of his own work: those, that is, by which the spiritual ends of the ministry are best served.

(*c*) Where a choice is open, preference may lawfully be given to public engagements which, besides their other claims upon him, promise to promote his influence or usefulness at home, amongst the people of his charge.

(*d*) Other outside work can be taken up or let alone just as he finds it laid to his hand by Providence, or believes that he can thereby render some signal service to the good of the community and to the kingdom of his Lord and Master.

CHAPTER VIII

HOME LIFE

IT is wedlock which constitutes the "home" in the true sense; and over a great part of Christendom, during nearly the whole of its history, it has been judged advisable in the interest of their sacred office that ministers of the Church should enjoy no "home life" at all. "Celibacy of clergy" was in the first instance an obvious inference from the ascetic theory of morals which almost from the outset infected Christian thought. He who ministers about holy things will always be expected to order his conduct by what his age accepts as its highest ideal. So soon, therefore, as superior merit was assigned to virginity over wedlock, the natural consequences followed. Prohibition, first of second marriages, next of marriage contracted after ordination, as in the Orthodox Greek Church to-day, and then of continued intercourse subsequent to ordination, were so many steps leading up to the final enforcement in the West of complete celibacy as a condition of priests' orders. The growing stringency of the rule kept pace with the growth of sacramental doctrine; for it is above all in the celebrant at the sacrifice of the altar that Catholic feeling demands the utmost priestly purity.

Regarded as a disciplinary regulation, this compulsory celibacy in the Roman Church has had the effect, possibly the intended effect, of securing a more subservient priesthood, entirely at the disposal of its superiors, and free to give to the Church a devotion unshared by competing family claims. Probably those only who have known the

system by experience and observation from the inside are
in a position to say at what price this result has been
attained, or how far it has been worth the cost. At any
rate, I presume no Protestant regrets to-day that at the
Reformation the rule was dropped, almost as a matter
of course; in part, because it was so closely inwoven with
the sacerdotal theory of office that it stood or fell with
that, but mainly because it could plead no sufficient
justification from the New Testament or from the practice
of the Apostolic Age.

Not only did our Lord call St. Peter himself to the
Apostolate when he was already a married man, but Peter
continued in after years to enjoy the society of his wife,
even on his missionary tours.[1] Although St. Paul gave
a preference to the unmarried state "by reason of the
present distress," and elected for himself to remain single,
yet even as an Apostle he claimed the right "to lead
about a wife" like Peter and the others.[2] In the Pastoral
Letters it was assumed to be the rule that both presbyter-
bishops and deacons were to be family men. The solitary
phrase[3] which, in the opinion of many, forbids second
nuptials to a presbyter, sanctions by implication his first
marriage, if it does not do more than sanction it. To
fix with confidence the original force of the words "the
husband of one wife" seems now to be beyond our power.
The phrase may prohibit the ordination of a celibate;
or it may forbid a second marriage to the presbyter;
or, as the foremost Greek exegetes understood it, it may
allude to contemporaneous or bigamous connections which
the laxity of pagan manners rendered frequent—such, for
example, as a new alliance contracted within the lifetime
of a divorced partner.[4] No Reformed communion, so far
as I am aware, has officially adopted any one of these

---

[1] Matt. 8[14], 1 Cor. 9[5].   [2] 1 Cor. 7[26ff.] 9[1-5].

[3] In 1 Tim. 3[2, 12] and Tit. 1[6].

[4] So Theodoret, for instance, Theophylact, and Chrysostom.   Cf.
Appendix B in Fairbairn's *Pastoral Epistles* (1874).

interpretations by giving effect to it in its requirements for ordination. All of them without exception have vindicated for their clergy freedom in the matter; certainly they have never required them to be married men.[1]

What has been regained for the Protestant minister being just his natural right to order his home life on normal family lines, nothing can exonerate him from the responsibility of so ordering it that it shall promote and not hinder the success of his ministry. It is plainly not a matter on which any general rule can be laid down. On the whole, as the result of nearly four centuries of experience, the balance of opinion in Protestant countries now leans pretty heavily in favour of family life, at least in the case of settled pastorates in quiet times. For one reason, because it contributes to the healthy development of the minister's own character; also, for the assistance and encouragement in his work which he may derive from suitable house companions; but chiefly perhaps, in order that from his own experience of domestic life in its duties, temptations, and trials, he may the better counsel other parents, instruct their children, and bring solace to their homes in days of sorrow.

These considerations create, I think, a *primâ facie* probability in favour of family ties, but nothing more. Not only do they depend on the character of the inmates and the kind of home-life which they lead; but in no case can the advantages be all on one side. There is always a minority of instances in which domestic advantages must be sacrificed for the work's sake. For certain posts a celibate alone ought to be eligible. Who would wish a married man to volunteer for the chaplaincy of a leper settlement, or to pioneer missionary effort among unvisited cannibal tribes, or even to accept an appointment in a fever swamp? Men do such things, no doubt, who find women heroic enough to share their lot. But one may be permitted

---

[1] Lea in his *History of Ecclesiastical Celibacy* (3rd ed., 1907, i. 98) tells us that in modern Russia "marriage is obligatory on the parish priest."

to doubt the wisdom of exposing wives or children to such
risks ; and no age has been without its examples of those
who, in the words of Jesus, have " made themselves eunuchs
for the kingdom of heaven's sake." [1] Instances much less
conspicuous may be occurring nearer home. Whatever be
the comforts of house-comradeship, circumstances will arise
which either place them beyond his reach, or make the
young minister feel that he can serve Christ better by
renouncing them. Questions of personal temperament may
enter, or questions of private means ; or family duty, as to
a widowed mother or an orphaned family of nephews and
nieces. He will not always have a free hand. His domestic
associates may be selected for him by Providence. But in
so far as he is free to choose, he has to consider what state
of life or what sort of household promises, in view of all
the conditions, to add the most, not to his personal happiness,
but to his spiritual power and to the probable usefulness of
his ministry. There are risks on every hand. If the
ordinary life of the family has in it great capabilities,
it also conceals grave difficulties. The call of Christ lays
exacting demands on those whom He selects for the honour
of it ; and single-hearted consecration to it is not always
easy to harmonise with the competing claims of earthly
kindred. A minister who shirks arduous or hazardous
duties in order to spare his wife anxiety or shelter his child
from infection, is not, I am afraid, unheard of ; and the too
cosy home may easily grow seductive to an indolent
temperament. Allow the utmost weight one can to other
reasons for a celibate clergy, such as a mistaken asceticism
or a priestly conception of office, it will still be hard to
convince oneself that a rule so widespread and so difficult
of enforcement drew no part of its strength from real
temptations in family life, with which the devoted servant
of Christ in every communion will have to reckon. Of
what that may mean, one can catch some notion who
listens to the stern saying of our Master to a certain

[1] Matt. 19[12].

disciple : " Leave the dead to bury their own dead ; but go thou and publish abroad the kingdom of God." [1]

Often, therefore, it may become a question hard to solve how far the spiritual " soldier on service " ought to " entangle himself in the affairs of this life." [2]   The young minister who is free from family ties will be spared in any case some distraction of energy and some loss of time.   He is much less dependent upon salary.   He can more readily shift his sphere of duty at home or go abroad on foreign employment.   In days of public disaster he will have less to sacrifice for the cause of Christ.   To a man who for such reasons wishes to gather his life well in hand and sit as loose as may be to whatever would divert him from the " one thing " he does, it may easily occur that ties of kindred ought not to be multiplied beyond those in which God has already placed him.

It is, of course, on the question of marriage, though not on that alone, that considerations like these commonly bear ; and there is no such presumption either for or against the wedded state as can release the bulk of men from the duty of a deliberate and well-weighed choice.   In the minister's case, the leading element in his decision will probably be one which concerns himself more than anyone else.   The reflex influence of a family home upon the minister's own spirit, in the way either of sustaining him in his daily duties or of incapacitating him for their discharge, is almost incalculable.   It is an aspect of home-life to which writers on Pastoral Theology are quite justified in calling special attention.[3]   In no other calling is a man so dependent on home influences for keeping him day by day in the fittest condition for doing his public duty as in the holy ministry ; simply because in no other calling does the quality of work depend so absolutely on the moral and religious state of the workman.   It needs no words to show that the quiet punctual orderliness of a well-conducted

---

[1] Luke 9[60], cf. Matt. 8[22].   [2] 2 Tim. 2[4].

[3] *e.g.* Schweizer in his *Pastoraltheorie* (Leipzig, 1875, §§ 97–99).

household must contribute materially to maintain serenity of temper, with a constant readiness for duties which can only be performed when one's spirit is at leisure from itself. To secure regular hours for prayer and reading, to have them free from interruption, to find the moral atmosphere of the parlour or nursery in harmony with that of the study, to be able to go forth from home to one's work in a self-collected and reverent mood, and to return to it as to an arbour of refreshment where one is sure of sympathy,—all this means a great deal to the busy pastor, and it is precisely this which a suitable partner and a carefully ordered household ought to furnish.

But they will only do so, of course, where his house-mates are in such practical sympathy with the spirit of his sacred calling that nothing is tolerated in the normal arrangements or atmosphere of the home which is uncongenial or distracting, nothing to foster indolence or self-indulgence, nothing either to damp his ardour or to restrain him from his duty. Under adverse conditions, the mischief which may be wrought by unsuitable companions in the home circle is proportionately great. It is not from the graver trials of family life that hindrance is to be apprehended. No: the family man has indeed given hostages to fortune; but sickness or bereavement will but ripen in him as in other children of God the graces of patience, tolerance, and compassion, fitting him to be a better messenger of consolation to his people. It is rather the petty irritations of domestic intercourse, especially when the household is a narrow or a pinched one, that are to be dreaded. And it is here that love finds occasion for continual self-denial in small things. A man is not to repress the noisy glee of his children or vex the soul of his wife with grumbles, merely that his study may be undisturbed by household din. Selfishly to fence himself from worry at the expense of all his house-mates would be a poor way of cultivating the pastoral spirit. On the other hand, sympathetic house-mates for their part will do what

they can to guard his private hours of labour from unnecessary invasion. In a hundred details must every member of
the little circle be prepared for small unnoticed sacrifices—
sacrifices which win dignity only from the cause in which,
and the Master to whom, they are made. Neither must
the family expect, nor dare the minister concede, any time
or attention bestowed on their personal convenience which
is inconsistent with a conscientious performance of his
public duties. Here the claims of kindred have to be
gently but firmly set aside in loyalty to a higher obligation.
"Who," said the Lord at one memorable moment in His
own ministry—"who is My mother, and who are My
brethren?"[1]

Enough surely has now been said to emphasise the
unspeakable consequence which attaches — should he
decide upon married life—to a minister's choice of a
partner. This does not mean that the first thing to be
sought for in a pastor's wife is a helpmeet in his official
duties. In many circles, modern methods of organising
woman's work, philanthropic or religious, have created
most useful posts for ladies who possess the gift of public
speech or who can conduct meetings of their own sex.
This is tending, I think, to create an impression that
the best wife for any minister must be one who is herself
half a minister, fit for every variety of curate's work
in the parish. This seems to me a mistake. Although,
when other things are equal, it is obviously desirable, as
it is expected, that the lady of the parsonage or the manse
should be competent to take an active share in such
Christian service as falls nowadays to other ladies, yet
it is of far greater moment that she should make a
suitable house-companion for her husband.

Of course, that means a companion who suits him
not only as a man, but likewise as a minister. If a wife
is to be a helpmeet, the least that can be asked for is that
she be in the fullest possible sympathy with his ministry;

[1] Matt. 12⁴⁸.

herself devoted in her own way to the same ends to which he has devoted his life. A devout Christian, attached to the branch of the Church in which her husband serves, inspired by such a measure of zeal for the glory of her Lord and the growth of His kingdom, that she is prepared to share inevitable sacrifices for these objects:—this, it seems to me, is the first requisite. Sacrifices there are sure to be: very probably of pecuniary profit and social position which her husband's talents might have won in another profession; possibly even of his health; sacrifice in any case of home privacy and of his society in leisure hours for the sake of public engagements. A wife who is too solicitous about worldly display or her own comforts, or even so anxious to coddle her husband that she restrains, instead of sustaining, him in the discharge of incumbent duty, is nothing short of a hindrance rather than a help.

For the rest, what she needs above all is prudence, and in most cases the qualities of a good housewife. For the income of a pastor is usually a narrow one; yet his bills must be punctually paid, his housekeeping should not appear penurious, and his home ought never to be untidy. The domestic arrangements of the minister, in respect of order and hospitality, need not differ from those of other well-conducted Christian homes of the middle class; unless it be by an even greater simplicity of living or avoidance of display, and by a hospitality which is professional rather than promiscuous. His income rarely allows of extravagance, either in table or in dress. In only too many cases, not in one type of Church alone, it is really inadequate to the legitimate claims upon it. However restricted it be, an effort must be made to set aside something—more than is called for from others whose means are the same—for charitable and religious objects. This is a necessity of his position which is apt to press heavily upon the ill-paid minister. Yet it concerns his honour and the credit of his office that he should pinch at other points in order to be generous here. He will be exposed to many appeals, and will run unusual risks of being taken in by the unworthy. Nevertheless, for a man who represents the spirit of his Master, it is better to be occasionally imposed upon than ever to be churlish or unkind to the poor. I know that the shameless mendicancy of modern city life is a grievous trial to many a minister. It is well known to the professional beggar and the begging-letter writer and the swarm of lazy impostors who prey upon the charitable, that the clergy are a class on whom distress has a professional claim. The wise minister in a large town will find the benefit of informing himself about every local charity. But guard his purse from the unworthy as he may, he must be prepared to devote to charity a liberal percentage of his slender income.

The judicious management of their resources is therefore a matter to which the minister and the lady of his household—be she wife or sister—must not grudge a good deal of conscientious and even prayerful attention. If to diligence and domestic economy, the mistress of the manse can add the supreme grace of silence that knows how to endure without complaining, and neither to bear tales, nor betray secrets, nor add needlessly to the pastor's anxieties, then her presence in his dwelling will nearly double the usefulness of his pastorate. All honour to those obscure virtues of the home! To be thrifty, neither penurious nor mean; to pay every debt honourably and promptly; to preserve the self-respect of gentle folks on the income sometimes of a superior artisan; to deny themselves personal comforts rather than complain or reveal their poverty to the world; to bear and be silent even when, to the discredit of his people or of some careless official, the stipend is not punctually forthcoming; to keep such sordid anxieties from their congregation, even, as far as possible, from their own children; to retain a quiet trust in God's providence, and go tranquilly about His service, though the purse be exceeding light:—these belong

HOME LIFE

them wins no fame, except in heaven. Not to do them
would dishonour the name we bear before an unfeeling
world. Many a manse and many a curate's parsonage
has concealed such heroic virtues; and conceals them
to-day.

To "have his children in subjection with all gravity"
was very early specified as a qualification for the episcopate.
The rule is perpetuated to-day in a popular expectation
that the children of the parsonage shall be patterns of careful upbringing. It is by no means always the case. There
are difficulties in the way, peculiar to the ministerial calling.
The minister's family has to reconcile itself to his absence
on many evenings which most private citizens can spend
at home if they choose. In this way the care of growing
boys and girls is apt to be thrown more than is quite
desirable upon the mother, without the support to which
she is entitled from the head of the house. Other seasons
ought therefore to be found, or made, at which the father
can bring his paternal influence to bear, especially as the
young people are approaching adolescence. To be taking
care for the Church of God will be no excuse for failure to
rule well his own house; and the lads who grow up unfamiliar with their father or untutored by his grave and
kindly wisdom, are all the more likely to go wrong.

But it is possible to err by excess, as well as by neglect,
of rule. I do not credit what one sometimes hears, that
the proportion of clergymen's sons who make shipwreck in
after years, is above the average in other callings. Statistics
are said to reveal an opposite result. At all events, it is
notorious that a high percentage of those who achieve
marked success in professional or business careers, come
from the homes of the clergy. The manse has proved
itself a fruitful nursery for the pulpit. Not seldom does
ministerial office tend to become hereditary. It is true
nevertheless that one's natural expectation is now and then
falsified by a minister's son who turns out badly, bringing

not sorrow only, but discredit on an honoured father; and such a breakdown when it occurs is sure to attract more than the usual measure of attention. Were it either possible or needful to trace cases of this sort to any defect in parental discipline, one might suspect them to be revolts against undue severity in the training of the home. In some instances, at all events, they have had this origin. The tendency in previous generations has been, and to some extent still is, to over-strictness; notably in puritanical circles, and with reference to such external points as the observance of the Lord's Day. When a rigorous code of conduct was conjoined with a narrow theology, it might be suffered during the early years of childhood without much visible harm; but where restraints which were legitimate or innocuous in childhood were prolonged after youths had reached some degree of personal responsibility, and of the sense of freedom which that brings along with it, they were very apt to be succeeded by a recoil which might easily become licence.

CHAPTER IX

CITIZENSHIP

THE attitude which the Churches and in particular their ministers ought to hold toward politics and social questions is a matter on which a good deal of discussion has recently taken place. It has revealed acute differences of opinion which discourage the hope that any common line of action, or even common principle of action, is likely soon to be agreed upon. By some the advice is urgently given that the ministry should confine itself to its " proper work " of preaching the Gospel, striving to save individual souls from sin. In other quarters loud and insistent voices are calling on every minister of religion actively to engage in social reform as part of his proper work, and in particular to advocate legislative measures which aim at the moral or economic elevation of the labouring poor. May there not be wisdom in the suggestion that there is room and need enough for ministers of both sorts, so that each man may feel himself free to follow that course of conduct in this matter which commends itself to his own judgment, or which best suits his temperament, his gifts, and his sphere of labour ?

But since in no other department of his duty does the young minister encounter greater perplexities than here, it is certainly desirable, if only it be possible, to mark out some guiding lines for his assistance.

1. In the quiet exercise of his political rights as a private citizen, at least, no difficulty is likely to arise. That he is as free as others, and certainly as much called on, to form

his own opinions on politics and to give them effect at the polling-booth, no one questions. His sacred office cannot release him from the responsibility which attaches to all citizenship.

2. Whether under any circumstances, and if so, under what circumstances, he is well advised to become an active and public party man, mingling in political strife, is less clear. When, if ever, for instance, may he speak on a political platform or canvass in an election?

The obvious objections which it is usual to urge against such a course arise partly from what is good for himself, and partly from what is due to his office. Like his medical brethren, though even more than they, the minister is understood to be set by his sacred calling happily aloof from, and in a sense above, the claims of mere partisanship; just in order that his time may be free for higher service to the public, and that his thoughts may not be diverted from higher concerns. Not that the din and dust of a political contest must necessarily unfit every one who engages in it for religious work; still less that a Christian who enters upon it from pure or noble motives is not thereby serving Christ as well as his country. But the minister of religion has prior claims upon him; and he can hardly descend into the arena without suffering distraction from themes and from duties which deserve his undivided attention. Still less is it safe to do so in the interests of his office. He represents to the eye of the public a purely religious society which has, or at least ought to have, no political colour. The best of Christians may be found in either political camp. The great majority of controverted questions in the public life of the State, even when they are not purely political, offer no such clear issue to the Christian conscience as must range all religious persons under the same banner. They may indeed have moral aspects and probable moral issues; but these are complicated in almost every case either by the political principles involved, or by prospective gain or loss to this or that

political party. The result is that men of the highest
Christian character differ in their party allegiance, according as family traditions, or early education, or personal
convictions, or the interest of their order, chance to sway
them. For the pastor under these circumstances conspicuously to espouse a side, must mean to place himself
alongside one portion of his flock in antagonism to another
portion of it. It must be so, as long as our Churches are
what Churches ought to be, and are not yet become gatherings of people who all think alike on affairs of State as
well as on the Gospel.

Nor is it simply from a prudential wish not to divide
the allegiance of his parishioners or alienate a part of his
congregation, that an official of the Church needs to keep
his duties as a private citizen carefully apart from his
public position as a minister of religion. It is because, if
he engage in the public advocacy of a political cause
through the press or on the platform, his advocacy will be
regarded neither by friend nor foe as the action of a mere
private citizen—but also as that of a minister of religion.
Nor ought it to be, since the minister can never divest
himself of his official character, or of the prestige which
that gives him in the eyes of many. The weight of his
advocacy cannot but be increased by the fact that he is
a minister of religion. To carry over in this way into a
political camp, for purely political ends, an influence which
comes to him from his sacred office, is to divert that
office to an end quite foreign to it. Moreover, this must
tend in the long run to weaken his prestige in the sphere
where it is legitimate. I mean, that he who misuses his
authority as a teacher of religion to support his opinions
as a politician, is sure to forfeit some of that authority,
even when it is religious truth he is enforcing. Especially
will those who differ from him in politics trust him the
less in religion.

Are we not touching here on one of the deepest
causes for that loss of clerical influence over large sections

of our population, which every reflecting person observes and all serious persons deplore? I have said that Churches ought to have no political colour. It is one of the worst fruits of ecclesiastical division in England, that our several communions, being drawn to a large extent from distinct classes among the people, have come to reflect the political complexion of their respective constituents. The ecclesiastical history of England has produced recognised types of churchmanship which merge into the outstanding parties of the political world. Even the venerable Church of England, which ought to mirror the mind of the whole nation, has had such long and close historical associations with the ruling and privileged classes, that it is confidently expected to cast its influence on the side of rank, of the country gentry, of land owners, and of the professions.[1] Dissent in England has, through its unfortunate history, acquired an opposite, but an even more avowed bias. There are Churches which depend on the prosperous and well-to-do middle class to such an extent that they are almost identified in practice with middle-class ideas or interests. Denominations, on the other hand, which have done their best work among the labouring poor, can hardly be blamed for championing the cause of labour or advocating the claims of poverty, although they may be able to bring to either little financial and even less social strength.

All this, however easy it may be to account for it, appears to me to have had the greatest and most deplorable results on the life of England; and one of those I

[1] In his sermon preached before the Church Congress at Barrow in 1906, and reprinted recently in his volume entitled *The New Theology and the Old Religion* (1907), Bishop Gore had the frankness to admit that the Church of England is "not in touch with the mass of the labouring people." It has failed, he says in stronger words than I have used, "to be the Church of the people in an effective sense in town or country." "The opinions and the prejudices that are associated with its administration as a whole are the opinions and the prejudices of the higher and upper middle classes, rather than of the wage-earners" (p. 282).

take to be the indifference, if not contempt, with which all Churches, with their official representatives, are regarded by considerable numbers of our fellow-citizens. Has it not gone far to rob every Church of the weight it would carry were its aims more exclusively and more conspicuously "not of this world"? Of course, no single minister in any communion, especially no young minister, can do much to counteract this state of things. But at least he should resist as he best may the pressure which bears upon him from the prevailing prejudices of his own Church and from the political ideas or passions which have grown to be traditional in it. This he needs to do if he is to guard his personal independence, both of opinion and of action ; still more if he would secure purity and elevation of motive in everything he attempts as a worker for the kingdom of heaven. He needs to do it if he would win spiritual influence. Sacred and precious is that power which gathers through the years around any servant of Christ who is felt to have no mixture of earthly aims in the zeal with which he furthers his Master's cause; who, when he speaks in his Master's name, is known to have his eye set on no lower end than to lead men up to God, to holiness, and to heaven. To this rule of action it ever comes back. Fidelity to his own high mission is for every minister the first of duties. And the secret of his useful-ness, which he must cherish as his best jewel, is just the moral power which that fidelity will give him over the hearts and consciences of men.

3. So far we seem to have reached a safe general rule, applicable to the majority of questions in politics. But it is felt by many that this avoidance of political partisanship is liable, in our own day especially, to exceptions, so that the path of duty has become less easy than it looks. There are two kinds of political matters in debate on which difficulty must arise. The one is where ecclesiastical interests are very closely touched. Of this, proposals for the disestablishment of a national Church

6

afford an obvious instance. The other is where the moral or religious welfare of the people, or of large sections of the people, is involved: a numerous group, lying on the borderland between politics and sociology, including legislation for primary education, for the discouragement of intemperance, the suppression of gambling, the protection of the Sunday rest, and similar matters.

It is impossible to deny that on both those groups of subjects, when they enter into politics, official guardians of religion have more than a right, have a responsibility, to make their voices heard.[1] But then they do so, not as party politicians, not even as politicians at all, but as Christian men and Christian ministers. In other words, such action as they feel constrained to take is not private, but strictly official, action: action incumbent upon them as ministers of religion no less than as patriotic citizens. The effect of this is, of course, to alter its character materially. By elevating its motive above the ordinary level of party, it ought to impart to it a tone of moderation, dignity, and Christian charity befitting whatever a man does in the holy name of religion. Those who embark on the advocacy of legislative measures affecting the Churches or the religious and moral welfare of the nation, have need to take care that their zeal for a holy cause is as free from baser alloy as it professes to be, and that their judgment is not warped nor their tone embittered by sectarian and party aims. The minister who succeeds in thus exempli-

[1] Cf. Newman, *Parochial Sermons*, i. 183–184: " If, indeed, this world's concerns could be altogether disjoined from those of Christ's kingdom, then indeed all Christians (laymen as well as clergy) should abstain from the thought of temporal affairs, and let the worthless world pass down the stream of events till it perishes; but if (as is the case) what happens in *nations* must affect the cause of *religion* in those nations, since the Church may be seduced and corrupted by the world, and in the world there are myriads of souls to be converted and saved, and since a Christian nation is bound to become part of the Church, therefore it is our duty to stand as a beacon on a hill, to cry aloud and spare not, to lift up our voice like a trumpet, and show the people their transgressions and the house of Jacob their sins."

fying in his own person that religious temper in which every serious problem of the sort ought to be approached, can do much by his public utterances to commend to others a similar temper, and to secure that, so far at least as his influence extends, it is the bearing of legislative schemes upon the sacred interests of righteousness, peace, and humanity which is kept in view.

The difficulty which ecclesiastics experience in preserving this correct Christian tone is immensely greater in the former of the two groups of questions I named than in the second. It is comparatively easy to keep one's eye single and one's motives high when it is a measure for the moral elevation of the people that one champions. But the temper which ecclesiastics display when fighting for the privileges of their order or the supposed interest of their Church, has too often been anything but worthy. Days of vehement ecclesiastical debate in the past political history of our land—the days, for example, of the Commonwealth in England, or of the Reformation and the Covenant in Scotland—were by no means models of sober discussion conducted in a courteous or religious spirit. If in either half of the island, or in both, we have before us a similar period of strife,—such a strife, say, over the relations of the State to the Church as some countries of the Continent are passing through,—it may come as a test of our Christianity. May it be given alike to those who desire and to those who fear change, to clear their hearts of unworthy motives, personal or sectarian, to rid debate of rancour, and to aim, with as little as may be of human prejudice, at the honour of our Lord and the advancement of His kingdom!

4. What has been said above applies to those social ills which it is proposed to remedy by legislative measures. But outside of legislation lies a very wide field for social philanthropy and reform, upon which is now concentrated a larger amount both of discussion and of effort than was ever the case before. It seems to me unreasonable to ask

from the overworked pastor and preacher in any of our towns much personal service in this new department of Christian service. Some portions of the field, indeed, for example, the intricate and technical problems connected with labour and capital or with the treatment of pauperism and the unemployed, lie too remote from his professional studies and require more specialised knowledge than he is likely to possess. They are for the economist, the publicist, or the statesman. Other matters, certainly, like the housing of the people, or the regulation of the liquor traffic, although they likewise call for experts to handle them well, do touch the Church very closely, because they relate to conditions which are adverse, if not fatal, to her own task of preaching the Gospel to the poor. They are not matters, therefore, from which the Christian Church can hold itself aloof. Nor indeed can a society which exists, as the Church does, for the express purpose of advancing God's reign on earth, neglect as beyond its scope any wise effort to provide human beings with the means of healthy, sober, and virtuous living. But social reform is not the concern of the Church alone : it is for the philanthropist and the patriotic citizens, whatever be his attitude to the religious life. Nor is it the Church's direct and primary business, for the performance of which her ministers are set apart. In so far, therefore, as it is the duty of a Church to do more than second the efforts of other people, or encourage her members to become volunteers in the "noble army" of philanthropy ; in so far as she finds it laid upon her in these days to combine organised social work with her own evangelism, such work, it seems to me, is best done by the Christian laity, inspired only, and, if need be, organised or led, by their official leaders. The spiritual duties for which the ministry has been set apart must ever be fenced from invasion, even by the holiest and most urgent of philanthropic efforts that have for their object the material welfare of the people. At present, one of the sorest troubles with which a conscientious minister has to contend, is the dissipation of energy and waste of time occasioned by a multitude of outside enterprises, societies, committees, and charities of every sort, in which he is expected to show interest by taking an active share. Excellent work most of it; work with which he must sympathise, because it lies in the line of the Master's kingdom and breathes more or less of the Master's spirit. But is it necessary for him to do it, or even to take any prominent part in the doing of it? Is it not by the freewill exertions of the Church's private members, under the inspiration of the Gospel which their minister preaches from Sunday to Sunday, that all this social beneficence, whether organised as Church work or not, ought to be carried on? In spite of all that has yet been done, there is here a clamant and growing opportunity for the consecrated ministry of Christlike men and women: might not the pastor's sympathy with it be more often taken for granted?

Two things, I think, in the future, ministers may fairly be asked to do. The one is to acquaint themselves at first hand with the social evils to be remedied, and to give some study to the methods attempted for their remedy, in order that they may be more competent to preside over that hive of activity—a modern "institutional" or home-missionary congregation. Not only must it limit their usefulness and lessen their influence to betray indifference or ignorance on what so many take to be the main task —it is certainly one of the main tasks—to which Christ is calling us to-day: it is even unworthy of their position as examples of the Christian spirit. And without some special study no one is competent to give sympathy which is intelligent, or guidance which is helpful.

The other service is one that falls to the preacher. The attention now devoted to sociology has made it urgent on divines to examine, and on preachers to expound, with greater thoroughness than heretofore, the social applications of the ethics of Jesus. Christianity is a religion for this world and for the daily life; but this side of it has not hitherto received adequate attention. It is from the pulpit that the teaching and example of our Lord have to be brought to bear upon the present-day relations of class to class and of man to man in the common life of the State. Sermons, therefore, ought neither to be so abstract as to lose touch with facts and with the responsibilities that spring out of facts, nor so exclusively aimed at the culture of the interior life as to have no eye for civic duties and national well-being. It is more than safe, it is right, for the capable preacher to urge his hearers to act out their Christianity as citizens, as employers or employed, as traders, masters or servants—in short, in every relationship of life. He will be at no loss for texts, and need not travel beyond his New Testament. But he will be helpless enough in this region and make awkward blunders, unless he has prepared himself by a careful and prolonged study of New Testament ethics.

As a rule, the preacher may very well content himself in his public teaching with explaining ethical principles and indicating their general bearing on everyday affairs. Their detailed application under the variable and entangled conditions of society must be left to the individual conscience. But this does not forbid him to censure with some precision prevalent forms either of vice or of injustice; to censure them with greater precision, I would say, than has for some generations been usual in the Protestant pulpit.[1] Situations may even arise, when a very outspoken application of Christian principles to public life is permissible. For example, when gross injustice is bearing hardly on the poor; or when there has been lawless excess or revolt among the masses; or when profligacy is flagrant in the higher circles; or when some widespread vice like gambling is eating as a canker into the commonwealth;

[1] Athanase Coquerel's remarks may be referred to: *Observations Pratiques sur la Predication* (Paris, 1860), translated by Bertram under the title *The Preacher's Counsellor* (London, 1867).

or when public attention has been aroused by a conspicuous instance of commercial fraud. Perhaps it is seldom discreet in a junior minister, or one whose voice carries little weight with the public, to constitute himself in this way a public censor. But anyone who from his age or position is entitled to do so will usually know how to avoid the risks which attend it. He will deliver his message under a sobering sense of responsibility, taking care to distribute blame without partiality, to exaggerate nothing and defame no one, and never to afford the slightest ground for the suspicion that he is advertising himself or hunting after notoriety.

PART II

THE MINISTER AS LEADER IN WORSHIP

CHAPTER X

THEORY OF CHRISTIAN WORSHIP

I COULD wish that our English speech, like the German, had frankly borrowed the Latin word *cultus* to denote public and solemn forms of worship, such as every religious community gives to its devotions. In a truncated shape we do occasionally use the word; any particular form of divine service we call a "cult." But for the abstract idea underlying all cults we have no better name than "public worship," although such common forms are as much a necessity for man as religion itself. "Religiös zu seyn," says Nitzsch, "und Religion zusammen zu pflegen, ist dem Menschen wesentlich." No doubt religion, wherever it is ethical, inculcating moral motives and precepts, fashions for ,itself another mode of expression from the ritual one, through those social duties to which a man feels himself urged by his fear or love of God. Still, no religion is satisfied with an exclusively ethical manifestation of itself. Its religious faith seeks some more direct utterance in acts or words which serve no other end than to give outward form or body to its feelings towards the Divine.

So long as this is confined to a private worshipper, or even to the family circle, it hardly needs preconcerted arrangements. But wherever a larger social group, united on the basis of a common faith, gives to that faith a public expression, some agreement is requisite as to the time, the place, and the manner of it.   Usually, too, a representative or official functionary is required, either to perform the rites in the name of all, or at least to lead the people in their common acts.   At once there arises an order of divine service, a ritual; in fact, what may be called in the earliest and widest use of the term, a "liturgy."   For at first, as its derivation implies, λειτουργός denoted any officer who discharged a State function.   At Athens it was applied to citizens who at their own charge undertook certain onerous civic offices.   Even in profane Greek, it came to be extended (at least in Egypt[1]) to the service of the gods.   With this application to the sphere of religion, words from this root are frequent in the Septuagint, and occur once at least in the New Testament of a Jewish priest.[2]   Hence they came naturally to be used of apostles and prophets in the Christian Church, even of our Lord Himself.[3]   It was a limitation when the word "liturgy" became a technical term in the ancient Church of the West[4] for the office of the eucharist as the central act of Christian worship; and, of course, its modern restriction in English to a prescribed form of common prayer, is equally a departure from its primary width of meaning.   German authors are therefore within their rights when they employ "Liturgik" for the whole theory of public worship in the Church.

The characteristics of every religion are, of course, reflected in its ritual; so that our conception of the public services which are proper for a Christian congregation has to be formed from the governing ideas of Christianity itself, and from the experience common to Christian believers.   The first change which the advent of Christianity effected bore on the comparative importance

---

[1] Deissmann gives instances from the papyri (*Bibl. Studies*, p. 140).
[2] Luke 1[23].   [3] Acts 13[2], Rom. 15[16], Phil. 2[17], Heb. 8[2, 6].
[4] Not so limited in the East, according to Bingham's *Antt.* Bk. 13, c. 1.

attached to substance and to forms in worship. Between
the outward and the inward there ought naturally to exist
a close and constant relation. Outward forms were
moulded at first by the inner belief, emotions, and wants
of the devout, and to the end they need to be sustained
and inspired by them. But all external rites tend to outlive the feelings which gave them value at the first. They
come in course of time to be repeated as a tradition, or
with a blind trust in the efficacy of the form after its
meaning has departed from it. To some extent this will
hold of every cult. But Christianity as the religion of
the spirit is distinguished, not only by the simplicity of its
rites, but even more by the supreme value which it
attaches to the inward over the outward. The latter
alone without the former it treats as worthless.

When it appeared, the world had long been accustomed
to the pompous cults of the Empire; to the splendour of
holy places; to temples and images on which art had
lavished all its skill; to a sensuous ritual of animal sacrifice, music and drama, with State processions and symbolic
pageants, venerable for the antique myths and forgotten
mysteries which they enshrined. Behind this gorgeous
and imposing worship, celebrated by Imperial functionaries
and creating for the populace a yearly circle of festive
holidays, how much or how little personal piety could be
supposed to lie?

Beyond a vague inherited reverence for the gods and
an occasional votive offering for good luck, the religious life
of an antique pagan either held a most limited content, or
drew its inspiration more from philosophy than from the
popular faith. Nor was it much better with the religion
of Judaism. Few national rituals can have been more
impressive than that of the Jewish Temple in its best
days. But from its forms, too, the spirit had evaporated.
The priestly round of Temple sacrifice and liturgy went
on; although the religious hope of the nation had gone
to inflame political factions, and piety had become

crystallised into a scrupulous observance of legal tradition. Of both the Jewish and the Gentile cults in the first century, may we not say that the material apparatus of worship vastly overloaded its inner content, which had shrunk almost to a minimum ?

Into such a society the Gospel came, enriching of a sudden the souls of its disciples with an astonishing wealth of novel and absorbing experiences.   New thoughts of God as the Father of all men, revealed in His Son ; union of man with God realised at last in the Person of Jesus ; the expiation of guilt achieved by His cross ; the liberty from the letter which the advent of the Spirit gave; a sense of security and superiority to the ills of life ; anticipation of coming glory ; a life to be lived every day in intimate filial fellowship with God through the risen Lord:—all this and much more flooded the Christian consciousness, clamouring to be expressed in the assemblies of the brethren : a whole new world of inner emotions, desires, and hopes which grateful hearts burned to utter in the ear of God as the common possession of Christ's Spirit-filled Church.

What was strange was that, with this unexampled deepening and enrichment of the inner side of religion—its devotional contents, the forms for its expression became in the same proportion few, and simple even to meagreness.   The heathen thought Christians had no cult at all. Temple, sacrifice, and ritual had disappeared.   Forms and ceremonial there was next to none.   The exuberant life of personal experience broke forth in individual utterances that might even be ecstatic, and were at times ill-regulated. Concerted or common acts at first hardly existed.   The symbolic dwindled to a couple of familiar rites : a bath and a meal.   Everything else was spoken, not acted:— the chanted psalm, the Old Testament lesson read, the extempore prayer, the half-inspired address.   Always it was the Word that was the medium through which had to be conveyed from soul to soul, or from many souls to God

Most High, every variety in the rich experiences of the new religion.

The explanation of a change so striking must be looked for in the principles laid down by our Lord at Jacob's Well.[1] From the spirituality of God followed, He said, the spirituality of acceptable worship. It was not novel teaching. Brave voices had often protested in Israel against formalism and lip-worship. But the truth was to receive in the new religion a new emphasis and to yield new results. It was to have far-reaching consequences beyond the one which Jesus deduced from it at the time—the abolition of holy places. One is that no external form retains any worth at all in God's eyes when it is divorced from the inner feeling of the heart, whose outcome it ought to be. For the inward spirit of self-devotion which a devout soul feels in the presence of its God, not only is the best worship—it is the only worship which pleases the Father. There, in the lowly surrendered spirit of the man, is the true shrine wherein God dwells and His human child adores. Worship can no longer be a ceremonial—an outward performance. A second inference is that it cannot be done by proxy. The priest's service on the people's behalf and in the absence of the people, is not such service as the Father seeks. For each private worshipper has his own spiritual contribution which he must bring, uniting his personal devotions with those of his brethren. Common worship is the sum of the devout emotions animating the assembled worshippers. And yet another of these consequences is that the visible symbols, the manual acts, the material offerings of older faiths, have now to yield precedence as forms of expression to that simple Word which is the soul's purest utterance of herself—that by which spirits convey to other spirits (so far as they are communicable at all) their own deepest innermost states. As the Father is Spirit and reveals Himself by His Word, so it is by their words His spiritual children are now to speak to Him. When worship is thus

[1] John 4[19-24].

" in spirit," it cannot fail to be also " in truth " ; for any external medium which the soul finds to utter itself by, will be no empty shell, devoid of substance, no outworn formula or misleading pretence of piety. Poor as it may be, it will be a genuine channel for the outpouring of the heart's sincere devotion.

Having learnt from this pregnant saying of the Master that the only real and acceptable worship of the Father is inward and spiritual, it is natural to raise the question : Why should this inward and spiritual worship seek or require any outward expression of itself at all ? What, in other words, is the purpose or the value of the Church's common service of God in public ?

Two answers have been given. Since Schleiermacher, the best writers on the subject[1] have agreed with him in saying : The united utterance of Christian devotion simply obeys and satisfies the craving of all life after self-expression,—a craving strong in proportion as life is strongly moved by emotions which are shared in common by a social group. Wherever the minds and hearts of many are swayed by the same impulse, they seek of necessity a concerted form of utterance. It is therefore inevitable that devout Christian people, banded by Christ's will into a Church society, will strive to express their common emotions towards God in Christ, and will do this in the most perfect form attainable, primarily as an offering of their devotion to God Himself, but also as a natural bond of sympathy with one another.

Social worship falls on this theory under the category of human actions which are intransitive or merely expressive. It is the category to which the fine arts belong ; and worship, too, is subject in its own way to those laws of taste which prescribe to every expressional act its fitting

---

[1] Schleiermacher, *Christliche Sittenlehre*, and his posthumous *Praktische Theologie* (1850). See also, Ehrenfeuchter, *Theorie des christl. Cultus* (1840) ; Kliefoth, *Theorie d. Cultus d. evang. Kirche* (1844) ; Vetter, *D. Lehre vom christ. Cultus* (1839).

measure and most perfect form. Theoretically, this *rationale* of a cult justifies itself as at bottom correct. Yet, nakedly put, it jars against both the sentiment and the practice of average Christians. Devout people have long cherished a very different explanation. They go to church, they say, to be edified. It is a means of grace. Take away this expectation of personal profit, and they would feel as if their chief inducement to join with fellow-worshippers in the services of the sanctuary were taken away.

When these two answers to the question, the scientific and the popular, are looked at apart, it seems to me plain that each of them is inadequate. The former without the latter loses touch with concrete fact and remains an unattained ideal. The latter without the former lowers worship into a prudential means of self-improvement, and so misses the proper idea of worship altogether. But the two are neither mutually exclusive, nor to be held severely asunder. Even from a formal point of view, the theory of self-expression, when closer looked at, is found to involve self-edification as well. It does so in two ways.

First, by a law of our nature, every mental state, especially every emotion, is fixed, strengthened, and deepened by being expressed; and this all the more when it receives a social or a formal expression. Nothing heightens any mood of feeling more than to join with others under the sympathy of numbers in giving to it festive or solemn utterance. Then the ardour of each kindles into enthusiasm under the contagious ardour of the crowd. Now, all such intensifying of devotional states must tend to build up the religious life out of which they spring. So that common worship, whether designed for edification or not, must at all events promote it as a result.

In the next place, the religious experience of Christian people cannot possibly receive adequate, or anything like adequate, expression in their common devotions, unless their sense of imperfection and their longing after growth in grace play a large part in the service. For they play a very large part in experience. Confessions of failure, supplication for divine aid, efforts to nourish the inner life on the "strong meat" of the Word of God, will be prominent items in every cult which fairly reflects the average life of a Christian congregation; and none of these can be conceived apart from the hope and intention to purify and strengthen the inward life.[1]

These considerations, however, lead us past the merely formal side of public worship as an act of expression, to examine what lies behind it, namely, the devout life itself, which is the thing to be expressed. And this ought, if I mistake not, to set in clearer light the connection between these two theories of its design.

It may be taken for granted, I suppose, that the root-idea in religion, at least in all its higher stages, is union or reunion with the Divine, and that it is this, therefore, which men have everywhere sought by worship to realise, it may be, to restore, but, at all events, to express. The radical thought which remains constant under every cult is some sort of intercourse or commerce with the Supreme. Men draw near to the presence of their God, first, that they may offer such gifts, believed to be acceptable, as it is in their power to present; and next, that they may receive from the Divine Power benefits which they are conscious of needing. Both the giving and the receiving may be of the rudest or the most earthly kind. The transaction may descend in unethical religions to the level of a bargain, or even of a bribe or of a spell. It may also be transfigured, as in Christianity, into the loving, con-fiding fellowship of a reconciled child with his heavenly Father, whose moral approval is the best of boons, and to whose moral designs he can lend the co-operation of a son. But always the end aimed at is a bond of amity, which

[1] "Da die Kirche immer auch im Werden begriffen ist, so muss sie sich auch als Werdende im Cultus darstellen." Schweizer, *Homiletik* (1848), p. 68.

shall embrace the Worshipped and the worshipper in one
—each giving to the other of his own in a mutual passage
or interchange of goodwill. This is worship.

Now, what is it that Christians come near to God to
give, and what to receive ?

Christianity being the religion of perfected reconciliation between God and man in Christ Jesus, the worshipper's
faith apprehends peace with God as already *un fait
accompli*. He has not to approach with an offering
intended either to expiate for guilt or to propitiate the
favour of an indifferent Deity. To bring any gift, be it
mass or eucharist, penitential tears, vows of amendment,
or simply the homage of song or prayer, with the idea of
winning Heaven's grace, is to worship as a Jew or a pagan
might, not as a Christian. Not that we have no need to
come owning our faults and begging for forgiveness.
But the way of access to the mercy-seat being not only an
open, but, to Christian feet, a familiar road, the worshipper
needs but to recall, in order afresh to realise, his footing of
acceptance in the Beloved. More is not needed for that
emotion of filial confidence and gratitude to be reawakened
in his bosom, which is the keynote of a Christian's devotion.
Its keynote : since what has above all things to be
expressed in our address to God, is the adoring wondering
thankfulness of redeemed men—humble in its joy, and
chastened into tender awe as it recalls the price at which
their pardon has been bought.

There is but one gift, adequate to express this
gratitude of the reconciled, which it is theirs to offer. It
is what St. Paul in a classical passage describes in
sacrificial language as " presenting your bodies a living
sacrifice, holy, acceptable to God—your reasonable service." [1] It is himself the worshipper offers : the wealth
of his own redeemed personality, his own love, his own
will, his own body and soul devoted to bear and to do all
the will of his Father in heaven. More he has not to lay

[1] Rom. 12[1].

upon God's altar. Less he has no heart to offer, nor will less be accepted.

It is obvious that such a self-sacrifice to the service of God is not a thing to be confined to an hour of Sunday worship. It is of the daily life St. Paul is speaking. It is through the whole week, with its plain practical duties of submission and obedience, that our offering, like that of our Lord, is to be presented. So all life becomes eucharistic and sacrificial. The aroma of grateful affection and meek yielding up of choice, and the joy of pleasing another, and lowly adoration of the Blessed One : this fragrance of worship clings about each common act of duty, and fills homeliest service with sweet odours to our King.

Of such a life public worship is the flower. To possess its true significance, it ought to be an occasional and combined utterance, in concerted acts or words addressed to God, of an attitude of the soul which is habitual because it is deep as the roots of the soul's life. When a congregation of such priestly worshippers unites its many consecrated hearts and wills into a single oblation, condensing the meaning of all the weekly life into a festive ritual of eucharist and sacred song and lowly fervent prayer, it is but imitating, as to the spirit and inner meaning of the act, the supreme self-oblation of the great High Priest.

This is the one side of worship—its purely expressive side. So far it is true that it seeks no ulterior end. Like the doxologies overheard by the seer in the celestial courts, it is an end in itself. But worship is never one-sided. Our fellowship with God is not complete till we receive as well as offer. And the praises of the earthly sanctuary are always dashed and clouded by a painful sense of the unattained, or worse, of sinful shortcoming. When a man is worshipping he is usually at his best. He is giving expression to the ideal at which he aims, rather than to his actual measure of attainment ; what

7

he hopes and means to be rather than what he is. Being at his best, he must be most keenly conscious of his worst. The very words he uses serve to remind him how far his performance falls beneath his profession. From this sense of dissatisfaction springs up the longing for divine help to live as he worships; to be as good in fact as he is in idea or in desire. This is the boon he craves from God. Every petition of the worshipping congregation offered on its own behalf concentrates itself on this one supreme moral aim—assimilation to the divine ideal disclosed in Jesus. And this is the "profit" which devout people look for from their attendance at church. For this they listen once more to the Gospel message, and submit themselves to the correction and instruction of the Divine Word. They find it in an ampler effluence of Divine influence—a completer union of the indwelling Spirit with the inward movements of their own spirits.

Thus all social worship moves betwixt those two poles of the Christian life:—self-consecration as the utterance of grateful praise for redemption by the Son; longing for more perfect holiness in the Spirit. In the synthesis of the two does the Church's communion with God complete itself on both its sides, as a giving to God and a receiving from Him.

From the spiritual contents of congregational worship to the religious tone which befits it is a short step. Here also we must be guided by the characteristics of the Christian faith. These prescribe in the outward expression which we give to our devotions the three notes of reverence, confidence, and cheerfulness.

1. Christianity as the religion of filial fellowship with the Father is so far from lessening (as a thoughtless observer might suppose) the sacred awe which ever becomes a sinful creature in his approach to the Divine Majesty that it rather strengthens it. Christian piety rests on a much deeper consciousness of sin and of indebtedness to mercy than is found in any other faith. The very fact

of being brought closer to God, with the nearer view of Him which this affords, brings into relief the moral contrast, the distance between, and the condescension of Him who admits "dust and ashes" to a place so near His love. St. Peter's reasoning is justified by a sound psychology of the religious feelings.[1] Just because we are encouraged to invoke under the name of "Father" the Holy One, who not only is to be, but is, the impartial Judge of each man's work ; just because the price of our redemption was the precious blood of the Lamb without spot :—therefore is our sojourn on earth to be spent "in fear." This must breathe into our worship a profound awestruck reverence, scrupulous to shun the faintest trace either of flippancy, or of presumption, or of over-familiarity. It is an offence to the trained Christian sense when rash worshippers "rush in where angels fear to tread."

2. In entire consistency with such reverence, and to be combined with the reserve which it begets, is the filial confidence or (as our English New Testament has it) "boldness"[2] which is so marked a feature in the attitude of evangelical believers. It has more than one source. The standing before God which Christians enjoy as re-conciled and adopted sons, begets a grave and tranquil assurance, a sense of privileged security, which ought to be mirrored in the Church's prayers. Relieved from servile apprehension, God's children fall beneath their true position if they do not draw near with sacred boldness to the throne. Besides, it has to be remembered that the incarnation has introduced into religion a strange new note of friendly frankness, or even of homely familiarity with our Divine Lord, based on His own experience as a Man. Of this one result is that there is no circumstance too trivial to be laid before Him, nor any shade of feeling too personal or too subtle for Him to understand. Although such matters are in the main to be reserved for

[1] 1 Pet. 1[16-19].

[2] παρρησία. Cf. Heb. 4[16] 10[19], Eph. 3[12], 1 John 3[21] 4[17-18] 5[14].

secret devotions, to which they impart a peculiar charm, yet even the joint worship of the congregation shares in a measure the same beautiful character of a confidential outpouring in the sympathetic ear of the Son of Man, who is ever present to be the interpreter of its desires.

3. As a result of all this, there should be imprinted upon the worship of the evangelical Churches a prevailingly cheerful character. Private acts of devotion cannot be invariably confident, still less cheerful. For individual experience knows moments of depression, even of misgiving and bitter self-upbraiding; moments, too, of crisis, of struggle with doubt, and of darkness nigh to despair, when the soul can do no more than lie low on the ground with " strong crying and tears." Such exceptional moods are not for public utterance. What common worship has to express is normal religious experience, conscious indeed of shortcoming, yet conscious too of the victorious grace of God and of all that the Church possesses in her Risen Head. Therefore it ought to reflect the calm of her assurance and the peacefulness of her faith. A tranquil tone, rising into bright thanksgiving and hope, at its highest into jubilant praise : this becomes it best. Exceptional raptures, it is true, are for the closet, no less than exceptional agonies. Yet at its supreme moments the united voice of the congregation ought to show itself capable of swelling into doxologies and pæans of praise over the riches of its inheritance.

CHAPTER XI

WORSHIP IN THE CHURCH OF THE FIRST CENTURY

THE lifetime of Jesus and His Apostles was a period of transition, when the old worship and the new met and crossed each other. Although, as we have seen, our Lord foretold that the days of an exclusive cult on hallowed spots of immemorial sanctity, like Jerusalem or Gerizim, would soon be over, He set up no model to take its place. So far as we are told, He did not even initiate any separate worship for His followers so long as He was with them. On the contrary, He and they continued loyally to frequent the Temple festivals as well as the village synagogues. Yet He certainly anticipated that after His departure they would hold meetings among themselves for common prayer. The power which lies in concerted petition could be no alien thought to Him who said: " If two of you shall agree on earth as touching anything that they shall ask, it shall be done for them of My Father which is in heaven." And, lest the fewness of His disciples in any place should act as a discouragement to such concert in prayer, He was careful to fix the quorum of a worshipping assembly as low as " two or three." Even to this minimum number of associated worshippers He granted the charter of congregational worship in the startling promise: " Where two or three are gathered together in My name, there am I in the midst of them." It is more than the charter of congregational worship—it is the consecration of congregational fellowship. Even an

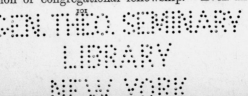

ecclesiola is fully equipped for its functions when to the " two or three " is added One more—the Master of assemblies Himself.[1]

A little further than this Jesus went. To a general sanction of Christian assemblies for worship, He added some slight hints on the contents of their service. At the request of the disciples (though only when requested), He dictated a brief model of united prayer, the germ of every later liturgy. He desired the baptismal rite of His forerunner to be kept up with a new significance as an initiation into the society of His disciples. Most important of all, He instituted at the Last Supper—so His first followers understood Him—a memorial celebration of His death. But all this, while it amply sanctioned social worship in His Church, and even defined some guiding lines, went a very little way towards a directory how it was to be conducted. If more detailed instructions were left with the Twelve, they have not been preserved. The contrast with previous cults could not be better marked. No service-book was ever more minute in its rubrics than that of Israel in its matured shape; but Jesus bequeathed no service-book to His Church. The spirit of the new devotion He inspired; its forms He left for the most part free.

It is certain that the Church parted company but slowly with the synagogue. St. Paul, who in one place seems to brush aside the sacred seasons and observances of Hebrew law, as well as of Gentile usage, with a touch of contempt foreign to his Master, as " beggarly rudiments " of the world's nonage,[2] is found on another occasion expediting his voyage from Europe to Palestine in order to be present at the great Hebrew festival of Pentecost, and when there joining reverently in Temple services.[3] Of the services in Christian assemblies, on the other hand, how little could we have gathered from his correspondence, if no abuses had crept in at Corinth. Had a great deal

[1] Matt. 18[19. 20].   [2] Gal. 4[1-11].   [3] Acts 20[16], cf. 21[23-29] 24[11-18].

depended on an exact imitation of primitive forms, one
wonders if more pains would not have been taken to
record them.

Yet, even in the canonical books, materials do exist,
though not complete. These, especially if we are allowed
to supplement them by documents from the generation
which outlived the Apostles, enable us to construct a
fairly full sketch of the Church's worship within the
first hundred years after its foundation.

More than one stage in the development of a cult,
both among Hebrew and Greek converts, can be faintly
traced in the New Testament. During the opening years
that succeeded the advent of the Spirit, the Apostles
clung, as far as they could and as long as they could, to
the ancestral services both in Temple and in synagogue.[1]
None the less, from the very first day, Hebrew believers
in the Messiahship of Jesus constituted a distinct group
inside Judaism, holding daily and weekly meetings of their
own in addition to those which as Jews they continued
to attend. These were held in private dwellings. The
service embraced already common prayers, praise, instruction by the Apostles, and, above all, a common meal that
closed probably with the Lord's Supper under the name
of "Breaking of Bread." [2] Our sources leave no reasonable
doubt that the eucharist, as the most characteristic act of
social Christian devotion, and the bond and badge of
believing fellowship, grew at once into a custom out of the
recent example, if not at the command, of Jesus Himself.
At first observed daily, it is not till later that we come on
traces of a weekly celebration each Lord's Day.[3]

A second stage of Hebræo - Christian worship necessarily began on the expulsion of the young society, to be
henceforth in the eyes of orthodox Judaism a separated
" sect." [4] Perhaps it is to this stage, which may have lasted
some time in purely Hebrew groups, that the Epistle of

---

[1] Acts 2⁴⁶ 3¹ 5²⁰· ⁴² 9²⁰ 13¹⁴ etc. [2] Acts 2⁴²⁻⁴⁷.
[3] Acts 20⁷, 1 Cor. 11²⁰· ³³. [4] αἴρεσις in Acts 24¹⁴.

St. James refers, with its graphic sketch of a presiding "synagogue" where, as in its Jewish prototype, Christian "elders" sat in seats of honour, and every male adult was at liberty to teach or exhort.[1]

In two later writings of the same school, the Epistle to the Hebrews and the Apocalypse, some scholars have seen traces of yet a third stage.[2] Both indicate change. By the time Hebrews was composed, the "leaders" (not here called elders) are described as "speaking the Word of God," as well as "watching for souls."[3] What is more striking is that in this treatise there is mention for the first time of congregational praise. Still more, that it is spoken of as a sacrifice ($\theta v\sigma i\alpha$) perpetually offered up to God on earth, just as the Apocalypse speaks of the prayers of saints as ascending, perfumed with incense, in the heavenly sanctuary.[4] Not only is the worship of the Church looked upon by the writer to the Hebrews as a sacrificial oblation, but the Lord as our High Priest is represented as carrying on ceaseless ministrations on our behalf in the courts above.[5] This imparts new significance to "the assembling of ourselves together." Worship means a drawing near to God with clean bodies and purified hearts to find admission—in spirit it must be—into the "holiest of all," the nearest and most immediate presence of God; while the poor prayers and praises which we offer here below are taken up into the upper courts, to be presented there with acceptance by our exalted Priest, before "the throne of the Majesty in the heavens."

The idea at the root of this, of a parallel worship going on in heaven as on earth, is advanced yet a step in the Apocalypse. For the author of that book, in harmony here as elsewhere with much late Jewish thought, sees in

---

[1] Jas. 2¹⁻⁴ 3¹ 5¹⁴, cf. 1 Pet. 4¹⁰. ¹¹.

[2] See Jacobi's art. in the *Jahrb. f. deut. Theologie* for 1873.

[3] Compare the parallel progress in Greek Churches to be observed in the Pastoral Letters.

[4] Heb. 13¹⁵, Rev. 8³. ⁴ 5⁸.   [5] Heb. 8¹. ² 9²⁴ 10¹⁹⁻²⁵.

celestial worship the ideal on which Levitical ritual in the
Temple had been fashioned.[1] The divine Throne, the Seven
Lamps, the Cherubs, the Lamb slain, the Censer of incense,
the Harping Choir: all reappear in their glorified pro-
totypes in the Temple of heaven. It is even noticeable
that this idealised worship, while it is the pattern on
which the Jewish was modelled, is set before us in a way
to recall early Christian services. It may be an accident
that the twenty-four elders sit on thrones round about the
throne of God, very much after the arrangement of
presbyters' seats in the Early Church. But at least the
ascriptions of praise which the seer heard so often in his
vision have quite a liturgical ring, and may well enough
have been imitated from hymns or doxologies already in
use, and familiar to the author in the churches of Asia
Minor. This must remain conjecture. What is certain is,
that not only do we see in the Hebrew section of the
Apostolic Church a Christian service fairly developed; but
that cult of neo-Israel retains under Christian dress the
great idea of sacrifice which had always formed the kernel
of Israel's ancient rites.

It is rather a different atmosphere into which we enter
when we turn to the Greek communities of the first
century. St. Paul is here almost our sole canonical source.
If from him we learn more about the way in which
Christians worshipped at Corinth than anywhere else, that
is only, as I said, because at Corinth the services had
become unusually disorderly. The items in their service
which he found occasion to name are common prayer, a
psalm, edifying discourses of several sorts, and the common
meal for which viands were brought by the members to be
consumed in public, and which was followed as elsewhere
by Holy Communion in the Supper of the Lord.

Some investigators have believed that in the Apostle's
First Epistle it is possible to distinguish two different kinds
of church meeting: one which he regulates in the fourteenth

[1] Cf. Heb. 8[5] 9[23. 24].

chapter, to which non-Christians were admitted, and at which prayers and addresses formed the leading exercises; and a more private gathering of the members at another time for the purpose of the Holy Supper alone. With the latter they connect the passage in the eleventh chapter.[1] If this be correct, then it was at the more open or public service, which was evidently conducted with much freedom, that addresses were delivered which, if properly managed, might convict the casual heathen listener, by revealing to him the secrets of his own heart. A deal of discussion has taken place over the three kinds of discourse named by St. Paul; all of them delivered with the aid of the Divine Spirit, but under diverse conditions of the speaker's own mind. According to the most careful results, it seems likely that a calm and reasoned exposition of the contents of the faith was called "teaching"; that "prophecy" denoted a more impulsive and imaginative discourse, in which the prophet under some excitement was inspired to utter his "apocalypse" on an aspect of divine truth borne in upon him at the moment; while in the third class, known as "tongues," the state of the speaker must have been one of pure ecstasy—his power of conscious reflection being for the time in abeyance, and his utterance unintelligible to the ordinary bystander. Whether this last phenomenon occurred as a part of congregational worship anywhere else than at Corinth, we do not know. Other cases of it on record belong to a different category.[2] Prophecy at least seems to have been fairly frequent; for we read of it at Thessalonica and Ephesus, as well as Jerusalem and Antioch.[3] When both gifts passed away, there remained to the Church, as the only standing form of address in her worship, the most quiet and normal of them all.

[1] Jacobi's art. *ut supra* ; Weizsäcker in a subsequent paper in the same magazine for 1876; and Köstlin, *Gesch. d. christl. Gottesdienstes* (Freib. 1887).

[2] In Acts 2^4 10^{46} and 19^6.

[3] See 1 Thess. 5^{20}, Eph. 2^{20}, Acts 11^{27} and 13^1.

The table fellowship at Corinth comprised two parts, not separated by any long interval: the *agapé* or meal of brotherhood, and " the Lord's Supper." Possibly these were divided by the eucharistic prayer, to which the congregation responded by an " Amen." [1] It is difficult to account for the *agapé* as a meal distinct from the eucharist. Though it dated, as we saw, from the earliest days of the Palestine Church, it found no other parallel in Jewish worship beyond the annual family supper of the Passover. Its acceptance by Greek converts may have been facilitated by the custom of *symposia* in Greek society ; but it certainly did not originate from them, still less from the συσσιτία of Sparta or of Crete—mess-tables provided for poor citizens at the expense of the State. It is on the whole best accounted for by supposing it to be a reminiscence of our Lord's last supper, at the close of which He instituted the new memorial communion of His Body and Blood.

St. Paul's immediate design in discussing Corinthian worship forbids us to infer that other usages which he had no occasion to mention did not exist there. For instance, he says nothing of Scripture readings. Nor does he elsewhere name them, unless his advice to Timothy, " Give heed to reading," referred to lessons read in church.[2] Even if it did, we can hardly conclude with Jacobi that this portion of the service was only then beginning to be customary in Gentile congregations. The acquaintance with the contents of the Old Testament which is presupposed in all St. Paul's letters to his converts is difficult to explain, unless from the first the synagogue practice of reading Scripture systematically at every service had been taken over by Christian assemblies, Greek as well as Hebrew.

How the public praise was conducted is a point on which we are almost without information. Paul names " a psalm " as one of the contributions which a member might bring to the common worship ; [3] but whether he

[1] 1 Cor. 14[16].   [2] 1 Tim. 4[13].   [3] 1 Cor. 14[26].

means one of the Hebrew psalms or a Christian composition, or how it was recited or sung, we are not told. His counsel to believers at Ephesus and Colossæ to admonish one another or themselves with sacred songs, like the similar language of St. James, seems best understood of a private use of religious verse.[1] One or two passages in his letters are conjectured to be quotations from Christian poetry,[2] which we know on evidence cited by Eusebius [3] to have been composed at a very early date. But when or to what extent musical praise found its way into the worship of the primitive communities remains uncertain.

Another custom there was, however, connected with meetings for worship, although it can scarcely be called a part of it, which is well established as Apostolic—the " kiss of peace," or "of love," as a seal of the Christian's new-found brotherhood.[4]

In the Pastoral Epistles we reach the latest stage in the New Testament documents of Greek Christendom. It is marked by two, or possibly three, features unnamed in earlier writings : (1) the effort to secure as presbyters men who were themselves fit to teach ; (2) careful directions for intercessory prayer on behalf of civil rulers and of all classes, to be offered by male members of the Church only—" holding up holy hands " in the Jewish manner ; and (3) possibly the inclusion of public readings from Holy Writ.[5]

Scanty as these materials are, they give us the elements at least of a congregational service, made up of prayer, instruction, and the holy meal, with the possible addition of praise and Scripture lessons. Now, these are just the acts which we find entering into the Sunday services of the sub-apostolic Church when we pass beyond the canon to the opening decades of the second century.

---

[1] Eph. 5^{19}, Col. 3^{16}, Jas. 5^{13}.

[2] Eph. 5^{14}, 1 Tim. 3^{16}, less probably Tit. 3^{4-7}.   [3] *H. E.* v. 28.

[4] Rom. 16^{16}, 1 Cor. 16^{20}, 2 Cor. 13^{12}, 1 Thess. 5^{26}, 1 Pet. 5^{14}

[5] 1 Tim. 5^{17}, Tit. 1^9, 1 Tim. 2^{1-8} 4^{13}.

For example, the well-known report which Pliny sent to the Emperor Trajan in the year 109 A.D. describes the worship of the Christians at Bithynia. They met twice on Sunday (for that, no doubt, was the " fixed day " referred to): first, very early, before sunrise—possibly a precaution for the sake of concealment, and again at some later hour. On the second occasion, they came together for the purpose of taking a common meal; but this meeting, which had drawn upon them suspicion as an illegal or possibly seditious club, they had suspended in obedience to the governor's orders. The early morning assembly was evidently for worship. Two acts of devotion only are named by Pliny. The one was a Christian hymn of praise to our Lord, recited or chanted after some alternate fashion. The other is characterised by the Roman official as a *sacramentum*, a word which must bear, of course, not its later ecclesiastical sense, but its current classical one. Was this solemn oath or formula by which the Christians engaged themselves to lead a blameless life, the explanation of Holy Communion which these incriminated brethren had furnished to the authorities? On the whole I am disposed to think it was. It is difficult to conjecture what else they could so describe; whereas it is quite easy to see why they should reveal no more of their sacred rite to a heathen magistrate than simply its moral obligation as binding the brotherhood to a life of virtue. Assuming this view to be correct, it is the first occurrence of the eucharist as a morning celebration, separated from the evening *agapé*; as well as the earliest application to it of the term *sacramentum*, though in another than the later sense.

Not much light is thrown on the ritual of the larger and better-known Churches, or of any portion of Greek Christendom, by that curious directory, the *Didache*. Neither its date nor its place of origin is certain. The very early period, between 80 and 110 A.D., to which scholars inclined at first to assign it, has not held its

ground; and opinion leans to a later decade in the first
half of the second century. In any case, it is a strongly
Hebræo - Christian production, designed apparently to
regulate Church procedure in some out of the way rural
district, possibly in Syria or in Egypt. Its theology is
far from Pauline; there is no invocation of the Holy
Spirit; nor is its conception of the eucharist at all an
elevated or even distinctively Christian one. But it
agrees with other sources in making the eucharist, as
the Christian sacrifice of thanksgiving, the central feature
in the worship of every Lord's Day. The first act in the
service was "to confess their transgressions that their
sacrifice might be pure." Nothing is said either of the
reading of Scripture or of praise. The chief novelty is
that brief forms of prayer are prescribed to be said before
and after celebration of the eucharist, as well as at
baptismal services. A separate grace is to be recited
over each of the elements, and the cup takes precedence
of the bread. A few minor details are added to our
previous knowledge. Thus, the rule is laid down that
members who are at variance are to be reconciled before
communicating. Two days in the week are to be kept
as fast days. And the private repetition of the Lord's
Prayer is recommended three times a day at the hours
usually observed by devout Hebrews.

In connection with the occurrence of set prayers in
the *Didache*, it seems to me of special interest to turn to
the other "find" which Archbishop Bryennios made at the
same time. I refer to the six recovered chapters near
the end of Clement of Rome's Epistle to the Corinthian
Church (chaps. 58 to 63). The date is considerably earlier,
as early, according to Bishop Lightfoot, as 95–96 A.D.
Of these chapters the greater portion is occupied by a
long prayer, which recent editors and critics of Clement
judge to have been taken from the public services of the
Church of Rome, over which he presided. If this be so,
it possesses for the student of liturgical language a singular

value. Opening with a prayer for the Church coupled with words of lofty praise, it passes to supplication for various classes of suffering brethren. Then follow petitions for absolution and for peace, and the whole is closed by a long intercession on behalf of civil rulers, which winds up with a doxology. Scriptural and elevated in its phraseology, it sets a model, although composed within the lifetime of the Apostle St. John, of the same solemn and dignified style, both of thought and of language, with which later liturgies have familiarised us.

Similar forms of common prayer can hardly have been everywhere in use at that early period. At least we meet with no indication of them, rather of the contrary practice, in the full and careful account of worship, as he knew it,[1] which half a century later Justin Martyr laid before the Emperor in his *First Apology*. Drawn up about a hundred and twenty years after the origin of the Church, it practically sums up for us the results we have reached.

The service on the Lord's Day, as he describes it,[2] opened with readings from the memoirs of the Apostles and from the writings of the Prophets. When the Reader ceased, the President or Leader gave an address of instruction and exhortation. Evidently it was based on the lesson, as was the synagogue practice. Then all rose up and offered prayers, which included intercessions; and at the close of these, the members saluted one another with a kiss. Bread was next brought forward with a cup of water and mixed wine, contributed by the worshippers; over which the President offered up prayers and thanksgivings at some length, "as he is able," [3] the people responding with the usual " Amen." It is probable that in this eucharistic prayer were incorporated the words of

---

[1] Unfortunately we do not know whether it was written in Palestine or during Justin's residence at Rome.

[2] *Apol.* c. 35, 67.

[3] ὅση δύναμις αὐτῷ—a much discussed phrase. In the *Library of the Fathers* it is rendered by " with all his strength." But other senses have been suggested. It is hardly consistent with a prescribed form of prayer.

institution. Distribution of the elements by the deacons then took place ; and to the absent also they were sent through the hands of the same officials. The service closed apparently with a collection to be deposited with the President for the succour of orphans and widows, the sick, strangers, or any others who were in want.

If the above was meant to be a complete order of service, the absence of praise would excite surprise. But, seeing that in an earlier chapter (chap. 13) Justin had already spoken of thanking God in " hymns," it is safe to assume that the omission was accidental. Of the *agapé* as a distinct act, he also makes no mention.

To this sketch of ordinary weekly service in the middle of the second century, it only remains to add a brief reference to services which were not weekly. That from the commencement, Sunday, as the weekly festival of the Resurrection, had been set apart in place of the Jewish Sabbath for Christian worship, is sufficiently attested in the New Testament [1] and confirmed by the sub-apostolic documents just referred to. But the observance of the Passover season as a Christian " Holy Week " in memory both of the Passion and of the Resurrection, rests on a different footing. It is not mentioned in the canonical writings ; nor, so far as I am aware, in any extant document of the period we have traversed from the founding of the Church till the middle of the succeeding century. Very few years, however, after Justin wrote his *Apology*, there broke out (in 155 A.D.) the well-known and long sustained discussion between the Churches of Asia Minor and the rest of Christendom as to the mode in which the date of its celebration ought to be calculated. Into the history of this (so-called) quarto-deciman controversy there is no need here to enter. But its early emergence, together with the keen desire exhibited on all hands to bring the Churches to a simultaneous observance of

---

[1] Cf. besides our Lord's own appearances and the coming of the Spirit on that day, Acts 20[7], 1 Cor. 16[2], Rev. 1[10].

what was for all of them alike a season of unusual sacred-ness, and the fact that Apostolic authority was confidently appealed to on both sides—force on my mind the conclusion that the observance itself was a custom old enough to go back at least to the close of the Apostolic age, if not earlier. In his letter on the subject which Eusebius cites,[1] Irenæus tells us that much divergence of practice existed respecting the manner and duration of the fast which invariably accompanied the commemoration of the Lord's Passion. But on the fact that always and every-where this annual commemoration had been kept by Christians from the days of the Apostles, no difference of opinion can be observed. It was just because it was the one anniversary recalling our redemption which was sacred to every Christian Church, that the sentiment of Christian unity was wounded, when in a single region it was regu-lated by a different tradition from what obtained else-where, even though that tradition claimed to have descended through only half a century from the Apostle St. John. Seeing that the Passover week proved to be in coming generations the starting-point for the growth of the whole Church year, this fact becomes one of first-rate consequence for the student of Christian worship.

[1] *H. E.* v. 23–24.

CHAPTER XII

SIXTEENTH CENTURY REFORMS IN WORSHIP

THE forms of Divine service which Protestant ministers are required to conduct, date in substance from the sixteenth century. In spite of considerable diversity among them, they all resulted from the effort of Reformers to revert to the practice of the Church at some earlier and purer period of her history. Casting aside the Mass, as well as Mariolatry, the use of images, the invocation of saints, prayers for the dead, with other superstitious and sacerdotal features in mediæval service-books, an endeavour was made to return with more or less thoroughness to a mode of serving God in closer harmony with the spirit of the Christian faith, and even to an approximate reproduction of the Church's worship in its pristine simplicity. This is what the Reform was meant to be—what to a fair extent it actually was.

It is easy to see how new forms of worship, fundamentally at variance with mediæval ritual, sprang of necessity out of men's changed beliefs. Stated as broadly as possible, Protestant cultus differs from Catholic in two essential features:—First, its value depends, not on manual acts of a priest, but entirely on the religious attitude of each individual worshipper who takes part,—an attitude of his spirit known only to God; so that its forms are appropriate just in the measure in which they lend united expression to the devotional feeling of the congregation at the moment.

And, second, since this devout feeling in the worshipping people is a natural outcome of their faith, that is to say, the response which follows under the Spirit's influence from an intelligent acceptance of the Gospel of divine grace, the proclamation of that Divine Word through which faith is begotten and sustained, must be the most prominent, if not the central, act of the service. This at once gives to the open Bible, read or expounded, a position which in Catholicism had been assigned to the altar.

It is quite clear that these are both simple corollaries from what it is customary to describe as the two essential principles of the Reformation: its "material" and its "formal" principles respectively. The former change was involved in what theologians call "justification by faith"; for by that is meant that each man's acceptance with God, or the forgiveness of his sins, depends solely on his inward state as a penitent believer in the promise of God through Jesus Christ; while the second followed no less directly from the sole authority over Christian faith and life ascribed by Protestants to the Word of God revealed in Holy Scripture.

But although, as a matter of logic, reformed worship grew irresistibly out of reformed teaching, it is none the less startling to witness a revolution so rapid and so radical, in a department of human conduct where, if anywhere, traditional usages are slow to alter. When one reflects that the main ideas which gradually embodied themselves in the Catholic rites had entered the Church as early as the third century, and for how many centuries they had swayed the minds and regulated the devotions of Christian men with all but unchallenged authority; when it is remembered that for generations more than one could reckon, the priest, the Mass, and the confessional had been the holiest things known to Christendom; and when one's imagination calls up the venerable and often gorgeous ceremonial of the mediæval Church, how it appealed to every sense, and laid the arts of music, architecture, painting and sculpture under tribute to augment its solemnity and impressiveness:—I confess that nothing in the Lutheran movement strikes me with more astonishment than the suddenness and completeness with which large regions in Central and Northern Europe flung it all aside and went back to the simplest and most unadorned elements of worship as in the primitive days of Christianity.

It was inevitable that the gain should be purchased at the cost of some loss. Any violent rupture of historical continuity shatters links with the past which are of value. In this case, the sense of Church unity and cohesion, of which a uniform ritual had been at once a product and a symbol, suffered disastrously. Nor has any universally accepted order of service been able to establish itself in the Reformation Churches, such as might have restored to Protestant Christendom a unity of its own. Divine services, too, have suffered much in their beauty and impressiveness. If the old ritual did owe most of its impressiveness to what was sensuous in it, or symbolic, is it not through the senses that uneducated people are most impressed, and by symbols that they most easily apprehend the unseen? A good Protestant need not hesitate to admit that a severely spiritual cult lies under a disadvantage when the question is how to address unspiritual natures. Any service which is largely composed of verbal teaching must make heavy demands on the intellect, and call for a devoutness less aided by the imagination than is usually to be met with among average persons. The case has often been made a good deal worse than it need have been. In some countries, reformed worship has meant a service of God devoid of beauty, bald and severe to ugliness, as if piety and good taste were natural foes. And whereas it belongs to the very genius of the reformed system that the whole congregation is the worshipping unit, each member in which has his own part to take in the common acts, how often have the people seen their share in vocal worship dwindle to a minimum, through a too exclusive prominence given to the leader or an excessive reliance on his fitness to lead!

All this and more may be frankly conceded, while we still give God thanks for the change, devoutly recognising that what the new era gained far outweighs the loss. Mediævalism had been a relapse into lower religious conceptions and outworn modes of religious observance, unworthy of the Christian Gospel. It was a manlier devotion which took the place of its meretricious, if splendid, ritual; just as it was a more free and filial attitude toward God which breathed through it. Unattractive they may be to the indifferent or undevout, but in the unadorned services of our evangelical Churches penitent and faithful souls will always feel themselves at home; because there, amid no inconsistent or irrelevant accessories to distract the mind, they can give utterance to that inward worship of the Father "in spirit and in truth" which was consecrated by the Lord Himself.

The two great divisions of Protestantism, while agreed in spirit, differed in the thoroughness with which they strove in points of detail to reproduce primitive worship. Luther was cautious and conservative in his alterations. So long as nothing was left from which people could learn doctrine inconsistent with the Gospel, he was disposed not to break with accustomed usages. Given the essentials of evangelical devotion, lesser details seemed to him matters of prudential arrangement. In this way the Lutheran Churches retained a good deal which Calvinists rejected. Pictures were left on the walls. The crucifix and the lights remained on the holy table. At certain prayers the clergyman continued to turn to it with his back to the people. The Gospel and Epistle were still read every Sunday, and made obligatory as texts for the weekly sermon. Besides festivals which commemorate the great events of our redemption, a few other feasts of the Church year were likewise retained, such as All Saints', Michaelmas, and St. John's Day, not as in themselves sacred, but as affording opportunity for extra services which it was profitable to utilise. In the same spirit, Luther's revision

of the Mass, not only the earlier one in 1523, but even his
more drastic recension three years later, while it dropped
everything which implied a sacrificial oblation of the elements,
with a crowd of minor ceremonies, allowed certain of the
ancient prayers to remain, along with the versicles, the *Kyrie*,
the *Pax vobiscum*, and the Creed. It is upon one or other
of these revisions that the Lutheran States have modelled
the various *Agende* or service-books which have since been
sanctioned for public use.

The Reformed Churches of Switzerland, followed by
those of the Palatinate, of France, Holland, and Scotland,
with a more express intention to be guided by the New
Testament, went somewhat further. Even they did not in
point of fact reproduce in every particular the worship of
the Apostolic Church. For instance, they revived neither
the love-feast nor the kiss of brotherly love. They did not
dispense with prepared prayers at the Lord's Day services;
nor did they any longer celebrate the Lord's Supper on
every Sunday, according to immemorial and invariable
usage, but reserved it for special occasions. They continued
to recite the Apostles' Creed in worship. Moreover, they
retained, although the New Testament is silent on the
subject, the five great festivals of the Christian year—
Good Friday, Easter, Ascension, Whitsunday, and Christmas;
and they gave to the weekly festival of the Lord's Day a
stricter and more legal aspect by identifying it in point of
divine authority with the Hebrew Sabbath. In other
respects, however, they stripped the worship to its essentials,
making it as bare and simple as they could; casting organs,
for example, and pictures out of their places of worship,
abolishing the fixed lessons, and exchanging the traditional
prayers for newly devised forms.

What in the end affected Calvinistic worship more
deeply than these matters of detail was the excessive
emphasis laid upon doctrinal instruction. The Swiss went
further than Luther, not perhaps in exalting the preaching
of the Divine Word, but at least in giving to the intellectual

element in religion a preponderance over both the
emotional and the æsthetic elements. The sermon became
to them, not simply the main thing at every service, but
the central or controlling part of worship, to which its
other acts were contributory. What this meant was that
imperfection, adhering to the actual life of Christians, was
more prominent in their religious consciousness, and was
allowed a more prominent position in their public worship,
than the ideal of Christian life in Christ—the perfection
which is already the Christian's own by the gift of God.
It resulted of necessity that self-edification, or the cultivation of spiritual life in the soul, with the correction of its
faults, was kept ever before the mind of the worshipper as
the chief end to be aimed at in Divine service. Worship
tended to become little else than a means of grace. It is
true that this one-sidedness, with the under-estimation of
worship as an end in itself to which it gave rise, was less
apparent among the continental Reformed of the first
generation than it became on this side of the Channel
during the next century. It was then, under the influence
of a rigid orthodoxy and an introspective piety, that
Puritan cultus, among both Presbyterians and Inde-
pendents, put on the unlovely appearance with which it
has so often been reproached.

Transplanted to English soil, the same diversity in
practice which in Central Europe had from the beginning
divided Lutheran from Calvinist, assumed an acuter form
and gave rise to more vehement debate betwixt the two
parties which divided the national Church. English
Reformers, influenced more from Wittenberg than from
Geneva, had revised the Missal in a spirit still more
conservative than Luther's. Ceremonies had been abolished,
not because they " had their beginning by the institution of
man," but either on the ground of their abuse in time past,
since " the abuses could not well be taken away, the thing
remaining still," or for the less weighty reason that " the
great excess and multitude of them hath so increased in

these latter days that the burden of them was intolerable." [1]
A reform so tender in its handling of accustomed forms in
worship, effected less change than took place in any other
part of Protestant Europe. With a very large proportion
of the population adhering to the Roman allegiance, policy,
no less than sentiment, counselled the retention as far as
possible of usages with which the people were familiar. A
very large number of festivals and saints' days, the
cathedral system nearly unaltered, daily prayers in which
the old offices of the "Hours" appear in abridged form, an
order for Holy Communion which follows in the main the
early liturgies, a large number of collects taken from the
Gregorian and Gelasian sacramentaries:—were all features the retention of which enabled conservative-minded
Englishmen to pass from the old to the new state of
things with the least possible sense of dislocation or of
novelty. And whatever else may have come about in consequence, one result has been, that no existing liturgy
excels the Anglican for the beauty of its prayers or the
richness of its materials, nor has any other Protestant
communion preserved so much of the stateliness of the
Roman cult.

It was natural that from the first a party should exist
in England, encouraged by continental divines, which sought
to have the Church assimilated in a more thoroughgoing
fashion to the example set by the Swiss Cantons. But the
objections of the early Elizabethan Puritans referred to
relics of the old ritual which were of secondary consequence.
For the services, in particular the Order of Holy Communion, had been substantially purged, even in the revision
of 1559, from the Roman teaching on the subject of the
Mass. Of any change in the elements or any offering of
them to God in sacrifice, no mention was left. The Supper
is called simply, "a perpetual memory of that His precious

---

[1] Preface, "Of Ceremonies, why some be abolished, and some
retained," first prefixed to the 1549 edition of the Book of Common
Prayer.

death." The elements are described as " these Thy creatures of Bread and Wine." " His most blessed Body and Blood " are expressly termed "spiritual food." All that is characteristic of the Mass has disappeared.[1] What exception was taken against, were such external details as sacerdotal vestments, kneeling at the reception of the eucharist, the use of the name "priest" for presbyter, the sign of the cross at baptism, god-parents, saints' days, the retention of the word "altar," and the ring in the marriage ceremony. From a list of " nocent " ceremonies like this one could hardly have foreseen that English Christianity would permanently split into two antagonistic camps, with all the bitterness, intolerance, and narrowness of which that has proved the prolific parent throughout the subsequent history of English society. As little, however, could it have been foreseen that, as a result of the remaining leaven of Catholicism, our age should witness such a widespread revival, not only of Catholic ritual, but likewise of Catholic teaching on the subject of the "Mass," as constitutes to-day the peril of the ancient and venerable Church of England.

As the discussion between High Churchman and Puritan developed, it became necessary to ground both attack and defence on some general principle. To urge merely that the practices complained of savoured of Rome, or that they gave offence to tender consciences, or that foreign Reformed Churches had discarded them, or that a simpler ceremonial was to be preferred—were all of them too weak pleas to prevail against immemorial use and wont. Too weak, at all events, among a people slow to change, and in a Church tenacious of historical continuity. For English divines had striven, while dropping the later abuses of mediæval worship, to fall back on Catholic antiquity and the consent of the Catholic Fathers; so that the canons, no less than the creeds, of councils, down to the fifth or sixth century,

---

[1] As is well known, the tenet of Baptismal Regeneration did not so completely disappear from the Order for that sacrament.

were freely cited as authorities. A "middle way" so characteristically English, in which the great majority of English Churchmen ever since have seen the best recommendation of their Church, could only be abandoned at the bidding of some imperative principle. It became necessary, therefore, for the Puritans to take their stand on the position that nothing ought to be introduced either into the life or into the worship of the Church which is not sanctioned in the Word of God, if not expressly, at least by some general rule laid down in Scripture. It was Calvin's position : that the Word of God is for His Church the sole supreme directory for practice, as well as standard for doctrine. "They did not deny but certain things are left to the order of the Church, because they are of the nature of those which are varied by times, places, persons, and other circumstances, and so could not at once be set down and established for ever." [1] But as the main rule to guide in all such matters, they laid it down that " the Word of God containeth the direction of all things pertaining to the Church." [2] Hooker admitted that Puritanism " hath grown from no other root, than only a desire to enlarge the necessary use of the Word of God." [3]

The ablest advocates of this view were Cartwright and Travers. But the Church, put to her defence by her own sons, found to the full as able apologists in Hooker and Whitgift. It is above all to Richard Hooker's monumental work that the student will turn.[4] Article XX. of the Thirty-nine adopted in 1562 and issued in the following year by Royal authority, had laid it down as the teaching of the Church of England: "The Church hath power to decree Rites and Ceremonies, and authority in Controversies of Faith. And yet it is not lawful for the Church to ordain anything that is contrary to God's Word written, neither may it so expound one place of Scripture that it be repug-

---

[1] Cartwright quoted by Hooker—Keble's ed. i. p. 405 footnote.
[2] *Ibid.* p. 289 note.   [3] *Ibid.* p. 287.
[4] *Of the Laws of Eccl. Polity*, 1593, with later dates for Bk. v.-viii.

nant to another." [1] This is in substance the thesis which
Hooker had to maintain. His main line of argument, set
out with opulence of reasoning and in classic English, is
well known and easily stated :—

The sufficiency of Holy Scripture means its sufficiency
for the end for which it was given ; and that was " to deliver
a full instruction in all things unto salvation necessary, the
knowledge whereof man by nature could not in this life
attain unto." For this purpose Scripture is complete.
But it does not follow that it must lay down directions
concerning everything which men either ought to do or
lawfully may do. For God has other ways of conveying
His will to us; such as, the light of natural reason and the
positive laws which regulate human actions in societies,
civil or spiritual. Scripture itself assumes that men are
able to inform themselves as to what is best to be done on
many matters, and counts on their doing what by reason
and nature they find to be good or right, although there
be no express direction to that effect in the written
Word.

No doubt all this is true and pertinent in many departments of human conduct. At the same time, it is quite
possible to doubt whether it applies to the introduction of
ecclesiastical ceremonies into Divine worship. For the question what liberty Christ has left to His Church in that matter
is a much narrower one. The Church is the special creation
of Jesus Christ, His house in which He alone is Master;
and if it can be shown that binding and permanent directions on ritual, no less than on doctrine, have been laid
down in the New Testament, which both disputants accepted
as Christ's statute-book, then it may well be that beyond
these Church rulers are not at liberty to go. It will then

---

[1] It has been much disputed whether the opening words of this Article
were inserted by competent ecclesiastical authority or by the Crown. Some
have supposed they were inserted in the copy subscribed in Convocation,
by Queen Elizabeth herself, in support of the claim made by the Crown to
decree ceremonies. Cf. Hardwick, *Hist. of the Articles*, London, 1895, pp.
140-144.

be a society administered at all points under the statutes
of its Founder ; with a certain discretion, no doubt, but a
strictly limited discretion, in the application only of these
binding statutes. The distinction which the Puritan party
drew between the substance of Christian worship and its
accidental or variable circumstances, is one which it is
hardly fair to describe as only a difference of degree.
There is a material difference between leaving to Church
rulers, as Article XX. does, a perfectly free hand " to decree
rites and ceremonies," so long as nothing is ordained
contrary to Scripture, and limiting their power to " circumstances concerning the worship of God . . . common to
human actions and societies." [1]

The question has never again been debated with the
same thoroughness or ability. It has lost at the present
day much of its former interest. We are not now so sure
as men were three hundred years ago that the New Testament does lay down binding and permanent directions,
either on modes of worship or on the government of the
Church. There are many who would even give a wider
application than Hooker himself gave to his dictum, that
the end for which revelation was given and for which alone
it is sufficient, is " to deliver a full instruction in all things
unto salvation necessary." Yet the history of ceremonial, not
only in past ages, but even within our own time, attests the
tendency of Churchmen to encumber Christian worship with
additions which are too significant of erroneous ideas to be
called " details," or which mar its simplicity even when they
do not corrupt its spirituality. As a simple measure of
precaution, therefore, it would have been well for the purity
of Christ's Church had the limits laid down by Puritan
controversialists been more respected as limits beyond which
it is neither necessary nor safe to go.

But even if in principle we cut down the Church's
liberty in legislation to such modest limits, it is obvious
that room will still be left for honest variations in practice.

[1] Westminster Confession of Faith, i. 6.

The minds and tastes of individuals, of different nations in Christendom, and of successive generations, are variously constituted. Some will always see a perilous innovation where others find nothing more than a reasonable or beautiful ordering of the "circumstantial" in worship. Even the Pauline canon, which is perhaps the best rule of all: "Let all things be done unto edifying," [1] will not always carry us clear of difficulty. The ritual which is helpful at one time, or in one place, may be "nocent" at another. The most stringent purists do not stand to-day exactly where they stood even a generation back; nor would any evangelical Church in this country be satisfied with forms of Divine service so meagre and unadorned as satisfied at one period the extreme schools of Puritan dissent.

[1] 1 Cor. xiv. 26.

CHAPTER XIII

ORDER OF WEEKLY WORSHIP

THE outward acts of a congregation which, variously arranged and performed, go to make up Divine service as we practise it on the Lord's Day, are few in number and extremely simple. Musical praise by choir and congregation; prayers; readings out of the Old and New Testaments; the recitation of a creed; a sermon; the offering of our gifts to God; celebration of baptism occasionally, and, as often as we will, of the Lord's Supper: these constitute, if I mistake not, a complete list. It is nearly all a service of godly words, spoken or sung; and although both praise and prayer admit of considerable varieties in form, yet one feels that if the whole compass of a Christian people's emotions and desires in the presence of our Father is to find utterance, study must be given to use to the full these few and simple elements at our command. For the devout states of the worshippers, which are to be the spiritual contents that fill up these forms and lend to them their whole value, are both more numerous and more complex. In one or other act, if the service is to be a full one, the congregation has to give expression to a great many moods of its devotional life: to adoration, to contrition, to gratitude, to trust and peace in believing, to its consecration to the Divine service and its surrender to the Divine will, to brotherly love and the sympathy of the Christian body with its suffering members; to a crowd of desires also, that always press for utterance in the ear of God: desires for forgiveness, for comfort, for help in temptation, for growth in knowledge and in holiness, for the advancement of the kingdom of Christ; everything, in short, which enters into the normal experience of pious believers.

Now, it is to the adequate and orderly presentation, within the few minutes allowed by custom to a Sunday service, of such varied feelings and desires, nothing over-done and nothing omitted, that the earnest effort of the leader needs to be chiefly turned, in so far as he is left responsible for the conduct of the service. Were it in one's power to construct an ideal programme for the weekly worship, what would be the points to be kept in view? Probably there are just three merits which it would be important for such a service to combine:—

1. That each act of worship be devoted to a definite purpose and bear a character of its own, having its distinct contribution to make to the completeness of the whole;

2. That no devout feeling or desire, common to the wor-shippers and requiring expression, be left wholly unex-pressed; and

3. That the acts succeed one another in what may be called a natural sequence; following, that is, so far as may be, the order of normal Christian piety. That the moods which spontaneously arise in Christian hearts during their deliberate approaches to the throne of grace do usually succeed each other in some order natural to the new life, will probably be conceded; although everyone might not set them down quite in the same sequence.

In other words, the worship-acts ought to be distinct, comprehensive, progressive.

But the leader of worship has not usually been left in this matter without guidance. Only in Churches on the Independent model, where each congregation constitutes an autonomous unit, is the minister free as a rule to construct an order of service of his own. Even there, I imagine, traditional usage in a particular Church will frequently prescribe to any new pastor the order of service he is expected to observe. In larger Church bodies, at all events,

the minister is always required more or less strictly to
follow an order laid down for him by ecclesiastical authority.
There are two degrees of guidance he may receive, by which
his responsibility is more or less shared and lightened. In
the Catholic and Anglican communions everything is dictated with all but faultless exactness by a "liturgy"; that
is to say, by an Office of Common Prayer, covering the
entire service, and prescribing for his use and that of the
people their respective shares in the service, from which
neither he nor they are at liberty to deviate. In the
Presbyterian Churches of Great Britain and the British
colonies, and in those of America which sprang from
British emigrants, a lesser degree of guidance is afforded
by the Directory of the Westminster Assembly, in which
an order of service is laid down, with the general character
of its separate acts; but the phraseology of the prayers in
particular is left to the discretion of the leader. Lutheran
and Reformed Churches on the Continent, with the Kirk of
Scotland in her earlier history, adopted a combination of
the two; portions only of the service consisting of prescribed
or written forms; though, if I mistake not, their clergy have
never been rigorously tied to these liturgical forms, as in
the Anglican and Roman rituals.[1]

The basis of all Reformed service-books was Calvin's
"Book of Geneva,"[2] still in force in French Switzerland, in
France, and among the German Reformed. Introduced also
into Scotland, it was accepted, with some enlargement, as
the "Book of Common Order" for the Kirk. Through
A'Lasco's adaptation of it for the Church of the Foreigners
in London, which was translated into Dutch, it became the
chief source of the liturgy of Holland and of the Dutch
Reformed Church in the United States. The Palatinate,

---

[1] This certainly was not the case in the Scottish Church. "A directory
with forms for optional use" is Dr. M'Crie's account of it. (See his *Public
Worship of Presbyterian Scotland*, Edin. 1892, p. 106.)

[2] Issued in 1536 under the title, *Forme des Prières Ecclésiastiques*, but
subsequently revised and re-issued at Geneva in 1556.

with other Reformed Churches on the Lower Rhine, likewise adopted a form based on the same model.

In theory, the difference between a liturgy and a
directory affects only the language employed in public
prayer. For everything else, the rubrics of the one may
be as precise and comprehensive as those of the other.
In practice, however, the rubrics of the Westminster Directory, though nominally binding upon most English-speaking
Presbyterians, have long ceased to be closely observed.
Where that document has not been subjected to recent
revision,[1] it may almost be said to be obsolete; with the
result that a good deal of diversity has come to obtain in
Presbyterian worship. Numerous suggestions for its reform
have within the last century been made by Church Service
Societies or individual ministers; but an authoritative re-
casting of the Puritan Directory of the seventeenth century
is an urgent need, which the Scottish and American Churches
might combine to supply.[2]

With so much liberty prevailing outside the Churches
which use a liturgy, the actual practice in many evangelical
communions, both in this country and in America, is not
readily ascertained and hardly admits of exact comparison.
Any casual observer might be forgiven if he were more
impressed by their diversities than by their substantial

[1] As it has been in the Presbyterian Church of England and by the
Federal Assembly of Australia and Tasmania.

[2] The *Euchologion* issued by the "Church Service Society" of the Church
of Scotland is well known and has been pretty extensively used. More
recently a similar society in the United Free Church of Scotland, the
"Public Worship Association," has provided for its ministers ample material,
first in the way of subjects for prayer (*New Directory for the Public Worship
of God*, Edin. 1898), and now also by forms of prayer selected from a wide
range of sources (*Anthology of Prayer for Public Worship*, Edin. 1907).
Although prepared for Scottish use, all these will be found helpful by others
who are called to lead in non-liturgical Churches. None of these has received an official *imprimatur*. But some time ago the General Assembly of
the Church of Scotland permitted the issue of a service-book for the use of
worshippers deprived of the services of a minister (*Prayers for Social and
Family Worship*, revised ed., Edin. 1892).

9

agreement. Not that uniformity in details would be in itself any great merit. Christian freedom to differ, and the adaptation of worship to the needs of different communities, are principles too precious to be sacrificed to a cast-iron sameness, were it even more desirable than it is. Yet agreement there may well be where there is no uniformity. And I think that underneath superficial variety the prevailing forms of evangelical worship do bear a broad resemblance to one another. They belong to the same type. In the arrangement of their parts, especially, they either conform, or, in the hands of a capable leader, they may readily be made to conform, to a fairly uniform scheme. How far that scheme is one in which the features laid down above as desirable can be traced, will best appear from a rapid review of the ordinary Lord's Day service.

1. The Preface

The main service of a congregation on the Lord's Day is always introduced by a " preface " of some sort.[1] For at any solemn function, civil or sacred, the abrupt and the hurried are to be avoided ; and reverence dictates that in drawing near to God the mind should collect itself, striving to fix its thoughts on Him and to realise His presence.

This is done in a variety of ways : either

(*a*) By a simple call to worship ; or

(*b*) By reciting a Scripture verse while the people rise : it may be always the same ; *e.g.* the formula given in the Book of Geneva, " *Our help is in the name of the Lord, who made heaven and earth,*" has long been current among continental Presbyterians ; or it may be selected, as in the Church of England, from a suitable list.

Or (*c*) by a brief prayer of lowly adoration coupled with invocation of the Holy Spirit's aid in worship, as in the

---

[1] The "*Introitus*" of the German liturgies ; which is usually a brief responsive prayer, said by clergyman and people, followed by the *Gloria Patri.*

Westminster Directory. This is now common, but is often made too long.

Or (*d*) by the singing of a psalm or hymn, as was long the invariable practice in Scotland. Only the leader needs to see that the verses chosen are appropriate for the opening. Every act of praise, no less than of prayer, should, of course, bear a character of its own, befitting its position and purpose. Here the object is to attune the heart to the spirit of devotion and give a keynote to what is to follow.

Where a combination of two or more of these is attempted, care has to be taken that the whole Preface, as well as each act in it, is not made too long. All through the service, in fact, it is the duty of the leader, so far as he has control, to arrange that, while there is no appearance of haste, neither is there any part that drags, or repeats itself, or is prolonged to tediousness, or encroaches on the time of the rest. There is so much to be done in a brief space. The secret lies in knowing beforehand exactly what desire or feeling has now to be expressed, giving it utterance in quiet, concise, apt words, enough and no more— then passing on with grave deliberateness to the next.

2. CONFESSION OF SINS

The congregation having now placed itself consciously in the presence of God, the instinct of every devout heart is to recall in that presence its own uncleanness and unworthiness, with which among believers is invariably associated the thought of the new and living way by which we have access to the Father. Consequently the service proper opens most fittingly with a General Confession of Sin and a Petition for Divine Forgiveness. The Church, admitted to the presence-chamber, begins by taking the lowest room.

According to Achelis,[1] this formed a regular part of early worship until the custom of private confession to a priest came

[1] *Prakt. Theologie,* ii. 146.

in, and it was restored to the German Mass in the twelfth
century. Its universal introduction at this stage into the
order of every Reformed Church was due to the influence of
Calvin, who adopted it in his Book of Geneva; but the form
of "General Confession" everywhere used is now said to
have been the work of Œcolampadius of Basle. It first
appeared in the Zurich Service-book of 1525. That this
important feature dropped out of the services of Scottish
Presbyterians after 1645 was a result of its omission from
the Westminster Directory, and has been a serious im-
poverishment of the worship. It has lately been restored
in their revision of the Directory by the English Presbyterians. Leaders of worship in Congregational or Presbyterian Churches who desire its reintroduction will be more
likely to frame a confession for themselves than to fall back
upon any Reformation formula. Without entering into
much detail, it ought to acknowledge in simple and un-
exaggerated, though in humble and contrite, language, such
faults of character and shortcomings in Christian duty as
are to be found in all of us, so that the entire congregation
can honestly appropriate every word of it.

In the Lutheran and Anglican Churches, whose ministers
are empowered to pronounce penitents to be absolved, the
"General Confession" is followed by a prescribed form of
absolution. This Calvin is said to have omitted only
through fear of giving offence.[1] The Church of England,
while expressly claiming for her clergy such a power, is
careful, like the German liturgies, to give to the declaratory
formula a general, not a personal, application, and follows
it up by a bidding prayer for "true repentance" in which
the most scrupulous of Protestants may join.[2] In most
evangelical congregations, it will probably be deemed
sufficient to recite a Divine promise of forgiveness for

---

[1] See Baird, *Chapter on Liturgies* (London, 1856), p. 21, footnote.

[2] "He pardoneth and absolveth all them that truly repent and un-
feignedly believe His holy Gospel. Wherefore, let us beseech Him to grant
us true repentance and His Holy Spirit," and so on.

Jesus' sake and, pleading His merits, to append to the act of confession a simple petition for penitence and pardon. This, however, ought never to be omitted.

3. SCRIPTURE READINGS

From this point the worship is that of men who, however imperfect, have afresh committed themselves to the Divine mercy, and who now realise their acceptance in Christ as sons of God.

One of the earliest needs of the new life is for fuller teaching, guidance, and support out of the Word of God. "Speak, Lord," is its voice; "Thy servant heareth." Very naturally, therefore, do the people at once assume the attitude of disciples while the Holy Book is read. Ere we directly address our petitions to the Most High, it is fitting that we should meekly hear what He has to say to us. Man's prayers are a response to Heaven's revelation.

It was an old custom in the Church of Scotland to mark the gratitude of the forgiven by placing before other Scriptures a reading or chanting of Psalms, as the Church of England does. The brevity of a modern service may make it difficult to spare time for this in addition to the two usual "lessons." Each of the latter, however, is usually followed by an Act of Praise, which may, if desired, be taken from the Psalter. These Acts cannot be intended merely for variety, or to give the reader a pause. They express the joy with which a pious soul welcomes and responds to the Word of the Lord, "as one that findeth great spoil." Hence they ought never to be on a minor key, but bright bursts of grateful praise. For one of them there can be nothing better in itself than the *Te Deum*. Its length is here its only drawback; but if used in this connection and not at a more advanced stage, its length seems to make it fitter that it should succeed the second reading rather than come in between, as it does in the " Book of Common Prayer."

In many Churches the selection of the passages to be

read is left to the leader, who discharges the duty most frequently by choosing well-known portions which have some connection with the subject of the sermon to follow. The practice has fixed itself so firmly in many quarters that it would now be difficult to uproot it. Yet I am convinced it is a faulty one. There are two pleas on which it is justified. The one is that it imparts unity to the service. So it does, but the unity is merely that of a single thought made dominant at each service. To be consistent, indeed, the prayers also, no less than the lessons, would need to be coloured (as sometimes they are) by the theme of the preacher's discourse. By this means a kind of unity is no doubt gained; but it is at the sacrifice of what is of far greater consequence, the unity of a complete service of Divine Worship, in which each devout mood of the people, with all their wants, finds adequate and harmonious expression, in the degree of its importance in religious experience.

A second plea is that in Protestant worship the Word of God is the prevailing feature which ought to give character to all the rest. That is true ; but to make the Word of God felt all through every service as its leading factor, is a very different thing from making the particular subject selected for that day's sermon by the preacher, the governing thought in the whole worship of each Sunday, to which everything else is to be subordinated. Wherever a true feeling for common worship is strong, the devotions of the assembled people will assert their own claim apart from the sermon.

Now, so soon as an independent value is conceded to the Scripture readings, and the need of the flock to be fed in the pastures of the Word is made the guiding consideration in their selection, it is seen to be desirable that the public reading of the Bible from week to week should follow some intelligible order and aim at approximate completeness, in order "that the people may become better acquainted with the whole body of the Scriptures."[1] When a preacher, to

---

[1] Westminster Directory.

fit his text or to please his taste, selects at random, the usual result is that a limited number of favourite or familiar passages are repeated again and again, while the great body, even of what retains a present-day value for edification, is never read at all. Ignorance of the Bible is confessed to be on the increase among us. It is less and less read in the family, possibly even in the closet. If a systematic acquaintance with the facts and teachings of Holy Writ is to be gained at all by many of our people, it must be gained at church.

It is a misfortune that no quite satisfactory and well-known lectionary exists to which a minister can have recourse. The Church of England has inherited an ample one, but it is compiled for Matins and Evensong on every day in the week, with the unhappy result that worshippers who are only present on Sundays hear one lesson out of every seven, and are carried at a leap over the intervening six. The old "pericopes," as they are termed, that is, the Gospel and Epistle, are for Sundays only, it is true; but they possess no continuity, besides being brief and adjusted to the Church year. To draft a course of Lord's Day readings, for one year or for two, is a needed service for all our Churches. If the Scottish Churches, for instance, were to undertake it in combination, it would be found helpful far beyond their own borders. In the meanwhile, each minister can construct one for himself. It is only needful to take care that the suitable contents of the canon be divided into coherent sections, each possessing some unity of subject, and not exceeding in length on the average, say, from twenty to five and twenty or thirty verses. To read these ordinarily in consecutive order need not exclude an occasional interruption when a Sunday occurs that wears a character of its own: such as Easter, or Children's Day, or a church anniversary, or the last Lord's Day in the year.

4. THE CREED

If the congregation is to profess its faith at all in weekly worship, this seems to me the right place for it; a fitter place than where Calvin put it in his Liturgy, quite at the close of the service. For the "Belief" is our response to the Gospel teaching just read out of Holy Scripture.

One chief end for which the Church of Christ exists is to bear witness to the world of the Message of her Lord; and this end at least is served by the Creed as often as it is recited in public. But the devotional recital of a Creed means something more than this. It is a spontaneous utterance on the part of each worshipper of his personal faith, addressed, not to the world, but to God. It is an act of trust in the acts of God for the redemption of the world. It makes, therefore, a distinct contribution to our common devotions as the expression we give to our Christian piety, and if it be present at all, it must fill a place that is all its own. Hardly any other devotional exercise is more characteristic of the Christian religion than to confess the Triune God, telling out what He has done for us, through the redemptive acts of Jesus Christ, to the glory of the Father, and of the Son, and of the Holy Ghost.

The custom had existed in the Church from the fifth century,[1] and the Apostles' Creed passed into Protestant service-books, among others into the Common Order of the Kirk of Scotland. That it was dropped out of Scottish worship under later Puritan influence, and never found admission at all, so far as I am aware, into Independent congregations, has been the loss of a link, where we have not too many, with the rest of the Church Universal.

Its reintroduction where it has fallen out of use will probably be a matter of time. Some ministers who apprehend objections to its weekly recitation are inserting it in the Communion Service. Probably few congregations, however, if fairly consulted, would object. Here and

[1] Bingham, *Antt.* x. 4. 17.

there the usual attenders at a particular church include a
number of persons whose personal belief is too indefinite or
has been too deeply shaken by present-day difficulties to
permit them to repeat with full assurance all the clauses in
the Creed. Such cases are exceptional. An obstacle to its
adoption which is more widely felt lies in the unhappy version of that much-debated clause which runs in English :
" He descended into hell "; or rather, it lies in the difficulty
of agreeing upon a more accurate rendering of the original.[1]
To substitute " Hades " for " hell," which would restore the
true sense, has now been rendered more easy by the use of
that Greek word in the Revised Version of the New Testament. Or, the clause being a comparatively late insertion,
unknown before the recension of Rufinus (c. 390 A.D.), its
omission might be defended. At any rate, it seems hopeless
to propose the use of any other symbol. Otherwise much
might be urged in favour of the so-called " Nicene," more
accurately, Constantinopolitan Creed; especially the fact
that it comes nearer than any other to absolutely universal
acceptance, being the solitary Confession of Faith that is
of authority over all Oriental, as well as Occidental,
Christendom.

5. THE SERVICE OF PRAYER

The worship of the congregation now moves a step
forward to a more intimate converse with the Most High.
We have been disciples, and we have professed one faith ;
we are now to be filial suppliants and intercessors with the
Father. Hitherto it is the intellectual side of religion
which has received expression. What we have received
from God has been His Word of instruction and of gracious
promise through His Son; what we have presented to Him
has been our sacrifice of praise for the great mercies of His
Gospel, with an avowal of the Church's belief in Revelation
facts and truths. A different side in religious experience,

---

[1] εἰς τὸν ᾅδην. See Schaff's *Creeds of Greek and Latin Churches*,
p. 46.

one of equal moment, remains to be reflected in our worship: its practical aspects and needs as a life of emotion and of desire, spent in daily contact with the trials and duties of this world, a life of human want, responsibility, and temptation.

Here, just as in the previous section, worship must be true to its idea as a fellowship of man's spirit with God in mutual acts of giving and receiving. But it is not here, in God's house, it is outside it, in the home and the mart, that the great sacrifices of life can be offered, the ceaseless oblation of grateful obedience and of surrender to the Divine Will. Not here, but there, that the soul which waits on God must draw into herself in a ceaseless tide the gift of His Spirit's energy, to purify, sweeten, and enrich her life. All that can be offered in Church is merely the devotional expression of this daily commerce in giving and receiving. That devotional expression takes the dual shape of thanksgiving and petition.

Thanksgiving is praise cast into the form of personal gratitude as the worshippers recall their own past experience and note what countless benefits they have all received, as members of the human family, or as members of the Church of God, from the unwearied, open-handed liberality of Him from whom cometh down "every perfect boon." An Act of General Thanksgiving is therefore the first offering wherewith we now draw near to speak unto the Father.

But life is as full of our own needs as of His gifts: needs always urgent, sometimes bitter. The heart of each worshipper comes laden with its private wants; and the congregation has desires of its own, no less than those which touch the welfare of the universal Church. Conscious, therefore, of present needs and anticipating more to come, what can we do, but make our requests known unto God, craving at His hand fresh gifts of His love, not inferior to those for which we have thanked Him: benefits temporal, but much more spiritual, for ourselves, and also for others?

If this be a just *rationale* of the long prayer, or if it be preferred, of the series of short prayers, which forms a feature in nearly all services, it will be apparent why it should fall into three main divisions and no more:—a Prayer of Thanksgiving; a Prayer of Supplication for the congregation then present; and a Prayer of General Intercession.[1] At the close we fitly sum up our desires in the Divine Prayer which Jesus taught, in whose words all can unite.

Of these three, the second may well be the freest portion of the whole service. For here, more than anywhere else, the leader, who is also pastor, prays with and for his own flock, out of his close acquaintance with their local circumstances and needs. None so able as he to interpret to God those longings, born of the hour and of the place, which his own spirit shares with the most spiritual of his people: longings for whatever he and they know the flock to stand in present need of; the quickening, for example, of such as are members only in name; the recovery of any who have gone astray; the training of youth in the home; the preservation of brotherly harmony; the succour of the tempted; the comfort of the sick or the bereaved; the success of the congregation's efforts to win the irreligious around. This, of course, he is able to do when he is at liberty to vary his petitions from week to week as his pastoral experience dictates. At this point supplication can scarcely be too precise, nor can it be too fervent or imploring.

It is otherwise with the Thanksgiving, and still more so with the Intercession. The latter is, of course, a higher act, one of the highest of all; for in it a priestly community, in association with its high-priestly Head, is interceding on the world's behalf. For this reason a calmer or more restrained tone, as well as a more formal style, is suitable than in their entreaties for themselves. It naturally comes last. There is less room for variation or for detail.

---

[1] The service-books both of the Reformed Churches and of Westminster deferred the prayer of intercession till after sermon.

The petitions should be precise, no doubt, and cover as great a variety of objects as time will allow: always including (1) the whole Church, (2) civil rulers and the common weal, with (3) every class of the afflicted and needy; yet always couched in such general terms, concise, aptly phrased and free from repetition, as do not require to be much altered from day to day.[1] Few men can compose such a prayer on the spot.

Here then we are made sharply aware of the question, once keenly debated in this country, between the advocates of liturgical and of free prayer:—if, indeed, we do not find here a suggestion of the best way to solve it. The comparative advantages and disadvantages of each are by this time too well understood to make it necessary to fight the old battle over again; and probably there are not a few who would prefer to either a combination of them both. In fact, no service entirely wants the liturgical element in which the Lord's Prayer is regularly recited. In certain other prayers, such as the Confession of Sin and the Intercessions, a form for habitual use is so appropriate that, where it is not imposed by authority, ministers are found who compose or adopt one for themselves. Prepared forms likewise suit occasions which, like baptism or marriage, bear closely on unusual circumstances and do not recur too frequently. On the other hand, the unvarying repetition of the same words throughout a long service is apt, in the experience of many, to degenerate into a mechanical recitation of phrases only too familiar, which tends to narcotise the mind. This is certainly not admitted by loyal members of the Church of England, habituated from childhood to the Prayer Book; but it would probably be felt by worshippers accustomed to a freer method. A prayer conceived for the occasion, they maintain, is more

---

[1] Yet a leader who is free to make changes may give variety, if he will, by introducing more detailed petitions, now into one, and now into another, of the three main groups named above; but all three ought to be remembered on every occasion.

likely to be the utterance of devout feeling in him who frames it, and consequently better adapted to arouse attention and beget devotion in those who listen to it. At any rate, the changeful experiences of a Christian flock, with the incalculable movements of the Spirit of God in the hearts of leader and people, find no room under rigid forms. Some plan, therefore, which provides a reasonable measure both of concerted and of *extempore* utterance, seems to commend itself.

That, however, is a matter for Church authorities. In the meantime, what each officiating minister has to aim at is, to avoid the usual faults of the system under which he serves, while endeavouring to secure its benefits and training his people also to use and to enjoy it.

The leader in a liturgical service has no doubt a much lighter responsibility than burdens his brethren of the non-liturgical Churches. Nevertheless, he too has besetting sins to guard against. To read prayers (where it is not necessary from the size of the building to intone them) in a worthy manner, putting into every reading of them the earnestness of personal devotion as one who is actually praying with the people, and to escape such vices of delivery as a monotone, or a sing-song, or an over-rapid and indistinct gabble—this is possibly less easy than it looks; for it has not always been attained by the clergy.

On the other hand, one whom his Church has honoured with the weightier duty of leading in free prayer, needs to bestow on its right discharge a great deal of attention, if he would avoid the graver perils which beset him. What these are no one needs to be told. Loose and disconnected prayers, full of repetition and circumlocution, yet omitting some material topic, often substituting didactic statement for petitions, couched in a dull, verbose or slipshod style —these were for long a familiar reproach against the Presbyterian—and also, if not equally, against the Congregational—ministry. There has recently been, if I mistake not, a change for the better. More care is given to the conduct of worship. Few of the younger ministers probably take as little pains as their fathers did to qualify themselves for the discharge of a duty more sacred than preaching and probably quite as difficult. What is to be desired is a general training as well as special preparation. The general training required is partly to study the nature and purposes of public cultus, the character of Christian worship, its parts and the tone appropriate to each, together with the relation of the leader to the body of worshippers, what and how much he should express of their common feelings and desires; but also to familiarise himself with devotional material. There is a language of devotion in which the minister does well to steep himself. It has been the product of centuries of devout life. It is not a mosaic of Bible phraseology, but it is modelled on Scripture examples and even more on its spirit and tone. It is a rare essence, distilled from the experience of all saints, fragrant with their concentrated devoutness. With classic specimens of its literature, which are not numerous, a man would need to be conversant who should catch the mingled dignity and simplicity, depth and sweetness, boldness and reverence, gravity and cheerfulness, warmth and chaste reserve, which befit the temper of Christian piety at its best.

After such a preliminary discipline, less preparation will be wanted for each Sunday's prayers: less, but not none. On this point it is difficult to lay down a rule. Shall the minister write out his prayers, and learn or read them? or simply meditate the order of thought and endeavour to possess his heart at the time with the spirit of devotion? Here, as in preparing sermons, what suits one best will not suit another. Some young ministers will find it needful to begin by composing prayers beforehand, and possibly to continue doing so for a year or two. Yet I think, after some practice, it will generally answer better to fix in one's mind what each prayer is to contain, with its specific value or design in the structure of the service, so that nothing of consequence be overlooked; then let the mind, once embarked on the flow of devotional feeling, utter itself in the words which the Spirit prompts. Such a prayer, though less crisp or finished in style, is likely to breathe a fresher and more fervent mood for being to a limited extent impromptu.

6. The Hymn

It does not appear to me desirable to interrupt these prayers, or this long prayer (as is done in the Anglican service and often in other Churches), by an anthem or similar act of praise. This can hardly have any better reason than to relieve the strain of what after all need not be a very protracted exercise. But a hymn naturally follows at the close, of a different character from any previous act of praise. Since the opening hymn, the prevalent note in all that has been sung by the congregation should be, more than, I think, it often is, one of grateful praise to God, for what He is in Himself and for what He has done for us. This hymn, however, from its position between the prayers and the sermon, may most fitly be a rich and warm utterance of ripe Christian experience—a song of trust, or of hope, or of breathings after holiness; in any case a subjective song, answering to what in Germany is denominated the *Hauptlied*, or main hymn. In the choice of it, it is not amiss if the leader have regard to the subject of the discourse which is to follow.

Where an anthem is included in the ordinary service, as is now frequently the case, it is probably better, on musical grounds, that it be left to the choir, the rest of the worshippers joining only in spirit, yet indicating their participation by a standing posture. Every other act of praise, however, is to be such as the people generally can unite to sing. This is in many places of worship the only part of the worship in which they are accustomed to take an

audible share. Enthusiasm for the improvement or cultivation of Church music, however much to be welcomed, is
carried too far when the vocal praises of the worshippers
are sacrificed to it. For a similar reason, the innovation
of wholly musical services on Sunday evenings is to be
discouraged. The weekly seasons of Divine service have
too many and too precious uses to be surrendered to
organist or choir-master. The minister must also recollect
that, although he does not lead the music, it is his duty
to retain the leadership of the people's praise, by himself
selecting what is to be sung or chanted. It will be his
wisdom at the same time to do so after frank and
sympathetic consultation with the musical leader.

7. THE OFFERING

The modern money-collection, or "offertory," may be
viewed as either a survival or an equivalent of the gifts in
kind contributed by members in the primitive Church, out
of which were taken Bread and Wine for the Lord's Supper,
as well as food for the Love-feast. Whether it be cere-
monially presented on the Communion Table or not, it is an
integral part of worship; and, for all who bear in mind its
symbolic significance, an important as well as unique
element in it. From a material point of view, its money
value as alms for the poor, or as a contribution to the
expenses of the house of God, is not in most cases a matter
of indifference. But in His eyes who sat over against the
treasury, we must believe that its religious value as an act
of devotion is estimated, not by its amount, but by the
generosity which dictates it, by the proportion it bears to
the giver's means, and by the consecration to God of his
whole substance which it implies. Like the first-fruits in
ancient Israel, it is a part which represents the whole. Its
inner meaning as an act of worship I take to be that our
devotion holds back nothing from the service of Him who,
for our sakes, became poor, but lays at His feet, along with

ourselves, our possessions also, to be used in His honour and for the welfare of His kingdom. If it means this surrender, the smallest of coins becomes eloquent.

8. THE SERMON

That the sermon has been removed from the Order of Holy Communion, where it still stands in the Book of Common Prayer, and has been made in every other Protestant form of worship an invariable and integral portion of morning and evening services, is a change which we owe to the new emphasis laid at the Reformation on the truth that "the Spirit of God maketh the reading, but especially the preaching of the Word an effectual means of salvation." The Reformed Service-books gave it a place before the Intercessory Prayer; thus dividing the prayers probably in order that the sermon might be the central act in worship; and this position it retains in many Presbyterian Churches. It is doubtful how far this really enhances its importance, and the cutting into two of the "devotional exercises" has had the unfortunate effect of creating an impression of their subordinate value, as though they were no more than accessories to the preacher's discourse, which they either serve to introduce as "preliminaries" or to follow up. Such an unfortunate impression is got rid of when the body of common prayer is ended before the preacher's address begins.

The sermon is to be fully treated in Part III. Its prominence as a means of grace, taken by itself, would hardly require us to handle it separately as a distinct function of ministerial office; not even when we add the amount of labour which it entails upon the minister. Its peculiarity rather lies in this, that it is the one act of Divine service in which the leader does much more than lead. In every other he is simply the foremost worshipper, the mouthpiece of the assembly, who guides its acts and voices its devotion. But as the preacher, he detaches himself from the congregation. He addresses, not God along with them, but them on

10

behalf of God. A new relationship has entered, that of an orator to his audience. So that, while the sermon is taken up into congregational worship, and from that fact derives a character which religious addresses do not bear under other conditions, yet it remains a speaker's or "orator's" discourse. Moreover, the intention to edify, which throughout most of the service is secondary and kept in the background, steps at this point into the foreground. It is in this way that preaching comes to be a distinct function, claiming for itself a large division of practical theology.

9. Close of Worship

The brief "prayer after sermon" for the Divine blessing on the words of the preacher, like the petition "for illumination," which by old custom precedes the sermon, marks our dependence on the Holy Spirit, in whose hands even the Gospel message is but an instrument, impotent unless His power operate through it. It is well to swathe the Word in prayer.

But now, unless the offertory has been postponed till this point (which is the Prayer-Book order), nothing remains, when there is to be no celebration of a sacrament, but to bring the service to a close. It should not end, any more than it began, abruptly.

Two short acts, and no more, are usual. The first is praise, which in many congregations is a hymn echoing the sentiment of the sermon. But if the main hymn before sermon was selected with this reference, it is better that this should be expressly a closing act—a dismission, or a doxology, or at evening worship a vesper hymn.

Then comes the real act of dismission, which is always a prayer, but a prayer of a very peculiar kind. The minister invokes the Divine blessing upon the people. How are we to understand this act?

One of the quaintest and most venerable features in the ancient ritual, which, I think, lingers nowhere among

Protestants save in the English Liturgy and in Lutheran *Agende*, was this mutual greeting exchanged between leader and congregation:—Minister: "*The Lord be with you*"; Answer: "*And with thy spirit.*" The closing benediction resembles it, only it is not mutual but one-sided; more official and less fraternal. Although in pronouncing it the minister is simply uttering a petition, for he does not declare the people blessed, but asks for a blessing on them; still he does so in some official capacity. He separates himself from them, for he does not as in other prayers include himself; and its official character is visibly symbolised by the posture usually adopted in it.

It is hardly to be wondered at, therefore, that a good many people scruple at this, because they suspect in it a savour of priestliness, and dislike it accordingly. No doubt the Trinitarian benediction which is usually employed is the New Testament substitute for the Aaronic blessing;[1] and that was pronounced by the Hebrew priests. Nevertheless, there could be nothing sacerdotal about its employment by St. Paul,[2] and therefore there need be none when it is spoken by the Christian minister.

In what capacity, then, does he bless the people; for "without all contradiction the less is blessed of the better"?[3] The simplest explanation of a formula which certainly calls for explanation, is probably the one given by the divines who sat in the Jerusalem Chamber in the seventeenth century. "It belongs," they said, "to the office of the pastor to bless the people from God." From *Lightfoot's Journal* one learns that this result was only reached after a long discussion.[4] It seems a safe solution. No one need take exception at the pastor of a flock parting from his assembled people, as St. Paul took leave by letter of his Corinthian converts, with a formal and solemn prayer that "the grace of the Lord Jesus Christ, and the love of God, and the

---

[1] Num. 6[22-27].   [2] 2 Cor. 13[14].   [3] Heb. 7[7].

[4] See Form of Presbyterian Church Government, and cf. *Lightfoot's Journal* of date 8th Nov. 1643.

communion of the Holy Ghost" may be with them all. May we not likewise catch through the lips of its ordained minister the voice of the great Church of God, interceding for this small company of its membership, and calling down upon every one of them the threefold benediction of the New Covenant?

Let the act be done with solemnity. Never may the leader in worship relax the intense strain upon his own spirit until he has put his whole soul into these great closing words.

CHAPTER XIV

SACRAMENTAL SERVICES

On certain Sundays, which it is well should recur at fixed dates, so that people may count upon them, worship either morning or evening, instead of closing in the usual way, is prolonged to include a sacramental service. The rule for both Baptism and the Lord's Supper requires public administration; for both, private celebration is in most Churches a permitted exception. It is true that they do not stand quite on a level in this respect. Holy Communion is by its nature a social act; and although I believe its occasional observance by a select group of Christian friends in the sick-room of a chronic invalid to be not merely a legitimate, but even a desirable, privilege, yet it ought never to be administered to the sick person alone, like the *viaticum* of the Roman Church. Baptism, on the contrary, is an individual rite; and, wearing in the case of infants a family or domestic character, it is much more tolerant of household administration. But this liberty has in the past been greatly abused; and the present tendency in Presbyterian communions to insist on publicity, as the Scottish *Book of Common Order* required, is certainly wise. The admission of a new member into the Church entails responsibilities on the society as well as on the individual. In Baptist congregations it must always take place, for obvious reasons, in a part of the church buildings arranged for the purpose; nor have I often heard of adult baptism in any communion taking place at home, although such an exception would be permissible. The case is not materially altered when it is an infant member who is to be formally received and enrolled. The rubric of the Church of England requiring children to be brought to the font "immediately after the the last Lesson" at Morning or Evening Prayer, "when the most number of people come together," is certainly not now observed. It is probably the length of the Order for Baptism which has made it obsolete. But the reasons given for it still hold for any Church: "As well for that the Congregation there present may testify the receiving of them that be newly baptized into the number of Christ's Church; as also because in the Baptism of Infants every man present may be put in remembrance of his own profession made to God in his Baptism."

Ministers of other Churches no doubt encounter the same objection to incorporating a baptismal service into the Lord's Day worship, namely, that it unduly prolongs the service. To meet this difficulty either by curtailing the usual service or by crushing the Order of Baptism into as few minutes as possible, is equally undesirable. Where the difficulty is seriously felt, perhaps the best plan is to hold the baptismal rite in church immediately after the dismissal of the morning congregation, inviting all who are piously disposed and not pressed for time, to remain during the few minutes which it occupies, just as communicants do when Holy Communion is to follow.

It may well be that household administration for insufficient reasons or for none at all, and the hurried fashion in which it is sometimes administered in Church, have both contributed to depreciate the importance attached to this Holy Sacrament. At all events, low views of its meaning and value are too common in our Churches. By some parents it is regarded simply as a family ceremony for the dedication or for the naming of their child. By others it is said to be omitted altogether with no sense of loss. One even hears of persons being admitted to the Lord's Supper in riper years who never are baptized at all—the minister being either ignorant of the fact or indifferent to it. One cause which has helped to create this heedless attitude is the disuse in bygone generations of adult baptism, from the universal custom of christening every child as a matter of course. Against such indiscriminate administration the Baptist Churches in England have at least been a standing protest. In Scotland, the law of the Presbyterian Church refusing the rite to all but the children of Church members has tended to uphold, in theory at least, a worthier conception of the ordinance. But it is the rise of missions, with the consequent reception into the Church of adult converts in large numbers, which has probably done most to restore to this sacrament its full significance in the thoughts of many Christians. It tells us much of the unaggressive, non-missionary state of British Christianity in the seventeenth century, that the Puritan Directory of that date took no notice whatever of the baptizing of adults. Nowadays, with the growing indifference of non-religious classes in our population, even to the forms of religion, the baptism of persons in riper years is far from an infrequent duty of the home minister; and he needs, before admitting applicants to Communion, to satisfy himself that they have already received the earlier sacrament of initiation.

Whenever either sacrament is administered, its importance justifies the universal custom of enshrining it within a special form of service of its own. As soon as a love for material symbols invaded the early Church, and ceremonies which had no Apostolic warrant came to be multiplied by popular piety, with or without ecclesiastical sanction, it was natural that these should cluster thickly around both Baptism and the Eucharist. For these two were the only rites of material symbolism which the Church had received from its Founder. Everything else in the Christian cult was thoughts expressed in words. Here ideas were embodied after a manner far more usual in earlier and less spiritual faiths, in manual acts and material substances. It was a recognition of that symbolism in nature of which Jesus in His parables had made constant use for teaching purposes. It was, if you like, a concession to the infirmity of human faith in the unseen. Most men apprehend truth best in a figure. Here, at least, were two Christian rites of unimpeachable authority, to which much else that was symbolic, whether drawn from pagan mysteries or from Jewish ritual, could readily attach itself.

This occurred, as time went on, to a much greater extent in the celebration of the Supper than in the simpler rite of Baptism. Yet there also a number of additions were early made, which are still retained in the Roman ordinal but have been discontinued in Protestant services. To this discontinuance, indeed, I recall but a single exception, the sign of the cross on the forehead of the baptized, the retention of which by the Church of England was a bone of contention with her Puritan members. The form of administration among Protestants is therefore singularly uniform; except where post-Reformation objections to pædobaptism and the belief in immersion as the only valid mode, have introduced divergencies.

Where his Church has furnished him with no Order of Baptism, a minister has it in his own hands, by his mode of conducting it, either to disparage this sacrament in the eyes of the people, or to do it honour. The indispensable acts which constitute the unchanging framework of the service are few, and leave room for a good deal of variety in other parts.

1. The first of them is the *reading of the words of institution* (Matt. 28$^{16-20}$). An address of instruction or exhortation founded upon it, or upon other passages in the Gospels, is optional. But, in view of the ignorance and indifference which prevail regarding this great Christian seal of cleansing and new birth, it must be often advisable, and because it is a difficult duty the young minister does well to take special pains in its discharge. Especially is this called for in the administration of baptism to infants. To be faithful to the doctrinal position of his Church, a Reformed pastor has to correct on the one side a frequent

tendency of ill-instructed parents to lean on the mere performance of the rite as an indispensable guarantee to them
of their child's salvation; on the other side, to bring out its
significance and value to the offspring of believers, as confirming to them the promised grace of the Gospel and
marking the privileged place within the fellowship of the
Church which is theirs by birth.

2. *The questions* addressed to an adult candidate or
to the parents (or sponsors) of a child need to be known
beforehand by those who are to make the responses, and
therefore ought not to be left, as is customary in Scotland,
to the discretion of the officiating minister, but be prescribed
by authority and never deviated from. They always embrace two things: a "creed" or equivalent profession of
belief;[1] and a promise to discharge certain duties. The
purpose of both in the case of an adult candidate is obvious.
It is on the ground of his profession of personal Christian
faith and promise of Christian obedience that he is received
into the Church. God-parents in the Church of England,
as in the Catholic Church, make the same profession of
belief and undertake the same vow to lead a holy and
obedient life, not in their own behalf, but "in the name of
the child," as its spokesmen. In its name, also, they re-
nounce, in the terms of a very old formula, the devil, the
world, and the flesh. It is therefore under an implied
condition that the child, when come to years of discretion,
will hold the faith and lead the life of a Christian, that he
is baptized in infancy. The unreality of such professions,
made in the name of an unconscious infant, has always been

[1] The representatives of the Kirk of Scotland present at the Westminster
Assembly contended for the use of the Apostles' Creed in baptism, to which
in their own Service-book they were accustomed, but were overruled by the
English Puritans. They got certain questions introduced as a substitute,
which do not now stand in the text of the Directory. "It has been supposed," says Sprott, "that they were struck out by the House of Commons"
(*Worship and Offices of the Church of Scotland*, 1882, p. 66). I presume he
is founding on the authority of the *Portland Papers*, i. 194. (Hist. MSS.
Commission, 13th Report; Appendix, Part I.)

felt to be a difficulty in the Catholic ritual. It is got over
in all Reformed communions by founding the right of a child
to be baptized, not on its own assumed future faith avowed
in its name, but on the present faith of its parent, and his
undertaking to instruct his child in Christian truth and train
it to a Christian life. When, in Churches of this order, a
sponsor is, in rare cases, substituted [1] for an absent parent,
he simply assumes for himself the same responsibilities.

3. *The administration of the rite.* Where it is desired
and may conveniently be done, immersion as an alternative
to pouring water on the head is in some communities expressly recognised, and, I presume, would be admitted in
all. But it is only among Congregational Baptists that the
mode of administration is deemed essential to the validity
of the sacrament.

4. A formal *reception of the new member* should follow;
with a commendation of him to the fraternal fellowship of
the brethren. This is suitably answered on their part when
the congregation unites in singing a benediction-prayer;
such as the Aaronic one: "The Lord bless thee and keep
thee," and so forth.

With what other prayers and acts of praise these four
essential acts are accompanied may usually be left to the
leader, because they naturally vary with the circumstances
under which the rite is administered. In every case, this
service is to be made as bright and as full of Christian hope
and love as it well can be; for it is a joyful day when a
young member is formally received into the brotherhood of
Christ's Church.

We have seen that the Church's worship as an expression of the Church's life is all one prolonged act of communion with God, having two sides: one of sacrificial
offering on our part, which is devotion in its primary sense;

---

[1] "In the Scottish, as in all other branches of the Reformed Church,
god-parents were joined with parents as sponsors" (Sprott, *op. cit.*, p. 61).
But "substituted" only in case of the parent's necessary absence.

and another of waiting upon God for His benefits, which is worship regarded as a "means of grace."[1] Now, in the several parts of Divine service those two are combined in unequal proportions. Thus, when a congregation devoutly listens to the Word of God, read or spoken, and when it offers up supplications for pardon or for grace, the receptive side of worship is clearly prominent. For then man's need waits with open mouth and thirsts for the Water of Life. In pure acts of praise, on the other hand, in the sacrifice of thanksgiving, and in the offering of its substance, the Church presents to God for an oblation something of its own, such poor gifts as it has to offer.

Applying this test to the Holy Sacrament of the Body and Blood, what makes it, as all admit, the highest act, as well as the most characteristic, in Christian worship, must be that here both sides in the Church's communion with its Lord attain their moment of greatest intimacy, and are combined in equal perfection. To eat His flesh and drink His blood, said Jesus, is "to dwell in Me, and I in him." Closer or more complete fellowship there cannot be. And it makes this union and communion with Christ only the more easy for men still living in the flesh to realise, and, when realised, all the more intimate, that it finds a twofold medium adapted to our twofold nature. Material symbols, no less significant and pathetic than they are simple, addressed to eye and touch and taste, unite with the Divine Word of Promise addressed to intellect and heart: a completed form of expression given to complete and perfect fellowship.

Hence we Protestants need have no quarrel with the Catholic because he cherishes so high an esteem for this sacrament as the supreme moment in Christian cultus. Our complaint is that he has materialised it, and by a crass and literal reading of its teaching has missed its spiritual contents. For the faithful in that communion, public worship consists in frequent attendance at Mass; and one is thankful to know that through such attendance multitudes of true worshippers

[1] See *ante*, pp. 95–98.

have offered a genuine and profound devotion. Nevertheless, the cult is complete and attains its end although there be no one present except the priest. For it is the manual act of the priest alone which offers the sacrifice that is believed to propitiate, winning Divine benefits alike for the living and the dead.[1]

It was disastrous to spiritual worship when men first ascribed to the earthly substances of bread and wine offered on the altar, a religious value or virtue of their own, divorced from those inward states of the recipient's mind and heart which alone can bring him into spiritual contact with the Divine Reality behind the symbols. Such a change began, as I suppose, as early as the third century, with a confused identification of the sacred elements with that real and efficacious Presence of our Lord's Body and Blood which they represented to faith. It took many a century for this confusion to work out its full effects in the West. In the East they have never been fully worked out. It only reached its logical issue in the mediæval dogma of transubstantiation. But the materialising of sacramental worship had gone far in advance of the dogma. Scholastic divinity only came behind with a theory to buttress or explain what popular devotion had been beforehand in assuming—that the consecrated Host *was*, and did not merely represent, or accompany, or convey, the Divine Victim offered on the Cross. The dogma justified the people in their devotion, and gave, as was but natural, a prodigious impulse to its worst forms. Then at last everything became material and objective : a cult made effective and complete by priestly acts, even in the absence of any worshipper. The retrocession of what had been spiritual in the rite behind what was material could go no farther.

To bring the sacrament back to its New Testament idea, it was enough that Reformation theology should restore to

---

[1] Cf. Thomas Aquinas : "*Perfectio hujus sacramenti non est in usu fidelium, sed in consecratione materiæ.*" See also Canones Trident. Sess. xxii.

its rightful place in religion that inner life of faith which it is the design of Christian worship to reflect. There can be but one real link to unite man's spirit with God and establish between them a living fellowship. It is not a material, but a spiritual, link: the trustful attitude of a contrite and humble soul, reposing on God's revelation of His grace in Christ His Son. Under the illumination of this controlling idea, which it is for every Protestant pastor when he leads in sacramental services to keep clearly before his own mind, both sides in the blessed act of Communion assume their proper aspect.

(*a*.) The offering which the Church has to present to the Father is not the ineffable sacrifice for the sins of the world once offered on the cross; but, recalling that one propitiation through the aid of the sacred memorials, each believing worshipper associates himself with it by faith, and, as one in spirit with his Lord, offers himself a living sacrifice of thanksgiving by a devout surrender of his own heart and will to the pleasure of the Father. The spirit of this self-oblation is indeed the same as that of his Lord's. He has kindled his devotion at Christ's own altar-fire. But it is himself he offers, because it is himself alone that is his own to give. And in no other act of worship does this surrender of one's personality, which is the inspiration of all Christian living, find an equally perfect expression.

(*b*.) Similarly—what the worshipper receives from God is the gift of His Son, not under a material form to be received by the mouth, but as He is offered to us in the Gospel, to be more and more fully appropriated by each man's inward faith. Christ he receives in all His fulness of Saviourhood; not only for remission of sins through His Body broken and His Blood shed once for all, but likewise in His energy as the Divine Food of the spiritual life, for inward nutriment and growth. "He that eateth Me," said Jesus, "even he shall live by Me." This incorporation of two lives, this mutual indwelling, is a great mystery. But it is a spiritual mystery; and the organ that effects it

is faith. In no other act of worship does the Christian's
participation in the hidden source of Christian life receive
so perfect an expression.

It is a characteristic rule in the Reformed Church that
the Communion service is invariably preceded by a sermon.
This bears in Scotland the name of an "Action Sermon,"
meaning that it prepares the communicants for the holy
action of the Supper. The practical result has been that
the sacrament follows the usual congregational worship on
the Lord's Day. The usage is in accord with the order
prescribed by the ancient liturgies and retained in the Book
of Common Prayer of the Church of England. But the
reason for it in Reformed worship must be sought, I think,
in the Reformed doctrine of the sacraments as means of
grace. They are taken to be ancillary to the Word of God
as the chief means through which the Holy Spirit operates.
They illustrate the Gospel as symbolic signs; they confirm
it as seals to the covenant of grace; they bring home its
general promises to the individual. But they possess no
independent value as vehicles to convey grace to the soul.
To attach the Lord's Supper, therefore, to a foregoing proclamation of the Gospel served to mark this relationship
between the two. It was a seasonable protest against the
incessant repetition of Masses, to which as mere perform-
ances (*ex opere operato*) Catholic teaching ascribed a merit
and an efficacy of their own.

While in this way the Reformed Church never separated
the Lord's Supper from the preaching of the Gospel, it did
not observe it every Sunday as a constant factor in the
weekly worship of the congregation. This is what Calvin
himself would have preferred; but Calvinistic Churches
have leant to a less frequent celebration. In some lands,
notably in Scotland, notwithstanding that the ancient
Order of the Scottish Church spoke of it as "commonly
used once a month," Presbyterians have gone to an extreme
of infrequency. Once or twice a year used to be customary,
not only in landward parishes, but even in burghs. The

explanation is not that they undervalued the ordinance; rather that they attached to it, under one of its aspects, a veneration so exalted as to border on superstition. If as a means of grace it was only a handmaid to the Word which it served to symbolise and seal, yet as the supreme act expressive of communion with Christ it was accounted a season of rare devotion, a festal privilege reserved for times of exceptional elevation of feeling. Not without careful preparation of the heart by self-examination, as St. Paul counsels, was it deemed profitable, or even safe, to approach the Holy Table where such intimate fellowship with the Unseen was to be enjoyed. To come unprepared was to risk the appalling judgment denounced by St. Paul upon "unworthy communicants."[1]

This reverential awe and fear to offend account, not only for the rarity of communion seasons, but likewise for the unusual devotions, in the closet and in the house of God, with which Scottish custom surrounded such seasons when they came round. The fast-days which went before, with the numerous meetings for public worship that attended them; the concourse of worshippers from adjacent parishes, and the number of clergymen who came to take part; the prolonged and solemn services of the Communion day itself; the small proportion of the people who, in Highland congregations at least, deemed themselves fit to partake; the rigour with which unworthy persons were "debarred" from communicating: these things all betray the tendency of Calvinistic piety to make of the Memorial Supper, not "daily bread" for the soul, but a very high and exceptional feast. It took the place, one may say, of the abolished festivals of the old Church year.[2]

Something of this feeling survives, but not much. In

---

[1] 1 Cor. 11[27-32].

[2] Some of these Communion seasons are remembered in the annals of the Kirk for the revivals of religion to which they gave rise. Others, like the anniversaries of martyrs (*natalitia*) in the post-Nicene Church, became scenes of scandalous licence.

all British Churches, the recent tendency has been to more frequent celebration of the sacrament. The abolition of statutory fasts in the Northern kingdom was at once a result and a cause of this tendency. Even Presbyterians are gravitating towards monthly observance, which is, I think, usual among the Free Churches of England. This is probably as often as congregations are in the habit of communicating where simultaneous Communion is the rule.[1] For at daily, or even at weekly celebrations in the Anglican Church, it may be presumed that no more than a small percentage of the people partake on each occasion.

In so far as this disposition to multiply opportunities for receiving the sacrament is due to any deepening of devotional life, one can only rejoice at it. At the same time, there are not a few in all the Northern Churches, not all of them of Puritan leanings or merely conservative tastes, who view it with misgiving. They regret the passing away of the solemn festivals, with the profound impression which they were fitted to produce on susceptible souls. They fear that a more frequent, may come to be a less reverent, celebration. All leaders in worship, therefore, especially those who are bound by no prescribed order in the service, would do well to be on their guard lest the hallowed awe which ought always to invest the Supper of the Lord should suffer at their hands; and this all the more in proportion to the frequency of its repetition.

Two incidental results, neither of which was probably foreseen, have resulted from more frequent observance of Holy Communion. One of these is that fewer worshippers except the communicants themselves are present at the ordinance.[2] This is at variance both with the theory and with the older

[1] Except, of course, among Plymouth Brethren, a body which owed its rise in part to a desire to revert to the weekly Eucharist of the Apostolic period.

[2] All the early liturgies dismissed the other worshippers before the Eucharist. But this was only a temporary rule in the Catholic Church, and possibly began and ended with the *disciplina arcani* — which lasted from early in the third till the sixth century. The reason for such reserve

usage of the Reformed Church, which has always regarded the
rite as a public proclamation of the Lord's death calculated
to impress onlookers, and to be especially profitable to the
immature members of the Church, whose presence, therefore, has always been desired. So long as its observance
recurred very seldom, it was possible to alter for one day
the whole order of Divine service, and secure that every
class of worshippers continued their attendance throughout
the "feast." But if it take place once a month or so, it is
obviously inconvenient to make any great change in the
usual worship, and the bulk of the non-communicants
present find it impossible to remain for what is practically
a second service. It is true they are generally invited to
do so. The continuity of the entire service is in many
cases indicated by not pronouncing the dismissal benediction until after Communion.[1] I am afraid, however, that in
practice communicants are for the most part left alone, as
they usually are in Anglican places of worship.

The other result referred to has, on the contrary, been
an advantage. Frequent Communion has favoured simultaneous reception. The old Scottish method of numerous
"tables," each of them accommodating merely a fraction of
the membership, often allowed persons to partake who
could not otherwise have done so; but it was objectionable,
less because it greatly prolonged the exercises of worship
without adding anything to their religious contents, than
because it did not give visible expression to the unity and
brotherhood of the congregation as a whole. Where the
custom is for communicants to partake, as in Lutheran or
Anglican worship, in small groups at the altar rail, there
is, of course, still less to suggest this corporate aspect of
the Supper. The prominent thought there is individual

or secrecy is still uncertain. It possibly grew up under the influence of
heathen mysteries and their ceremonies of initiation. Cf. Frommann, *De
Disciplinâ Arcani* (Jena, 1833) ; and R. Rothe, *De Disciplinæ Arcani Origine*
(Heid., 1841).

[1] After long debate, this question of closing the first service in the usual
way was left open by the Westminster divines in the seventeenth century.

11

privilege, not Church fellowship. But the idea of the Supper as the bond of Christian brotherhood, to which St. Paul alludes in his Epistle to the Corinthians,[1] is one on which, by their whole manner of observing it, the Reformed have always laid a good deal of emphasis. The very posture adopted, the spreading of a table, and the passing of the elements from hand to hand, although probably due in the first instance to a desire to copy as far as may be the details of its institution in the upper room, are fitted to bring out very clearly this idea of a family meal, at which the brethren realise their relationship to one another by sharing in common in the same sacred food. It can matter little in itself whether one receives the elements standing, as the Lutherans do, or kneeling, as in the Church of England, or sitting at table, as is customary in the Reformed Churches. It is possible that kneeling, the traditional as well as lowliest attitude, was changed because it had become too closely associated in the public mind with adoration of the Host. A disclaimer of this intention, like the " kneeling " rubric inserted in the Book of Common Prayer, many might feel to be too feeble to break that association. It was an additional reason for the new attitude of sitting round a common table that it utterly shut out any notion of reception at the hands of a priest. But I suspect the strongest motive for its adoption was a wish to conform, as far as Western manners permit, to the example of those who reclined around the Lord "on the night in which He was betrayed." Be that as it may, it has the merit of laying stress on the equality and fraternity and unity in Christ of all believers—truths which it is our wisdom to retain and cherish.

When the Communion service proper is about to commence, it has been widely felt that the people should be briefly reminded of the solemn responsibility which attached to the act. I think it probable that it was this feeling

---

[1] 1 Cor. 10[17] : "We being many are one bread, and one body : for we are all partakers of that one bread."

which inspired the famous formula found in every ancient liturgy : τὰ ἁγία τοῖς ἁγιοῖς. That came in too late in the service, however, to be of any real use as a warning to the profane; for it immediately preceded actual reception. Very much to be preferred are the elaborate exhortations provided for the use of the clergyman in the Prayer Book of the English Church :—one to be read when " warning for the celebration " on a preceding Sunday; the other "at the time of the celebration." These may be compared with advantage with the similar form given in the Westminster Directory, which only requires to be turned into direct from " oblique " speech, to be an admirable guide to the young minister to-day.   Of all these the design is twofold: to warn unfit persons, and to invite and encourage timid penitents who shrink from so high a privilege under a sense of their own unworthiness.   That many ministers of the Church of Scotland, substituting addresses of their own for the sober form recommended by their Church in her official Directory, did at one time exaggerate the warning, and fail to urge on hesitating consciences the inviting side of this preface, is no reason for dropping it altogether.

So soon as this short address is over, bread and wine can be brought forward and arranged on the Holy Table.   This is all that now remains to us of the primitive custom of an oblation of gifts in kind, from which the elements were taken for the Supper of the Lord :—unless, indeed, it survives under another form, in the collection for the poor which frequently accompanies or follows the service.

The bread is in Protestant worship as in the East an ordinary leavened loaf.   It may be that the unleavened " wafer," long used by the Roman Church, more closely represents the Paschal cakes of Jewish ritual.   But it cannot be proved to have been always the custom even in the West, and it is strongly objected to by every Oriental communion.[1]

I cannot but regret that the sixteenth century Reformers abandoned the mixed cup of wine and water

---

[1] Cf. Neale's *Holy Eastern Church*, vol. ii. : Dissertation on Azymes.

which, apparently from the very beginning, was universal in the early Church of all lands, with, it is said, the single exception of Armenia. For this primitive practice, fanciful reasons came later to be assigned; as, for example, that it symbolised the union of the two natures. Patristic ingenuity invented fanciful reasons for every usage the origin of which was lost in antiquity. But for this one no more recondite explanation was required than that our Lord and His Apostles, like other Jews of their day, no doubt drank diluted wine at the Last Supper. The proportion of water to wine was never fixed; and the few early heretics we read of, who, on ascetic grounds, abstained from the use of wine, simply drank water alone. It might even be difficult to maintain, as a general proposition, that in the chief rite of a world-wide religion, meant for every zone of the globe wherever men are found, the contents of "the cup" must invariably be "the fruit of the vine," and nothing else. Among ourselves not a little trouble has arisen over "ecclesiastical wines," turning principally on the dispute whether these beverages answer to the correct description of "wine" or not. Had the diluted cup been retained at the Reformation, it is conceivable that the scruples which in our own day have led to the wide substitution of non-alcoholic beverages for the heady wines our fathers used, might never have been seriously felt.[1]

We now proceed to the Communion service itself. Its indispensable portions are few—no more probably than four: (1) Recital of the Words of Institution from one of

[1] A few years ago, Dr. Harnack of Berlin surprised students of Christian antiquity by an attempt to prove from Justin's references to the Eucharist, supported by a passage in Cyprian's correspondence, that down into the third century, water was in common use instead of mixed wine and water. See "Brod und Wasser" in *Texte u. Untersuchungen*, B. vii. (1891). The evidence has since been carefully examined, especially by Zahn (*Brod u. Wein*, 1892), Funk, and Jülicher. It is far from adequate to sustain Harnack's wide inference; but there is no doubt that for one reason or another (ascetic abstinence or a wish to avoid scandal) water alone was occasionally used in the early Church in the eucharistic cup, and not always by heretical sects.

our four sources, usually from the earliest of them in First
Corinthians. (2) The Eucharistic Prayer of Consecration.
(3) Distribution of the Elements. (4) A closing act of
Praise. But the leader ought to resist the temptation in
non-liturgical Churches to abridge to its essentials or to a
minimum a service of so much consequence for religious
life. There will therefore always be an introductory part,
which cannot omit at least an act of praise and a brief
petition or collect, uplifting the heart to God, and answering
in idea to the *Sursum corda* of the ancient Church.
Reformed liturgies, both Zwinglian and Calvinistic, judged
this a fit position for the creed, which the Church of
England placed earlier; and I observe a disposition among
Presbyterians to restore its use here. The praise at this
point will naturally be not so much jubilant as lowly and
adoring—its model the *Ter Sanctus* of the seraphim in the
prophet's vision.[1] This inspired song every early liturgy
embodied, as well as the words of institution, in the
eucharistic prayer itself, which thereby became extremely
long as well as broken. It seems preferable to treat both as
independent acts.

When those two insertions have been removed from the
Church's great prayer before Communion, quite enough
remains. For it requires to group together in a single act,
not too prolonged, and in language the most reverent and
befitting, four or five distinct devotional states, all of which
are so appropriate to this solemn moment, that they may
be presumed to coexist in the breast of every communicant,
and consequently to crave utterance through the lips of
the minister who leads. Arranged in their natural order,
they are as follows :—

(*a*) An acknowledgment of our unworthiness and unfit-
ness for so high a privilege ;

(*b*) A thanksgiving for the Father's love in our redemption
through the incarnation and work of our Lord
Jesus Christ ;

[1] Isa. 6[3].

(c) A profession of humble trust in His atoning death
    for the remission of sins, which we are about
    to commemorate;

(d) An invocation of the Holy Spirit to bless the
    elements, consecrating them into a means of
    grace to our souls; and

(e) A dedication or devotion of ourselves to God as
    the crowning act of our " Eucharist."

I do not see how any one of these can well be left out.
The last does not find a place in Catholic sacramentaries,
for there the sacrifice is not the self-oblation of the
worshipper, but something infinitely different; from Protestant services it surely should not be absent. It may,
however, be deferred till after participation.[1] The invocation of the Spirit is likewise omitted, this time unaccountably, from the Roman Mass—an omission unfortunately
repeated in the English Prayer Book as well as in the
Scottish "Book of Common Order"; but the omission has
been regarded as a serious blemish by Eastern Christendom.

The "manual acts" of the officiating minister become
of importance at this point, for two reasons: first, because
it has always been felt that in obedience to the words: " *This
do in remembrance of Me*," each recorded action of our Lord
at the institution ought to be closely followed; and also
because a wide-spread belief has prevailed that these
actions, which are the same in all our sources ("*He took*"
—"*He blessed*"—"*He broke*"—"*He gave*") possess, as parts
of a symbolic rite, separate symbolic significance.

In two particulars, nevertheless, there has been a very
general departure from the order observed at the Last
Supper.

1. We have the authority of two Evangelists (Matthew
and Mark) for believing that Jesus said grace twice, first
over the bread and then over the cup; and St. Paul's
expression, "the cup of blessing which we bless," so far
as it goes, rather confirms this. This double saying of

---

[1] So in the Anglican Prayer Book.

thanks has never, I think, been the usual practice of the Church; though instances do occur of a literal imitation of the Master's example. The *Didache*, for example, prescribed two little prayers, first for the cup and then for the bread;[1] and in Scotland, in the seventeenth century, Gillespie speaks of a brief thanksgiving introduced in distributing each kind, in addition to the earlier prayer over both.

2. In every one of our four accounts, it is said that Jesus "took" the bread or cup before, not after, He "blessed" or "gave thanks." This is said to have been the undeviating practice in Scotland "for at least two hundred years after the Reformation."[2] It certainly is so ordered in the Scottish "Book of Common Order." The Westminster Directory is silent on the point. The Church of England rubric requires each kind to be lifted in the course of the prayer, just at the moment when the words of institution that refer to it are being pronounced. According to Dr. Sprott,[3] it was about the middle of the eighteenth century that the custom of "lifting" before, not after, the prayer began to be given up in Scotland. Not, however, without a protest. Among the Antiburgher Seceders it occasioned a division, and one minister is reported to have suffered himself to be deposed from office rather than treat the matter as one of indifference.[4] It would surely be as well to adhere to the old usage in strict compliance with our Lord's example.

As to the symbolism of these "manual acts," few will nowadays see in the "lifting" of the bread an emblem of the setting apart of the Saviour to His work of redemption, as some of the old Scottish divines did. But there can be little doubt that Jesus meant significance

[1] In agreement with Paul's order in 1 Cor. 10, though not in chap. 11 or in other authorities.

[2] Wright, *The Presbyterian Church*, p. 168.

[3] *Op. cit.* p. 115.

[4] See Macpherson, *History of the Church in Scotland*, Paisley, 1901, p. 345.

to attach to His "breaking" of the bread, or, at least, that the early Church understood Him to do so. It is true that we cannot now found this on the word κλωμένον in 1 Cor. 11²⁴, since that word has been omitted from the best modern texts. But that the action was retained in the Apostolic Church and was regarded as important, can be inferred, I think, from the very early name—"*the Breaking of Bread*"—given to the rite, as well as from St. Paul's expression: "The bread *which we break*, is it not a communion of the body of Christ?"[1] The meaning which the first Christians saw in it must have been either a setting forth to the eye in symbol of the violence done to the sacred body which was given up for us all, or the share which every partaker has in the "one loaf," which represents the one mystical body of the faithful.

In the next act, of "giving" the symbols, with the emphatic words: "*Take, eat*," "*Drink ye all of it*," it is reasonable enough for faith to see an emblem of that unspeakable act of love by which our Lord, who gave Himself once to death, still gives Himself to each of us without ceasing as both our propitiation and our spiritual nourishment. The idea is, of course, continued in the expressive action of every communicant when he takes and eats and drinks, appropriating by faith the Divine gift.

Mutatis mutandis, these acts are repeated in both kinds; but because our Lord took the cup as it stood ready and is not said to have poured wine into it, we do not, as part of the ritual, pour out of the flagon into the cup or chalice, though this is done in the Mass by the Roman priest. But the minister must follow Christ's example by taking the cup into his own hand as he pronounces the invitation: "*Drink ye all of it*," and then by giving it untasted to one of the communicants.

The custom recently introduced into some congregations of what is called the "individual cup" must be judged of

[1] See Acts 2⁴². ⁴⁶ 20⁷, 1 Cor. 10¹⁶.

by the hygienic reasons adduced in its favour. At first sight it appears to miss the sense of unity conveyed by common participation. After all, however, no large congregation which partakes simultaneously ever does drink literally out of only one cup; and it can make no difference in principle whether the wine be distributed into five or five hundred separate vessels. But, however sound this reasoning may be in logic, the sentiment of partaking in common is seriously wounded when no two drink out of the same vessel. What still more seriously offends against the idea of corporate communion in one "cup," is the objectionable innovation of using two different kinds of beverage at the same celebration—one fermented and the other not.

Suitably to close the service nothing more is called for than prayer and praise; but both should bear a well-marked character. Gratitude for the high privilege received and entreaty for grace to live in daily fellowship with Christ, will occur at once to every communicant. From such personal experiences the people should be led to rise to the thought of the Church universal. For each fresh season of Communion sets the local congregation, however small, into conscious fellowship with the vast company of Christ's faithful followers over all the earth. It even sets the living into union with the faithful of every age who in their generation commemorated the same Lord by the same memorial acts. Here, therefore, it seems to be at least as appropriate as at an earlier stage to intercede in accordance with ancient practice for the good estate of the Church catholic, and to revive the memory of departed saints in the Church triumphant. A prayer for the speedy consummation of the kingdom at the second advent of the King will fitly conclude. We only keep the feast "till He come."

Throughout the whole of this solemn service of worship it is essential to preserve the utmost possible order, silence, and freedom from distraction. Ministers cannot be too careful that each detail is arranged beforehand, so that tranquillity may reign in the sacred edifice. This stillness, however, only reflects the inner mood which he should strive to secure in the worshippers. To do this let him strive above all to be himself in a subdued, peaceful, and devout frame of feeling. The spirit of the service is one of tender emotion. Not intellect is called here into play, but the heart. There should be little said. Anything unfamiliar only distracts. It is an hour when the individuality of the minister needs to be suppressed. Here, if anywhere, he is not an exhorter, but the leader only in a common act. How often do his words jar on the meditative mood of the communicants rather than assist it! Unless he himself be moved and bowed by the mighty emotions of the hour, his leadership can only mar, instead of fostering, the devotions of the people.

CHAPTER XV

WEEK-DAY SERVICES

A FEW old ministers still survive who recollect the days when
a couple of services on a Sunday nearly, if not quite, made
up the tale of their public duties. It might be felt right to
hold, in urban parishes at least, what was called a " weekly
prayer-meeting"; but it was so poorly frequented that in
Scotland it sometimes met in a vestry or side-room, and
added little to the pastor's labours. For the rest of the
week the church premises showed a locked door. In
England the framers of the Prayer Book had contemplated
the daily reading of morning and evening prayers in every
parish church,[1] as well as in cathedrals; but during the
early decades of last century the rule seems to have been
all but universally disobeyed. It is now as generally observed, at least by High Church incumbents. The hours,
however, for matins and evensong suit the convenience of
very few save persons of leisure. In the case of many
devout Anglicans, early Communion must often take their
place. If busy people in other churches are to benefit by
a week-day service, it needs to be arranged for a fairly
late hour in the evening, after the day's engagements are
over. In nearly all their places of worship, therefore, the
" prayer-meeting," or what is now termed the " week-night
service," has long been a recognised tradition.

---

[1] A similar rule obtained in the old days of the Kirk of Scotland. Twice
a week a sermon took the place of common prayer with Scripture lessons. See
Sprott, *Worship and Offices of the Church of Scotland*, Edin. 1882, p. 105 ;
M'Crie, *Public Worship of Presbyterian Scotland*, Edin. 1892, pp. 114, 167.

Of late, it is true, a crowd of miscellaneous meetings has threatened to swamp the old established mid-week worship. There is scarcely a church or chapel, large or small, whose doors are not open at some hour and for some purpose on several days in every week. The recent development of Church life in England and America, by multiplying the organised activities of every town congregation, has added immensely to the responsibilities and labours of the ministry; so that it grows every day a more pressing question whether the subdivision of groups and the multi-plication of meetings has not already gone too far for the real efficiency of congregational machinery. It seems to me probable that a movement for the concentration of energy will shortly have to set in to counteract the present dissipa-tion of it. Be that as it may, the numerous other gatherings which occupy so many evenings, such as class meetings, Bible classes, guilds, literary societies, bands of hope, Christian endeavourers, working parties, social entertain-ments, and the like, appeal, as a rule, to special sections of the congregation, and are designed for other than purely devotional purposes. They belong, therefore, in so far as the minister has to do with them, to the pastoral department of his office. Whereas, on the one evening invariably set apart for Divine service, nothing sectional is contemplated, but the presence of as many of the flock as possible is desired.

To this mid-week worship most ministers of experience continue to attach a high value. It not merely breaks the long interval of secular occupation between one Lord's Day and the next; provides an opportunity for devotion to persons who find few such opportunities at home; and brings pious members of the Church into kindly intercourse with their pastor and with one another: but, above all, it has two definite functions which it ought to fulfil in the economy of the congregation's life. It ought to supply religious inspiration to every other part of the congregational activity; and it ought to be a central service of intercession, incessantly calling down upon every part the power and blessing of the Holy Ghost.

Both of those are uses the value of which cannot be exaggerated. The more manifold, exacting, and subdivided becomes the organisation of a modern Church, drawing into one or other of its agencies the varied gifts of its members, branching out, moreover, into social ministry, material and educational no less than religious, the greater risk arises lest the spiritual consecration, which ought to link all such agencies to the person of the Redeemer and animate them with His Spirit, should evaporate. Then must the Church's ministration to human need degenerate into a busy, bustling philanthropy, useful, but not distinctively Christlike, or even religious. To avert such a risk as this, and warm all Church business and every workers' meeting from the central fire of pious love to Christ, is the first benefit to be derived from an earnest, loving, and well attended mid-week worship. To render this benefit it needs to be well attended. How can it supply motive-power for all the work of the Church, if the workers are not present?

The other function of intercession is no less important. The Church lives by its prayers just as individual Christians do. Barren of results, at least of the highest results, must its work be, unless it be steeped in an atmosphere of prayer. It must ask before it can receive. I believe this is widely felt, and deeply felt, by the ministry; and just because it is so, do we everywhere hear regrets, not always loud but deep, over the decay of the "prayer-meeting." I question if there is any other part of an average minister's work which he finds so disappointing. Thin attendance, lack of interest, absence of the young and active members, want of helpers to take part in the prayers, a general coldness or formality in the service, a few loyal people only turning out for duty's sake: such complaints abound, and the heart of many a minister is made sad. While the opening of each winter season sees ingenuity successfully expended in devising fresh and varied plans, say, for attracting and instructing young people, for example, or for stimulating the interest of older members in missions, domestic and foreign, nothing ever seems to infuse fresh life into this old-fashioned " prayer-meeting "—so many minsters tell you : it lingers on in a feeble, if not moribund, condition.

One practical result has been that even where the con-gregational " prayer-meeting " has not changed its name to a " mid-week service," it has changed its character, and become to all intents and purposes a shortened edition of the Sunday worship, a little less formal, perhaps, with less labour bestowed on the " address " than on the " sermon," but otherwise conducted on identical lines. The steps in this metamorphosis are easy. No man can profitably occupy a whole hour in devotional exercises when no voice but his own is heard from beginning to end. In a few places the minister is fortunate enough to have members in his church in sufficient numbers who are both competent and inclined to assist, and the service may go on with spirit as simply a service for devotion. But where this is not the case, an " address " is unavoidable. And insensibly the order then approximates to the type most familiar to both leader and people, that is, to the Lord's Day worship.

Such a week-day worship of an hour's duration with a sermonette, may be the best thing that can be done. If successfully conducted, it will in a measure accomplish both the ends we desire—nurture devotional feeling in the flock, and intercede for a blessing on its operations. But it is not a " prayer-meeting," and, with one's best endeavours, it cannot quite fill the place of one. A consciousness of this is inducing some ministers to attempt a supplement of some sort to the usual week-night service. They begin to realise that for the purpose of intercession, pure and simple, the attendance of the active and busy workers themselves, however desirable, is not indispensable. A few praying people will do. Where the minister has strength and the people inclination, a short meeting to ask a blessing on the various labours of the day is sometimes held on the

Lord's Day, it may be for ten or fifteen minutes only, either before morning worship opens or at the close of evening worship; and that is better than nothing. It would, however, be worth a good deal of pains to get together, some time in the week, even a small company of warm-hearted members of the flock, who, if they can help in no other way, will combine to be God's " remembrancers," pleading while others labour, interceding for the blessing of " the Lord of the harvest " upon the ploughing and the sowing, by giving to each item in the congregation's work and to every group of workers in its field, a stated place in their petitions. We ought not to despise such a gathering for prayer and nothing else because its members are few. It ought, I think, to be an axiom in this matter that it is not numbers that count, but concert and devout importunity. The Divine condition is: "If two of you shall agree on earth." The Divine test is: "Always to pray and not to faint."[1] I think the best of our "workers" would try to be members of the "praying band" as well. But why should not such a band, in whose breasts pious desires are warm, even if it were composed of those who come out to few other meetings, or can give but little aid in other ways, be just as truly a piece of service for the kingdom as any other, as teaching an infants' class, for instance, or visiting the sick poor, or singing in the church choir? It would fill its own niche, and have its recognised place and use among those more active associations which are at present in vogue.

Its meetings need not exceed half an hour in duration. Everything should be as free and brotherly as possible. All who come might be encouraged to take some part, were it but by suggesting a topic for intercession. It would be the office of the leader to arrange beforehand concerted subjects of petition for each occasion, securing the utmost variety; to receive suggestions and report private requests for prayer; to interpose between the prayers a helpful promise from

[1] Matt. 18[19], Luke 18[1-8], cf. 11[5-13].

Holy Writ or a hymn verse; to keep the meeting to the business in hand by quietly checking irrelevance or prolixity in those who take part; and to close punctually. In such a brief service there should be little else than petitions, brief, pointed, and intense, like arrows shot towards heaven. It may be a dream, but I can imagine such a prayer-meeting to tell like a benediction on the whole hive of energetic and varied "workers" who constitute the modern ideal of congregational life.

Be this as it may, the practical problem for most ministers is how to invest a mid-week service of an hour with so much interest and value as to attract to it a considerable proportion of the people, and at the same time to furnish a material contribution to the best life of the congregation.

My own impression is (and it is only one's impressions one can give) that it is a mistake to make the order a reduced copy of Sunday worship, or at least, to repeat this on every occasion. Such a sameness argues a lack of inventiveness. Uniformity breeds dulness. No special need of the congregation is met which the Sunday services do not meet. Offering no fresh features, it awakens no fresh interest. Yet the conditions are different from those on the Lord's Day, and to be met in a different way. Every Lord's Day is a weekly festival. It is, so to say, a "State occasion." The congregation is present, at one of the diets of worship at least, in its unity and completeness. Young and old combine, as at no other time, to present before God their common faith and life with as much solemnity and fulness of utterance as are attainable. It is fitting, therefore, that the worship should express all the common emotions and desires of Christian experience, under regulated forms which cannot greatly vary from week to week. But here the circumstances are quite altered. A portion only of the membership—as many as can spare an hour in the midst of week-day toil and worldly cares—are come together in a much less formal fashion. They are all busy folk, and

the children are absent. Is it not better to aim at something as little reminiscent of familiar Lord's-Day forms as
may be? Something which need not be invariably the
same, nor regulated with equal strictness? In order to
create interest and maintain it, giving people a motive to
attend strong enough to draw them away from their usual
secular engagements, surely what is wanted is, first, a distinct purpose on each occasion, and then, variety from week
to week. Let each meeting wear as far as possible a
distinctive character, and it will have an interest of its own.
Let that character be changed as much as possible at successive meetings, and the interest will be kept fresh. It is
seldom convenient to continue the weekly service over
more than a portion of the year; and for the weeks of
(say) seven months or so, few ministers would find much
difficulty in drawing up a varied programme, adapted to
the needs of their own flock.

One group of evenings, scattered over the year, ought
always to be strictly devotional, given up either to prayer or
to praise. The prayer-meetings may, of course, be organised
on the lines described above; with topics selected beforehand
and qualified persons arranged to assist; with definite
petitions bearing, some on the congregation's own operations,
some on more personal requests for prayer sent in privately;
with commonly an interval allowed for silent supplication,
or at times liberty given for any who choose to volunteer to
lead in prayer. An occasional hour so spent, if carefully
prepared for and not too frequently repeated, would meet a
want felt by many of our best people. A quite different need
is met on other evenings by a praise-meeting, at which the
resources of the hymn-book are laid under contribution, and
the assistance of the choir, after special rehearsals, is called
in. The programme of sacred song, arranged by the leader
some time previously, will be more or less ambitious from a
musical point of view according to the attainments of the
congregation; but it can always follow a given order of
religious thought, so as to possess unity and interest.

12

Bible teaching of various kinds will supply material for profitable hours of a different character. Then is the minister's opportunity to deal with aspects and applications of truth less suitable for the Sunday sermon, either because they are too technical or because they run too much into detail. The practical bearings, for instance, of the ethics of Christ on the family, on business, on social duties or problems, are matters in which many Christians of all classes are taking in our day a keen concern. In the pulpit they can only be handled rarely and in large outline. A study of these, based on all the relevant material to be culled from the New Testament, would stimulate self-examination, call people's attention to unnoticed faults in daily conduct, and help to mould opinion on public questions. Not less is it a duty of the hour for the minister to guide his people into the fresh ways of reading their Bible which recent scholarship has made inevitable. The best results of criticism can be made intelligible to the humblest Christian, and there are few readers of Scripture who do not welcome wise and plain instruction on many points. The date, purpose, and characteristics of single books, or the unfolding of a great truth from one epoch of revelation to another, or the diverse lights under which it is viewed by the several inspired writers:—there is simply no end to the variety which may be imparted to a " Bible-hour " by any well-informed expositor of the sacred volume. It is a sort of teaching much needed, and by not a few nowadays much desired.

Information on philanthropic and missionary efforts, both at home and abroad, forms another group ; keeping well to the front those fields of labour to which the people are in the habit of extending financial aid, or in which they themselves are taking an active share, yet sketching now and then the progress of Christ's kingdom in regions where less known agencies are at work. But any minister who cares to diversify in this way the character of his week-night service can readily add to the specimens I have named :

the aim being that every class in his flock may find something to profit as well as interest them, and that the dulness or stagnation so often complained of may be kept far away. It asks for initiative and versatility in the leader. Certainly it means taking trouble, and making one's preparations some time in advance. But have we any reason to count on many people putting themselves to inconvenience in order to be present, if we grudge the trouble of providing what may prove fresh and attractive as well as helpful?

PART III

THE MINISTER AS PREACHER

CHAPTER XVI

WHAT IS PREACHING?

PREACHING is an art; and the principles which regulate the practice of it must spring out of a correct theory of its nature and design. No amount of instruction either in the principles or in the rules of any art will ever make an artist. Nothing can do that but practice. Yet a preliminary study, both of the theory of preaching and of the rules which long experience has suggested to experts, ought to be of material service to a young preacher. It sets before him an ideal, and supplies a standard by which to estimate good or bad workmanship. It puts him on his guard against wrong methods of working. He knows better what to avoid and what to aim at. Self-discipline and practice must do the rest.

For the purposes of our art, then, preaching may be described as that continuous and public testimony which the Church is always giving, through discourses by her official members, to her own living faith in Christ, as rooted in and sustained by the written Word of God.

To understand this definition, it is fundamental to assure ourselves that the pulpit takes the Church for granted, and utters the testimony, not simply of a solitary believer, but of a divinely founded society. There was a

Church before there was a Christian preacher. Peter, even at Pentecost, on the birthday of the Church, spoke in the name of a hundred and twenty believers. A propagandist of the faith finds it his sorest trial when, alone and unsupported by Christian comrades, he has to preach the good news on the strength of his own personal experience. Yet the loneliest foreign missionary, the single confessor in a heathen land, has at his back the universal Church of all lands. He witnesses to the belief of a multitude that no man can number. And he knows it. What sustains him is the consciousness that he has behind his solitary voice the testimony to Christ of Christendom and the Christian centuries.

In the case of a pastoral preacher, selected by a congregation or trained and commissioned by a great Christian community, it is far more obvious that, be his personal convictions ever so strong, he never stands merely aloof or over against the people, as one who speaks his own faith and not also theirs. The Church has other ways of expressing her witness to the Gospel. She does it by her creed, by her sacraments, by her hymns. This particular way is by a public discourse into which, however, much more than into these, there enters what is personal to the speaker. Nor is every public discourse an official testimony as this is. Public discourses may on occasion be delivered by private members of the Church. Nothing that can be said on the theory of ministerial preaching, whether missionary or pastoral, can for a moment limit or prejudice the inherent right of every Christian to declare his faith on suitable occasions and in his own way. It rather presupposes that as a duty lying upon the whole brotherhood. If it were not the right and duty of Christian discipleship to testify to the truth as it is in Jesus, it would be hard to see how a testifying order of disciples came to be organised at all. Private witness-bearing, in the home or in social intercourse, is a duty of every Christian. Public witness-bearing, when and where occasion invites, is a privilege open to any competent adult, now as in the primitive assemblies. But when, for reasons of order or of profit, or in obedience to what is taken to be the will of Christ, all utterances for the edification of the brethren at the stated assemblies for worship are committed to chosen men specially trained or believed to be specially fit, it is plain that their official discourses must take for granted the common faith. No doubt the sermon is something else and something more than a creed; but it takes the creed for granted. The man will not be tolerated if he contradict those cardinal Christian verities on which he and the people are presumed to be at one.

Plainly we have reached here at the outset our first antinomy, or pair of mutually limiting elements betwixt which the preacher's art has to move. The personal and the representative or official are united in him, and in his discourses. Each of these has to come by its due and no more. Each is essential and has its separate value. The more full his accord on the one hand with the specific type of Christian belief and piety which obtains in the Church he serves, so much the more representative a speaker does he make. On this representative character does his official commission as a preacher rest; and his possession of such a commission affects in many ways the character of his preaching. It lends him confidence. It adds weight to his words. It gives dignity to pulpit utterances, and imposes on them a certain reserve. It checks the expression of vagaries of private opinion or of abnormal and eccentric experiences in religion. It distinguishes the preacher from the lecturer, or the platform speaker, or any self-constituted advocate of his own individual notions or beliefs. The fact that he is authorised to speak out of the heart of a great community what it holds for deepest and truest in the things of God, may become a fetter, but it ought to be an inspiration. While it sobers the speaker by a sense of his responsibility, it ought to elevate him to his best.

On the other hand, what is personal to the preacher

needs equally to come by its rights. To his own personal
convictions, won by experience, he must testify, not to the
borrowed beliefs of other people ; else he is no true witness
at all, but the pitiful echo only of a voice. Unless he be
free to utter in his own way and with the intensity due to
personal assurance what he himself has been taught by the
Spirit of God in the struggles and victories of his inner life,
you make of him the most dismal of machines. No doubt
all through the service the leader, if he is truly to lead,
needs to be himself in living possession of the feelings and
desires of the congregation. But in the sermon far more
than anywhere else, both the thing spoken and the form of
its utterance are to be the man's very own. For it is, what
no other part of worship is, a speech addressed by one man
to his fellows ; forged, therefore, in his own living brain and
heart, cast into an intellectual mould of his own, and pro-
jected by the heat of his own emotions. The more true,
therefore, to himself the preacher is, the better for the
purposes of his oratory.

Rightly to adjust these contrary factors in preaching—
the personal and the official—tests the preacher's skill.
For although they always coexist, they coexist in varying
proportions in different kinds of preaching, as we shall see,
as well as in preachers of dissimilar temperament and at
various periods in the history of the pulpit. Yet the presence of either may be so much in excess as to constitute
a fault.

The same remarks apply to a second pair of factors
which appear in our definition of preaching: the variable
and the permanent in the subject-matter of it. I refer to
the "living faith" of the actual Church at any given time
on the one hand, and the "written Word of God" on the
other. If the pulpit is to be a genuine witness-bearing by
living believers, then it is not the belief of any past age
which it has to utter, but what we ourselves who speak
do believe and know of God's truth. Often enough, no
doubt, a dead orthodoxy has rattled the bones of creeds and

of systems of divinity, out of which all moisture and vitality had long departed. But that is not true preaching. The pulpit ought ever to stand in close relations with the thought and life of the Church of to-day, acting upon it, but also acted upon by it. Both in its substance and in its form, it should mirror the influential beliefs of our generation, its attainments, its aspirations, its struggles, and its duties. This is why preaching has decayed as often as Christian life has decayed, but has gained in power whenever God revived His Church, and changed its form when His providence brought fresh aspects of truth to view, or set her amid the currents of a new period.

None the less is there a deposit of saving truth embalmed in a permanent literary form—a norm of belief and life to be reckoned with amid these fluctuations of the generations. By it has the old to be fortified and the new to be tested. To it as to a standard must the Church recur for correction of error; to it as to a fountain for fresh and deeper draughts of revealed truth. Out of it must the life of every generation of Christians be fed; and from it has come again and again the inspiration that breathed fresh life into a somnolent or corrupt Church. To Holy Scripture, therefore, ought the pulpit to abide faithful; for it is out of its treasures, ever better understood and more livingly apprehended, that the preacher fulfils his double office of edifying the saints and winning the world to Christ.

To harmonise these two elements is another of the preacher's tasks. If his discourses err on the one extreme, they become too subjective, experimental, or pietistic; if on the other, they grow over-doctrinal, scholastic, or exegetical. It is neither a class-meeting nor a Bible-class he is conducting in the pulpit; but it is with Christian life and Bible revelation in living union that he has to deal.

At its widest acceptation, preaching contemplates two distinct results; for it is the Church's chief instrument for effecting both of the great ends for which the Church exists: self-propagation and self-edification. Alike in its contents and in its methods, it must be profoundly affected according as the preacher sets himself to produce the one or the other result: to beget repentance and faith in the unregenerate or to nurture and mature Christian life in those who are already believers. This gives rise to a broad distinction betwixt two kinds of preaching, which, however seldom we may find them quite separate in practice, it is yet necessary to treat apart in our homiletic theory. I shall call them pastoral and evangelistic. Both of them date from the very foundation of the Church. They are carefully marked in our New Testament sources by different names; though, from the nature of the case, we hear more in the first days of Christianity of missionary or evangelistic, than of pastoral or congregational, preaching.

For the former the technical New Testament terms are κηρύσσειν and εὐαγγελίζεσθαι. Neither word quite forfeits in Scripture the metaphor which underlies it. St. Paul twice calls himself by the title of a "herald" or public crier who makes public an official proclamation;[1] and in an earlier passage he plays on the use of the word in the stadium: "Lest, after making proclamation to others, as the herald at the public games, I myself should be rejected as a disqualified competitor."[2] The companion verb, εὐαγγελίζεσθαι, frequent in the Gospels and in Acts, is used by St. Paul in the same connection of his missionary preaching of the Gospel to heathen cities; and it, too, seems never to lose the flavour of its original sense as an announcement of glad tidings. The choice of terms like these is full of instruction. This earliest and greatest branch of the Church's ministry by word needs to be carried on even within Christendom by the most public methods, as the proclamation of a grave and authoritative message from

---

[1] 1 Tim. 2⁷, 2 Tim. 1¹¹.
[2] 1 Cor. 9²⁷. For the noun κήρυγμα, see Rom. 16²⁵, 1 Cor. 1²¹ 2⁴ 15¹⁴, Tit. 1³, 2 Tim. 4¹⁷. It is used only by St. Paul. The verbal form is much more frequent.

God, which yet carries the best and gladdest news that
ever greeted the ears of men.   Since the modern revival
of missionary enterprise at home and abroad, we are not
likely to overlook it; although we are far as yet from
giving it the place it deserves either in the study or in
the teaching of Homiletics.   Many of the German authorities,
in fact, especially since Schleiermacher,[1] have confined
themselves to the pastoral sermon alone.   It was by way
of protest against this one-sidedness that Rudolph Stier in
1830 issued his *Kurzer Grundriss einer biblischen Keryktik*.
This new-coined name he proposed to substitute for
"Homiletics," in order to convey the idea that all preaching whatever is addressed, as he put it, to "the natural
man in his blindness and sinfulness."   The protest missed
its aim because it was no less one-sided.   When Beyer[2]
would have the modern preacher take Apostolic examples
for his model, he is not wholly on wrong lines.   Only he
does not sufficiently distinguish betwixt missionary preaching and addresses for the edification of the Church.   Of the
latter we possess no such illustrative specimens from the
Apostolic period as we have of the former in St. Peter's or
St. Paul's evangelistic discourses to Jew or Gentile.[3]   Nor
had it yet received a name of its own.   In St. Luke's
account of the midnight meeting in an upper room at
Troas,[4] for the first and only time in the New Testament,
we find the verb which afterwards furnished a name—
"Homily"—for this class of Christian addresses, used
possibly in a sense which approximates to its later technical
signification.   Wherever else in the New Testament the
verb ὁμιλεῖν occurs, it retains its ordinary meaning of con-
sorting or conversing with anyone.   But the religious
intercourse of those early Christian teachers with their

---

[1] See his posthumously published *Praktische Theologie* (Berlin, 1850).

[2] *Das Wesen der christlichen Predigt nach Norm und Vorbild der
apostolischen Predigt* (1861).

[3] Acts 2, 3, 10, and 13 ; and 14 and 17.

[4] Acts 20[11] : ἐφ' ἱκανόν τε ὁμιλήσας ἄχρις αὐγῆς.

converts took the form of conversational instruction in the things of the spiritual life. So the Greek word "homily" which Xenophon had applied in the *Memorabilia* [1] to the same easy familiar style of teaching, was given to every pastoral address, when in course of years the earliest form of the Christian sermon was developed.

The division in practice between these two ground-types of preaching is rarely a clean-cut one. To a purely heathen audience the missionary's address must be wholly evangelistic. In a congregation composed of none but genuine Christians, the pastor's address would be wholly pastoral. The former case does occur in the foreign mission field, as in bazaar or street preaching in a heathen city. The latter never occurs, for every Christian congregation is wider than the true Church, and includes hearers whose Christianity is only nominal. As a rule, therefore, preaching needs to be of a mixed character. The proportion in which, on any given occasion or to any given audience, it is the preacher's duty to combine the two, is a matter left to his discretion. In practice it gives frequent rise to much perplexity. But we can quite well hold the two distinct in theory, and a complete homiletic would allot to each a treatment of its own. Here, since we have in view the settled ministry in our home congregations, I shall speak first and most fully of pastoral preaching; adding only some notes on the modifications which result when the evangelist is called on to address an irreligious, or at least an unconverted, audience.

[1] *Memor.* i. 2, 6, 15.

CHAPTER XVII

PASTORAL PREACHING: I

THE feature in pastoral preaching which first arrests attention is that it is a part, and an important part, in the public service of God. The preacher who realises that, when he delivers his sermon, he is about an act of worship, will find, I think, that from the very nature of worship in general there arise for his guidance at least three canons.

First, as to the matter of his discourse, it is restricted to the sphere of religion. For surely it needs no proof that nothing can have a legitimate place in any act of solemn devotion which does not bear upon our relations with God. The rule is hardly a limitation of the field that lies open to him, since all human life, when seriously contemplated, and (not less) truth in its manifoldness, have religious bearings; but it does define the point of view from which every subject is to be handled in the pulpit. Over whatever interests or affects his hearers, it is conceivable that he may find occasion to range. Only it must be regarded in its relations to the religious life or for a religious purpose, before it can claim to lie within the preacher's scope. What is historical or scientific or philosophic or secular, as such and for its own sake, is out of place.

Next, as to the tone and manner of the preacher, that is to be reverential and devout as befits a sacred occasion and a devotional act. This canon of reverence prescribes to the speaker in the first instance the mood in which he is himself to be. But it also extends to the mood of feeling which his language and his gestures have a tendency to awaken in his hearers. This suggests, I think, the true answer to the question: May the pulpit admit what is witty or jocose? It should admit nothing of which the effect or the tendency must be to impair the devotional attitude of the worshippers, by arousing associations in their minds which are ludicrous or simply diverting. We rule out in this way the vulgar jests and merry tales of a certain school of preachers in the late Middle Age. Only, in applying this canon, we have to bear in mind that different ages, or different classes in any age, receive very different impressions from the same discourse. Flashes of wit, homely anecdotes, colloquialisms, and the like, have often been harmlessly indulged in, not only because the hearers tolerated such things or relished them, but because they were so much a part of their everyday religious life as to awaken no sense of indecorum or of irreverence. If I am not mistaken, the Catholic pulpit has not on the whole maintained the dignity of preaching quite so well or so uniformly as the Protestant has done; the reason being, as I suppose, because in Roman ritual the sermon has been dissociated from the holiest acts of worship, delivered from a different part of the building, and commonly at another time from the service of the altar. On the other hand, Protestant preachers have been accused of carrying formal dignity too far, now to the extreme of frigidity, again to that of pomposity. There is a risk of what is called "dying of propriety." If the spring of reverential awe is within a man's soul and not assumed, it ought to leave him perfectly natural and true to himself; only it will be to his best and highest self. For that very reason he ought to be as far from pomposity as from levity. For the pompous is always the self-conscious, the affected; and surely, if ever a man is not to be inflated by his petty self-importance, or to pose as bigger than he is, it must be when he speaks for God with the fear of His presence upon him.

The third canon suggested by the place which preaching
holds in Divine service, is that it strive after artistic
perfection, alike in matter and in form. This applies to
every act of worship. The music, the hymns, the prayers,
the reading, are all to be as good as we can make them.
For two reasons : partly because we are giving expression
to the deepest and worthiest that is in us, and whatever is
expressional aims at beauty of form ; partly because worship is an offering which we make to the Most High, of
whom our best is unworthy. The same rule must apply
to the sermon. What is slovenly, in bad taste, or poverty-
stricken, is not worthy of Him in whose service it is
uttered. A random talk in the pulpit, an ill-jointed discourse, a negligent style, a clumsy delivery : these things
not only offend good taste ; they sin against the law of
sacrifice. Shall I offer to my Maker what costs me
nothing ?

The late Bishop Phillips Brooks of Boston denies any
place in the sermon to this quality of artistic perfectness.[1]
He does so on the ground that the sermon is spoken for a
purpose. It exists " to persuade and move men's souls " ;
and this is, he affirms, " thoroughly inartistic," because
" art contemplates and serves the absolute beauty." One
feels there is a mistake here ; and it springs, I think, from
confounding a work of pure art which exists for its own
sake alone, with that artistic perfection which applied art
may confer on a useful object. The sermon certainly is
not a product of " pure art." It serves undoubtedly a
" further purpose." So does a Greek vase. Its purpose is
the homely one of holding liquor. Yet on it the artist can
lavish the utmost grace of outline and the loveliest designs.
Such is the art of the preacher. At this point we come
in sight of those relations of Homiletics to Rhetoric of
which so much has been made in homiletic literature.
Since it is by ordered speech the preacher has to minister
to the service of God, and to persuade men, let him do his

---

[1] Yale *Lectures on Preaching*, 1877, p. 109.

best to make perfect for its purpose and beautiful in its usefulness, every discourse by which he seeks to lead men on to higher faith and holiness.

Besides these rules springing out of the very idea of worship, there are certain characteristics of Christianity, which as they impress themselves on every part of Christian worship, so also must their influence be felt in the pastor's preaching.

1. For example, we saw that, in contrast with both pagan and old Hebrew ritual, the spirituality of the Christian religion implies that the worshipper is brought into communion with God " in spirit and in truth "—not, that is to say, by the aid of sensuous or material symbols, which are shadows of truth, but through the word addressed to the reason and the conscience. In harmony with this must the preacher also " commend himself by the manifestation of the truth to every man's conscience."   In other words, it is on the naked force of religious and moral truth that he must rely. Efforts to play upon the passions except through the understanding, are unworthy of the Gospel. Even appeals to the imagination through the senses merely are out of keeping with it. For ecstasies and tumultuous conditions of the soul, created by a heated fancy under the excitement of numbers, have merely a momentary effect, and do not produce those permanent ethical results at which the Gospel aims. It is from this point of view that we must judge of what in the modern pulpit is termed " sensationalism." Sobriety and sanity are marks of a genuine enlightenment by the Spirit of God ; and the sermon, like the whole service, ought to be simple, manly and sober. The preacher may agitate the soul of the sinner, and, in extreme cases or among the more excitable races, such agitation may discover itself through its effects upon the body, but the means to be employed must always be moral and spiritual truth,—not adventitious or meretricious aid from harrowing pictures of physical torment, the exhibition of a crucifix to the eye, even sen-

suous details of the Passion, or the mere influence on the nerves of a falsetto voice.

2. Moreover, Christianity is the religion of completed revelation. It is not, in Paul's phrase, " a veiled Gospel." The Word of God is spoken in Christ, not in hints, or figures, or mysteries for the initiated, but plainly, to be understood of all men. The preacher's first duty, therefore, is to be intelligible. Not ignorance, but knowledge, is the parent of Christian devotion. We are not hierophants, but proclaimers of an open message. Let the preacher therefore make his meaning plain to his audience by using words commonly understood ; the days for tongues that no one understands are over. And let his discourse be both rational and coherent, bringing light to the intellect as well as warmth to the heart. To wrap up one's meaning in a cloud of words ; to obscure it from the average man by learned, technical, or far-fetched terms ; to pour forth rhapsodies ; or to hint at half-unfolded thoughts, " mystic, wonderful," such as can only be discovered by meditating over them :—none of these things is for the pulpit.

3. Once more, ours is a worship based on the certainty of faith. Its attitude is that of men who " know that the Son of God is come," and " that in Him we have eternal life." There is a tone of assurance proper to such an attitude. " We use great boldness of speech." It is out of the heart of this settled confidence in the Church's possession of truth and life in Jesus Christ, that every preacher is supposed to testify. He is a witness, or he ought to be, to what he personally knows. He is addressing a congregation of fellow-believers who also know. It is true that our lot is fallen on days when such confident belief is become more difficult, both for those who speak and for those who hear. To not a few in our audiences the words of that speaker will carry most power who has himself doubted, if only he has resolved his doubts and overcome them. Nor is the Church entitled to require that even her preachers shall have reached assured results on

every question in religion.   Enough if they have attained
through personal experience to the assurance of faith on
the essential verities of the evangel, and within that region
at least are not afraid to say : we know.   For the preacher
is no speculator or investigator, discussing questionable
theories in religion, or ventilating novel discoveries.   He
believes and therefore speaks.   There springs from this a
certain dogmatism, if I may call it so, that is peculiar to
the pulpit, and perfectly consistent with personal modesty.
It is consistent likewise with a desire to awaken in the
hearer, or to confirm, a reasoned faith.   And if to the
people's faith he would add knowledge, he will be at pains
to exhibit the reasonableness of revealed truth, its harmony
with itself and with other truths, its adaptation to human
needs, and the like.   He will argue and define and illustrate,
putting all he knows in the clearest and most convincing
light.   Yet it is what he knows.   He makes a mistake if
he utters the message of salvation in halting or apologetic
tones, claiming for it no more than a bare probability, or
putting it forth like some happy guess, as likely to be true
as not.

4. In the last place, ours is the worship, not of timid
bondmen or dubious suppliants, but of free-born sons of
God who have "received the reconciliation."   As we found
before that this imparts to all Christian service a note of
peace and joy, so that ought to be the dominant note in
preaching.   It is quite true that the glad news is relieved
against a sombre background.   Guilt and judgment with all
the solemn facts of human sinfulness which shut us up to
seek comfort in the Gospel—these are only part of that
background.   Gethsemane and Calvary are another part of
it.   The price of our redemption has to be counted.   "Knowing the fear of the Lord, we persuade men."   Earnestness,
solemnity, urgency, are the graver notes which sustain and
enforce the preacher's appeal.   Still, it remains true that in
all preaching, but in the pastoral pulpit more particularly,
doleful and warning notes are to be firmly subordinated to

13

evangelical comfort. If not in every sermon, yet certainly in one's ministry as a whole, there should reign a temper of devout restfulness, hope, and peace with God. A too exclusive denunciation of Divine wrath, or dissection of human frailty, or exposure of sinful character, or dwelling on the dark side of religious experience : these are things which have some-times imparted to preaching a character of gloom which misrepresented piety and shadowed the lives of the saints. No : ours is a good and a glad, as well as a serious, message ; never to be spoken with levity, it is true; but also not with austerity.

It has been pointed out in a previous chapter that two things are aimed at in our worship which blend, though unequally, in its several parts : its direct and its reflex or secondary aim. The one, to present before God in His honour some worthy expression of our religious life with its pious affections and aspirations ; the other, to crave and to receive at His hands more grace for the further upbuilding or maturing of our very imperfect Christian life. Although possibly both of these may be detected in every act of worship, yet they blend in very unequal proportions. And, next to the simple reading of God's Word, it is in the pastoral preaching of it that the element of direct worship is not lost but subordinated, while the edification of the worshippers comes to the front as the leading end in view. The object of the preacher, when he preaches as a pastor, is to edify. Building on a foundation already laid, he leads the people of God forward from what has been attained to the yet unattained. To use inspired language, his work is to " build up the body of Christ," till his people " all attain unto the unity of the faith and of the knowledge of the Son of God, unto a full-grown man, unto the measure of the stature of the fulness of Christ." [1] Such a work as this breaks into two factors—an intellectual and an ethical ; for spiritual growth is a synthesis of the two:—increase in

[1] Eph. 4[12. 13].

knowledge and increase in virtue. A twofold aim has therefore to be kept in view—to instruct and to correct. Or, to use Paul's language again, if he would "present every man perfect in Christ," the pastor must "admonish every man," as well as "teach every man in all wisdom." [1] On the one side, the truth which has been already accepted by all, has to be exhibited with greater purity and completeness on the basis of God's finished revelation in His Son, that with growing knowledge, ignorance or mistake may be removed and feeble faith wax stronger. On the other hand, the imperfectly sanctified Church is to be led to seek more perfect conformity with the ethical ideal in Jesus Christ, that its faults may be rectified, defects made good, and every member in the body brought nearer to the stature of a mature spiritual manhood.

This dual aim, once grasped, defines with much precision the relation of pastoral preaching to revealed truth. It gives the preacher as his instrument nothing less than the complete revelation of God, yet always in its bearings upon Christian life. Since the result he aims at is so comprehensive as a perfect Christian life, he must be at liberty to employ for its production every part of Christian truth. Like the Apostle at Ephesus, he must not "shrink from declaring anything that is profitable," and the "whole counsel of God" may be, for one purpose or another, at one season or another, profitable.[1] It would not, I think, be accurate to say that he may not pick and choose among the truths or the duties of Christianity. For of both duties and truths there are some which, for their own central importance, or for their needfulness to a particular congregation at a given time, deserve to be selected for more frequent handling. But the pastor claims for his province none the less the entire contents of Christian revelation, the "treasures of wisdom and knowledge" that are "hidden" in Christ. He has the right to use them all so far as he has learnt them; but he is responsible for using them for the

[1] Col. 1[28].   [1] Acts 20[20, 27].

profit of the flock, and therefore in the measure and in the way in which they severally contribute to its edification.

Thus we reach what is perhaps the most important of all homiletic rules, especially for a pastoral preacher: Christian truths are always to be handled in their practical bearings upon Christian life. It is the first lesson a young minister has to learn. A theologian the preacher is presumed to be; but the theological training through which he has passed has not always taught him how to use his theology for practical profit. It may even have divorced in his mind doctrine from experience. The first thing, therefore, he has to learn as a preacher is that it is not theology simply which he is set to preach. Not an exact definition of dogma in terms of scientific divinity, nor the articulation of doctrines into a system, nor their apologetic defence or proof, constitutes his primary business. I do not deny that the profit of his hearers may at times call upon him to do any of those things. When their faith is like to be shaken, he may have to defend it; when they are in danger to be misled for want of an accurate or exact acquaintance with a doctrine, he may have to explain it. But such things he does at the rare times when edification demands them. It is a mistake to imagine that men's religious profit is in proportion to their minute familiarity with orthodox definitions. That has sometimes made a disputatious, rather than a godly, people. The life of piety is fed by Divine truth in its depth rather than by its logical definitions. The infinity of Divine thoughts enlarges the soul. Circumscribed within dogmatic formulas, they may be contracted in their power, as well as stripped of their attractiveness. But in his effort to combine truth with experience, there are two extremes, not one only, into which the preacher may fall. While it is true that preaching which is doctrinal and not much else is sure to be over-intellectual, frigid, and lifeless, breeding orthodox rather than vital Christians, what used to be termed "experimental" preaching is just as apt to beget a self-centred, introspective religion.

The business, then, of the pastoral preacher is to cor-
relate Christian truth and Christian living with one another,
employing the former for the upbuilding of the latter. Undoubtedly every portion of revealed teaching has a side or
aspect, rather it has many aspects, towards piety and morals,
which fit it for homiletic treatment. Entering into the life
of the soul, truth works there like a live thing. In manifold ways it works according to each man's needs, susceptibility, or willingness to welcome it. The formal " five uses,"
which it became a fashion early in the seventeenth century
for divines to append to each discourse by way of application,
wear nowadays a whimsical air; but do not let that obscure
from us the lesson which lies at the bottom of the old-
fashioned custom. Every truth we preach is " profitable "
for many things—" for teaching, for reproof, for correction,
for instruction in righteousness," and for " comfort." [1] Such
" uses " of doctrine it is our business to find out, although
I hope we shall apply them in a less forced and mechanical
way than those forefathers of ours did three hundred years
ago. The skill to do this has to be learnt. As a rule, it is
by practice young preachers need to acquire it; and it is a
pity they should so often have to learn it largely by their
mistakes. From books, except from sermons themselves,
there is little help to be got. For the homiletic value or
application of a doctrine is a field that has scarcely been
worked. Most modern German writers on homiletics devote
a section to what they call " material" homiletics, that is,
what one ought to preach; but they do not discuss in detail
what practical employment is to be made of this or of that
doctrine of the faith. The only deliberate attempt to do
this with which I am acquainted is the work of Dr. Heubner
of Wittenberg, entitled *Christliche Topik.*[2] He has endea-

---

[1] The five uses were taken from 2 Tim. 3^{16} and Rom. 15^4. The passages
refer in the first instance to inspired Scripture.

[2] Potsdam, 1863. An earlier book, with apparently a similar design:
Fuhrmann's *Christliche Glaubenslehre von ihrer praktische Seite bearbeitet*
(Leipz. 1802), is known to me only by its title.

voured under each head of doctrine to set forth its religious or ethical bearings, with a view to help the preacher in the use he makes of it. It is very doubtful, however, whether any literature would here be of much assistance. The preacher has but two main aids to lean on—experience and Scripture.

1. First of all, he needs to study with attention the bearings of Divine truth in his own life as a Christian man and in the experiences of others, especially of his own congregation. A man preaches best, of course, what has come home to himself in the needs or struggles of his own inner life; from which it follows that in proportion as a minister grows riper with the passage of the years and assimilates more of religious truth through widening and deepening experience, in that degree ought his preaching to grow richer and more mellow. If this seem to reflect at all on the pulpit work of the younger ministry, let it be borne in mind that it is only a compensation after all which the years bring to old preachers for their inevitable loss of fire and energy. May we then, as some do, lay down the rule: preach only that truth which you have learnt from personal experience? By no means. To counsel a young minister to make no effort to apply Divine truth to cases which are not, or at least are not yet, his own,—to console, for instance, before he himself has been afflicted,—is neither necessary nor safe. It is true, he may not fulfil such a duty of his office so well as he will do after he has been longer in the school of Christ. Nevertheless, the Christian life is so much of a unity, and the elements of human experience are at bottom so simple, that every Christian may be said to possess already *in gremio* all that is essential to the religious life, and thus to be competent from the first to understand in a measure, and to sympathise with, experiences remote from his own. He holds in his hand at least the living Word, whose treasures it is his privilege to open up in their mani-foldness, all of them "hidden" in Christ Himself as the personal centre and sum of Gospel truth. These the all-

wise Spirit of Christ dispenses to every variety of need.
Were it otherwise, every pastor, even the oldest, would be
shut out from large regions in the spiritual life of his
people; for the religious experience of the ripest of us
remains to the last a very partial thing.

Besides, the pastor has in this matter a wider range of
observation than falls to almost any private Christian. It
is in the faithful study of his people's varied experiences
as they come before him in pastoral care that a preacher
gains acquaintance with types of religious life diverse from
his own, and discovers how the truth of God can be handled
so as to minister to their requirements. This alone makes
him in any genuine sense of the expression a pastoral
preacher. To separate pulpit duty from the office of pastoral
superintendence over the flock, as has often been proposed
and occasionally attempted, would mean to alter its character considerably, if indeed it did not cut the nerve of its
usefulness. At least I am afraid it would have this effect
in any Protestant Church. The Lenten preacher of the
Roman communion is often a different person from the parish
priest; but then he has open to him a very effectual method,
which Protestant preachers have not, for coming into the
closest contact with the religious life of the people—I mean
the confessional. If our ministers are to speak in the
pulpit out of a knowledge of their hearers at all approaching that intimacy with men's inner religious condition which
a father confessor acquires, it must be gained by the closest
pastoral intercourse. To be widely and familiarly conversant
with specimens of religious experience, both in its strength
and in its weaknesses, is for the preacher hardly less essential than to be saturated to the deeps of his own being with
Christian truth.[1]

2. To rectify, however, and to supplement our own very

---

[1] As yet the psychology of the religious life in general, of conversion in
particular, and of Christian sanctification, is an almost untouched department of study. The day may come when it will yield a new instrument to
the hand of the preacher.

limited acquaintance with the application of Divine truth to human life, it has pleased God to put into the preacher's hand a quite invaluable guide in Holy Scripture. To every other means at his command for learning this supreme art of his calling—how to bring revealed doctrines to bear upon the edification of the flock of God—this is always to be added : let him be a thoroughly biblical preacher.

There are more reasons than one why it has been an invariable rule, never seriously questioned, though not always equally obeyed, in the history of the pulpit, that all teaching and all exhorting in the congregation's worship should be grounded on the exposition of the sacred Book. In the earliest age, we have learned from Justin Martyr that the address of the president in a Christian assembly was simply an exhortation to practise the lesson read from " the memoirs of the Apostles." This conception of the homily as a running commentary on a considerable passage, often carried through whole books on successive Sundays, lasted for a long while in the Church ; and although a topical sermon on a briefer text took a place alongside of it, it has never wholly died out. But the mere length of the text, or even the use of a text at all, is a purely formal matter which may be left over till we come to examine the structure of the sermon. What is more important is the relation of the contents of pastoral preaching to the Bible as a whole. Here the traditional understanding has been that, text or no text, the utterances of every pulpit orator ought to be through and through an *emanatio totius Scripturæ*—the outflow of a mind and heart charged to repletion with Bible teaching.

Let me repeat that this canon concerns the substance of pastoral preaching rather than its form. It is not obeyed, for instance, by weaving together a *cento* of scriptural phrases. Frequent quotation of texts, whether to establish a doctrine or to enforce a duty, is now less usual in the pulpit than it used to be ; probably less usual than is quite desirable. Of great modern preachers, Newman is perhaps the one who made the freest and the happiest use of this

old practice; and I believe he might be imitated in this
with advantage. Many congregations hear too little
deference paid to the very words of Scripture. Still, a good
memory for texual quotations will not of itself make a
biblical preacher in the best sense. Neither will a free
employment in one's diction of the characteristic or technical
terms of the Bible. If we need to import into everyday
language a pulpit phraseology at all, it is better, no doubt,
to borrow it from our English Bible than from the divinity
school; and to a certain extent this is unavoidable. To
express its own ideas, Christianity had to mint a terminology
of its own. It selected a number of common terms, which
it charged with its own deeper fulness of significance, and
these must remain its circulating medium to the end of
time. Such words as "repentance," "conversion," "faith,"
"grace," and "new birth," it is safe as well as necessary to
employ; for with them everyone is familiar, and most
people understand with fair correctness their Christian
connotation. Of the later or latest coinage of scientific
divinity there are few of which the same can be said.
Purely technical terms of the schools are rarely admissible
in addressing an average congregation. "You will never
find," says Cardinal Maury, "in the great masters of the
pulpit, a single scientific word."[1] But when it is urged that
pastoral preaching should be biblical, it is not of the
language one is thinking, but of the ideas expressed, and of
their setting, and of their illustration, and of their religious
bearings and moral implicates. What is meant is that the
thoughts of the preacher, besides being rooted in biblical
teaching, are to move mainly along its lines, so that his
whole way of conceiving of things—his way of thinking
about God and man, and sin and redemption, and life and
duty, is to be the scriptural way of thinking about such
themes. And, what is a still more subtle quality, it is
meant that the spirit of his thinking is to be that of Holy
Writ. It does well to betray the indefinable, yet quite

[1] *Essai sur l'Eloquence de la Chaire*, p. 258, Paris, 1845.

recognisable, flavour of the Holy Book. This comes only when the preacher's own religious life is steeped in Bible study. He must be all the year round not " a man of one book," to be sure, but conversant with God's Book before everything else, if he is to speak habitually, as if out of its very bosom, with the accents of inspiration echoing in each tone and the fragrance of it clinging to his breath.

One reason for this close dependence of the pastoral pulpit upon Holy Scripture is, no doubt, the theological one already hinted at, that Scripture is the norm for both Christian faith and duty, and that, since it is not his own ideas he is there to ventilate, but a message he has to bring from God, the people must be left in no hesitation how far he has behind him the authoritative record of revelation. But besides this reason springing out of Protestant doctrine, there is another more practical one, that Scripture is the chief text-book for the religious life. And it is so, just because of all books in existence it is the one which never treats religious truth apart from the lives of men, or human life apart from religion. That interweaving of truth with experience which it is the pastor's aim to achieve in his sermons is here achieved to perfection. From beginning to end of the wonderful literature, Hebrew and Christian, which we bind together and call our Bible, there is not a page that is not concerned with God, His doings or His thoughts, and yet there is not a page of abstruse or abstract writing about theology, not the vestige of a creed or of a system of divinity ; but it keeps throughout in the closest touch with the manifold affairs of human life and history. In a myriad ways and by a crowd of instances, great or small, it is concerned to show how Divine teaching found its way into the hearts of men, and how it wrought there; how variously they related themselves to it, well or ill; and how, as often as it reached them, it showed itself a word of living power, to convict, to subdue, to cleanse—in a word, to remodel human character and the interior life of human souls. An incomparable record of astonishing compass, leading the preacher into the very secret he seeks to know: that is, how God's truth is to accomplish its saving work upon the men and women whom he is set to build up in the Christian life. It never served this purpose for the pastoral preacher so well as it does to-day, since its human aspect as a religious literature has come to be studied, for the very problems which most fascinate the modern scholar are precisely how, through endless earthly channels, Divine thoughts came to men of old, moulding the lives of Prophet and Apostle into a diviner likeness, and lifting them into the fellowship of God.

CHAPTER XVIII

PASTORAL PREACHING: II

NATURALLY, it is the junior minister who, before he has acquired skill by practice, is tempted to treat of doctrines in the abstract, without tracing in sufficient detail their workings in the religious life. In a prolonged pastorate other difficulties arise, besides the difficulty created by the mere intellectual strain of over-production. Even this alone, however, may be seriously felt. Where the undivided pulpit duty falls, as in the Protestant Churches of Britain and America it usually does, to a single minister, his office is extremely exacting. Apart altogether from other duties during the week, to address the same audience twice every Lord's Day is a severer demand than is made on any other class of public speakers. When such a steady and rapid output of sermons is kept up, as it often is, with no change of sphere nor any more than a very occasional break for fifteen or twenty years, it is obvious that there must be, a great danger of intellectual exhaustion, showing itself in monotony or in repetition, both of the matter and of the form of his discourses. The most candid way in which such an overtaxed minister can repeat himself, is also, I conceive, the least harmful either to himself or to his people. It is that after a considerable lapse of years he should feel free, with no damage to his reputation, to fall back occasionally on old material, more or less worked over and brought up to date. Some men shrink from doing this openly, under an impression that it is disliked by the people. But to have recourse to it in a furtive or veiled fashion can

be wholesome for no one.   Nor is there, I believe, any real
need to do so.   When an old sermon has been the product
of honest toil and possesses both grit and body, the repetition of it is often welcome, and will rarely be objected to by
former hearers:—not to say that congregations are constantly in a state of rapid change.   To permit the use, with
or without acknowledgment, of another man's sermon, as the
Church of England tacitly does, affords an equal measure of
relief, certainly ; but the practice is absolutely condemned
in other communions, and, even where it is permitted, it is
open to the serious objection that it violates the conception
of preaching.[1]   The borrowed discourse is no longer the
speaker's own personal testimony, spoken out of personal
experience and conviction.   It is a recital, at most an endorse-
ment, of another's testimony, which is a different thing.

But, long before he has reached through over-production
a stage of intellectual barrenness, at which he is fain to fall
back on used material, the pastoral preacher, addressing
weekly the same audience, finds it difficult to secure variety
in his discourses.   Not so much in his subjects as in his
manner of discussing and presenting them.   Every man's
mind has its limits, and works in a way of its own.   He who
has to be perpetually delivering addresses, all of which are
confined to the region of the religious life, can scarcely avoid
settling into a groove.   It is so much easier to construct a
new sermon on lines very like the old ones, approaching
each subject in a similar manner or arranging his matter on
a similar framework.   Sameness of this sort in the form of
his sermons comes to mean dulness.   Regular hearers get
accustomed to the speaker's method, even to his mannerisms ;
and the freshness of thought or of its presentation, which at
first gave zest to his production, wears off.

[1] On the lawfulness of preaching borrowed sermons, I am not aware that
there is any question in the Church of England.   On the wisdom of it, however, opinions have been divided.   Archbishop Whately, for example,
advised it (*Quarterly Review*, vol. iii. p. 488) ; Daniel Moore condemned it
(*Thoughts on Preaching*, 2nd ed., Lond. 1869, chap. iii.).

How then is the minister to secure the requisite diversity in the form of his sermons? Not by the old plan of constructing them by artificial rules or with the help of the " topics." The efforts of the older homilists to gain diversity of treatment by an artificial classification of sermons based on some logical scheme were not successful, and are now abandoned. It is true that the early suggestion of Hyperius of Marburg [1] in the Reformation age proceeded, not on the structure of the discourse, but on the practical ends aimed at by the preacher; and this might still perhaps be remembered with advantage. His five *genera* were— sermons (1) to teach doctrine, (2) to confute error, (3) to train in piety, (4) to reprove sin, and (5) to comfort sorrow: to which a mixed *genus* made a sixth. But the Lutheran text-books of a century later, after the Thirty Years' War, assorted sermons by far more artificial differences, and laid down rules for producing them in a greater variety of ways. At first modestly content with four or five methods, they soon reached five and twenty; nor did the chase after new sub-varieties take breath till a list of quite a hundred had been compiled.[2] They even took to naming these varieties, as a Dutch florist might a new tulip; so that you get the " Jena " method of sermon-making, the " Leipzig," the " Helmstadt," and so forth. The manual of that period, a more sober one, it is true, which has had in this country the greatest vogue, is the essay by the famous French preacher, Jean Claude.[3] Translated by Robinson of Cambridge for the use of dissenting preachers, and re-issued in 1776 by Charles Simeon with

---

[1] In recent years, interest has revived in this writer on homiletics, whose work was in advance of his time. He was the first to see that the Christian pulpit must fashion its own form untrammelled by classical oratory. His book, *De formandis Concionibus sacris* (1553, 2nd ed. 1562), appeared in London in 1577 in an English version, *The Practis of Preaching, otherwise called the Pathway to the Pulpit, Englished by John Ludham, Vicar of Witherffield.* The original was reprinted in Germany by Wagnitz in 1781, but this edition also is now scarce. His five genera (like the "five uses") were taken, of course, from 1 Tim. 3^{16}.

[2] *e.g.* in the *Hodogeticum* of the elder Carpzov (1656).

[3] *Traité de la Composition d'un Sermon* (1688).

a hundred "skeleton" sermons of his own appended, this little book formed the basis for Sturtevant's ponderous and dull volume,[1] last edited by Henderson in 1866. It has thus enjoyed a wider and longer repute than falls to the lot of better treatises on homiletics, but it does not deserve its fame. I am afraid that much of this formal technique in sermon-building and assorting is but labour lost, as far as the modern preacher is concerned. Our shorter sermons require, and present-day taste prefers, a far simpler and more natural "disposition" of what we have to say; nor do the "topics" of the ancient rhetoricians, nor any other artificial schemes, render us much assistance. As Dr. Watts said : "Persons of any invention or imagination need not go knocking at the door of the topics to help them out of their difficulties."

The truth is, that an experienced preacher who achieves diversity in his preaching, does it simply by giving his chief attention to the subject of each sermon, allowing that to prescribe its own appropriate manner of treatment. One of the first things he has to learn is that his discourses are not to be all modelled on a single block. There is no doubt a ground type discussed in every handbook on homiletics; but there is no need to force every subject into that typical mould as if it were a bed of Procrustes. To turn out every week the regulation article, with its introduction, three divisions, and an application, is but apprentice work. The learner may have to follow the rules of his craft. The master will use his freedom. The sermon would never have become a byword for dulness had pulpit methods been more elastic. This brings us back to the fact that the secret of variety lies primarily in the variety of a sermon's theme, aim, and religious tone. These must be suffered to fashion the form of it. And of this variety in the subjects there is no lack, if only we will be biblical preachers. The Bible at least is manifold enough. History and biography, incident and emblem, poetry and apothegm, the didactic treatise, the

[1] Sturtevant's *Preacher's Manual* (1830).

devotional lyric, the parable and the exhortation :—each has its fitting mode of presentation. Surely we have made a poor use of the opulence of literary material at our command. How can men prelect so monotonously on a literature so diversified ?

Without attempting at this time of day to invent absolutely novel kinds of pulpit addresses, I think good might result from the revival, with a difference, of an old kind which has fallen into desuetude. What killed the " expository lecture" that was once so common was the fatal ease with which it degenerated into a string of disconnected comments on the passage, verse after verse or clause by clause. This cheap method brought discredit on "lecturing." If it has for the speaker the advantage of facile preparation, it is most wearisome to listen to, for it ceases to be a continuous address at all. I suppose it was the "homily" of the early Church run to seed. Useful in the hands of Origen or Augustine, its inartificial form and colloquial style, to which the latter Father repeatedly alludes, require to be remodelled now. Given greater pains to work it into the unity of a coherent discourse, it lends itself to admirable use in dealing with Scripture in its larger masses. The two points in which it differs from the most textual of ordinary sermons are these: first, that the speaker assumes the humbler rôle of an interpreter, who stands aside, as it were, to let the written Word tell its own story ; and, second, that, instead of selecting only from the contents of the passage so much as will serve a purpose of his own, he makes it his aim to explain and focus everything which is really of consequence for the understanding of the passage as a whole.

To do this well is not easy. It is more difficult than sermon-making. Its difficulty obviously lies, not only in seizing the central thought or lesson of the passage selected, but in making all its parts, with the details needful for their elucidation, contribute to impress upon the hearer that central lesson. It can only succeed, therefore, when one is careful to choose a section of Scripture which is a whole in itself—a unity. It fits most readily to a parable, for instance, or a psalm, or a short story—some incident, historical or biographical, which stands out well from the surrounding narrative. It used also to be the favourite method in going consecutively through the paragraphs of a didactic book like an epistle; only here greater care is called for in the right division of the paragraphs.

Discourses of this kind are appropriate to the work of a pastoral preacher, and have always been found instructive by Bible-loving Christians. They permit the preacher to touch upon topics which he could with difficulty select for any other treatment. They make hearers who attend with regularity familiar with the drift and connection of revelation as a whole. In this way the revival of the old-fashioned "lecture" in a modern dress would help to meet the newly awakened desire of many intelligent worshippers for a kind and amount of Bible study which the usual sermon cannot give. For the public is rapidly waking up to the progressive character of revelation. The historical and literary features in the Bible are matter of everyday knowledge. Men feel that it is a collection of archaic and Oriental documents, every one of which asks for separate study and needs help in the right use of it. The task of the modern preacher shapes itself accordingly. He is bound honestly to apply those modern methods of hermeneutics which he has learned to regard as sound. He can no longer with impunity put the whole Gospel into every book, or treat Scripture as a magazine of proof-texts, or interpret poetry as if it were prose, or wring profit out of narrative by spiritualising it. He is bound to discriminate between one age of revelation and another, between one inspired author and another. The pulpit expositor of the future will be expected to make it clear to his hearers how the light dawned gradually on ancient prophet and seer; how their lessons for their own time still yield principles which bear a modern application; how casual sayings of Jesus in Galilee

14

remain fountains of perennial truth, and gain fresh value for ourselves; how His ethical maxims can be guides in present-day duty; and how expositions of Christianity, written for a few converts at Corinth or Rome, can still inspire and regulate Christian life under the complicated social conditions of the twentieth century. All this means exposition; and exposition of a new kind, unlike in many ways to the comments which edified our forefathers.[1]

Lack of variety is by no means the worst danger which besets the pulpit ministrations of a pastor. He will find it to be a graver difficulty to leave no important part of Divine teaching untouched, and give to each the prominence it is entitled to. If he would be a good workman, declaring "the whole counsel of God," and "keeping back nothing that is profitable," he needs to arrange his work for the pulpit with deliberate forethought. No material department either in the faith or in the duty of a Christian is to be overlooked in the course of his ministry, nor undue prominence given to any. Amid the vicissitudes of a congregation's history, while its component parts change, and often change rapidly, it has a certain unity of its own, and a common life, either advancing or declining, which has to be nurtured. Besides variety, besides even the regard to be had week by week to temporary conditions, it is obvious that something like system in the exhibition of both truth and duty must be striven after.

I do not know any matter on which a conscientious minister finds it less easy to satisfy himself than this. He will get little assistance from the text-books. The subject is rarely alluded to in the usual manuals, and I know of none in which it is discussed with thoroughness. What is certain is that a proper balance and symmetry will not be observed in the teaching of a long ministry, if it be left to

[1] Consult such recent books as, *e.g.*, Watson's *God's Message to the Human Soul* (Lond. 1907); or Garvie's *Guide to Preachers* (Lond. 1906); or Forsyth, *Positive Preaching and the Modern Mind* (1907).

chance. I do not recommend a man to tie his hands beforehand by any hard and fast scheme laid down a long while in advance. But I think he ought to keep a record of his preaching, and look back from time to time over the course it has taken, to note what has been excessive in it, or what missing. He will thus make sure that he is not hiding any vital portion of Gospel truth, nor putting truths into a false perspective, nor harping incessantly on the same theme, nor narrowing down his message to a thin layer of elementary commonplaces, nor giving to doctrine an undue preference over duty or to duty over doctrine. What seems to me quite wrong, although, I fear, it is rather common, is to go on season after season, preaching on any text that happens to strike one, without ever inquiring whether one is fairly covering the ground or "rightly dividing the Word of truth." Some settle into favourite lines, and for months keep hammering at a subject which happens to have taken possession of them. Others are so eager in the hunt after fresh ideas, that they fritter their energies away on out of the way or insignificant points. You might attend their ministry long enough and never learn how men are redeemed and regenerated at all. I say nothing of the cowardice or disloyalty which would suffer any preacher deliberately to suppress part of the truth because it is unfashionable or unpalatable; because I do not suppose any of my brethren to be guilty of that. But there is among the doctrines and duties of Christianity a homiletic perspective—a measure of relative value for the Christian life, which it is easy through inadvertence to overlook, or by applying a mistaken standard, to misread.

There is likewise a perspective—an order of importance —in our systems of theology. But he would make a serious blunder who should take that for his guide in the pulpit. The place of a truth in the scientific system is determined for the most part by logical, in preaching by vital and practical, considerations. Neither school divinity, therefore, nor confessional symbols are here a safe guide.

No one needs to be told how both preaching and religious life at certain periods suffered from confounding the theological with the practical value of a dogma. The great period of systematic divinity, for example—the sixteenth century—put its school system too much into its preaching. Although the Westminster Confession, like the theology of its age, made the doctrine of election a pivot on which the whole doctrinal structure turned, it was nothing short of mischievous folly to give to that mystery a place equally central in the pulpit. Because theology had been built up by federal theologians on the theory of a twofold covenant, preachers indoctrinated our Puritan ancestors in that scheme, imprinting, as one result, upon the religious mind of Scotland a scholastic mould which lasted for generations. There is at present no theological system equally dominant, at least in this country. But there are movements of thought which for a time sway unduly the mind of the public, and theologoumena which fascinate smaller groups of devout people. Against such influences the preacher needs to be on his guard, as well as against favourite branches of study which have for himself a legitimate intellectual attraction. One is vastly interested in the bearings of evolution on religious thought; another in the higher criticism; a third in kenotic theories; a fourth in eschatology. But these are for the study: they must not be suffered to monopolise the pulpit.

By what rule, then, shall we fix the proportion of prominence which each part of truth is to receive? Probably by the closeness of its relation to Christ—to His Person and His Work; or—which comes to the same thing —to the life of a Christian in union with Him. For whether our theology be Christo-centric or not, I suppose we shall all agree that our religion is so, and therefore our preaching is to be so too. We have laid it down already that it is the religious value of any truth in the practical life of a Christian which is the preacher's concern, in fact, which entitles that truth to a place in his preaching at all.

The same test must determine what that place is to be. But all truth is vitalised and receives value for the devout life when it is set into relationship with Jesus Christ as the personal centre and sum of all Gospel teaching. "In Him are all the treasures of wisdom and knowledge hidden."[1] He is the life-centre of the whole revelation of God, in whose light every part of it is to be construed, who binds every portion of it into one organic whole of truth. Can we measure the vital quality of a doctrine, or its value for the upbuilding of the Church's life, by any other standard than this : the closeness of its connection with His blessed Person and His saving Work ?[2]

In most of the great branches of the Church of Christ, in the Catholic, the Lutheran, the Anglican, and some of the Reformed, the minister has, in the festivals of the Church year, a guide to the place he shall assign to cardinal Christian facts and the doctrines connected with them. For one half of the year, from Advent till Whitsuntide, the chief events in our redemption, our Saviour's Birth, Passion, Resurrection, and Ascension, and the advent of the Holy Spirit, are celebrated in chronological sequence, so that the meaning of these supreme events for Christian faith and living comes automatically before the minds of preacher and people at least once a year. Whatever else may be said of the Christian year, this at least must count in its favour. It does secure that the central facts on which repose the foundation mysteries of the creed cannot be entirely elbowed out of sight by any other teaching that is less imperative or less vital.

Where there is no observance of these commemorative days, each minister is trusted to take his own plan for keeping before the congregation the events which they com-

[1] Col. 2[3].
[2] In his lately-published volume, *Positive Preaching and the Modern Mind* (1907), Dr. Forsyth has addressed to preachers an urgent and a timely call to observe this proportion in the value of doctrine, putting first things first.

memorate. If at the seasons when the rest of Christendom
is remembering the Birth or the Passion, the Resurrection
or Pentecost, he does not choose to select the same events
for his theme of discourse, at least let him take care to do
so at some other time.

Among the Free Churches of England there is creeping
in of late what may be called a "Church year" of a different,
and, in my judgment, less valuable description. Efforts are
made to combine Churches in the observance of "Children's
Day," a day for Foreign Missions, Hospital and Citizen
Sundays, a "Temperance" day, and I know not what
besides. These are voluntary observances, and consequently
escape the objection which many entertain against festivals
imposed by ecclesiastical authority. The innovation may
have its use, if kept in moderation, by affording to the
pastor occasions for considering topics which otherwise
might be forgotten; but at present it is threatening to
burden the Churches with a crowd of anniversaries of subordinate consequence, at some sacrifice of what is of greater
value.

In the recurrent celebration of the Lord's Supper, a
minister finds most fitting opportunities for concentrating
devout thought upon the central mysteries of our Saviour's
death and risen life. Where the Holy Meal is observed
as frequently as once a month or even oftener, it may not
answer to deliver on every occasion what in the Scottish
Church is called an "Action Sermon." But once in two
months, at any rate, the day's discourse may quite profitably
bear on the event commemorated, in one or other of its
almost innumerable aspects or implicates. For the chief
rite in Christianity has been fashioned with Divine skill to
gather to a point the vital truths of our religion as well as
to invest them with moving and tender associations.

Besides giving in this way a central position to central
truths, every prolonged ministry ought to be made as
comprehensive as possible. It is not possible in a year
or two to cover anything like all the bearings of the Gospel

on human experience and everyday life.   But somewhere
or other in the course of a protracted term of service in the
same flock, every minister would like to feel that he had
ranged widely and touched with some minuteness on all
the more usual experiences of Christian people, and on the
relative duties of personal, family, or social life.   Help may
be obtained by plotting out for his own guidance series
of sermons which have an inner connection with one
another.   When this takes the form of going in order
through a portion of Scripture, such as the Decalogue, or
the Sermon on the Mount, or the parables, the people will
be privy to his plan, and the series had better be brief and
not too continuous.   At another time he may block out a
course on scattered texts which shall be knit together by
some ruling idea in his own mind, not necessarily apparent
to his audience.   By methods like these the pastoral
preacher strives to gain internal completeness for his
pulpit work without any sacrifice of that external variety
which is part of its charm for the weekly worshipper.

CHAPTER XIX

EVANGELISTIC PREACHING

UNDER this rather loose title it would be possible to embrace all proclamation of the Gospel, whether inside Christendom or beyond it, which is sharply distinguished from the Pastoral Preaching described in the last two chapters by having for its aim, not to edify, but to convert. For the whole of the Church's self-propagating activity, we have no better name than Evangelism—no other equally comprehensive and at the same time familiar. But it manifestly covers vast fields of labour, with which the minister of a congregation, whose duties we are considering, has little or nothing directly to do. It branches out into both home and foreign missions, where the Gospel appeals to men under such diverse conditions that a large variety of agents, as well as of methods, need to be employed. The systematic study of those methods is only in its infancy; for the special training of those agents hardly anything serious has so far been attempted. All that lies obviously outside our present scope, and might claim a treatise, or several treatises, for itself.

It does not by any means follow, however, that the ordinary minister has nothing to do with these outlying fields of evangelism. Take foreign missions, for instance. It is the Home Church which is the true conductor of every enterprise to plant Christianity in heathen or Mohammedan territory. For both men and money it is responsible; bound, therefore, to sustain it, if not also (which is the ideal best) to organise its operations. To

my thinking, therefore, every young minister, on completing
his training, does well to regard the world as his field, in
this sense at least, that he will feel any call from his own
branch of the Church to serve her abroad, to be no less
weighty than the invitation of a home congregation.   In
our day the pressure of an inward obligation is impelling
numbers of ardent students to volunteer for distant service
—an augury of promise for the future.   But even where
that impulse to volunteer is absent, ought there not to be
presumed in every candidate for ministerial office a readiness to listen sympathetically to any summons for such
service which may reach him, and to weigh it as in the
sight of Christ.   Before Providence shall have fixed his
sphere of duty, he is potentially an evangelist or a
missionary, as much as a pastor.   Nor is his concern with
the propagandist side of Church activity ended on his
acceptance of a pastorate.   On the contrary, every pastor
is supposed to carry the needs of the world on his heart,
and ought to charge himself with quickening among his
flock, zeal and liberality for the cause of missions.   That
his own post is here and not there can only be treated as
an accident of his calling.   For the field is one, and Christ's
servants are at home in every corner of it.

With what are termed "Home" or "Inner" Missions,
directed to the irreligious or the unbelieving within
Christendom, the pastor, especially of a town cure, naturally
comes into far more intimate and constant contact.   He
may be called on personally to organise or to superintend
one.   No urban parish, hardly any urban congregation,
fails to lay demands on its incumbent, not merely for oversight and advice in its mission-work, but for an actual
share in the conduct of evangelistic services or the delivery
of evangelistic addresses.   Let him not grudge it.   Whether
such duties devolve upon him as a matter of course or not,
it seems to me that every minister does well to keep more
or less in touch with such work, to study its methods, and
to lend it occasional aid.   He has no better means for

warming his own spirit, or infusing into his pastoral
sermons the true evangelical fervour, than to go himself
at frequent intervals where the non-Christian elements of
our population are to be met with, and himself carry to
them at first hand, fresh from his heart, the original
message of his Lord: "Repent ye and believe in the
Gospel." [1]

But that is not all. The pastor has no need to leave
his own pulpit in order to be also an evangelistic preacher.
In every congregation, no matter how "close" its communion may be, and still more in every place of worship
where miscellaneous audiences are accustomed to assemble,
will be found groups of people in divers states of religious
experience, who may not be, and probably are not, in
inward and fruitful fellowship with Christ. The existence
of these nominal Christians, more or less regular in their
attendance at Church services, at once introduces into the
pastoral pulpit a large infusion of evangelism. No minister
dare preach solely for the edification of genuine "saints."
He is compelled to consider hearers with various shades of
belief or of indifference, at various degrees of distance from
living faith, whom he may be in no position to identify with
confidence, yet whom it is his business, if he can, to win
back to God.

I am afraid that in some quarters those pseudo-
Christian or "unconverted" hearers are far too seldom
remembered by the present-day preacher. Perhaps at one
time they were remembered too incessantly. Perhaps there
are still ministers, reared in a strongly evangelistic atmosphere, who read their commission to preach the Gospel
somewhat too narrowly, and deem no sermon complete
which is not an explicit statement of the way to be saved,
or a direct invitation to the sinner to come to Christ. But
if I am not mistaken, the danger to-day lies at the opposite
extreme. I think we do not hear often enough the plain
setting forth of Christ as Saviour, the rousing appeal, the

[1] Mark 1[15].

urgent invitation, the pleading with sinners, even with tears in the voice, to forsake their sins and be reconciled to God. Too rarely is the preacher an ambassador on behalf of Christ, as though God were entreating by him. What was once the staple of all evangelical preaching has grown strange to the ears of many modern congregations. Yet there is always a fringe of loosely-attached adherents who frequent our services, as well as the casual hearer who in populous centres wanders on Sunday from one place of worship to another, but belongs to none. I do not forget that, when a preacher has an audience to address which is always for the most part composed of the same people, the solemn warnings and moving appeals of an evangelist may through constant iteration lose their power. Nevertheless, in every ministry ought they not to have a fairly frequent place?

Apart from this floating element, chiefly met with in town churches, something must be said of certain groups to be found in every congregation, who stand still closer to the pastoral preacher, and for whom he cannot but own himself directly responsible. These differ much from one another, and need very different styles of treatment.

The most difficult to deal with are the self-deceived— the most elusive class of all, because they are hidden from human detection, lost among the pews in the crowd of reputable Christian folk. One fears there must everywhere be a few of this class, regarding whose genuine piety, even if their names stand on a roll of membership, no one has less misgiving than themselves. Few tasks can be attempted more delicate than to lead them to a truer acquaintance with their own condition. The most skilful or practised preacher must often hesitate how he is to pierce the mail of self-complacency, to insinuate suspicion of their real shortcoming, or to beget a deeper and more vital experience of religion in the breasts of those amiable and blameless persons who are not far from the kingdom of God, yet on whom Heaven's judgment is: one thing thou

lackest.[1] Any handling of such hearers which is either
indiscriminate or unsympathetic can do nothing but harm.
Besides, there is always a risk that words meant for their
case may be misapplied by others, and so make sad without
cause some honest yet timorous soul. The wisdom which
the preacher needs can come only " from above."

A second group requiring quite different treatment will
be found among young people of both sexes, belonging to
Christian families, who might be expected to be communicants, yet for one reason or another are not. For them I
should suppose the best thing may be a winsome presentation of what Christ, if He be frankly surrendered to, can do
for a young life, to unfold what is best in it, to realise its
noblest ideal, to deepen its currents, enriching while He
hallows, and gladdening while He sobers. The path to a
fuller trust needs to be smoothed for the feet of such
hesitating disciples, and their steps allured to a more
resolved and conscious following of the Lord and Master
of their souls.

Just at present, too, there is a fair percentage of
cultured society to be found now and then at least in
church, whose attitude to Christianity hovers between a
traditional recognition of its claims, at all events of its
ethical requirements, and a critical or negative scepticism.
For the most part, this state of mind is best met by a positive and reasonable presentation of Christian truth. Yet
one who knows that it is there and who has an intellectual
sympathy with it, can quietly frame his presentation of the
truth in such a way as will meet it effectively, though not
obtrusively. Not every minister is competent to deal by
way of direct argument with prevalent forms of doubt; and
the public has come to be rightly tired of flimsy and
shallow apologetics. Where a man finds that express
controversy in defence of the faith is called for on his part,
let him first make sure that he has fully informed himself
so as to be qualified for the task. Even then it may be

[1] Mark 10[21].

advisable to reserve the subject for some special season, rather than introduce it into his usual ministry.

A preacher of the Gospel, who takes his office of evangelist seriously, and would discharge his conscience by commending his message with wisdom no less than fidelity to hearers of every class, needs above everything else to acquaint himself with their several states of mind that he may discover by what avenue they can be best approached. Minor questions of method, however, will likewise crop up: whether it is better to address them directly or obliquely; whether to devote an occasional sermon wholly to evangelism, or to insert a passing reference in a discourse mainly adapted for genuine believers; and so on. All methods are at his option, and circumstances must determine. He will rarely judge it discreet to follow the simple-minded old device of a twofold application at the close to "saints" and "sinners." Modern taste smiles at that. What is of more consequence, experience has shown that it misses its aim. If people are left to sort themselves neatly into two classes, the very persons who most need your warnings will pass them on to their neighbours. Our evangelism has to be more adroitly planned than that. Probably most preachers will feel it right to prepare a discourse now and then with a specific design to decide waverers, or disabuse the self-deceived, or arouse the un-reflecting, or sting into activity the drugged and slumbrous conscience. Then the speaker will consciously bend his strength to accomplish by God's help one definite result; though he need not openly avow his purpose or challenge a special hearing from the class he has in view. But if a preacher be in his heart an evangelist, and carry about with him a sense of the need of the unsaved and of his own responsibility for their conversion to God, occasions will be constantly arising in sermons not expressly con-structed for their benefit, when a word fitly spoken by the way will hit its mark. These he will be quick to utilise. Whatever plan he adopt, he should have no uncertainty in his own mind, nor confound in his private intention the two broadly contrasted aims of his preaching, but be always clear as to what class of hearers he has in view.

Feeling acutely the difficulty of combining, by any satisfactory method, Gospel appeals which single out the nominal Christians in an average assemblage of worshippers, with one's ministry of the Word for the upbuilding of believers, the plan of an occasional " mission-week " has recently been hit upon. Of this my own experience has been too slight to entitle me to judge of its utility. Any one can see, however, that under the name of a " mission," several different objects may be in view; and probably not much will be effected unless the conductors of it set clearly before themselves the class of persons they seek to benefit, and adapt their methods accordingly. A " mission " may first of all be conducted inside the church, with the aim of benefiting the congregation itself. Then there are at least three distinct results, ordinarily aimed at by the stated ministry, which such a series of exceptional meetings, kept up for a week or ten days, and addressed by a " missioner," may be hoped to yield in a richer than the ordinary measure : namely, (1) the deepening of the devout life in godly people through a continuous or prolonged waiting upon God ; (2) the overcoming of hesitation or removal of obstacles in the way of young persons, junior members in Christian families, or senior scholars ; and (3) the awakening to a truer knowledge of themselves and of their spiritual need of any in the congregation who " are at ease in Zion." It is possible that those three aims may all be combined by the promoters of a " mission " of this description, and by God's blessing may be accomplished by it. Provided the usual congregation, or a fair proportion of it, can be induced to attend, night after night, to hear the strange voice of a " missioner," proclaiming with more than usual insistence the claims of the Gospel upon us all, and especially Jesus' demand for a surrendered and consecrated life of service, good may be done to all the groups of persons

I have named.   And if nothing else be aimed at, no elaborate
or public preparation for the "mission" is called for in the
way of advertising or canvassing the district by door to
door visitation.

But a " mission" for the ingathering to Church connection
of irreligious or "lapsed" persons is another matter, and
needs, I think, to be promoted on quite other lines.   Its
success will be measured by the number of persons brought
by it within the sound of the Gospel or under its power,
who had drifted away from the Christian Church, although
they might be offended were we to deny them the Christian
name.   Such aggressive efforts call for evangelism of a
different type.   If a congregation organise one, it does so,
not for its own profit, but in the warmth of its outgoing
zeal.   The effort sustains a similar relation to home mission
services conducted all the year round in a " mission room "
or " Gospel hall," which the congregation's own week of
special meetings bears to its Sunday worship.   The
" missioner " may in this case also be an outsider, lay
or clerical ; but it is coming to be recognised as desirable
that such meetings should be as far as possible under the
control of the local clergyman himself.   In any case, the
class to be addressed being different, a different manner
of preaching will naturally be adopted.

Every form of evangelism, whether at Church meetings
for worship or anywhere else, is marked off from the
pastoral sermon by more than one peculiar feature deserving
of attention.

The first is the more restricted range of truth open to
the evangelist.   We have seen how wide is the field which
the pastoral pulpit ought to cover, all revelation being
given to make "the man of God perfect."   But for the
awakening and turning of sinners to God, elementary and
central truths are alone suitable.   The choice open to the
speaker will, of course, differ with different audiences.   He
must always start from ground common to himself and his

hearers. St. Paul rested his message to Felix, to Greeks at Athens, or to the people of Lystra, on quite different ground from the reasoning out of the Old Testament which he employed in the synagogues.[1] The foreign missionary can only build on the moral sense common to all men, or on true religious ideas embedded in their native faiths, or on the seeking after God which St. Paul tells us is implanted in the human heart. With professed Christians in our congregations, including habitual frequenters of " mission rooms," we have, of course, a very large amount of common ground on which to proceed. In all home evangelism, therefore, it seems to me, we have mainly two things to keep in view : (a) to inform the conscience or rouse it to repentance ; and (b) to persuade the hearer's will to prompt acceptance of the Gospel message.

As to (a): those whom we address, be they Church frequenters or not, are persons who bear the Christian name, but whom a form of religion contents without the reality. This betrays either that their conception of what true Christian religion involves is defective, or that conscience is inert. In the former case, the evangelist has to instruct the conscience by revealing the nature, the fruits, and the tests of vital faith in Christ, so that they may recognise how far their life comes short of what a real Christian's would be. The sources of such self-deception being numerous and subtle, this is delicate work which calls for much care. Vague denunciation of hypocrisy or railing at a false profession is of no use. What such hearers require is kindly but serious instruction on the inner side of piety, and on its unmistakable evidences in outward conduct. Where the conscience is not ill-instructed but inert, that is, where a person knows at the bottom of his heart, if he would own it to himself, that his religious profession is hollow, yet is made nowise unhappy by that secret knowledge, there he needs to be stimulated to wholesome alarm. The peril of mistake, the demand for sincerity and

[1] Acts 24²⁵ 17²²⁻³¹ 14¹⁵⁻¹⁷. Cf. the sermon in chap. 13.

thoroughness in one's relations with the Almighty, and the dread of Divine judgment, may all have to be pressed, in the hope of stinging into action a dormant or apathetic conscience. With coarse natures, we are here at some disadvantage through the decay of the old unquestioning belief in future penalties. There is no doubt compensation with minds of finer culture in their superior sensitiveness to inward honesty and reality. But there are some who are susceptible to nothing less ignoble than fear ; and the apprehension of judgment no longer affrights such persons as it used to do.

(b) In the more agreeable duty of urging upon the penitent or awakened the gracious offer of the Gospel, its essential facts may generally be taken for granted ; only the evangelist must beware of assuming too easily that the meaning of the facts is correctly understood. The Gospel has to be explained before it can be accepted with intelligence. In every Gospel address there should be the plainest possible statement of all that is essential to be known. Mere reiteration of the call to " come to Jesus," to " believe and be saved," is of little use unless it is accompanied or prefaced by clear teaching on the work of Christ as the ground as well as warrant of faith. Beyond that he need not go. At the same time, this exposition of the Gospel ought never to be of an abstract theological character. It has to be kept warm and human by making much of the love of God, and of Christ's pity and sympathy as our High Priest. A tender alluring presentation of the personal Saviour, whose self-sacrifice for us has laid bare the heart of the Eternal Father, is the evangelist's supreme gift. Such preaching can never be too simple, too gracious, or too winning.[1]

In proportion as an evangelist's audience differs from an ordinary congregation of Christian worshippers, other deviations from the pastoral type of preaching set in, besides this more limited range of topics.

[1] See Canon Mason's *Ministry of Conversion* (Lond. 1902).

15

For one thing, the address loses by degrees its character as an act of common worship. The less Christian the hearers, the more, of course, are the characteristic notes of Christian devotion absent. This explains why at such services the usual acts of worship tend to become themselves evangelistic. At a "revival" meeting, for instance, and sometimes in mission halls, the hymns chosen either are a singing of the Gospel, or they express sentiments appropriate to a penitent coming to Christ. The prayers, too, become petitions for pardon, or entreaties to the Holy Spirit to use the Word for the awakening and conversion of the hearers. On these lines there is still room for worship of a sort, since there is still a nucleus of belief in Christianity common to speaker and to audience. In evangelising non-Christian races, even this fails. When a missionary stands up to deliver his message in an Indian bazzar or a Chinese village, there can be no common worship at all.

For the same reason, and in a like degree, the evangelist is much less an expositor of Holy Scripture than the pastoral preacher. In addressing a home audience, he may generally take Gospel facts and truths and illustrations and arguments freely from the Bible. Assuming these to be familiar, he makes them the warp and woof of his discourse. But it is a mistake for him to burden a plain message with minute or detailed explanation of Bible language. His text should be an easy and well-known passage, where evangelical truth is put so unmistakably as to need no pains to bring it out. Even the use of a text at all may be given up when his audience is a heathen crowd, or a rude and ignorant street gathering at home. The sooner the speaker goes on to direct testimony, with appeals to the conscience and the heart, the better. Let the time that is spared from expounding Scripture be devoted to every method of persuasion; for such sermons need to be nearly all "application." The preacher must get at once into sympathetic touch with his hearers. He must speak to their peculiar diffculties, temptations, and sorrows. He must come into close grips with their conscience. He needs to adapt his discourse, as it proceeds, to their changing moods, noting the subtle signs they give of being moved by his words. A very free and impromptu style of address suits best.

Lastly, it is clear that this kind of preaching leaves freer scope to the preacher's individuality. Any checks which his position, as the representative or leader of the Church in its worship, imposes on a pulpit orator are here withdrawn. The desk or platform of a hall, still more the corner of a street, admits of a freedom in speech, an unconventional bearing, freaks of manner, and indulgence in private idiosyncrasies, which everyone would feel to be out of place in a pulpit. What is of more consequence, it not only admits, it calls for, a more individual testimony. The speaker speaks for himself. He is less the organ of a common witness-bearing to common experience. He is thrown back more on his personal religious knowledge of the Gospel. If I have to face alone a crowd of unbelievers, I must tell at first hand just what I know and have tasted of the Gospel's power to save. Such unsupported testimony, as every practised evangelist is aware, puts a severe strain on the spiritual resources of the solitary herald. This is why such preachers like to have at their back a strong platform of earnest Christians. They like to know that sprinkled up and down an audience are a few praying people. Even in open-air addresses, it is judged well to station a group of fellow-believers by the speaker's side, to add to his words the weight of their consenting testimony.

CHAPTER XX

PREPARING TO PREACH: CHOICE OF A TEXT

THE minister in regular work, who has to deliver one or two sermons every Lord's Day, will, if he be a prudent man, spare himself that wasteful and irritating hunt after a subject which costs some men much loss of time. He will take care always to have a stock of suggestions at hand, from which he has only to select the most appropriate for the next occasion.

The rule is that a good sermon is not one sought after, but one given. That is to say, its central idea, the germ of thought out of which it is all to grow, has at one time or other spontaneously offered itself with living power to the preacher's mind. It comes to him in the course of general reading, or of Bible study, or of pastoral and social intercourse, or of private devotion. Anything may suggest it. Few men who are intellectually and spiritually alive, and whose minds are habitually working round the truths of religion, can fail to find, provided they are on the watch for them, striking and fruitful thoughts, which at least have a *primâ facie* interest for them as if they had received them for themselves. That is the first essential. And it is a good rule not to be satisfied to preach on anything until it has thus quickened in one's own soul, become alive there with a promise of growth.[1]

---

[1] "In every discourse, if it have life, there is a parent idea or fertile germ, and all the parts of the discourse are like the principal organs and members of an animated body" (Bautain, *Art of Extempore Speaking*, 3rd ed., Lond. 1860, pp. 150–151).

Such creative moments are precious: to be made the most of. The mind is far from being equally productive at all seasons. When these times occur, let them be at once seized. Let the ideas which they offer be detained and fixed in writing. A MS. volume for the purpose should be at hand. A blank page or two is to be given to each fresh suggestion of a theme; the exact idea to be set down without delay, just as it occurs; and if time permit, let the mind keep on working while in the vein. The occurrence of such a fresh and vivid view of truth is like the opening of a spring. Tap it and secure its waters, lest it run to waste.

It is when a man has been thus found and gripped by a truth of God that he may be expected to preach best. Unfortunately, sermons have sometimes to be delivered on aspects of truth which have not thus come home with the force of a message to the preacher himself—almost with the freshness of a discovery. Yet Dr. Horton has done service by emphasising in his Yale Lectures the duty of every minister to seek to be filled and possessed by the truth before he stands to speak it forth in his Master's name. He calls it the "coming of the Word of the Lord" to the man; and so it is.[1] One need not be in a hurry to use these subjects to preach from. Ideas once started grow and ripen in the mind insensibly, even when one is not thinking of them. Now and then, in a leisure hour of quiet musing, let the half-filled pages of one's "seed-plot" be turned over. Recall the original line of reflection; define with more precision the thought which struck you; add whatever has since occurred in your reading or thinking that is cognate. Perhaps on second thoughts the idea looks thinner, or less original, or less prolific, than it did at first. It may have to be rejected. If there be in it the making of a sermon, carry on the process of incubation a little farther. Appropriate materials will gather round it: illustrations, related ideas, developments

[1] *Verbum Dei* (1893).

along fresh lines, practical applications of all. All great sermons grow.[1]

When the time comes for deciding on a subject for next sermon, one is selected from the note-book list in view of three considerations: that the preacher's mind lies to it; that the people need it; that it is wanted to keep one's handling of the truth balanced. I think I have named these three in their just order of consequence. But Phillips Brooks places the need of the people first.[2] He may be right, for the pastoral consideration deserves much weight. On the other hand, it is rarely worth while to fight against a positive disinclination to handle a particular subject at present; while the matter which is ripest in one's mind, or to which one feels most drawn at the moment, is that which promises the best results. It matters less, however, in what order we put these considerations in choosing any single subject, than that they be all habitually present to the judgment to qualify one another. " The sermon preached only with reference to the people's needs is heavy," says Bishop Brooks. " The sermon preached for symmetry is formal. The sermon preached with sole reference to the preacher's wish is whimsical. The constant consideration of all three makes preaching always strong and always fresh." [3]

So far I have said nothing about a text, because the germinal conception of a fertile subject to speak about is the main point to start from. In most cases, that will present itself in connection with a passage from Holy Scripture. Either it is out of some written word of God the idea has leapt to the light; or else, at the heels of the idea, a written word flashes into recollection. When that happens, the passage first thought of is quite likely to prove the fittest text for the future discourse. But it may not; a better may have to be sought for; or the conception of a possible sermon may have occurred unaccompanied by any

---

[1] Compare Mr. Moody's plan of collecting material in separate envelopes, as reported by his son in his *Life* (p. 381 f.).

[2] *Op. cit.* p. 153.   [3] *Ibid.* p. 156.

Scripture passage. At all events, this is the place to consider, not only why a preacher needs a text at all, but also
what sort of text he ought to choose.

The homiletic practice of taking the theme of every
sermon from a passage of Holy Writ, has been an all but
invariable tradition in the Christian Church. Here and
there, it is true, an innovator has been found to select, in
preference to any words of Scripture, a verse of a hymn, or
a popular proverb, or a sentence out of the catechism; or
even to open with no text at all. But such experiments
have been few and far between.[1] In last century, one or
two writers followed the lead of Voltaire in the eighteenth,
by questioning the utility of this venerable usage. It was
in his *Siècle de Louis Quatorze* that Voltaire had expressed
the wish that Bourdaloue, in reforming the pulpit, had
banished this custom from it. And in 1837, Claus Harms
ventured to say that preaching from texts had been detri-
mental, not only to the art of preaching, but also to
Christian knowledge and even to Christian life. Vinet
was more cautious, but leant to the same opinion. In
the end, however, neither the German nor the Frenchman had the courage to propose that the custom should be
dropped.[2] One may concede all that Vinet has urged against

---

[1] Schmidt (*Gesch. der Predigt von Luther bis Spener*, Gotha, 1872) gives at
p. 119 quite a number of volumes of sermons on hymn-verses published about
the time of the Thirty Years' War. The custom was not new in Germany,
however; cf. *ibid.* pp. 74–76. As instances of preachers who dispensed with
a text, Hüffell names Theodoret in the ancient Church, in the mediæval
Rabanus Maurus, Bernard, and Geiler von Kaisersberg, and Luther and
Ewald among moderns (*Wesen u. Beruf*, Giessen, 1830, i. 217).

[2] " Dürften wir auch noch die Behauptung wagen dass das Predigen nach
Texten nicht allein die Ausbildung der Predigtkunst sondern ebenfalls die
christliche Erkenntniss, und selbst, was noch mehr sagen will, das christliche Leben, sehr gehemmet habe? . . . Indessen, nur ausnahmsweise
möcht' ich selber nur passiren lassen, ausser anderen Gründen, aus dieser
pastoraltheologischen : Die Gemeinde verliert die Gewähr, oder, was sie
für eine Gewähr hält, dass eine solche Predigt, wirklich Gotteswort sei."
Harms, *Pastoraltheologie*, 1ter Theil (Kiel, 1837, pp. 65, 83); cf. Vinet's
Homilétique (Paris, 1853, p. 109). The question is discussed at length in
Dr. Carl Clemen's *Predigt und biblisher Text* (Giessen, 1906).

it in the case of topical sermons, where it is difficult always to fit the text to the theme and the theme to the text, and yet conclude that the reasons in its support are of overwhelming strength.   The strongest is that to which even Harms bows, that it lends to the central idea of the sermon the authority of the Divine Word.   Hence in Old English, as one can see in Chaucer, it was called the "authority" (*auctoritas*).   The great fact, of which the text is an index, is that every true sermon grows up out of the living Word of Revelation, and, because it has that behind it, is to be both spoken and listened to, not as a "word of man's wisdom," but as the message of the Eternal for our salvation. Surely that fact ought to be made visible and kept before preacher and audience alike.   It is no answer to say that a man may take a text and yet preach unbiblically.   He may; but if he does, his text condemns him.

Minor advantages will readily occur.   It secures to each discourse a character of its own, no two texts being exactly alike.   It affords to the hearer a peg on which to hang the substance of the discourse for easier recollection.   It bespeaks at the outset a reverent hearing for what the preacher has to say.   It lays to his hand an endless variety of those human interests and picturesque images in which the Bible is so rich.   And it gives the pastor an opportunity for leading his people into deeper acquaintance with their Bible.   But the main thing is that it reminds speaker and congregation of what a sermon ought to be—an utterance of God's Word revealed to Christian faith, not human opinions or speculations.

If in reality, and not as a mere form, the text is to carry this value as an "authority," it is clear that it needs to be selected with care.   It is needless to say that not every combination of words in the Bible is fit to be preached from. Words even occur which taken by themselves, apart from their context, contain not truth, but an untruth : like "Let us do evil, that good may come."   Plenty of passages also, in the Old Testament especially, are incapable of yielding such instruction or profit as a sermon ought to afford. Bare lists of names in a genealogical table, rubrics in the Levitical service-book, many topographical or archæological details in Hebrew annals, do not naturally convey any religious lesson. It is true that some preachers have delighted to startle audiences by announcing such an unpromising text, trusting to extort a meaning out of it by ingenious tricks of interpretation. Such a *tour de force* or homiletic legerdemain is unworthy of the pulpit. There is, no doubt, a happy knack which a few men possess, of picking out unhackneyed sayings which do really teach truth, yet teach it in a fresh fashion. But no preacher is well advised who makes it his habit to search out far-fetched or fanciful or allusive texts, the connection of which with what he is going to say is remote or strained. Still more ought he to disdain the vanity or the eccentricity of bizarre texts, which can only be utilised in a fashion so odd that the hearer is either astonished or amused by it. Cheap tricks of this sort usually mark an inferior preacher. Great orators prefer great texts; and as a rule wise preachers choose plain ones, which easily and naturally sustain the thought they desire to illustrate.

Moreover, if the theme or subject of discourse is to rest upon the passage selected, then the text needs to have unity, and, as far as possible, completeness. It would be easy to extract at random a bit of narrative, for example, or a fragment cut from an apostle's argument, on which to found a few unrelated remarks, but which never could be made to yield any single topic. Nor is it well to choose morsels that carry no complete sense, but require to be supplemented in order to make a whole. To build a sermon on a single vocable, or phrase, or clause in a sentence, is rarely permissible. The text may be brief enough; and some of the briefest are also the fullest; like "Jesus wept," or "God is love." But it should have substance in it to furnish material for a discourse. There is a nibbling way of treating the sacred book which snips off from it little tags, bits that may no doubt suggest or infer much more than they say, but which by themselves say very little. It is better surely to take a portion which, whatever its length, has within it bulk and depth of meaning adequate to fill the sermon and to feed the flock.[1]

Nor am I persuaded by what Austen Phelps has advanced in their defence,[2] that what are called "motto" texts should be otherwise than sparingly employed. To prefix to a sermon, as one might to a chapter in a book, a borrowed saying, however felicitous, of which no further use is to be made, does not answer the purpose of a text. It seems to me a more wholesome, as well as manly, course to find a passage of God's Word which, in its true sense and organic connection with the rest of revelation, can be fairly summed up in the theme you propose to speak about.

The first thing, then, to do with such a text is to study it. Examine its meaning exegetically, with the best helps at your disposal, making sure of the precise force of its important words and of its relation to the context. Compare it with its nearest cognate passages to discover what is peculiar to itself. Sometimes help can be got from the history of the text in the Church, or its use at crises of religious experience; for texts have their annals and their associations. "A text," says Athanase Coquerel, "is always richer than we think."[3] If such a process should make our preaching strongly biblical, no harm will be done. How texts can be used to sustain theological dogmas is not for the moment, what it once was, the chief point of interest. But what say the original documents of our faith, as read by modern men in the light of modern questions? So, too, in handling moral texts, the first thing is to ascertain the Christian meaning which the New Testament breathes into

---

[1] Cf. Spurgeon: "You must not for ever hover round the mere angles of truth" (*Lect. to my Students*, 1st Series, Lond. 1876, p. 78).

[2] *Theory of Preaching*, 1882, p. 44.

[3] *The Preacher's Counsellor*, Lond. 1867, p. 109.

Greek terms for virtues of character, how that differs from their use in Aristotle, or other heathen moralists, and why it differs—that is, from what root in the Gospel teaching the words drew their new sense. Only after fixing in this way the New Testament force of the terms, can the preacher go on to apply them to present-day conditions and duties.

In all this, the preacher needs to keep an exegetical "conscience void of offence." It is a homiletic offence of the first magnitude to make Scripture mean anything else than it does mean. The safe rule is the one which Hagenbach formulated in these terms: "Conscientious preaching requires that no explanation of Scripture be given which cannot be scientifically justified." That does not hold good of the text only. It holds good of every passage cited for proof, or even for illustration and enforcement of truth, except where Bible language is merely borrowed in the well-understood way of literary adaptation. There is such a thing as quoting the words of Scripture or of secular authors for a purpose never dreamt of by the author, or even in a sense not justified by their original meaning. St. Paul occasionally quotes in this way from his Bible.[1] Within the limits of good taste, and where no false inference can be drawn by the average hearer, this is allowable. But whenever the hearer is likely to suppose that we are citing the words of Scripture in their original or intended sense, then it ought to be in that sense we cite them. The text, at all events, must always be taken and used in its strict meaning.

It is a difficult question, what attitude the modern pulpit is to take up in respect of the very ancient and far-descended habit of spiritualising or allegorising the narratives and the figures of sacred history. This habit, learned from Jewish expositors, has been in vogue among Christians at least since the third century. During the

[1] For example, when he quotes Ps. 19^4 in Rom. 10^{18}: "*Their line is gone out through all the earth.*"

patristic and mediæval periods it was often driven into strange extremes. When Isaiah speaks of seven women taking hold of one man, we should no longer think with Origen of the sevenfold operations of the Divine Spirit.[1] Few moderns would so far spiritualise the parable of the Good Samaritan as to understand the twopence paid to the innkeeper as a figure of the two sacraments, as a Middle Age orator is said to have done. On the other hand, few preachers would hesitate to employ the cure of Bartimeus as a parable of spiritual enlightenment; and I think many of us, in discoursing upon our Lord's words on the Cross, "I thirst," would feel free to extend its application from His bodily need to His deeper longing of spirit for the accomplishment of His mission. Yet Dr. Hoppin of Yale would condemn both.[2] The venerable pulpit tradition is out of fashion; but it has not died out yet. Where are we to draw the line? It is clear that we are badly in want of some sound rule, and this it is not easy to lay down. I suspect that spiritual feeling, held in check by a sober judgment, must practically be our only guide.

This question of the "accommodation" of Scripture and its limit is commonly discussed in connection with the choice or use of a text. In truth, it is a much wider question. It concerns the whole employment of Scripture for edification, both in its narrative portions and above all in its typology. So far as the latter is concerned, I do not see how we are to rule the Old Testament "types" wholly out of court. The New Testament writers certainly led the way. They even traced it back to the example of our Lord Himself, who used the story of Jonah, for instance (whether by way of accommodation to Hebrew methods of exegesis or not), as a parallel to His own burial and resurrection. In so far as theocratic personages in

---

[1] Cited by Ebenezer Porter of Andover in his *Lectures on Homiletics and Preaching* (Lond. 1835).

[2] *Homiletics*, revised ed., Lond. 1881, pp. 314–317.

Israel held in their own day a relation to the people of God analogous in some respects to the mission or work of the Messiah, afterwards to be revealed, it must be legitimate to employ them for the purpose of illustrating features in His work of salvation. The Aaronic high priest certainly typified His better Priesthood, or the whole Epistle to the Hebrews is based on a mistake. Figures like Joseph, the rejected of his brethren, or Moses, the redeemer of his people, or Joshua, the captain in the holy war, are so adapted to prefigure Christ, that it is difficult to show they were not in the wisdom of God designed to do so. Certainly the instinct of Christian piety has always delighted to see such foreshadows in the economy which prepared a people for our Saviour's advent. It is a difficult use of history to make, and it has been grievously overdone. When we venture beyond the guidance of Scripture to invent types for ourselves, it is even a risky use to make of it. Still, a fantastic allegorising of history is one thing : a cautious typology is another.

There is, however, another mode of drawing lessons out of Hebrew annals which is liable to no such danger, and which is more to the taste of the modern mind. I mean when the examples of the Fathers, and the teaching of Providence through their experience, are applied, after a simple and natural fashion, either for warning or for imitation. The Bible is the book of Providence, but with the key attached. Its characters are thoroughly human— "men of like passions" with ourselves. What happened to them "happened by way of example," and their history was "written for our admonition." It teems, therefore, with the most beautiful and instructive lessons for all time. The preacher has no need, for instance, to handle Joseph as a type of Christ. He can read from his career a lesson on the Divine overruling of events, or on youthful purity, or on fidelity to a godly upbringing, which every hearer will feel to be thoroughly apt and profitable. Here he runs no risk of indulging his fancy by inventing unreal parallels.

He preaches from life to life. He teaches by concrete
example. Other biographies and the annals of other
peoples might teach, it is true, similar lessons. Only in
this story it has pleased God to put in our hands a key
to the hidden purposes of His ways with men. We are
told through His prophets the secret meaning of events,
domestic or political. The ways of God with His people
of old proceeded on the same principles of righteousness
and grace as govern His dealings with ourselves. And
we know what these principles were; for it was by this
Hebrew story that He revealed Himself, and by it He
leads us into the hidden purposes which, still as of old,
by our lives as by theirs, He is working out for the
coming of His kingdom.

CHAPTER XXI

PREPARING TO PREACH: PLAN OF THE SERMON

THE sermon being a personal address by a speaker to an audience, its structure falls under the rules which govern that branch of the art of rhetoric called oratory. That preaching ought to be as oratorically perfect as we can make it, is required, not only, as we saw before, by its place in worship,[1] but also by its practical aim. It ought to be skilfully adapted to its purpose. Faults of oratory are not the worst of which the preacher can be guilty. It is far worse to be insincere, or frigid, or false in his teaching. But defective skill in the art of speaking is a much more common fault. Ill-arranged ideas, want of proportion in the divisions of a discourse, slovenly style, and the like, are frequently to be met with. And they are not merely inartistic, they are hindrances to the effect of the sermon; they interfere with the profit of the hearer.

The application of rhetoric to the pulpit began early.[2] From the time of Origen, indications multiply that the Greek schools were beginning to influence the preaching of the Church. At first a very informal conversational style of address had sufficed for small meetings of the brethren, held mostly in private rooms. During the third century, congregations in the larger cities began to worship in special buildings and with more publicity. The presence of strangers encouraged fuller exposition of Scripture, and, in the hands of Origen especially, the homily became a con-

---

[1] See *ante*, Chapter XVII.
[2] *E.g.* the sermon εἰς τὰ θεοφανεία ascribed to Hippolytus.

tinuous and elaborate commentary verse by verse, in short, an expository lecture.

When men of culture, trained in the universities of Greece, were advanced to the chief sees, still more when Christianity became the religion of the Empire, when its cult was celebrated in imposing basilicas erected by Imperial munificence, and when eloquent bishops could sway the passions of the citizens or influence the politics of the Court, it was unavoidable that the homily should develop into an oration. Then everything favoured the growth of a Christian oratory, by no means free from the faults of pagan Sophists in that age of decadence, yet offering a field for the highest efforts of the practised speaker.[1] From Augustine to Melanchthon, homiletics was treated almost exclusively as an application of classical rhetoric; and the tradition has been largely followed by later writers.

Not without an occasional voice raised in protest. Augustine himself counselled the preacher to modify heathen models by the example of St. Paul; and earnest Christians have often urged that the Gospel must create a manner of its own, as distinct from that of the Greek or Roman tribune, as its aims are higher. But this is no more than can be said of all applied oratory. In every department of public speaking, the rules which teach how to speak well are subject to modification from the occasion, the theme, or the design of the particular discourse. In pulpit speaking, therefore, just as in the oratory of the senate or the bar, general rules have to be applied under prescribed conditions. The sermon is a solemn address, spoken in public worship for the conversion or religious edification of the hearer, and always attaching itself to the exposition of the Gospel. It is under these conditions that it aims at producing similar results to those which were contemplated by the ancient orator. In that section of his *De Doctrinâ Christianâ*, which is really

[1] Cf. Villemain, *Tableau de l'Eloquence Chrétienne au 4me Siècle* (1849).

our earliest treatise on homiletics, Augustine cites from Cicero as the preacher's three aims: "ut doceat, ut delectet, ut flectet."[1] But the three are not of equal consequence. Its sacred character and spiritual purpose subordinate very strictly the desire to please to the desire to profit. They rigorously forbid the use of mere ornaments of speech for their own sake. They reject, above all, every disingenuous argument, clap-trap appeals to prejudice, points made merely for momentary effect, and other tricks of the sort. In brief, the solemn issues that depend on the pulpit emphasise what Theremin calls the "virtue" of the orator, that is, those moral qualities in the speaker which lie at the basis of the truest and noblest eloquence.[2] In this way Christianity may be said to have purged the art of speaking of its baser elements.

It certainly has given to the orator far grander themes and graver tasks. The themes are grander, for they reach to the profundities and altitudes of Divine truth. The tasks are graver, for they aim at no less than the reconciliation of man with God, and the reconstruction of his spiritual life. The inspiration which alone can uplift a speaker to themes and tasks so sacred must needs be drawn from a higher than Greek or Roman source. It is only with the forms of speech that rhetoric can deal; and it is pretty certain that its value for the preacher has often been over-estimated by writers on homiletics. Its formal rules may possess for most of us little more than a negative utility in warning us how to avoid faults which mar the effect of the most earnest speaker. Even were it so, still every preacher ought to know what these rules are, and have them before him in the preparation of his discourses; since, after all, the virtues of a good speech must be in substance the same

---

[1] Bk. iv. c. 12. He has not quoted the *De Oratore* accurately, however. Did he intentionally change *ut probet* into *ut doceat*? The comparative importance of the three is discussed by Augustine.

[2] *Die Beredtsamkeit eine Tugend*, Berl. 1837. Reprinted in *Bibliothek der theol. Klassiker*, 1888.

16

for sacred as for secular eloquence; and, for the highest
purposes of his mission, Christ's messenger must be left as
free as any other to employ every noble means of effective
and persuasive utterance which stands at the service of any
orator.

The first virtue, then, in a well-ordered sermon, as in
every work of art, is unity: "l'art lui-même," says Vinet,
"ayant pour premier objet de créer un tout, par le rap-
prochement d'éléments dispersés."[1] But again I must add,
not for art's sake alone; for the sake of its usefulness also,
every sermon ought to be a unity. It is indisputable, as
Vinet argues, that an address, listened to, not read, is more
easily followed, more agreeable to the hearer, better
remembered by him, and more likely to leave a lasting
impression on the mind, above all, on the will, when one
animating idea informs every part and the whole moves
steadily forward to a single aim, than if it be rambling,
heterogeneous, or incoherent. I do not know whether Dr.
Shedd was correct when he affirmed that "sermons are
more defective in respect to unity of structure and a
constant progress towards a single end, than in any other
respect."[2] But if there be justice in this criticism of
current preaching, the minister will do well to pay special
heed to this primary condition of effectiveness.

To the unity of a sermon there are three things which
chiefly contribute: two of them essential, and a third
desirable. It needs to have a single theme and a single
design; it is well if these prescribe also unity or
"keeping" in its tone.

1. UNITY OF THEME

What is meant by the "theme" is simply a proposition
which states with precision the subject of discourse. That
I assume the preacher to have now pretty clearly in his

---

[1] *Homilétique*, p. 47.
[2] *Homiletics and Pastoral Theology* (Edin. 1869), p. 129.

mind. I suppose him to have taken from his store of subjects a germinal idea around which materials have gathered. He has also selected and studied the text which seems to him best adapted to express, or at least to support, his fundamental conception. But at this point he must be advised to give to the subject the utmost precision or definiteness of which it is capable before he proceeds further. It is not enough to throw it out in the form of a loose title, such as one might prefix to a book, after a fashion recently introduced by some preachers. It will much assist the unity of his discourse if he will set it down in writing, for his own use at least, in the form of a proposition. Since in any case it is to be the formative and governing truth developed before his audience, that under which every subordinate idea must be capable of being gathered up, he will find it extremely helpful to have it before him as a clearly expressed statement or thesis. That is his " theme."

The " theme " thus stated is to bear a fixed relation to the text. It should be at once true to its ascertained meaning and fairly exhaustive of its contents.

It is true to the text when it springs out of a correct exegesis of it, and does not go beyond its full religious import as a part of revelation. Unless it do this, the text ceases to be a Divine authority for what is taught in the sermon. The preacher may say nothing that is not true, but unless it be the truth contained in the text, the book of God is misused. To build a discourse on a misinterpreted passage has been a frequent sin in the pulpit; but it is a high homiletic misdemeanour, for which it is no apology to plead that you are preaching nothing heretical or unbiblical. You are preaching it from a wrong text.[1] Disappointment may be felt at losing, through strict obedience to this rule, a few familiar texts which have been misused by generations of preachers. But the Bible is full of unexceptionable ones,

[1] Cf. the examples given by Broadus, with his account of the sources of the error, in his *Treatise on the Preparation and Delivery of Sermons*, 2nd ed., Lond. 1871, pp. 53 ff., 70–78.

and a closer study of its genuine meaning under stricter modern methods of interpretation will disclose finer applications than any we can lose. Especially when it is added that our theme may transcend the literal sense of the text-words, provided it do not go beyond their full import in the light of completed revelation. We are surely entitled to place a Scripture passage under the ampler illumination which the finished revelation in Christ has cast back over its earlier portions. If the Bible be the record of a continuous discovery of God which was designed to attain full-orbed completeness in Jesus Christ, then it is permissible, applying St. Peter's canon of interpretation, to look beyond the original significance of an event or an oracle as it could be understood at the time. The prophets, he says, did not fully know all that the Spirit meant by the revelations of which they were the transmitters. They prophesied of a grace that was afterwards to be revealed; and so they ministered, not unto themselves, but unto us.[1] In searching for this fuller spiritual force in ancient words, one has always to start, of course, from an historical reading of the oracle—what it signified to the age and to the men to whom it was given. But we are not forbidden to ask how much more of God's thoughts it may have to say to us, " upon whom the ends of the world are come." Not seldom does the local, the temporary, the far away fact or word of Hebrew origin break like a husk in Christian hands, to set free a principle, a truth, or a lesson of enduring value for the Church of God.

I said the theme is also expected to be fairly exhaustive of the text. In one sense, no doubt, we cannot exhaust the force or the contents of a great text; for the Word of God is infinite in depth and reach. Each young generation of preachers comes to the old words, to find in them fresh aspects and applications of truth. Only when the important ideas in any text are brought into focus, to be summed up under one paramouut thought, and that

---

[1] 1 Pet. 1$^{10\text{-}12}$, cf. Gal. 3^{23} and 1 Cor. 10^{11}.

thought is your theme, then it may fairly be said to exhaust
the text. Some texts are so short and simple that they
constitute the theme. Others embrace a plurality of
propositions, expressed or implied. Then one is bound to
search for a single thought large enough to cover all of
them, central enough to combine them into unity.[1] In
other cases, the text may be a whole narrative. Still, the
paramount idea has to be seized. Nor will a strong-brained
or manly preacher care to spin sermons out of the fringes
and corners of a big subject, but will fasten by preference on
the heart and substance of it as a part of the revelation
of God.

2. UNITY OF AIM

The aim or "scope" of a sermon is the practical effect
which the preacher designs to produce upon his audience.
A sermon is not an essay, nor an abstract disquisition or
exposition of a truth. It is an address spoken for some
practical purpose. The whole plan of its construction will
be determined by the object which the speaker has in view.
Nay, the very way in which he apprehends his subject, the
viewpoint from which he regards it, must vary according to
the use he proposes to make of it. Here, therefore, at the
outset he needs to come to an understanding with himself—
to answer for himself the question: What do I expect to be
the result of this discourse ?

Most subjects lend themselves to a multiplicity of uses:
must then a preacher select one out of the number and aim
strictly at that alone ? Nothing is more common than to
hear a preacher, as he draws near the end of his discourse
indicate several "lessons" to be drawn, or several sorts of

---

[1] An example will illustrate this :—

TEXT : St. John's Gospel 8[46-59].

THEME : How Jesus testifies of His Godhead before the unbelieving.
He testifies (a) to His sinlessness, 8[46] ; (b) to His glory, vv.[50-54] ; (c) to His
eternity, v.[58].

persons whom the same lesson may benefit in diverse ways. Is this wrong?

From the point of view of pure oratorical art, I conceive it is undeniable that the more an orator can unite his efforts to convince or to persuade upon a single point, the more effective will his oratory be. That is the most powerful form of speech which drives consciously to one definite result; making all its arguments, for example, its motives, and its appeals converge upon a line of action to which it seeks to persuade the hearer. Such simplicity of aim can usually be secured in an evangelistic address; because its one end is to turn the sinner to God. But the edification of the Church is a much more complex result, which is promoted in a vast variety of ways. The practical requirements of his congregation do not always permit the pastoral preacher to consider one class of his hearers to the exclusion of every other, or to ignore through a whole sermon the bearings of the truth in hand upon various characters and conditions to be found among his flock. Plain everyday preachers, therefore, who simply consult the profit of a mixed audience, constantly find it expedient to embrace under one general aim a plurality of particulars. But even so, he must have one general aim at least, which admits of being stated. The spiritual profit he hopes to secure may be reached by sundry methods, or the truth may do its work differently on persons in different circumstances. Yet there ought to be no dubiety in his mind as to the general effect, or the kind of impression, which he intends his discourse to produce. About that he ought to be quite clear: and the more closely he is able to define that to himself, the more likely is he to be successful. Otherwise a sermon is extremely apt to drift, and, being aimed at nothing in particular, the result is that it hits nothing.

3. Unity of Tone

With the subject and design of each sermon, its "tone" ought to be in keeping. By that is meant the pitch or key of feeling in the speaker and in his manner of speaking. There are many moods of emotion, any one of which may be dominant. A discourse may be, for instance, restful or impassioned, contemplative or insistent, solemn or cheerful, homely or ornate. And what is intended by this rule is, first, that it should depend on the theme and the aim of each sermon which of those moods is most appropriate; and then, that, whichever it be, the whole should be in harmony with it. This does not mean, of course, that a monotone of level feeling is to reign from the opening to the close. On the contrary, the note struck will swell or fall as the progress of the discourse requires; especially is a *crescendo* movement towards the close always in place. Only, one part of the discourse ought never to strike the listener as in violent disharmony with the rest.

Such skilful "keeping" imparts to each discourse a character of its own, aiding unity of impression, and is a quality of high value in oratory. But it is hardly to be looked for from untrained speakers. Moreover, the range of tone possible to each speaker is limited by temperament. Some men are habitually intense; some uniformly sedative. Everyone is entitled to give play to his natural manner; and it is well to recognise that a man may preach well in any way that is natural to him. At the same time, each of us will do well, I think, to cultivate as wide a range as we can compass, and not settle down into one stereotyped mood of feeling in all discourses alike. The endless variety of truth is fitted to evoke from any man various responses in the way of emotion, provided he will let it play freely upon the whole of his nature. To get into the spirit appropriate to each sermon's subject and intention; then to let that mood of feeling have free unconfined utterance: this will secure unity in each discourse with wide diversity in one's pulpit moods.

Guiding lines having thus been fixed in the preacher's own mind, which serve to define the future sermon and secure its unity, he may proceed to plan an outline of what he is to say. In any ordered speech four members are distinguished by the rhetoricians :—(1) The Introduction or Exordium; (2) Announcement of the Proposition or Theme to be treated; (3) the Development of the Matter under two or more divisions; and (4) a Conclusion or Peroration. No mechanical scheme of this sort ought to fetter the practised preacher; nor does it conduce to the pleasure of a hearer when the joints of the skeleton are obtruded. Yet an order of procedure so simple and reasonable will commonly be found to underlie a good discourse even when it is not very visible. To keep it in mind while drafting the outline beforehand will assist the speaker, however free he may feel himself to be when in front of his audience. And what I have to offer by way of suggestion can all be said under these four particulars.

(1) *The Introduction*

It is a mistake, I think, to assume that a sermon must always have a preface. To invent an artificial opening for its own sake, when no real use is to be served by it, appears to me to be a blemish. Vinet indeed, with a Frenchman's fancy for rhetorical art, lays down the rule that the preacher should lead the audience skilfully up to his real subject by starting some idea of a simple character which is not part of his subject, but only lies near to it.[1] It is good art, he says, to wind one's way into a theme through a little avenue of approach : what Cicero called " *aditus ad causam.*"[2] Yes; but the principal use of an exordium in the view of the ancients was to conciliate the audience. That is rarely necessary for a Christian preacher. An evangelist address-

---

[1] *Homilétique*, p. 356 ff.   [2] *Ad Brutum.*

ing a hostile or indifferent assembly may require to bespeak favour; the pastoral preacher addressing his usual congregation has no such need. Time is precious, and none of it, I think, should be wasted on introductory matter unless it is judged requisite in the interest of the sermon for one or other of the following reasons:—

Either the theme does not arise so obviously from the mere reading of the text as to be at once and readily apprehended by the hearer. If he has to be assisted to see how the subject springs out of the text, this is the place to do it. The terms of the text may call for a slight explanation; or, in order to bring out its exact force, the context may have to be recalled; or the purpose of the preacher may require the passage to be set in a special light. If for any such reason the audience needs to be led from the text to a better acceptance of the subject drawn from it, there is room for an exordium.

Or should a congregation be, though not unfriendly, yet sluggish or unsympathetic, an opening is called for which will seize their attention or predispose them to listen. Some congregations have the unfortunate habit of settling themselves, at the outset of the sermon, either into a critical attitude if the preacher be a stranger, or into decorous listlessness if he be too well known. To pique curiosity or awaken interest in the subject is then indispensable; and one's chance of gaining a good hearing depends very much on the first five minutes.

It is therefore of moment that, if there be an introduction, it should be lively, piquant, and brief, couched in choice and studied words. But in his effort to make it striking, the speaker should beware of pitching it on too high a key. Few faults are worse than to fall from an ambitious start into commonplace. Let it be quiet, though interesting. The main thing is to create an impression in the audience from the first that you have something to say worth hearing, and are so much in earnest that you mean they shall listen to it.

(2) *Announcement of the Theme*

Some skilful speakers reserve any express statement of
their subject till near the close, trusting to lead the audience
forward by steps which are not seen to be conducting
towards it until it come out at the end of the discourse.
This requires a practised orator with intelligent hearers,
intent to listen. As a rule, it is safer to state at this point
what you propose to speak about. This satisfies the congregation that you at least have a clear idea in your own
mind. It assists dull hearers to follow you better. It
enables good listeners to connect every part of your address
with its governing idea. But the subject has to be stated
briefly and neatly, with the utmost simplicity and perspicuity, avoiding at this stage decorative diction, whether
epithets or tropes.

(3) *Development of the Matter under Divisions*

The bulk or body of the sermon is, of course, to be
devoted to working out its main idea by bringing to its
elucidation, proof, or enforcement a variety of subordinate
and helpful materials of one sort or another. " Le discours
est la proposition développée, et la proposition est le discours
en abrégé." [1]

Two sources to which one may go for these materials give
rise to the two leading kinds of sermon. When the ideas
which form the substance of a discourse are drawn out of
the text itself, which may well happen if the passage chosen
be large and complex, then the sermon is called " textual "
or synthetic.[2] When the subject only is yielded by the text
and the subsidiary ideas by which it is developed are sought

---

[1] Fénelon, *Lettres sur l'Eloquence.*
[2] EXAMPLE.—TEXT: 2 Thess. 2[13, 14]. THEME: The Calling of the Christian. DIVISIONS : 1. Its Author= " He called you." 2. Its outward means
= " By our Gospel." 3. Its end, which is twofold : (*a*) Immediate end is
faith and holiness ; (*b*) Ultimate end is to obtain the glory of our Lord.

for elsewhere, the sermon is said to be "topical" or analytic.[1]
A judicious preacher will practise both kinds, guided on each
occasion, partly by the contents of the passage, and partly by
the character of the subject. Textual sermons are often
easier to produce than topical ones, since they call for
less inventiveness or fertility of mind. The speaker's skill
is shown in binding up into a synthesis what the passage
gives him, or so much of it at least as can be made available
for his purpose. On the other hand, the topical sermon
admits both of a freer handling and of a more complete
discussion of the subject. The text is virtually dismissed so
soon as it has yielded up its theme. For the rest, the
preacher is thrown upon his own invention. He is at
liberty to fetch arguments from Scripture, reason or
experience, illustrations from every region of nature or
of history, applications of the truth to any department of
human conduct, or motives of every description to move the
hearers as he would have them moved. Having so much at
his command, he has no excuse if he does not select what
will contribute most to the precise design which he has set
before him. Good sermons in either manner abound. The
textual is probably more in favour in our time; but the
topical sermon will always remain a choice instrument in
the hands of powerful and intellectual preachers.

With either class of sermon, but most of all with the
topical, what old rhetoricians styled "invention" has now
to be undertaken; and it is this crucial portion of his task
which most tests the preacher's intellectual training and
habits of study. Of the study of the text I spoke in the
foregoing chapter. What has now to be studied is the
subject itself. It may require reading: either to inform
oneself of what others have said about it, or to collect facts
in illustration, or to verify literary parallels and allusions,

---

[1] EXAMPLE.—TEXT : 1 Tim. 1[11] : "The Blessed God." THEME : The
Happiness of God. DIVISIONS : 1. What it is. 2. That it belongs in
perfection to God only. 3. How far creatures are capable of a like
happiness.

or to keep one's theological teaching straight. But what it requires most of all is downright hard thinking. A few commonplaces any one can jot down at half an hour's notice about any Bible subject you like. But to penetrate to the heart of a deep theme, to seize upon what is central in a great one, to detect its relations to other truths and to human life, to catch the splendour or the mystery of it, to work it up into fresh forms by a vigorous exercise upon it of both brain and heart, so that it is not apprehended merely, but assimilated and made one's own :—this is more than it is given to every man to achieve, and more than a crowd of indolent men will take the pains to attempt. Yet this is exactly what every real preacher needs to do.

I admit that it is possible for a smart phraser to catch for a time the ear of a congregation. But his emptiness will be found out. People do not care in the long run for what is not fresh—the coinage of one's own mint. When I say that sermons are to be "original," no one will take me to mean that the truths or the ideas are to be such as no man ever thought or spoke before. Who is so foolish as to ask that? All truth is at the heart of it as old as the hills, and our message has been ringing through Christendom for nineteen centuries. Only it is the property of absolute truth, Divine truth, to enter into fresh combinations in each living soul that is possessed by it, to take on itself in each man's mental workshop a shape it never had before, and so to come forth from his living personality newborn, like Pallas, in the radiance and the strength of eternal youth. This is what people expect at the lips of a preacher. They have a right to expect it. Therefore no true preacher ought to grudge the toil of brain and spirit through which alone the truth can become his own possession—better, can come to possess him.

The prime counsel to anyone who is getting up a sermon is, therefore, think; think for yourself; not taking too much out of books; above all, not trusting to what a commentary can give, or a homilist's outline, or another

man's printed sermon. All such crutches are for the
preacher vanity and a snare. To use them often saps
intellectual self-respect. It enfeebles one's power of
thinking. It reduces one to a parrot-like repetition of
other men's ideas. Give to old metal at least the fresh
stamp of your own brain.

In thus collecting material by reading, by study, and,
above all, by thinking, one need not gather with a sparing
hand. It is prudent to accumulate everything one can—
ideas, facts, sidelights, inferences, illustrations, quotations :
set it all down ; for one cannot yet tell what will be helpful
when the sermon comes to be built into a whole. What
may be profitably said on any given topic is enormously in
excess of what either can be or ought to be said in a single
sermon. Young preachers, therefore, are not commonly
gravelled for want of matter; the fault they frequently
commit is to put too much or too many things into one
discourse. For now comes the last of the indispensable
steps in sermon preparation : the selection and arrangement
of the material to be used. And it is hard for the beginner
to sacrifice so many of the vivid conceptions and happy
illustrations that have by this time occurred to him.
Selection one knows there must be ; few have any notion at
first how drastic and pitiless it has to be. Luckily, what
cannot be said to-day will keep, if it be worth anything, till
another time.

To guide one in this work of selection, two principles
are given us by the two "fixed points" I spoke of : the
proposition or theme, which is to be the governing thought
of the whole discourse, and the aim or design which it keeps
in view. The former tells us what may be said; the other
what it is best to say.

1. Nothing is admissible which has not a twofold relation to the theme : a connection with it at once logical and
natural. A logical connection, that is, one justified by the
laws of thought; and a natural connection, or one which is
easily recognised by the audience. The former requirement

excludes what is irrelevant, the latter what is far-fetched. The former needs no defence; for it is a law of all reasonable discourse whatever, that it be relevant to its subject. But the second is no less a law of the spoken discourse, where the hearer cannot pause as a reader might, or turn back a page, to make sure what relation your remarks bear to the matter in hand. He needs to see that at once as soon as he hears them. Even in addressing trained or picked audiences, a speaker has to be careful to leave no unspoken gaps in the thinking, nor spring upon the listener unexpected statements, whose relation to what precedes is hard to find. The preacher's audience is never, or hardly ever, a picked one. It is a gathering of all sorts of people, of all ages and both sexes, marked by no feature in common save their common faith, and sure to number some persons who are neither clever nor intent to listen. He should never show his own ingenuity by dragging in far-fetched observations at the cost of leaving such hearers in a fog.

2. This reference to the subject of discourse determines only what is admissible; to discover what is most pertinent or fittest to be said on any occasion, one must have regard to the end or aim of the speech and the character of the audience. The ideal sermon is one in which, out of the mass of permissible matter, those things are selected which are best adapted to tell on a particular audience so as to produce a particular result. Whether the preacher's aim be to instruct, or to convince, or to evoke religious feeling, or to persuade to a course of action—be it what it may— his business from first to last is to make for his object, choosing those points which are most effective for the end he has in view. Thus a good sermon is tied, so to say, by those two "fixed points" behind and before.

While one is selecting one's points or the material to be used, it has probably fallen of itself into groups or what preachers call "heads of discourse." But this final step— "disposition," the rhetoricians term it—is too important to be left to itself.

It is characteristic of any preconcerted address as distinguished from a casual talk, no matter how important, that the speaker, knowing beforehand what he means to say, shall say it in lucid order and consecutive arrangement, finishing each point ere he proceeds to the next. This makes it inevitable that his discourse should fall into masses, whether these be numbered, named, and formally announced, or not. Every organised discourse must thus possess structure, its paragraphs being properly related to each other and succeeding one another in proper order. Such a method there must be in the speaker's mind, and well-nigh every speaker finds it advisable to set it down on paper for his own guidance. There is much diversity in the fulness with which preachers work out their ideas in their written plan or outline. The beginner at least is counselled to block out with considerable detail how each division is to be handled: noting the line of discussion, the subsidiary ideas, the references to life and experience, the illustrations. An artist is not usually content to sketch in the rudest outline the composition of his future picture. He makes a careful study of each of its main parts.

One of the most frequent faults to be met with among preachers of the present day is the lax or structureless arrangement of their discourses. A prevalent tendency is to let the sermon flow on like an essay, with no marked breaks, each part linked to the preceding, as it seems, by the loosest or most casual suggestion. It is a frequent method in the Anglican pulpit, where the sermon is so often brief and inartificial. If the preacher would avoid such a formless essay, let him build up in his study a firmly-knit and organised framework, all the members of which are articulated into a central backbone of robust connected thinking. Phillips Brooks seems to me wholly right in protesting against the current ridicule of "divisions" as unwise.[1]

This leaves us, of course, quite open to consider when

[1] *Op. cit.* p. 177.

or how far the congregation should be told beforehand what
the order of the sermon is to be. The custom is one on
which a good deal of difference exists. It used at one time
to be an all but invariable pulpit habit. Fénelon, who
is opposed to it, remarks that "it is not usual with ancient
orators or the Fathers, but has been inherited by modern
preachers from the schoolmen." [1] The most recent fashion
is against it. The leading advantage gained by indicating
from the outset what order it is proposed to observe, is that
it assists a dull hearer to follow with ease, and afterwards
to recall, the course of thought. Few would preach a
sermon to children without well-marked stepping-stones or
even pithy catch-words; and for a similar reason an uneducated or slow-witted audience is the better for them.
In the case of a sermon that is abstruse or argumentative,
even an average congregation will trace the unfolding of
the preacher's meaning more surely for knowing beforehand
what his line of thought is to be. Every wise speaker aims
at being at least luminous; and most audiences grow impatient of what it requires an effort to follow, and hate to
be perplexed by a tortuous or obscure discussion. On the
other hand, no audience cares to be treated like children;
and, when the division adopted is quite a conventional one
or is obviously suggested by the text, it sounds like an
insult to their intelligence for a dull preacher with a solemn
air to lay down his "heads" *ore rotundo*, possibly repeating
them twice over. To intelligent and practised auditors, the
charm of a discourse may consist in anticipating the line
of treatment or in watching it gradually unfold as the
address proceeds. Such an audience is apt to grow listless
if it has been told beforehand what the argument is to
be. Better let it open out piece by piece, and gather it
up at the close. No hard and fast rule, it is clear, can
be laid down. In each case a skilful preacher will be
guided by the character of his sermon or the insight of his

---

[1] *Dialogues sur l'Eloquence*, Dial. II. Vinet, in discussing the question,
cites authorities both for and against. See his *Homilétique*, Pt. ii. chap. 3.

congregation. Only, if he decide to mention his "heads" at the outset, let him do so quietly in terse clear words or sometimes in memorable phrases.

There is little room for choice left to the modern preacher as to the number of divisions his sermon may contain. The Puritans, who preached by the hour-glass, could indulge in a good many main "heads" with sub-divisions under each; but the brief half-hour or so pre-scribed by modern habit does not justify subdivisions at all, as a rule, and reduces the heads to a very few. To make too many fresh starts robs a speech of continuity and diminishes its effect; for a long list of particulars recalls a table of contents, and leaves no time to dwell on any point to the degree that is indispensable for oratorical momentum or impression. Hence there can hardly be more than four with advantage; rarely so many. The frequency with which three occur is no reason for avoiding that number; it only testifies to its convenience.

Errors on this point are rare: a more frequent fault is, to be so taken up with one division, usually the first one, that it gets more than its share of attention, insufficient time is left for the rest, and the symmetry of the whole is spoilt. The origin of this is a want of balance in the measure of interest or of pains bestowed on each part during one's preparation of the sermon. Do not suffer any division to bulk disproportionately before your own mind. If you do, another danger arises—of weakening the hearer's interest through over-elaboration. His mind should never be suffered to grow slack by a too slow movement of thought, but be carried forward from point to point before any idea has had time to become stale. Movement is the life of oratory. No single part is to be dwelt on as if it were the whole; but only as a part in its relation to the governing idea. When it has been long enough before the audience to make an impression proportioned to its relative import-ance, it is time to go on to the next.

But these transitions it is confessedly difficult to manage

17

well. Opposite extremes have to be avoided. The continuity of impression proper to a speech is lost by any stop
in the flow of thought, so complete as to create the effect of
a quite fresh commencement. To let an audience down in
this fashion is to forfeit what has been gained in the way
of interest or of warmth of feeling; and it is doubtful if
an equal measure of attention can be recovered again.
This is one reason why sermons so frequently prove less
effective in the closing than in the opening quarter of an
hour. On the other extreme, it is a mistake to fill up the
interstice between one part and another so completely that
boundaries are obliterated. For if the speaker glide imper-
ceptibly from each division to the next, the advantage of
having divisions at all is largely sacrificed. The tired listener
gets no breathing time, no sense of relief. What is worse, he
has no sense of progress. The reposeful consciousness of
having advanced a stage is replaced by a breathless chase
after the speaker.   Nothing therefore is gained by attempting
to conceal the fact that a fresh " head of discourse " is to begin.

Both of these opposite risks will be best avoided when
there is a natural connection between the parts, so that
each division leads on the next, and the hearer's mind
advances to the new matter as to something higher.   On
every account preachers ought to pay special heed to this
law of advance in sermon-construction.   There are, in truth,
no more than two chief rules to govern the relation of one
part of a discourse to the rest.   The one is that the divisions
be logically co-ordinate, that is, that a conception which
is in logic subordinate is not to be placed alongside or on a
level with another which is higher or more general.[1]   But

[1] This is best seen by an example of the violation of the rule. THEME :
God is not moved to save man by any merit in him :—
    1. This is a truth of the highest importance to the sinner.
    2. It is as important for the saint as for the sinner.
    3. While it keeps the saint humble, it also helps to make him holy.
It is obvious that (1) and (2) exhaust the bearings of the subject, and (3)
falls as subordinate matter under (2).   This example, like others in the footnotes, is taken from a printed sermon.

this indispensable rule is too obvious to be often violated by any clear thinker. The second one aims at a superior kind of excellence, not logical, but oratorical, and is more difficult to attain. Indeed, it is not always possible of attainment; but where it is, it should be striven after. It is that the ideas should succeed each other in an order which constitutes a progress, each being in one way or other an advance upon its forerunner "in interest, in vigour, in emotion," and all of them carrying the hearers forward to the intended conclusion. If you merely set a string of parallel particulars alongside one another, with no further relation between them than that they are equally drawn from your subject, you can build up a good and reasonable discourse; but it will not be one of the highest order. It must lack that movement towards an end which every speaker instinctively seeks after. Daniel Webster, the American orator, is said to have defined eloquence as "always a progress, on, right on, to an object." If the life of oratory be movement, then advance is the power of its life. In support and explanation, M. Coquerel's counsel here may be quoted with advantage :—

" I cannot too earnestly press upon our young ministers to break themselves to this necessity of their task, to this condition of their success. They must mature their plan in such a manner as to classify the ideas, the groups of ideas, the arguments, the examples, the exhortations, in the order of their importance. They must overturn their plan if it has not led as its result to this indispensable order of the matter; they must even, when the sermon is written, change the disposition of its parts, transpose them, and, by means of new transitions, modify their series, if it is discovered that the strong arguments have taken a place before the weaker, the moving appeals before the more tranquil, and aspiration full of fervour before the remindal of an example, an apostrophe or a prayer before a calm argumentation. This is the price of success." [1]

[1] *Op. cit.* pp. 105-106 of the English translation.

(4) *Conclusion*

What I have just called the "law of advance" throws the weight of a sermon forward, to rest where it ought to do on the close; call it peroration, or "application," or what you will. All masters of the art bid us be particular about the conclusion: "the trying and perilous part" of the discourse.[1] To end feebly is to lose half the battle; because it fails to leave the desired impression planted firm and full upon the minds of the hearers.

That there ought to be a conclusion appears from the uses which it serves. These are two at least. First, to satisfy the audience that the natural and intended close has been reached. It is one thing to stop—no mortal can tell why; and quite another thing to conclude, because what you set out to do has been done. A good sermon is bound to end where it does, and the "conclusion" ought to satisfy the hearer of this by giving him a feeling of completion. The other use of a peroration is to gather to a point or climax, not the theme now so much as the design or scope of the speaker, so as to leave the audience in the mood, or full of the purpose, which he desires to create in them. Just as the introduction led up to the theme, so does the conclusion bear closely on the aim of the discourse—the practical issue with a view to which the whole has been planned.

This near relation to the design of the sermon cannot fail of course to impart to the conclusion a practical character. But it is by no means indispensable that it should assume the shape of an exhortation, or of an express "application," as it is termed. If the bearings of the subject on life and duty have been kept steadily in view all along, this is not necessary. If they have not, it is apt to be formal. People are little moved by admonitions that are railed off in a place by themselves, or that only come in by rule at the end as a concession to pulpit traditions. The

---

[1] Hoppin, *op. cit.*

mere suspicion that anything of that sort is said *pro formâ*
or in cool blood, is fatal to its moral effect.   Besides, it looks
as if, until the "application" is reached, both preacher and
hearers might safely forget that the Gospel has to do with
the actual needs of living men.   One must never suffer an
audience to take the sermon for an academic or intellectual
exercise through five-sixths of its length, only redeemed for
pulpit use by a sting in its tail.

But when a preacher speaks all through as a pastor,
with his finger on the pulse of his people's life, in sympathy
with their religious difficulties, trials, or shortcomings, and
with a message for them from God in his mouth, he can
find many an effective mode of closing quite unlike the
conventional "application."   It may be by a rapid summary
of the line of thought pursued; or by a sudden rising from
details to a wider outlook which commands them all; or by
a sharp contrast, even, which sets off the main lesson with
unlooked-for vividness as by a foil; or by reverting swiftly
to the opening, to end upon the thought from which he
set out.   In any case, it ought to be the most animated,
or, at all events, the most intense, part of the whole discourse.   Not long, however; nor, though for sheer impressiveness the most weighty, need it be the most ambitious
in style.   Rather the reverse.   If the sermon has been
impassioned, it is often wise to let the audience down to
a quieter level of feeling ere you close.   This is to be done
either by addressing the conscience, an address usually
marked by calm solemnity rather than by excitement; or
by a deeper utterance of religious emotion, and religious
emotion is calm when it is deep.   No preacher who knows
his business will be afraid of emotion.   What is a sermon
but an utterance of the speaker's own religious life in order
to enkindle or to intensify religious life in his hearers?
And of all life the very heart, the central fire, is feeling.
On one hand of it stands truth: with that the speaker
begins; it is his instrument for awakening feeling.   On the
other hand of it stands action: to that the hearer is to be

led. Between the two, linking them together, there must be high, spiritual, noble emotion. Truth published in love breeds it and feeds it. Once generated, it sets the will in motion; impels it to righteous effort and generous deeds. No mistake is greater than when a young preacher sets out with a dread for emotional preaching, or with a contempt for it.[1] Now, whatever warmth of feeling, moral or devotional, has been kindled in the minister's own spirit or in a sympathetic listener during the course of the address, ought to glow in the peroration, attaining there its completest and most artistic utterance, that the audience of worshippers may be sent away subdued, melted, or inspired with holy love for holy things.

How is such a conclusion to be studied or prepared beforehand? To realise in cool blood what it shall contain is barely possible. I grant it; but it ought not to be prepared in cool blood. All through the preparation of a discourse it is desirable that the minister should himself be in the mood of feeling which befits it. Have we not heard sermons where the thoughts were solemn to pathos, yet they were discussed with the air of detachment that becomes a critic? A man's theme may lead him to the very fount of tears where simplicity and tenderness are asked for, and he may treat us to flights of fancy or flamboyant rhetoric. Enter on the drafting of a sermon as a purely intellectual exercise, and you will be frigid till the close. But the preparation is to be itself a rehearsal. One needs to get into the spirit of the address when quietly ruminating over it in the study, until one comes to experience its emotions as they are to be experienced in the delivery of it. While you are musing, the fire must burn. I do not care how it is managed: it may be on one's knees.[2] Let the preacher keep human souls before him as he studies at home: flesh

---

[1] Cf. the late Dr. Joseph Parker's defence of preaching "with tears in it," in his *Ad Clerum*, p. 70 (Lond. 1873).

[2] One of good old Cotton Mather's "Counsels" is: "Study your sermon on your knees" (*Manducatio ad Ministerium*, 1710, sect. xvi.).

and blood hearers whom it is to be his business next Lord's Day to move, to rouse, to warn, to comfort, to persuade, to save. Let him suppose himself already in the pulpit, bent to reach and subdue the hearts and wills of his audience; then it will not be so hard to discover of what sort his closing words should be. Nature will tell him, moved as he is himself, what will move them; by what swift, brief, intense gathering up of all the passion of his theme, sweet be it or solemn, he can bear down upon these souls before him, and lift them up with himself to God.

CHAPTER XXII

DICTION AND DELIVERY

Up to this point, diction, or the language in which the preacher is ultimately to clothe his thoughts, has not come at all prominently into view. It can be left to the moment of delivery. The preparation of a careful, even full, plan or outline of all that is to be said, and of the order in which one part is to follow another, is practically indispensable; but nothing else is so. Whether the work of preparation is to be carried a step further by writing out the sermon in full before it is preached, though an important question, is a secondary one. The precomposed and the extemporised discourse have their respective recommendations and drawbacks. Whichever plan may be on the whole the better, there are some men who will do their best work in the one way, and some in the other. I suppose each of us can only find out his own aptitudes and limitations by experimenting with both. But in deciding the question, one has also to take into account the advantages and defects of each method.

The chief benefit of writing out one's sermons is to secure a better English style. Composing pen in hand, a man can weigh his words and pick them. He can prune and polish his phrases. He can construct his periods with skill. He can give to his sentences balance and cadence. He can delete awkward, obscure, and feeble expressions. He can avoid what is tautological, or inexact, or inflated. He acquires a more copious vocabulary, and superior tact in using it. In short, it is in his power to train himself to write in a style which shall combine the three qualities commended by the rhetoricians, of perspicuity, force, and beauty.

Every one must recognise that this is to gain a most material aid to effective preaching. Language is our instrument; and whatever enables us to wield it with greater mastery, contributes to our power as speakers. According to Cardinal Maury, it is the supreme merit of their style which has assured a long life to the masterpieces of the French pulpit.[1] The advantage of a finished style, however, is not one the value of which is equal for every audience or for every preacher. It takes a fairly cultured congregation to appreciate the niceties of language, or to be offended by looseness of construction. And there are some speakers whose skill in composition is never likely to be very great. If a man who at his best can only write flaccid or indifferent English is called upon to address people who are not at all sensitive to such defects, he may not after all gain so much by writing out his sermons as to be worth the time and labour.

Besides, the effort after style has accompanying risks. Chief of these is the risk that through over-elaboration in the absence of an audience, a preacher's diction become too literary, too remote from spoken language. In the study one is apt to compose like a book, not like a speech. One comes even to forget how great the difference is between diction intended to be read and that which is addressed to an audience. The directness of a speech is apt to go. The fulness of utterance in which not much is left to be supplied, the ease in passing from one point to another, the amplitude of exposition, the needful repetition of an idea to catch every listener, the use of the personal pronouns, the apostrophe, the interrogation, the impromptu air:—all these features of spoken style are apt to suffer; and instead of an address, you may get, what one too often hears from the pulpit, a disquisition or an essay.

[1] *Essai*, sect. 37.

Of course, the recommendations and the defects of extemporising are just the converse of these. He who stands up to say what he has not previously written is pretty sure at least to speak to the people, which is after all the main thing. He gains in ease and naturalness. He is direct and pointed. His address wears a look of reality. It is easy for him to adopt a familiar tone ; and although a young preacher fresh from the classroom may be chary of a semi-conversational manner, all really popular speakers employ it as the basis of their address, only rising in exceptional passages to a more solemn or elevated style. This does not mean that the average pulpit level is not to be above the bald, disjointed chitchat of friendly talk. At its lowest it ought to be more like the intelligent and correct monologue of a cultured and practised speaker when he is addressing his friend on a more than usually serious subject. The leisurely pre-meditation which has gone before, the sacredness of the occasion, and the sympathy of numbers ought all to lift the pulpit orator to a level of chastened passion and well ordered forceful speech, such as conversation in private never or rarely attains. But, then, extempore speech has the defects of its virtues. It easily becomes slipshod. There is risk of becoming impoverished in the vocabulary at one's command. The same poor, thin phrases recur ; the same forms of construction. Sometimes the right word comes, sometimes not. Sentences will trip and get dis-located. Grammar even may suffer. Periods end feebly or run on with loose articulation. You repeat yourself ; even lose your thread. It is hard to keep such a mode of sermonising, when exclusively practised, from degenerating into a maundering, ill-put-together talk.

There are clearly strong points to be scored, then, by either method, if only it be a success; but whichever a man selects, he will need to secure himself against its pitfalls.

A second reason sometimes adduced for writing out

sermons previous to delivery, is that this leaves the
preacher less dependent on the mood of the moment. A
man can choose his time; and it is commonly his own
fault if he compose his sermon when out of sorts, or over-
jaded, or in the wrong mood. Having once secured his
manuscript in a happy hour, when fresh from meditation
and full of his subject, he is less dependent on the sympathy
of an audience or the inspiration of the hour of worship.
The truth is that a great many sermons have to be delivered
under most disheartening, uninspiring surroundings. A
chill church, thin pews, unappreciative hearers, fog in the
atmosphere and dulness in the spirit—a thousand things
may occur to work languor in the brain, and to disqualify
the best of us from speaking at our best. When one
listens to a secular orator achieving an oratorical success,
it is on some special occasion, on a subject of the day,
before a packed and eager throng of partisans ready to
punctuate his hits with their plaudits, and reporters below
to give his words a wider circulation. Then, to be sure, if
a man can speak at all, he ought to speak well. The
preacher has none of these attendant stimuli. Before the
same people, week after week, in some obscure, ill-lighted,
or half-empty chapel, it may be, with no public outside
waiting for his message : the conditions are not favourable
for eloquence. I know what can be said on the other side.
The minister of Christ speaks on the most momentous and
inspiring of all themes, with eternal issues depending.
He reasons, he pleads, he beseeches in the name of God.
He has words to say that are mighty to pierce the conscience and to break or melt the heart. Let him only be
alive to his message and to the needs of human souls :
should he want any other inspiration ? I recollect all that.
But is it not often easier for a man to realise these things
in the solitude of his study, when he muses and prays,
easier then to pour out his soul in " words that burn "
when he is writing with an imaginary congregation before
his mental eye, than it will be in that trying moment when

he must stand up to address an unsympathetic handful of worshippers ?   And if he goes to the pulpit with a discourse already composed in such a lively frame, when thought was fertile and emotion vivid, it may be easier for him to withstand the influences that depress, to revive the ardour of composition, and pour his thoughts through channels which they fashioned for themselves in a happier hour.

All this is true ; for some men very true.   But the independence of external influences which is thus gained is only comparative after all ; and it is purchased at a price. For, on the other hand, he who has composed beforehand is much less able to catch and respond to the inspiration, when that is favourable—or to create it if it be absent—of the place, the audience, and the hour.   In fact, he is not so vigorously summoned to do so, as if he extemporised.   He makes therefore, as a rule, less effort to put himself into sympathy with his hearers, or to rouse them into sympathy with his own mood.   Too often he is content to recite with propriety what he came prepared to say.   Whereas, an extempore speaker is lost unless he can rouse both himself and his audience.   That very necessity puts him on his mettle.   It peremptorily calls upon him to exert himself. It makes his mind move more nimbly.   It compels him to cast himself upon whatever help he can get from the listening people, be they few or many.   In such circumstances even a single quick responsive auditor becomes a valuable aid ; should the interchange of feeling betwixt speaker and congregation grow general and active, then the free speaker is in a position to take full advantage of it.   He has more liberty to deviate from his intended course of thought.   He can profit by those swift sideglances, happy and suggestive illustrations, touches of pathos, momentary appeals, or the like, which offer themselves in the heat of speaking, never can be reached in any other way.   Nothing then comes between the orator and his audience.   Nothing hinders him from rising on the rising tide of their emotions to his true throne—to heights of passion, and that sway over the minds and wills of men which is the highest triumph of eloquence. If the extemporiser must at times fall flat or fail, at least he has a chance at other times to attain his best. The written discourse keeps closer to the safe level of a speaker's average.

Between the relative claims, then, of these two methods, every preacher has to strike the balance for himself. Since excellent results can be attained on either plan, one's choice may be largely guided by other considerations; chiefly by these two: which method does most justice to one's own powers, and which promises the best results among the kind of people to whom one ministers. In the majority of cases, however, the counsel of perfection seems to me to be this: acquire a command over both methods by conscientiously and steadily practising both; with this additional precaution that each of them be practised in such a way as will reduce its disadvantages to a minimum.

To some extent, at least, both must be practised if the full benefit of either is to be secured. Those authors who have most strongly urged free speech in the pulpit are at one in insisting that an extempore preacher should train himself for his work by diligent practice at written composition. M. Coquerel, for example, thinks it necessary to postpone improvising until one has had a long experience of written sermons.[1] M. l'Abbé Bautain, who has written an excellent little book on "The Art of Extempore Preaching," heads one of his paragraphs thus: "That to speak well in public, one must first know how to write."[2] In the first of his lectures at Union Seminary on "The conditions of success in preaching without notes," Dr. Storrs of Brooklyn says: "Always be careful to keep up the habit of writing with whatever of skill, elegance, and force you can command."[3] So indispensable does he take such pen-practice

[1] *Op. cit.*, Eng. tr. pp. 123–151.
[2] *Op. cit.*, Lond. 1860, p. 66.
[3] London, 1892, p. 37. The *Hints on Extemporaneous Preaching* of an

to be, that he advises men who do not write their sermons, to write something else,—essays, lectures, or newspaper articles. But if it be so needful to write, why not compose at least one sermon a week ? Surely this ought to form a serviceable style for pulpit extemporising, better than writing for the press would do.

Nor is it one whit less incumbent on every preacher, whether his sermons be written or not, to acquire the power of speaking without verbal preparation. Occasions are constantly arising in ministerial work, as every minister knows, when he is called upon to speak extempore. Evangelistic addresses, for instance, are best unwritten. So with sermons to children. The mid-week discourse should be free. It is an intolerable strain to be obliged to put on paper every week two Sunday discourses and a week-day one as well. Besides, there are frequent calls for platform speeches at public meetings or at Church gatherings, when the modern pastor is expected to show himself ready and effective, sometimes on the spur of the moment. If for all such purposes a minister needs to acquire the power to command his thoughts in face of an audience, and utter them off-hand with self-posession, fluency, and a fair measure of force and correctness, why not use this power at least once a week in the pulpit ?

The other suggestion which appears to me to have value is that while a minister carries on the practice of both methods abreast, he should so manage each of them as to gain from it a maximum of advantage with a minimum of drawbacks.

1. When he has to preach a sermon which he has not written, let him take every precaution to guard against the chief dangers of improvisation. These are, I suppose, loose thinking, a bad arrangement of matter, and weak, flabby verbiage. I think the best way to avoid all three is first to

older American divine, Dr. Henry Ware of Harvard, are very sensible. They will be found reprinted at the end of Ripley's *Sacred Rhetoric*, (Boston, 1849).

spare neither pains nor time in the preparation of one's matter through all the stages described in the foregoing chapter. Only it is not enough that a digested and arranged scheme for the whole discourse from opening to close be set down on paper. He must get it into his head. One of the best advantages of free speech is its freedom. To attain that in its highest degree, no scrap of notes should be used in the pulpit; for any dependence on paper is so far as it goes a fetter. But it is impossible to dispense entirely with notes unless the plan of the discourse has been gone over mentally beforehand so often that it is now lodged securely in the memory. The speaker who trusts wholly to the moment for the form of expression needs to have a complete mastery of the road he is to travel, through all its stages.

For the success of extempore speaking, it is likewise of the utmost consequence that the minister go to the pulpit in a frame of earnest religious feeling. He needs to be in the spirit of his message; and if he is to be raised above trepidation or "the fear of man," let him see that his soul is charged with its urgency and with the sacredness of his office. Solitude and leisure for silent meditation and prayer are to be secured just before the service begins. M. Bautain, who presses this point, calls it the "final moral preparation."[1] When the Gospel messenger is full of his message and warm with zeal for God and love for men, then let him speak with confidence as the Spirit gives him utterance. Let him trust in the act of speaking to the impulse of the moment for the words in which to put his meaning; taking care only to keep the prearranged thread of the discourse well in hand. The charm of this kind of sermon is just to be impromptu, a live utterance of the thought and emotion of the hour, in which (as Milton has it in a famous passage) "words . . . like so many nimble and airy servitors, trip about him at command, and, in well-ordered files, as he would wish, fall aptly into their own

[1] *Op. cit.* chap. 17.

places." [1]   That is, provided they are there at the speaker's
command.   But for this the possession of an opulent
vocabulary is essential.   Louis Stevenson has told how he
trained himself to write by noting down choice words met
with in his reading and practising himself in the use of
them.   Some such method is still more helpful for a
preacher.   The stylist must be a connoisseur in words, deft
at the selection and the setting of them.   But the orator
needs in addition to have his stores within reach, ready of
recall.   Then may he with safety surrender himself to the inspiration of the moment.   It is not well to look backward now
to any chamber jottings, trying to recall phrases or forms of
speech previously set down.   Launch yourself courageously
on the broad bosom of your subject and make for the end
of your voyage—the impression to be left upon the hearer.
It is quite possible to do this without abandoning control
over the course of thought, or over yourself.   Never lose
self-command.   Hold your powers in rein, and let the
judgment keep its hand on the emotions.   Having calmly
decided ere you begin what course you are to steer, keep to
it.   A certain liberty the practised speaker may permit
himself, to enrich his address with brief felicitous additions
suggested on the spot; but if he abuse this privilege by
rambling too far from the course marked out, he throws
himself away, and will find it hard to recover himself
again.

2. Suppose, again, that the sermon is to be written out
in the study : is there any way by which the drawbacks of
a written style can be minimised ?   I think there is.

In the first place, write rapidly at a heat, and correct at
leisure.   Sir Walter Scott said that his best passages were
those composed with the greatest rapidity.   That is by no
means the method of every great author; but it is the way
to imitate with the pen the ease and fluency of speech.   It
may even be best, where it is practicable, for the whole to
be written at a sitting.   Slow or unpractised writers, whose

[1] *Apology for Smectymnuus.*

style is still unformed, cannot do that. But each main division, at all events, should be thrown off at a single effort; and when the work is resumed, it is worth while to read aloud with energy what has been already composed, in order to get back into the swing of composition (having first, of course, endeavoured by prayer and meditation to get one's mind back into the appropriate mood). If the thread be taken up in cold blood, the impetus is lost and the unity of tone is apt to be sacrificed. Nor should the writer ever suspend composition near the conclusion of a sermon.

Such rapid composition is only to be recommended, at least to any but the most practised writers, on the understanding that much will be done in the way of revision. Without careful correction, the manuscript, rapidly written, remains an extempore effusion, and might as well have been improvised in church. Recollect Roscommon's line :

"And write with fury, but correct with phlegm." [1]

The chief end of revision is to sharpen the edge of style, quite as much as to purify it, by pruning away unnecessary epithets, redundant phrases, technical or philosophical terms, inflated diction too high-flown for the thought expressed, and especially all obscurity of statement. Its object is not, as some suppose, a style smoothed or polished to the utmost. On the contrary, diction that is somewhat rugged or broken, especially if it betray the speaker's intensity, besides being closer akin to impromptu speech, will bear upon the listener's mind with forceful impact, when the lapse of finished and flowing periods only soothes his ear. Only care must be taken not to pare away the easy flow and fulness of what was written in haste to a point at which sentences become too abrupt or elliptical to be readily apprehended when first heard. The style best suited for a preacher's purpose is that which lets the ideas glide at once without effort into the intelligence of every hearer, yet at the same time drives them home to his heart

[1] *Poems* by the Earl of Roscommon, Lond. 1717, p. 39.

18

with the utmost force compatible with such ease of apprehension.

Though the fault is not at present specially common, some young preachers need to be on their guard against what is called "an ambitious style." That comes whenever the words are stronger than the thinking, or more ornate and passionate than the state of feeling justifies. No doubt, when an orator is impassioned, the oratorical temperament involves a certain amount of exaggeration, and oratorical effect probably demands it. No imaginative or emotional speaker confines himself to the cautious balanced phrases of a philosopher. He pictures, he amplifies, he uses hyperboles, that he may infuse into his hearer some of his own warm feeling. This is legitimate, but only so long as there is feeling behind no less real and keen than the language suggests. Inflation is at once detected. Indeed, the skilful orator speaks below rather than above his actual state of emotion, knowing that self-restraint is an element of power. Nor can any speaker tarry for more than a moment or two at his supreme point of intensity, but has to give himself and his auditors immediate relief by falling to a more usual pitch.

Another way to avoid the stiffness of written style is to follow a suggestion I have already had occasion to offer— that he who is writing for the pulpit should keep his audience before his mind while the pen is in his hand. If he come to the act of composition, as I have supposed him to do, with mind and heart full of a train of ideas designed to work some special profit for an actual congregation, there is nothing to hinder him from preaching while he writes. If he suppose himself to be addressing the people, then he will study to put every point as he would try to put it to a real listener, to whom he wished to convey his meaning with the utmost impressiveness. Some men, in fact, are accustomed to compose in this way without writing at all, walking up and down their room. They have the faculty of reproducing in church what has thus been rehearsed at home. Few can do that; but any one can write with an imaginary audience before him. It is a homiletic habit of composition by which the essay sort of sermon is escaped. The notion of a real speech is kept up, and the spirit of one is consequently caught. When in the course of composing or afterwards, one reads over what has been written, it is always wise to read it, or deliver it, aloud, as though one were preaching it, for this tests its fitness for its purpose. It shows whether it is direct enough, and lucid enough, and forcible enough, to go home to the hearer. It serves also to show how far the collocation of sounds is capable of easy enunciation, of rhythmical delivery, and of being pronounced with sufficient vigour for oratorical effect.

The sermon only comes into existence, in the true sense of the word, by being " delivered," spoken, that is, by the preacher as a real and present utterance of himself to his audience. We talk, indeed, of written or printed sermons, but in strict use of words the manuscript is no more than an aid to the speaker, and the published volume nothing but a report of what has been spoken. The sermon itself is a speech, and as such is born and dies in the hour of its delivery. Nor is this a verbal quibble, but a fact which no preacher can safely allow himself to forget. When it is remembered, no argument is wanted to convince him that his work is not over when the discourse has been prepared, not even when it lies fully written out upon his desk; that delivery is not an accident, but the very crown and end of all, for which the rest has been merely preliminary: so that to a perfect or finished sermon there goes a perfect and finished utterance of it from the heart to listening ears.

The minister who is most in danger of forgetting these things is the man who writes, and from the same manuscript may preach the same discourse, not once, but frequently. But even after a sermon has been written, the preacher has still to prepare himself to preach it. Like a written outline, it is but an aid to speech. It is to be used, not abused. The faculty which enables one to use in the pulpit whatever has been prepared beforehand is memory; and a manuscript is abused when memory is denied any share in the operation at all. While, therefore, there are several degrees of dependence on one's manuscript which are legitimate, there is one which I can only term illegitimate. It is when the pages are simply read aloud. When you see a man in the pulpit so entirely dependent on his manuscript that his eye must trace every line of it, and neither voice nor gesture differs from that of any educated person who reads aloud from a printed page what he may never have seen before, then you see what I mean by illegitimate use of it. The effect on the hearer is very much as if the address did not proceed from the man at all, but only passed through him, taking sound upon his lips. It has ceased to be a speech. It has become a lecture ; and this is fatal to the art of preaching. We may all have chanced to listen to such pulpit utterances ; but if I am not mistaken, the Church in Christendom which has sinned and suffered most in this way is the Church of England. Reading, pure and simple, of the clergyman's own composition or of another man's, at times from a printed or a lithographed page, has been the bane of the modern Anglican pulpit, and at one time went near to kill pulpit eloquence in that great communion. For, what is "delivery"? It is a giving forth to the hearer, in the best way attainable, of the best that is in the speaker: the projection, in other words, through voice and eye and gesture, of what lives and burns in his bosom of Divine truth and sacred emotion, so that by the mystic contagion of personality it shall possess and sway his audience. The true preacher is no reciter, or actor, who repeats the language or personates the mood of another, no, nor even calls up emotions which he himself felt once but does not feel now. It is the man's being possessed at the moment by the ideas and the feelings which he utters that makes the utterance of them real, living, not histrionic.

If a manuscript, then, is to be made use of at all, the preacher must free himself from such a slavish and me-

chanical reading of its pages, by calling in considerable
aid from the memory. There are three ways of doing this,
which differ in the degree in which the orator trusts to his
recollection; and all of them carry the sanction of high
example.

The one which, on the whole, has probably been most
frequently adopted, at least by great preachers, is learning
by heart. We call this " committing the sermon to memory,"
because in it the speaker's dependence on verbal recollection
is at its maximum. The masterpieces of the French pulpit
in the Louis Quatorze period, like many another famous
oration, were produced in this fashion. These French
preachers believed themselves to be following the classic
example of Greek and Roman orators. Certainly there has
been a general impression that the speeches of Demosthenes
and of Cicero, like Burke's great speech at the trial of
Warren Hastings, were elaborately composed and memorised.[1]
At any rate, if classic orators declaimed from memory, it is
fairly certain that Greek preachers in the age of Chrysostom
did not always adopt this method. Be that as it may, no
one doubts that splendid efforts of eloquence are attainable
on this plan; but it is on one condition—the discourse must
be learnt perfectly, not imperfectly. It is one thing, as
M. Coquerel warns us, to be able to recite it accurately " in
the solitude of the study," and another to " know it surely
enough, firmly enough, to deliver it in the pulpit and to
yield ourselves in delivering it to the warmth of elocution
which we possess." [2] To do this is easy for a very few; for
a good many it becomes possible by practice ; for some it is
impossible. If a man either cannot learn with verbal accuracy at all, or can only learn it well enough to say it like a
schoolboy's lesson with stiffness and effort, he had better try
some other plan. His labour will be wasted. Even in the
case of many who think they commit with ease and complete

[1] This is strongly questioned, indeed, by Fénelon, though his reasons do
not appear conclusive.
[2] *Op. cit.* p. 120.

correctness, the result is a bondage which spoils the delivery. One has heard of preachers who, if their memory tripped in a single phrase, were unable to proceed. I have known some who, during the recital, were consciously following in fancy the lines of their manuscript and mentally turning over its leaves. Others I have seen whose effort to recollect compelled them to keep their eyes fixed on a certain part of the opposite wall or a mark in the front of the gallery. Even Bourdaloue is said to have kept his eyes shut for the same reason. Such bondage, of course, is fatal to the comfort of the speaker; but it does worse, it robs his delivery of naturalness, spontaneity, and charm.

Escape from this difficulty is sought by an intermediate method, which aims at combining the freedom of extempore speech, with the precision of a written style. The manuscript is in this case conned and rehearsed until the ideas in their order can be readily recalled, and to a large extent even the language remains in the memory. This rehearsing is best done aloud. The manuscript is then discarded in the pulpit, as in the former case; only the preacher makes no deliberate effort to recall its words and sentences. He trusts at the moment of delivery to extemporisation; launching himself on his theme with no concern about verbal reproduction of his written pages at all. So much of the language as has stuck to his remembrance is suffered to come back to him if it will; for the rest, he depends on the inspiration of the hour. This plan suits many, perhaps a majority of speakers, very well. It does not burden the memory with task-work, if only the orator can rid himself of all anxiety to recall and repeat word for word. In the case of most men, a good deal of the diction, and that the best of it, will offer itself in the heat of delivery unsought for; and what thus comes to their lips will be more apt and choice than if the sermon had never been composed at all. But the success of this method must depend, partly on the extent to which the process of learning from the manuscript has been carried, and partly on the completeness with which the half-learned manuscript with its well-turned periods can be thrown to the winds as soon as the speaker is in the pulpit. Hankering after what has been written spoils it. The preacher must think of nothing but of his subject and of his audience, just as if he had never written down a word.

There is yet a third way distinct from both of these. Instead of trusting to improvisation to make up for defects of memory, the speaker trusts now to his paper. He has his manuscript before him, but uses it only as an aid to assist his recollection. It approaches to reading, as the last plan approached to extempore speech. Yet it differs from that slavish reading which I called illegitimate in this, that the preacher has made himself sufficiently master of what he has composed, to speak it forth with freedom under the feeling of the moment, aided only by swift, intermittent and momentary glances at the manuscript. Given a good eye, practice enables him to catch as much of the sentences as he requires, without bending over the page, or touching it, or even withdrawing his eye for more than a second at a time from that straightforward look at his audience in which lies so much of the orator's power. It is possible to throw into delivery on this method very nearly as much fire as if one spoke extempore, and not less of earnest directness of speech. The advantage is that the chiselled periods and selected phrases of a careful composition may be closely, all but literally, adhered to.

In choosing among the various methods open to him, the preacher is guided by the desire to deliver his sermon as effectively as it is in his power to do. All the authorities unite in extolling the immense importance of a good delivery; and it needs little experience in sermon-hearing to be aware that far more sermons are spoilt in the delivery than in the preparation of them. But it goes without saying that, differing widely as men do, each has a way of speaking which is his own and is his best. The conscientious preacher, therefore, makes it his endeavour to train himself, as part of his professional equipment, to be as good a speaker as it is in him to be. To a distressing extent young ministers are left in this matter to their own efforts. Were one not so accustomed to it, it would surely strike every observer with astonishment, that, for a calling which has to fulfil the major part of its office through public speaking, candidates are seldom instructed in the art, or, if at all, most imperfectly. The Roman Church is understood to subject promising seminarists, destined for the pulpit, to a very thorough preparation. But Protestant Churches, though they make more use of preaching, wholly overlooked for a long while this part of a minister's equipment; and even where some attention has of late been given to the matter, drill in sermon delivery fills but a slender share of the student's curriculum. Some help a young preacher may gain for himself from elocution classes (although these have not been always in the past of unmixed advantage); some from studying good examples in the pulpit or elsewhere; some from the criticism of a candid friend. But until the governing bodies of Churches and Colleges are moved to take up the subject with the seriousness which it deserves, we must submit to see higher gifts like scholarship and devoted piety neutralised to a painful extent by avoidable defects in delivery. It is not given to everyone to be a finished orator. But it is in the power of any educated man to be made, or to make himself, if he will, a correct and agreeable speaker. Is it unreasonable to ask of an order of men whose main mission in life it is to deliver religious addresses in public, that they shall at least understand the rules of voice production, pronounce the English language with purity, enunciate their message in distinct tones, avoid grotesque gestures, and know how to face an audience with dignity and self-command?

Useful as the art of elocution ought to be for overcoming such faults of voice or manner as mar either the ease or the pleasure with which a speaker is listened to, no art can replace the one indispensable and inimitable quality which gives to all oratory its power over an audience: I mean what the Abbé Mullois calls "the accent of conviction." I do not know where I have met with this sentence; but it is worth remembering: "The essence of preaching is testimony; the force of testimony is conviction; the source of conviction is experience." Out of the depths of his own most cherished and precious experience of the Gospel each preacher fetches that assured faith in its truth, that profound conviction of its power to save, which give value to his personal witness in the pulpit. Let us hear Thomas Carlyle: "As Demosthenes was once asked what was the secret of a fine orator, and he replied: 'Action—action—action'; so, if I were asked it, I should say, 'Belief—belief—belief'"[1] Or let us hear Goethe:

> "Wenn ihr's nicht fühlt, ihr werdet's nicht erjagen,
>   Wenn es nicht aus der Seele dringt,
>   Und mit urkräftigem Behagen
>   Die Herzen aller Hörer zwingt."[2]

Fortunately, this supreme virtue of the orator is within reach of every true preacher. Let him but speak his best out of a full heart: intellect and spirit both occupied at the hour of service by the thought of his theme and of the practical aim at which it is directed. Then let both voice and gesture be spontaneous, unstudied. Whatever previous labour there may have been to discipline the natural powers or to correct acquired faults, all that is over. At the time there must be no conscious art; no thinking about delivery in the act of delivering. Of his subject the preacher thinks, and of his audience; of himself not at all. Only in this way does he speak naturally; that is to say, naturally for him; out of his own nature. And it is a law of speech that every man speaks best when he is so possessed by what he has to say that no attention is left for his way of saying it.

[1] *Lectures on the History of Literature* (Lond. 1892, p. 73).
[2] *Faust*, 1st Scene of the First Part.

CHAPTER XXIII

PREPARATION OF THE PREACHER

APART from the preparation which he makes for every sermon he has to deliver, the minister who has given his life to this work makes it his daily business to discipline himself for its ever better and better performance. The necessity for the former escapes no one; but comparatively few realise that the training of the man to be a preacher is of much higher importance. The process is only begun in college years; it is to be the work of his life. And when this general preparation is well done, "preparations for particular occasions," as Fénelon said long ago, "will cost but little"[1]—certainly they will become surprisingly easier. I know no better instance of this than the case of the late Mr. Spurgeon. Of him it is told that in his later years at least his preparation for a sermon consisted in a few memoranda, the fruit of an hour or two's reflection on Saturday evening. Why was so little sufficient? Because the man had spent his whole life in equipping himself for this supreme function—the one thing he did. All his reading, study, meditation, devotion, intercourse with the world of men, had this for their paramount design—to fit him to preach the better ; until by long labour and incessant practice, it came to be as natural for him to preach as to talk.

It is not to the point to object that self-discipline equal to his will not make every one a Spurgeon. "Each man hath his own gift from God"; and there are constitutional

---

[1] *Dialogues on Eloquence*, Eng. tr., pp. 79–81.

qualifications born with a man which make him a greater
or a better preacher than his fellow. We can only
make the most of such gifts as we possess. But we are
bound to make the most of them; and my point is that
hardly any man turns out a first-rate preacher who does
not concentrate himself upon that as his one task. The
greatest American preacher of last century, Henry Ward
Beecher, lecturing at Yale, said this :

"Preaching will have to be your whole business. Now,
in a small way, everybody preaches. But if you are going
to be professional preachers, if you will make that your
life-calling, it is not probable that there is one of you who
was built large enough to do anything more than that. It
will take all that you have in you, and all your time. I do
not think a man could run a locomotive engine, paint
pictures, keep school, and preach on Sundays to any very
great edification. A man who is going to be a successful
preacher should make *his whole life run toward the pulpit.*" [1]

The words I have italicised hit the nail on the head.
But if one's " whole life is to run toward the pulpit," he
needs to start with and to keep up the highest ideal of his
work. I do not mean that he should set out expecting high
and instant popularity, or visible success. That is about the
worst thing he can begin with. But he should cherish a
very exalted idea of what it is to be a preacher, and consider
how terribly difficult it is to be a good one. The preacher
who has any adequate notion of the possibilities of his calling and of the pitfalls that lie on the road to excellence in
it, will not only judge charitably of indifferent practitioners,
he will be extremely dissatisfied with his own attempts, and
will work very hard and very long to improve upon them.

Then he must be prepared for sacrifices. No man
achieves excellence in any branch who has not made up
his mind to limit himself and surrender many things that
he may concentrate his powers on his one aim. It is the

[1] *Lectures on Preaching delivered at Yale College* (Lond. 1872, p. 53).
A suggestive little book.

athlete's training over again. Many pleasant occupations allure every cultivated man : scholarship, literature, science, wide reading in history, the practice of music or of art. These have to be ruthlessly forsworn, save within those jealous limits inside of which they are either serviceable for your calling or mere recreations after toil. As rival pursuits which withdraw time or strength required for your business, they have to be surrendered. This law of sacrifice is no harder for the minister of Christ than for the artist, or the politician, or the doctor. Only the transgression of it by a minister in a cure, who finds a living secured to him, is less swiftly and sternly punished than in the experience of some other professions. Are we to account in this way for the crowd of commonplace preachers, who are so content with mediocrity that they never improve ?

The lines along which a preacher's constant discipline of himself may proceed are various ; but the ends towards which they all run are two :—to beget in him a homiletic habit of mind, and to furnish him with homiletic material. What is called a homiletic mental habit is, in the words of Dr. Shedd, "such a habitual training of the mind as will impart a sermonising tendency to it." [1] In other words, a determination of one's faculties and pursuits towards preaching the Gospel as one's chief work and chief delight, begets the habit of viewing things in the way most helpful for pulpit use.

For example : it disposes a man habitually to contemplate human life and character in their relations to Christian truth. Just as a physician comes to notice instinctively symptoms of health or unhealth, or, when he visits a place, marks its sanitary conditions, so with the preacher. Men are to him in spiritual need of the Gospel. Their attitude to it, their susceptibility to it or the reverse, how it may best be applied to their case, how it will operate upon them : such points possess for his mind an interest that is paramount. Conversely, the homiletic mind acquires

[1] *Op. cit.* p. 93.

the habit of studying Scripture truths in their relation to the diverse needs of the soul.   Christianity is for the preacher primarily the remedy for moral maladies.   Not its speculative, but its therapeutic, value is what he cares most about. Again: a homiletic mind gets into a way of instinctively ordering and relating ideas in the manner best adapted for setting them instructively and persuasively before other minds.   With some preachers the tendency is "to skeletonise, to construct plans, to examine and criticise discourses with respect to their logical structure."[1]   These excel in the teaching or expounding department of pulpit work.   Others acquire the habit of recognising in every truth of religion its power to influence life, with the impulse to project it upon others in order to impress, inspire, or persuade them to action.   Such excel in the dynamics of the pulpit.   While there are yet others to whom the world of nature is for ever suggesting its affinity with eternal truths of the spiritual world, so that earth becomes for them one vast volume full of symbols and parables of heavenly things.   It is certainly true that such a bent of mind in one direction may be carried too far, with some loss of a wide and liberal outlook upon life.   This defeats itself; since to no man is a large all-round culture of more value than to the preacher.   Still, within limits that are not very often overstept, the homiletic habit makes the preacher fitter for his work and the work itself more easy.

With that there must go hand in hand the accumulation of homiletic material; and there are at least three main lines along which it has to be gathered.   They are (1) the exegetical study of Holy Scripture; (2) systematic reading of the best literature; and (3) familiar and sympathetic intercourse with other men.

1. No wise minister can judge it enough to hunt for ideas or to study texts in his Bible, just when he has a sermon to prepare.   Some busy men, it is to be feared,

[1] Shedd, *ut supra*, p. 94.

allow themselves to be reduced to this in the urgency of
"hand to mouth" work, when public engagements multiply
in their later years. For a junior, or for a rural minister,
no such excuse can be pled, if he neglect the systematic
study of Scripture apart from the exigencies of sermon
preparation. This does not mean the daily or devotional
reading of it, even in the original tongues. That has its
own value. What it means is, carrying on a minute and
exact exegesis of Scripture, in its main portions at least,
with the best available helps. I know that to plod steadily
through a commentary is felt by some to be a dull task.
It may be so, if the mind is merely receptive in the process.
It will not be so, if the student has acquired any power of
independent research. Diverse lines of investigation can
be struck out for himself : such as tracking the growth of
revealed truths, comparing the shade of meaning which
inspired authors attach to the great key-words of theology,
examining their respective ways of conceiving or presenting the Gospel, and the like. The Bible is the preacher's
treasure-field, into which he is to drive shafts, exploring
for himself; and there is no other way to keep his
preaching from growing stale and worked - out. He is
not coining gold into sermons by this process. But he
is amassing hoards of the pure ore, of his own extraction,
which will yield an ample coinage for homiletic use hereafter. I wish every minister could be persuaded how much
better material for sermons can be thus dug out of the
Bible by independent labour than the flimsy and cheap
discourses which a lazy man constructs at second-hand with
the help of homiletic magazines, ready-made "skeletons,"
or even some of those preachers' commentaries in vogue,
where the work is all done for us, and the food all but
cooked ready to be served up. To make a practice of this
is in my judgment to write oneself down a commonplace,
second-rate preacher for life. It is only a shade less
demoralising to the intellect than the custom one sometimes hears about, of borrowing right and left from other

men's sermons. Not such barefaced plagiarism as takes a whole sermon as it stands; but "cribbing" the conception of a discourse, its leading ideas, out of some printed volume, to be dished up afresh with a slender garnishing of one's own. How far that is done I am not aware; but it must weaken a preacher's self-respect, and yield him when done a poor sort of sermon. Anything may be helpful which sets one's mind to work; but nothing can be satisfactory which has not at the least passed through the manipulation of a man's own intellect and taken its shape there.

2. A second line of preparation to preach is found in general reading of extra-theological as well as professional literature. It has two purposes, to discipline and to enrich the mind. Austin Phelps of Andover, who has gone fully into this matter,[1] lays down the rule: "The object is discipline as distinct from accumulation." Of course that suggests the advice, given by many others as well, to pay chief and close attention to those few authors of all time whose "sceptred spirits" rule the thoughts of civilised men, and with whom one can never get too familiar as friends for life. It is sound advice to read, re-read, and study books—they are not numerous—of this select order. But when we have said this, have we exhausted the reading which the preacher needs? I am afraid not. "Accumulation" is not equally valuable with discipline of the intellectual powers; still, it cannot be dispensed with. If a man is to be abreast of the intelligent public he has weekly to address, and to keep up a continual freshness, his reading can hardly be too wide. He cannot afford to be quite ignorant of recent writers who are profoundly influencing the intellectual movements of his time. Audiences expect to find a public teacher well informed in many fields; and nothing that stirs the busy brains of our hearers during the week need come amiss to a capable preacher.

[1] In his volume entitled *Men and Books, or Studies in Homiletics* (Lond. 1882).

Yet to keep his reading within bounds and reasonably select, the minister must be on his guard against wasting time over worthless publications, or such as are at all events worthless for his purpose. Of a great deal of the minor authorship of the passing hour, he should make up his mind to be uninformed. It is scarcely possible to censure too severely that affectation of omniscience which is ashamed to confess ignorance, squandering time on the vain endeavour to turn over every monthly, and know something of every new book that society is talking about. It is really one of the sorest problems a minister has to solve, to understand his age without becoming its creature; sifting the important from the trashy in current literature, that he may know what needs to be known of the present without forfeiting all fellowship with the giants of the past.

With most busy ministers the puzzle is how to command the leisure required either for wide or for studious reading in any department. It simply cannot be done, unless a man will husband his time, measure out stated periods for it, and at all costs avoid desultoriness. It is fatally easy to dawdle over the newspaper, or to dissipate leisure by aimless dipping into any book that offers. Depend upon it, the preacher who lacks the moral fibre to compel himself to read by system will run to seed and achieve little. Nor is one's gain from books to be counted by the leaves turned over, but by the mastery which with our own brain we have won over their contents, or by the thoughts which they have stirred within our own souls. If self-discipline on the intellectual side be a duty, then as a duty let it be conscientiously undertaken.[1]

[1] The difficulty which a poorly paid minister experiences in procuring the books he has need of, is a very serious one. Clerical reading clubs offer only a partial remedy. Theological lending libraries are few in number, and might be multiplied with advantage. Intelligent members in our smaller churches could do their pastor no truer kindness than by adding to his often scanty stock; only they would act wisely were they to consult his own wishes in their choice of books. Well-meaning friends not seldom make mistakes by giving volumes that are unsuitable.

3. A third contribution to the preacher's equipment comes from his growing knowledge of men. This may be understood in more ways than one. Men of the world, immersed in its business, have often found matter for mild satire in the *sancta simplicitas* of the clerical order, and its helpless ignorance in the affairs of this world. To judge by the testimony of an American author whom I lately quoted, this venerable jibe against " the cloth " has lost none of its edge in the New World. " The popular conception of a clergyman," says Phelps, " is that he is, *ex officio*, in respect to the knowledge of mankind, an ignoramus. Be it true or false, this is the popular notion of the clerical character. It produces not a little of that feeling towards the clergy which vibrates between amusement and contempt. In the popular faith we belong to a race of innocents. If not all Vicars of Wakefield, we are cousins-german to that reverend greenhorn. Men of the world feel it to be refreshing when an able preacher breaks loose from the hereditary conventionalisms of the clerical guild, and thinks and talks and dresses and acts as *they* do." [1]

When allowance is made for a touch of caricature in this passage, it fairly reflects a widespread impression among laymen, which has just enough of foundation to make it worth thinking seriously about. Not every minister by any means is so unversed in secular affairs, or so deficient in worldly shrewdness, as his order is supposed to be. Still, it is true that ministers cannot help forming in some special respects a class apart from the world. Their very training largely unfits them for its business. Their absorption in the things of religion produces a certain aloofness from much that keenly interests men of affairs. They are even exonerated, less by law than by courtesy, from some of the usual responsibilities of society. Much of their time is passed in cloistered study, so that when seen they are usually occupied with sacred functions. The laity naturally associate them with solemn occasions when secular business seems an

[1] *Ut supra*, p. 21.

19

impertinence, may even environ them with a semi-priestly air of sanctity. An impalpable barrier, not easy to break through, thus comes to divide them from others, so that laymen rarely speak out before them quite as frankly as they do to one another.

For a part, though by no means for the whole, of this remoteness from secular life, the ministry is not to be blamed. It is unavoidable. Nor do I think it matters very much that a preacher is inexpert in the transactions of the Exchange, ignorant of the state of the markets, or unfamiliar with the latest fashions of polite society. Like other men who have a serious calling on hand, he is more than entitled, he is bound, to limit himself to its absorbing demands. No doubt, an irreligious hearer may parry the home-thrust of a Gospel appeal by the remark that it is a preacher's business to preach; when a busy layman who happens to deliver a religious address will be listened to with respect for his unworldly earnestness. But it stands to reason that, if we are to have an order of men set apart for this work at all, they must give themselves to it; nor is it likely the weight of their testimony to higher things on Sunday would in the long run be increased, if during the week they occupied their time in learning the details of other men's business. The preaching would only be worse done.

But intercourse with men is another matter. It seems to me a much more serious loss when the ministry as a class loses what was once its strength, close sympathetic daily intercourse with the people, till it neither commands their confidence nor shares their feelings. Has not this to a large extent taken place? Not to the same degree in every branch of the Church, yet to some degree in all, ministers of religion have drifted too far out of touch with labour, at least in the large towns, with results which every one bewails to-day. Decay of the old frank intimate association of the ministry with working people is now a consequence of the alienation from organised Churches of such large sections of them. May it not originally have helped to produce it? Can we hope to win them back unless ministry and people be brought once more into manly converse with each other—such converse in private on simply human lines as breeds first mutual respect, then mutual confidence and sympathy?

To the same lack of everyday intercourse with all but a picked section of the people may be traced the feebleness of the modern pulpit when it attempts to apply Christianity to everyday duties, or to the circumstances of special classes. Has it not also given occasion to the complaint—a bitter one for some of us—that while a sermon is actually the one form of literature left among us which is "popular" in the best sense, that is, which addresses itself to the broad humanity that is alike in all of us, rich or poor, nevertheless it is just the kind of public speaking which has become a byword for dulness? Must it not be that we preachers have lost the key to the public conscience and the public heart? That we have failed to understand the needs or the ways of thought or the daily affairs and interests of the people, so that the multitude will not come to hear us, charm we never so wisely? How many pulpit orators have we listened to who soared in a region of abstractions, seldom planting their foot upon the earth! Who dilated upon all things in heaven and earth except the things with which their audience was conversant! Who fulminated against imaginary sinners and extolled ideal saints! Who drew sketches of character or of experience which no one present could appropriate as his own! To shoot over people's heads is really not so bad as to fire off blank cartridges which can hit nobody.

I do not think such aimless firing argues an ignorance of human nature in the abstract, so much as a failure to recognise and address one's self to the actual condition of human beings. Most preachers have done a good deal in the study of man. Even their College years have taught them a little about the build of the human soul. As educated men they have daily access to a variegated world of literature—history, biography, poetry, fiction, and the drama—where are to be met the keenest observation and analysis of character and of motive. Above all, every preacher has his own heart for a field of study; and this has many a time made even a preacher who led a sequestered life insighted in the science of the human spirit, and adroit to track through all its windings the working of human passion. Men are at bottom alike. He who by the observation of his own heart has come to detect its frailties, its pretexts, excuses, and inconsistencies, as well as what considerations have power over him, and before what temptations he falls—ought to possess a key to his neighbour's bosom. It is human nature he is discovering in himself.[1]

But this is not all that is wanted to bring us into effective sympathy with actual men and women. People are not won by being treated as subjects for a moral scalpel. "Besides this general knowledge we are to have," writes Ward Beecher, "we should take kindly to individual men, for the very purpose of studying them." And, to illustrate his advice, he adds this curious little bit of autobiography:—

"I take great delight, if ever I can get a chance, of riding on the top of an omnibus with the driver, and talking with him. What do I gain by that? Why, my sympathy goes out for these men, and I recognise in them an element of brotherhood: that great human element which lies underneath all culture, which is more universal and more important than all special attributes, which is the great generic bond of humanity between man and man. If ever I saw one of these men in my church, I could preach to him, and hit him under the fifth rib with an illustration, much better than if I had not been acquainted with him.

[1] It would seem as if Catholic preachers must be separated from the laity even by a worse barrier than the Protestant pastor. If one would learn how they endeavour to overcome the difficulty, let him peruse the interesting sections 2–4 in Maury's *Essai sur l'Eloquence de la Chaire*, where he counsels the preacher to find in his own heart "the imaginary auditor, the abstract man, whom he sets himself to convict or to persuade." Who was it that advised a young preacher thus: "Think of your own sins and charge them upon the people"?

I have driven the truth under many a plain jacket. But, what is more, I never found a plain man in this world who could not tell me many things that I did not know before. There is not a gatekeeper at the Fulton ferry, or an engineer or deck-hand on the boats, that I am not acquainted with; and they help me in more ways than they know of. If you are going to be a minister, keep very close to plain folks; don't get above the common people." [1]

One might take exception, I dare say, to the great preacher's naively-confessed motive for " taking kindly" to 'busmen and deck hands "for the very purpose of study-ing them." His heart was here better, I am sure, than his words. True brotherly sympathy with men is not to be reached, no, nor true understanding of them either, by making them an object of professional observation with a view to pulpit use. But on the main point Beecher was certainly right: a preacher to the people must "keep very close to plain folks." To some men it comes far easier to do this, than to others. But to none can occasion for doing it be awanting. The parish clergyman is bound to it by his office. The quiet pastor cannot miss it in his pastoral duties. Even a popular city orator can be at no loss to find in the vicinity of his church or of his home, homes of the people and people in their homes to make him welcome, if only he come in the spirit of human brotherhood. It seems to me our English pulpit needs to be let down to this level of broad humanity, among the elemental forces. It has to relearn the language of the people, not speaking so exclusively as it does the dialect of middle-class culture. It need to use plainer and more pointed words in rebuke of people's actual sins, but also words of sympathy that comes from first-hand knowledge of their behaviour under their actual difficulties. Not all great preaching in the past has had this note about it, of close face to face contact with common life. But all preaching has had it which has deeply stirred the common people. Nor can our English pulpit, as it seems to me,

[1] *Op. cit.* p. 78.

regain its power to move and lead the nation until it learns this secret of genuine "popularity."[1]

The distrust, however, with which modern labour, strong in its new-found organisation, regards every existing form of organised Christianity, is too complex a phenomenon to be accounted for, save very partially, by the class character of modern preaching to which I have referred, or by its defective sympathy with what interests the working man. It has been the product of a number of influences, some social and some political, which operated in the past more than they do to-day. It can only be gradually and slowly overcome. Meanwhile, I do not see much, apart from this, to justify the stale cry about the "decay of the pulpit," or the exaggerated fear that "its day is over." What is true is that the conditions under which a preacher can work with success have within little over half a century undergone a change which is almost a revolution. But this is no more than has happened in other callings. The ministry is far from singular in having to adjust its methods to the rapidly changing times in which we live. Relatively to other forces in the national life, the preacher has suffered through, for example, the universal circulation of the newspaper and the magazine, the popularising of literature good and bad, and the multiplication of the subjects which engage public attention. There is no longer a parish in all the land where the Sunday sermon at church or chapel is now, what it once was, the one weekly agency to stir, or to educate, the rustic intellect. The interval between a preacher and his audience, even the humblest, has diminished, happily, and is diminishing, through the spread of education. This gives

[1] The evangelistic agency which in our time has most heartily adopted this line is the Salvation Army ; and to this fact its early success may have been largely due. The difficulty is not peculiar to our own country. The first portion of M. l'Abbé Mullois' *Cours d'Eloquence Sacrée* has for its avowed design to restore to the French Catholic pulpit a really popular style of preaching, in the hope to win the people back to religion. It has been translated by G. P. Badger under the title, *The Clergy and the Pulpit in their Relations to the People* (Lond. 1867).

him more intelligent, if fewer, hearers. It makes a heavier
demand upon his powers. It may increase in some cases—
in others it should lessen—the difficulty of arousing interest
in religious questions in minds which have been occupied
throughout the week with politics, or science, or sociology.
It adds in any case to the difficulty of satisfying their
interest when it has been aroused. Few preachers will
complain to-day that thoughtful persons are indifferent
to the problems of religion, however they may hesitate
to accept, or qualify their acceptance of, the creed of the
Church. But it may well be that the preacher's mode
of presenting his message needs to be modified, or that the
public asks for fresher and more intellectual discourses.

It is sometimes inferred that preaching has fallen off in
this country, because attendance at public worship is found
to be declining. I do not credit that. Declining attendance,
so far as it exists, is amply accounted for by changes in the
public attitude to the observances of religion. People do
not go to church so much as they used to do out of habit or
fashion. They go because they feel a need for it; and even
religious people feel less need than they did for two services
every Lord's Day. Other ways of spending Sunday, under
the breakdown of ideas and usages which fenced its sanctity
to our fathers, account for many an empty pew, without
entitling us to say that the sermon has fallen off.

So far as materials exist for a judgment, it rather appears
to me that the level of pulpit excellence has been rising, and
is likely to rise. Every day there is less to attract into the
ministry men whose heart is not in their work. The standard of ministerial education is steadily advancing. Pulpit
orators of distinction are "born not made," but it is by
training that an average man becomes a skilled preacher,
and it is on the whole of less moment that an age should be
rich in "great" preachers than that the rank and file of the
ministry should be competently equipped and effective for
good. The very difficulties which he experiences in gaining
the ear or answering the expectation, I do not say of the

outside public, but even of church-going folk, are putting
every young preacher just now upon his mettle. He is
driven to cultivate a manner of address which shall compel
attention. Sometimes he is tempted to resort to methods
which are questionable, to say the least. One hears a good
deal of the "sensationalism" of the new pulpit. It dabbles
in topics heretofore reserved for the newspaper "leader." It
advertises its subjects under catching titles. It spices its fare
with the talk of the hour. It placards the Cross in staring
colours and seeks for broad effects. It will have novelties
at any cost. Such advanced bids for popularity often
enough spring no doubt from motives which deserve respect,
but they are not to be encouraged. Along that line lies
danger for the true power of the pulpit. It is a poor
ambition to have one's Sunday evening sermon noticed
in the "local news" column on Monday morning. On the
other hand, any manly preacher who understands his age,
who lives keenly in its affairs, and has a real message for it
from God, can, without descending to stage tricks, bring
his pulpit into closer touch with its democratic life than we
have seen paralleled in England since the Commonwealth.

But, to win the ear of the people, it becomes more and
more the first essential to interest them by lessons that
leave an imprint on their lives, shunning ever as the one
unpardonable sin that venerable vice of the pulpit—dulness.
Sermons are become brief. But they will need to put more,
not less, into little compass, making straight for some clear
practical result. An energetic quick-living generation of
busy people, habituated to swift interchange of thought and
to business done by telegraph, will ask from the preacher
a sinewy, keen-edged and straightforward talk about faith
and duty—a message from God that can be translated
promptly into action. Preaching that fills the ear but aims
at nothing, that pleases like a well-played tune but does
not rouse to action like a battle-trumpet, is not the sort of
preaching I should expect men to care for in the strenuous
hurrying days that seem to be coming on the earth.

Working thus under conditions subject to rapid change, which, as they change, become ever more arduous, few ministers in any Church, unless they have settled down contentedly into a groove, escape occasional fits of disheartenment. The higher their ideal, the less are they likely to satisfy themselves. It is not necessarily an ignoble envy of better men which makes a man painfully aware of his inferiority. If performance is felt to fall dismally short even of his own intention, much more of what he esteems worthy of his sacred opportunity, any modest and sensitive craftsman may fear that he has failed through his own unskilfulness. Now, when such a sense of technical shortcoming haunts and oppresses an experienced preacher, either because the methods of his youth, which he is too old to unlearn, are become antiquated, or because his early training in scholarship or in the technique of sermon construction left much to be desired, a legitimate comfort may be drawn from reflecting that the efficacy of a sermon to edify and save is never measurable by its technical perfection. I do not say this to excuse avoidable defects; for, of course, no one is excusable for doing less than his best. Yet it is true that, for the highest ends of preaching, nothing counts for so much as certain spiritual qualities personal to the speaker; qualities which, thank God! are within the reach of every true-hearted servant of Christ. Two in especial may be named: personal character, and that indefinable gift which we can only call "unction."

Given a discourse which is born out of a faithful pastor's toil and sincerest love for his people, it owes more of its power to do them good to the weight of his proved character than either to eloquence or to homiletic skill. To casual sermons delivered by a preacher of note on some great occasion to a miscellaneous crowd, this hardly applies. But the profit gained from a minister's weekly addresses in his own quiet church, where every worshipper, down to the tiniest, counts him for a friend, depends mainly, or at least very largely, on the reverent affection and confidence which, through years of patient service, have been gathering round their pastor in the hearts of his people. So that, though we cannot all be great preachers, we may be such good men, valued for our work's sake, that our simple homely words shall carry power for his sake who utters them. He therefore need not fear a barren unblest ministry who comes forth to his people from his closet rich in their esteem, to pour himself out—his most treasured thoughts and hallowed desires—as a libation for God's honour and for the service of His saints.

This specially close relationship between the spiritual life of a preacher and the effect of his words, reveals itself best in that unmistakable but inimitable quality which is meant by "unction"[1] To compass a merely oratorical success, this gift is not essential; but for the highest results it is invaluable. It is hard to describe; but it is the note of a speaker who is filled with the Holy Ghost. A man who lives close to God, who thirsts after the salvation of souls, who delivers his message under an overpowering apprehension of Divine realities—that man may be guilty of countless breaches of technical rules, yet this spiritual note, if he has it, will more than compensate for them all. His word is "with demonstration of the Spirit and with power."

One cannot look for this quality unless the average level of a minister's religious life be high, his spirit kept devout and tender. Yet it does not invariably accompany genuine or even deep devoutness; for some very spiritually-minded Christians have proved ineffective in the pulpit. Probably, if one might guess at its origin, it comes at a moment when the speaker is speaking most out of the heart of his Master, under an exceptionally profound and solemn sympathy with the sinful man's huge need of the Saviour and the Saviour's huge pity for the unsaved sinner. I should hope a good many preachers have felt at times a little of this fellowship

---

[1] By French writers on homiletics the word "onction" is used, but bears a different sense: one nearly akin to the English "pathos." (Cf. Maury's *Essai*, § 73.)

with their Master; but, as we grow preoccupied with the routine details of getting up sermons and delivering them, discharging our office as we have often done before, no worse if no better,—the surpassing sacredness of our work, its unspeakable issues, and the awful Power that worketh through us, get hidden from our eyes, and thrill our hearts but rarely with that tremor of hallowed joy and dread which has so wonderful a force to awe and capture the souls of those who hear us. For this gift a man must wrestle on his knees.

PART IV

THE MINISTER AS PASTOR

CHAPTER XXIV

THE CARE OF SOULS

IT is a unique relationship which subsists between a pastor and his flock. In its intimacy, privacy, and sacredness, in the access also which it gives him to the homes of his people at every season of domestic joy or grief, it reminds one rather of the privileged bonds of kinship, such as bind brothers in the same family, than of any mere official relationship, chill and business-like, which can be created by social convention.

This peculiarity becomes intelligible on the theory of the pastorate currently accepted in the Evangelical Churches. They trace it ultimately to the new bond, not of blood, but of spiritual fraternity which Jesus constituted among His followers. "All ye," said He, "are brethren." To "love as brethren," children of the same Heavenly Father, is the simple law which sums up the whole attitude of Christians to one another. And of this newborn brother-love, the characteristic fruit and token are solicitude for each other's spiritual welfare.

Now, it is out of the bosom of this mutual privilege and responsibility of all the brotherhood to seek each other's growth in grace, that the specialised functions of an official pastorate were first developed. To a limited extent, it is

still within the power of all of us to minister to a few of
our fellow-members as under-shepherds, through whose
helpful and kindly care the Chief Shepherd can exercise
His own pastoral oversight. Were the pastor a private
Christian, he would still owe his brethren such watchful
care. But it would be rendered in his own name merely,
and limited to the circle of his private acquaintances.
Whereas he gathers up and concentrates in his official
person the care which the entire body he represents takes
in the religious wellbeing of all its individual members. He
is to each the voice, the organ, of all. Acting on behalf of
the Church, he is authorised to carry in its name to every
person within its communion, the counsel, the instruction,
the sympathy, the helpfulness, even the rebukes, which the
case of each demands.

When the care of souls thus becomes an official duty,
no change ought to pass over the spirit of it. Appointment
to office widens indeed the area of responsibility; it makes
watching on behalf of others no mere side interest, but a
life-work; and it entitles the pastor to speak with authority
in the Church's name where as a private Christian he might
have been silent. But the moral value of his pastoral acts
continues to lie, not in his office, so much as in himself:
for it depends on their being still a service of lowly self-
sacrificing brother-love, rendered in the spirit as well as in
the name of the Chief Shepherd.

Beyond question, such a position tests most severely the
temper of a man's Christianity. He is an official, and yet
the official disposition, in so far as it is opposed to the
fraternal, has to be vigorously combated. Two faults in
particular, which everywhere beset officialism, need to be
overcome, because they are at variance with brotherly
love: self-importance, the one, founded merely on the
possession of office; and the other, a hard mechanical tone
in the discharge of official duty. The former is at bottom
that overweening sense of superiority against which, under
the name of lordliness, St. Peter already found it necessary

in the infancy of the Church, to warn his "fellow-elders."
How often since then has it swollen to an incredible height
in ecclesiastics; not always in those of the Church which
boasts St. Peter as its foundation-stone.   With the slightest
tincture of that arrogant temper there come meddlesomeness, a dictatorial tone, harsh fault-finding.   Against it one
needs to fight with all one's strength.   Nor is there any
cure for it but being "clothed with humility"—that meek
humility which springs from ever deeper consciousness of
one's own defects.   Think of yourself as " less than the least
of all saints," then may you in no mock lowliness kneel to
wash their feet, being girt about with the towel of humility.[1]
The other danger is hardness of temper, when duties which
ought to be quick with sympathy and tender with the
tenderness of love become the perfunctory routine of one
who is appointed, even paid, to do them.   Then all the
charm of service is gone; its aroma has evaporated.

There is another way also in which his pastoral duties
become the most searching test to which a minister is
subjected.   Their faithful discharge is left in a large
measure to his own sense of duty.   More public functions
he cannot neglect without attracting public attention and
drawing upon himself, if not always censure from ecclesiastical superiors, at least open discredit.   But his care
for souls is largely a private matter.   Whether he omit to
pay a sick visit to-day because it happens to be inconvenient,
or how far he is disposed to be at pains for the recovery of
a lad who has gone astray—such things as these there are
few to observe and fewer still to call him to account for.
Here his fidelity, being less open to men's eyes, lies between
himself and the Chief Pastor whom he serves.   Granted
that a genuine love for souls and for the Lord of souls be the
prevailing motive in which one's pastorate took its rise and
from which, on the whole, it draws the breath of its life, yet
there are few so constantly possessed by it as never to need
the goad of stern imperious duty.   For this department

[1] Cf. 1 Pet. 5$^{1-5}$ with John 13$^{1-5}$.

of his office, to which all days are alike, covers of necessity a larger space than any other in the minister's life ; and there is no hour in his day when his services in this capacity may not be in demand.   He will often have to brace himself to obey an urgent summons when he is tired, or busy, or indisposed ; and the temptation can never be far away to reverse the apostolic rule and "exercise the oversight," not willingly, but of constraint.   Then, with its spontaneity, how much of the worth of such service will be gone ! Nor can the best of us, after every precaution against perfunctoriness, indolence, and negligence, say that we have done all that needed to be done or might have been done.   The pastoral office is so manifold, it is so crowded with opportunities, it can absorb such an endless expenditure of any man's best, that no one dare hope to exhaust its possibilities.   One comes to the end of one's strength, never of one's work. Well for us if only it can be said : He hath done what he could !

These are things often and anxiously weighed by every conscientious shepherd of souls.   If at times his spirit flag and the burden seem too heavy to be borne, there is but one source from which fresh strength can be drawn— strength of a genuine or worthy sort.   It is the co-operation of the *Pastor pastorum*.   Ministers, when they think of their pastorate, ought to pitch their thoughts high.   Great as is the burden, so great is the honour of it.   If I am not mistaken, there is no other part of their work which associates them quite so unceasingly, so intimately, or so confidentially, with their unseen Master, as care for individual souls.   It is closer than imitation, though that is in it.   The pastor does not merely walk in the footprints of Jesus' historical ministry.   He is not a vicar of the absent Head Pastor, left to his own resources.   He co-operates day after day in an actual Divine ministry which is going on now alongside of his own and through it: over-shadowing his, enwrapping it, directing its acts, and

graciously making incessant use of it. This, it humbly
appears to me, is the master-fact, the thought of which
ought to guide and to sustain all pastoral duty.

Weigh it well: of each soul we tend, Jesus is the
real active watchful Over-Shepherd. Say we have a share
in the oversight—it is the assistance which He condescends
to accept from us in a work with the direction of which He
has charged Himself. This, if it relieves us from the
ultimate responsibility for results, requires us (does it not?)
to be always trying to trace His dealings with the people of
our charge, and to fit in our poor contribution to those
operations of grace which all the while are going forward
in men's hearts by His providence, His word, and His
secret Spirit. I cannot think that any under-shepherd ever
worked in too close or too detailed an intercourse with his
Divine Chief. It is not presumption, nor is it enthusiasm,
it is a reasonable recognition of actual conditions which
govern this sacred partnership in labour, when a lowly
labourer on earth brings each anxious case beneath the
Chief's eye, begs for wisdom beyond his own to keep all his
dealing with it right, and craves and expects just that
message, of counsel be it, or of consolation, which the
Director of the work would have him carry in His name to
the soul in need. If he bear Christ in his heart, and with
a single eye use his best endeavour, can he be disappointed
of an answer? Is it not this which makes one's pastorate
the sweetest, tenderest, holiest part of all one's ministry?

But while each simple-hearted servant of Christ is
entitled to seek such guidance step by step, and while there
is no remedy for officialism, nor any cordial in discouragement, so potent as to realise that he is a fellow-worker
under "the Shepherd and Bishop of souls," let him not
forget that he has not been left without written directions
which he is expected to study and observe. The New
Testament is rich in such directions.[1] The Pastoral Epistles,
for instance, not merely lay down the qualifications which

---

[1] See Beck, *Pastoral-lehren des Neuen Testamentes* (1880).

Timothy and Titus were to require in a presbyter-bishop, they instruct these missionary delegates themselves how to deal with sundry groups of converts—with old men and young, old women and young, with widows and with slaves. Those are pastoral hints. Nor is there any more beautiful counsel on the spirit of the pastorate than St. Peter's to his fellow-elders, out of a heart filled with reminiscences of a great day by the Lake of Galilee, when he himself had been reinstalled to tend the several groups which compose Christ's flock. Although there enters into St. Paul's language to his converts a note of paternal authority, due to the fact that, if they had ten thousand tutors in Christ, they could have no spiritual father but himself; none the less can a modern minister find among under-pastors no worthier example than he, for self-sacrificing devotion, for adaptation of his methods to diverse situations, or for affectionate gentleness as of a nursing mother cherishing her babes. Nor can any reader miss the emphasis everywhere laid on the duty of vigilance : an unresting wakeful outlook, as of a sentinel in the night, to discern in time whatever peril may threaten a brother's advance in spiritual life, so as at the right moment to interpose and guard it. These all are lessons never long out of a good pastor's thoughts. But above all, he does well to keep ever in view the Gospel records of the Master's personal ministry. There can be no model to compare with Him. If the end of all our effort be to build up the kingdom or reign of the Father in the hearts and lives of our people, then it is from Jesus' teaching alone we can learn His conception of that kingdom under its present earthly aspects. If it be in concert with Him our ministry is to be carried on that He may work through us, then our safest guide must be His own example. His methods in the days of His flesh will furnish some indication of His methods still. Close study by recent scholars of the Lord's ministry has done something to bring out the lessons for his daily duty which a pastor may draw from the Good Shepherd's way of working, from His recorded

20

dealing with individuals, and in particular from His patient training of the Twelve.[1] Among these numerous lessons I name only a few.

It is from our Lord alone that a pastor learns the immeasurable value in the Father's eyes of each single soul gained for His kingdom, and how its recovery repays the utmost pains or sacrifice it may cost. Take along with this our Lord's scrupulous respect for the personal freedom, responsibility and right to self-determination and self-development which belong to every human being; and you have the two complementary truths by which as guiding lines one man's ministry of spiritual help to his fellow is defined. Jesus, while on the outlook for opportunities to help and never sparing Himself, is never found to force His help on anyone; nor did He ever hurry on the work of a soul's growth, but with endless tolerance gave it time. It was His method, without strife, or the argumentative discussions dear to the propagandist, to drop, as occasion offered, truths like seeds, in terse and easy language, leaving them to germinate in receptive hearts. For He seemed to stimulate independent reflection and to welcome honest inquiry, rather than to let His words be accepted with irresponsive or indolent credulity. No disciple was received in ignorance of what adhesion to His cause might cost, and His habit was rather to punctuate than to gloss over the hard terms of discipleship. Yet with men of an honest purpose, though dull and slow of heart to believe, none could have shown more consummate patience. Needless to say that He never refused to aid the suffering, in their bodily as well as moral ailments, although it is clear that He could only aid when, by a sympathy which always meant suffering for Himself, He had entered into their case. But that is only one example of the self-sacrifice in daily and small details which He exhibited, who had come to seek the lost, and to give His life a ransom for many.

[1] I may refer to three English works that will be found of use: Blaikie, *The Public Ministry and Pastoral Methods of our Lord* (1863); Latham, *Pastor Pastorum* (Camb. 1900); and Bruce's *Training of the Twelve*.

Finally, the homeliness of Jesus' manner, the simple style of His address, His habit of using in illustration of the deepest religious truth everyday affairs and the occurrences of home life : these with similar features which made Him, although the boldest and at times the severest of speakers, yet after all the Teacher who has spoken most successfully to the common people, are lessons which no pastor can over-look who will reverently watch the Master at His work.

Those services of vigilant oversight, guidance in the Divine life, and brotherly counsel, which it is the part of a pastor to render to his flock, were not only, as we have seen, the earliest to be committed to officials, they were also the earliest to be made a subject of study in the Church, and of literary treatment. The chief patristic contribution was the *Liber Pastoralis Curæ* of Pope Gregory the Great. It not only continued to be a classic manual for the use of priests all down the mediæval centuries, but is not even yet, I understand, antiquated in Roman Catholic seminaries. At the Reformation, the duties devolving upon the freshly instituted order of Protestant pastors began at once to receive attention, and the beginnings of a literature appeared, which has since grown to vast dimensions. Interest in the subject was keener among the Reformed than in the Lutheran branch, to the advantage on the whole of the Reformed Churches ;[1] although it must be owned that the legal strin-gency inherent in Calvin's system of ecclesiastical discipline produced some very unhappy consequences in the succeed-ing century. When other functions of clerical office, preach-ing especially, came to be separately studied by Protestants, there was a disposition to widen the old name of " Pastoral Theology " so as in a looser application to include the whole. Nor was this unnatural ; since it may be truly said that the pastor in his pulpit, or even at the prayer-desk, is the pastor still, aiming at the profit of the souls entrusted to his care.

[1] One Reformed Confession, the Later Helvetic, gives an excellent list of the duties of a pastor (Art. XVIII.).

However useful it may be to consider the several aspects of the ministry apart, it is not possible in practice to sever them completely from one another. But since in last century the whole science of "Practical Theology," as it has come to be termed, required to be subdivided, and its divisions to be accurately discriminated, continental authorities at least have agreed, with few exceptions, to restrict the name of Pastoral Theology to such functions as are not discharged in public assemblies nor designed for the congregation as a whole, but are directed to the individuals, whether singly or in groups, of whom it is composed.[1] Close, therefore, as are its relations both to worship and to preaching, the pastorate holds a clearly defined position of its own.

That is a very idle debate, however, which sets the preaching and the pastoral functions in opposition; which discusses which of the two is the more important, or which argues, either that the better preacher a man is, the worse pastor he must make, or conversely. Both being functions of the same office, it follows that to discharge the one well is no sufficient excuse for discharging the other badly. It is true that different gifts are called for each, and therefore some ministers excel in the one, some in the other. The only useful inference we can draw from that is, that so long as both are incumbent, a minister ought to give, if anything, extra pains to fit himself for the work to which he has least natural aptitude or liking. No doubt it is a question for the Church, that has been sometimes raised, whether we should do better in a large field of duty to set one man apart to preach and others for the private care of souls. Experience has not shown that in the Protestant Church such a division of labour works well. In our Churches, there is no way for a minister to keep himself in touch with the spiritual needs of his congregation, except by doing pastoral duty. The relation betwixt the two spheres is of the closest. Each promotes the ends of the other.

---

[1] See Achelis, *Praktische Theologie* (Freiburg i. B. 1890), i. 428 ff. He advocates the use of the name "Poimenik."

Getting to know his hearers privately, a preacher can adapt his public ministrations to their condition. Salutary impressions on the Lord's Day lose much of their hopefulness if they are not followed up during the week. People are much more impressed by the words of a man whom they have learned to know and to esteem; on the other hand, they are most disposed to confide their private experience to that pastor whose teaching in Church has moved or helped them. The two halves of our work dovetail into and sustain each other, if only we show ourselves equally loyal in the doing of both.

CHAPTER XXV

HOUSEHOLD VISITATION

THE first condition for any individual oversight of a parish or congregation is to become acquainted with those who belong to it. The shepherd "calleth his own sheep by name." Every pastor knows what a value people set on being personally recognised, and how hurt they feel when the minister is unable to name them or passes them on the street without recognition. In a very extensive city charge, widely scattered and subject to rapid change, even to do this will tax the memory of a pastor. In the multiplicity of his engagements, he finds it hard to keep himself acquainted with recent comers, and still more with their children. Yet only to know the people by sight or by name is the least possible degree of acquaintance. For effective pastorship, one needs to be informed of their circumstances, to gain some insight into their character, even to form an opinion on their religious condition. The further one can carry such a detailed knowledge, the better for one's pastoral work, so long as it is not an idle curiosity one gratifies, but a brotherly interest wholly dedicated to their spiritual profit. This is one of the many advantages of a small charge. But be the cure large or small, there is no way of obtaining such an acquaintance with the *personnel* of the flock, but house to house visitation.

When a minister enters on his duties in a fresh sphere, his earliest task must therefore be to acquire such information. Besides informing himself generally as to the history and character of the congregation, the people's occupations and circumstances, the moral state of the district, and the like, he has to make the round of his people's homes as soon as possible. In this task the incumbent of an English parish may often be left very much to himself. A Presbyterian minister shares the supervision of his flock with the elders, who as likewise ordained officers are associated with him in pastoral responsibility. In every part of his pastoral care he acts in concert with them, and if he be a wise man, will make as much use as he can of this body of coadjutors. The deacons of a Congregational church occupy a somewhat similar position. At the outset of a ministry the assistance of these brother-officers is specially valuable. They are already familiar with the people, each of them at least with those who reside within his allotted district, and can afford to their new leader exactly that information which he wants. Sometimes an elder or deacon can accompany the minister in his first calls. For it is at his introduction to each household that he ought to gather particulars respecting its inmates, the names and approximate ages of the children, the employments of the adults, and their several relations to the Church as communicants or workers. After this first call, people dislike such inquiries, which by that time they think ought to be unnecessary; whereas on an introductory visit they expect them and are gratified by them.

It is not always prudent to jot down such particulars on the spot; but they ought to be entered in a visiting book immediately on returning home. Such a register can hardly contain too much, especially of any facts which shed light on the religion of the home. With a like care must it be kept up to date, as often as changes occur, or a new family is added to the flock. In large congregations, the date of subsequent visits should be entered, with any fresh particulars ascertained. It is not safe to leave too much to recollection. Unmethodical pastors who grudge the time spent on registers of their work, or think such keeping of day-books too secular an employment, are making a huge mistake. Sacred work is none the less sacred for being done with business-like method, accuracy, and despatch. But I do not recommend the entry in a visiting-book, even though it be kept under lock and key, of any judgment the pastor may form, whether now or afterwards, of any one's spiritual condition, or of any private confidences with which he may be entrusted after his relations with his people have become more intimate. Neither of these is a matter to be safely committed to ink and paper.

Either during the course of his first visit of inquiry or from the pulpit, it is well to give the people clearly to understand on what footing and with what object he comes into their homes. It is, of course, to be followed up by subsequent visits, whether occasional or regular, not of a social, but of a pastoral character. While he always comes as a friend, with the frank and unprofessional manner which alone befits Christian brotherhood, it will be found to hamper his usefulness if the distinction between a purely social call and a pastoral one be not observed and kept in mind, both by them and by himself. This is, of course, specially requisite in the case of families moving in his own social circle. Both with them and with humbler folk, advantage is to be taken of every occurrence in domestic life which permits him to get closer to them. Births and deaths, illness and loss of friends, young people leaving home on entering upon life, business disasters, anything, in short, which touches nearly the family heart, is an opportunity for a pastoral call not to be neglected. He need not wait to be sent for. It is his opportunity, not only for becoming better acquainted with their inward experience, but still more for ministering to them the sympathy or the counsel which the occasion calls for, and which his office warrants him in proffering in his Master's name.

Shall he also undertake and keep up, year after year, a round of systematic house to house visitation? This has been since the Reformation a recognised practice in Reformed Churches, sometimes regulated, as in Scotland, by

ecclesiastical authority,[1] but always well understood to be
part of a minister's pastoral office. It has been otherwise
in the Lutheran communion. There it has not only never
been practised, but occasional efforts, on the part of the
Pietists chiefly, to introduce it have met with opposition from the majority of the clergy. Recent writers
continue to disapprove of it, not only as a waste of time, but
even as objectionable in itself.[2] What they say is that so
long as a clergyman contents himself with paying a visit
where there is occasion for it or where he has reason to
think it will be welcome, he is following a Divine leading
and going where Christ's providence or the Spirit of grace
has gone before him; but that to volunteer or force a visit
on people who do not want it, is an intrusion upon their
evangelical liberty, and likely to do more harm than good.
It is wise to bear in mind that visits paid when a special
occasion presents itself are the most urgent, because they
are the most promising. But the Lutheran objection to
going " where one is not wanted " contemplates the formal
and official visit to every house in his parish of one who
goes as the functionary of a State Church. From that
point of view it may be a wise abstinence on the part of
the German clergy; especially as the Lutheran custom of
optional confession to a clergyman gives to every one who
desires his advice an opportunity of going to him in private.
The objection, however, is pointed at a state of things which
in this country has passed away. Whatever may have been
the case formerly, when clerical authority was stronger, few
parish ministers would now dream of pressing their attendance where there is no desire for it. In the case of Church
members no such difficulty ought to arise. Where household
visitation has been customary, it is so far from being resented
that it is expected. Its utility must be judged of on its own

[1] Act of Assembly, 1708, respecting Ministerial Visitations. It will be
found in Fairbairn's *Past. Theol.* 1875, p. 295.

[2] Cf., *e.g.*, Palmer, *Evang. Pastoraltheol.*, Stuttgart, 1863, p. 381 ff. ;
Achelis, *op. cit.* i. 451 f.

merits; and the experience of pastors who still continue, at much expenditure of energy, to keep up the time-honoured habit, is, I believe, that where it can be done it is on the whole well worth doing.

Yet no part of ministerial labour has suffered more in recent days. Many causes incident to modern life have combined to make it more difficult and less effective. So much so, that many conscientious ministers confess that they really do not know what their duty is. It is not that these changes have put it beyond the power of most ministers to make a call, once a year or so, at every house where their Church members reside, or even on every one who habitually worships with them. With some parish ministers who think it their duty to visit every visitable family in their parish, the case is different. Rural parishes can usually be overtaken, no doubt; especially as there are always groups of Nonconformists in the population who are attended to by their own pastors. But in congested districts of large towns or cities, the non-church-going poor are either visited by a staff of assistant clergy, or they are left to Home Mission agents of one sort or another, lay-readers, district visitors, Biblewomen, or the like. The attention of the incumbent, who alone is legally responsible, is perforce confined, I think, to the superintendence of his curates and to the personal visitation of communicants at his church, very much as that of his Nonconformist brethren has to be. Then the work becomes in most cases manageable. The great majority of congregations are of moderate size. There remain, of course, a few cases where the worshippers are either much more numerous or are scattered over a much wider area. These will occupy a longer time, and the visits must be less frequent. But given resolution and persistent effort, the thing can be done, for it is done. The sole condition is that the pastor, even if he be a busy man much taken up with public affairs, shall feel this duty to be urgent; and urgent it can only be, if it can be so conducted as to become a really valuable instrument in the pastor's hands.

It is just here where difficulty has been created by changes in the social habits of the population. It used to be much easier formerly to find the people in their homes at the usual calling hours. Nowadays, business men leave home early and return late. The working-classes are massed in factories. Children are more frequently sent to a distance for their education. Domestic servants are no longer under their employers' religious supervision as they once were. The household is hardly ever to be found at home save for the morning and evening meals. A visiting pastor finds no one there in the afternoon but the mistress of the house ; and for mistresses, both rich and poor, it is often inconvenient to be caught at their home occupations. Add to all this that through the multiplication of congregational agencies in a modern church, societies of both sexes and various ages convening on the church premises on several evenings in the week, the minister has other opportunities, unknown to our fathers, for meeting the individuals of his flock and for influencing them. Is it to be wondered at if many a diligent pastor excuses himself, half against his sense of duty, for making half-hearted and intermittent attempts at household visitation, or ends by giving it up altogether ?

To such a surrender of an important means of usefulness we are by no means reduced. Clerical methods must just be adapted to altered conditions, and become less stereotyped. Such changes as I have mentioned in industrial and domestic arrangements are very far from affecting every minister's work in the same way or to the same extent. Different parts of the country, different towns or districts in the same town, different social classes and callings, have all their several customs ; so that, while the design of the pastor in his visitation remains the same, his methods will have to bend to local conditions. The purpose to be always kept in view seems to me to be threefold. First, to convey to the household a sense of its belonging to the body of Christ's faithful people who are all concerned in its spiritual wellbeing; next, to become better acquainted with the members of the household—as many of them as possible—in those matters especially which affect for good or ill their religious condition; and lastly, to drop, as occasion serves, some word of life that may bring them such comfort or counsel or correction as their present state calls for. If other ends are served—enlisting a fresh worker for the Church, for instance, or smoothing family unpleasantnesses, or affording to some one a chance to open out a secret grief—these are either of rarer occurrence, or they may be included under those three. Now, should a young minister discover that the old style of formal visits of a quarter of an hour or twenty minutes' duration, carried out on fixed afternoons in regular order and conducted on a fairly uniform plan, are so ill-adapted to the people of his charge, or to certain classes of them, that these purposes are no longer served, he need not scruple to devise a better. Provided the right end be kept in view, the more closely he adapts his procedure to existing circumstances the better. The convenience of the people, not that of the minister, has to be considered. Wherever an afternoon call will accomplish the purpose, as it will with certain classes, that time ought to be still preferred, in order that as many evening hours as possible may be reserved for work which can be done at no other time. If only an evening hour finds people at home and at leisure, then he must surrender some of his free evenings, or keep others free, for this work. With the working classes, this is likely to be the only time when the head of the house can be seen; nor is it otherwise with most business men, or with young men and women in situations. These latter will have to be sought at their lodgings, or it may be better to give them an interview at the minister's own house, but always at an evening hour. With men on night duty and any others whose hours of employment are unusual or uncertain, special appointments may have to be made. One ought, I think, to feel bound to no hard and fast rule, either by custom or by personal convenience, but be as free as possible to vary one's plan in different congregations or among different groups within the same congregation. To give the people notice beforehand when to expect a visit, is usually advisable. The only risk that arises from irregular visitation, is lest some get overlooked. To prevent this, each visit paid should be at once duly entered against the address in the visiting-book. A glance will then show what houses have been overtaken and what passed over.

In the conduct of each visit, a like freedom, it seems to me, ought to obtain. Neither a uniform duration nor uniformity of procedure can be maintained. There are a good many houses where the old method of a very brief service is still the best: a few Scripture verses read, a few words spoken, and a prayer offered for the inmates. When elderly or infirm persons are present, this is often most appropriate. At a *tête-à-tête* interview, on the other hand, the natural course is to engage your companion in a conversation leading up to religious matters and becoming in the end as frank and confidential as possible. This gives a pastor the best chance of all to win private confidences, which may enable him to minister to hidden hurts, and needs of the inner life. Evening visits, where old and young are met together, will take diverse forms, preferably that of a free talk, winding up with family prayers. The pastor's aim is to combine the utmost measure of simple familiar friendliness, void of every trace of professional stiffness, with a constant endeavour to lead in the direction of the highest things: his hope being that openings will arise for dropping some unforced but helpful or suggestive words in the Master's name. Two extremes are ever to be avoided: being drawn in conversation so far from your object that the talk degenerates into idle gossip; or thinking it needful to save the character of the visit by a sudden and awkward dragging in at the close of professional or pious utterances. When the number of houses to be visited is extremely

large, a minister may content himself in many cases with a
brief friendly visit of inquiry. Even then, however, I
think there should be something to distinguish it from an
ordinary social " call."

Whatever method or variety of methods a minister
adopts in household visitation, he rarely finds that the art
of turning conversation to religious profit is one which comes
to him by nature. By all save a very few it is a thing to
be learnt: not easy for many of us; to some extremely
difficult. The better certainly a pastor comes to know his
people, the easier it will grow; and in every congregation
some are found who meet their minister's advances halfway
or more. But glib talkers on religion are not always the
best people. It is usually wise, sometimes it is indispensable, to prepare oneself beforehand for each visit.
First by recalling what one knows about the personal or
family circumstances of the household; then by considering
what line of treatment promises in their case the best
results; finally, by an act of intercession—coupled with a
petition for direction for oneself. To avoid the risk of
awkward silences or the necessity to fall back upon plati-
tudes, some recommend the unready man to bethink him
beforehand of a text or Gospel lesson deemed suitable, so
that, in case no natural opening for religious converse occur,
he can frankly pull out his Bible and plunge into his
message. That counsel of despair ought very seldom to be
called for. There is usually something special to speak
about, which, if not quite recent, has at least happened in
the family history since the minister's last visit; or some
fresh departure in congregational activity in which they
might take part; or an aged disciple is present; or a child
has gone to school, or a lad to his apprenticeship. Anything may supply a natural starting-point from which a
moderately skilful visitor will know how to advance to
serious talk and appropriate lessons.[1] The most difficult

[1] In his useful and well-known handbook, *For the Work of the Ministry*
(Lond. 1873), Dr. Blaikie writes : " If I were now beginning a ministry, I

thing of all in most cases is to lead people on to express their own mind. Reticence on the deeper experiences of the soul is to be expected and is not to be censured. Yet there are hearts among us, not a few, that are weary of bearing their burden alone and in silence. A pastoral visit occasionally offers to such persons an opportunity to open their trouble ; but not often. It seldom happens that there is privacy enough during a family visit. But it may create a desire for a more private interview. If the pastor detect any indication of such a desire, he must create an opportunity. Probably he does well to announce a stated hour in every week when, at his own house or in the church vestry, he is known to be always "at home" to every one who desires to consult him. Many things will bring his people there; but the weary and the heavy laden will venture to come and unbosom themselves all the more readily because their minister has been recently inside their own doors and has shown himself sympathetic there.

An earnest pastor will often return from visiting, dissatisfied with himself and depressed by the slender result which he thinks he has achieved. He ought not to suppose his labour has been in vain. In any case it is worth while to be seen once a year or so in every home. It is an attention which Church members count upon and value. It rivets them to the Church. With some of them it is his only means of coming into contact. It makes them all feel that they know their pastor better. It paves the way for closer pastoral dealing at special conjunctures, when they arise. It makes his preaching more practical and gives him more attentive listeners. It comforts the old. It interests the children. Here and there, at least, a stray word in fit

should feel it of immense value to store my memory with facts derived from Christian biography, and similar sources, to be used from time to time in prompting pastoral conversation, and making it at once profitable and easy" (p. 286). It is not every one, however, who has the gift of using anecdotes happily. Others, like Mr. Heard in *The Pastor and the Parish* (Lond. 1865), think it is the minister's business to induce the people to talk to him rather than speak much himself (chap. v.).

season has been spoken. The most careless has been reminded that religion has to do with his home as well as with the house of God. Though every visit will not effect the utmost he intends, yet on the whole the hours which a minister devotes to this duty will not prove to be the least fruitful for the highest ends of the Christian ministry.

CHAPTER XXVI

THE SICK AND THE BEREAVED

WHATEVER amount of time, be it much or little, a pastor may be able to spare for continuous household visitation, there are other visits which have a first claim upon him. The spirit of his office, no less than the example of his Master, makes him a "son of consolation" to the sick and suffering. These he must on no account neglect, for it is the very glory of his office to bear all such upon his heart and to serve them with tender and assiduous care. They fall into several groups.

1. Every congregation will number at least a few chronic cases: either invalids of long standing, or elderly and delicate persons who can seldom attend church, at least in winter. These are to be visited periodically, say, once a fortnight to once a month, according to the size of the congregation or the pastor's other engagements. In this duty it is well to be as methodical as a doctor, duly noting each visit on the sick list, that no one be kept long in expectation after the accustomed day has passed. The fact which distinguishes all such cases and should govern one's treatment of them, is simply that they are deprived of the privileges of weekly worship in public. The purpose of a visit, therefore, is to bring to them in their homes some of the benefit they have lost through their infirmity. It is not always to be done in the same way: as, for example, by a short service of Scripture lesson, comments upon it, and prayer. This may be a good normal type; and when the visit takes that form, any others in the house who are

at liberty and so disposed can be permitted or invited to join in the little service. But a monotonous order is to be avoided. Some account of the Lord's Day sermon, a passage from a book one has been reading that seems appropriate, a choice hymn or sacred poem, news of church work in the congregation or beyond it, will all be useful to give variety. Even an incident in the daily work of the pastor is admissible for its interest, so long as he does not relate in one house what has transpired in another, or allow his chat to become gossipy. Best of all is an occasional serious talk on personal experience in religion, which is not infrequently possible; for among this class are often to be found the choicest of saints and the most deeply exercised in the interior life, to converse with whom does us more good than any benefit we can bring to them.

So soon as a minister has diagnosed the spiritual state of the invalid and established a friendly understanding with him, he will know how to proceed. The rule is to go prepared. Think over beforehand what the character of each visit is to be. Have something ready. Some ministers carry an interleaved Bible, or one with which a few blank pages have been bound up, on which are entered selected texts suitable for various cases likely to occur. This is not commonly a difficult part of the pastor's work; it is often one of the most refreshing for his own spirit. It is only in extremely protracted illnesses that tedium is apt to enter; and then he must be careful not to slacken in his attention or grow remiss in his visiting as though he were weary of it. Even when there is no risk of this, it is an excellent recommendation of Achelis[1] to enlist the kindly aid of a private member of the church, introducing him by consent of both parties, and arranging that he should periodically visit, read to, or pray with the invalid. In Presbyterian Churches there is always a district elder to do this; yet even his services need not render such friendly ministrations from a private member a superfluity.

[1] *Op. cit.* i. 490.

2. Illness of a more acute kind, not necessarily grave or dangerous, however, at least at first, falls under a different category, comprising many varieties. Against such calls a pastor is never secure, and a sudden summons is to be promptly responded to. Ministers frequently complain that the people, even when publicly requested to do so, abstain from sending early notice of an illness in their homes. When that is followed up by the unreasonable reproach that he ought to have come sooner, it is provoking enough. It is to be remembered, on the other side, that sickness which in the end proves grave may begin with a slight indisposition, and friends are often reluctant to trouble their minister unnecessarily. When the seizure is serious from the first, there is usually excitement in the home, with much to think of. In any case, it need hardly be said, no pastor should stand on ceremony. So soon as he is apprised of sickness, he does well to make an immediate call. He can then judge for himself how soon it should be repeated. Van Oosterzee's rule to visit a serious case every two or three days, one of dangerous illness daily,[1] is good enough as a general guide; only it is open to many exceptions according to circumstances. Nothing is so urgently expected or so gratefully remembered as close and devoted attendance where the sickness is at all serious —indeed, at every critical period in the history of a family. By the way in which he treats any such incident, the pastor may either attach a household to himself or alienate it.

Where a minister has a previous acquaintance with the patient, with his character, repute, and religious profession, as must usually happen in purely pastoral visits, he ought to be able to adapt his ministrations to the person's state of mind at least approximately. As a rule, his main object will be to calm and cheer the sufferer by leading him to see in this trouble the hand of his Heavenly Father who always corrects in love for our spiritual profit.

[1] *Praktische Theologie* (Heilbronn, 1878, i. 256).

Affliction is not invariably a rebuke for sins of the past, though it may be; but it always tests and exercises, that it may strengthen, Christian graces. The inspired *rationale* of chastening in the Epistle to the Hebrews [1] may serve as a general directory; but the precise form which the pastor's counsel ought to take must depend on what he knows, or believes he knows, of the person's state of mind. It is always helpful to keep clearly before one's own mind the spiritual exercises proper to one in sickness so long as the physical malady has not impaired the power of collected thought. Such, I mean, as self-examination, acts of penitent trust in God's mercy through Christ, patient endurance, and cheerful submission to the Divine will, and resolutions for an amended life in view of recovery. Which of all these be most called for in a particular case must be judged of from what one knows of it.

It will occasionally happen that a minister is called to see a sick person with whose previous character or present state he is wholly unacquainted. If the condition of the patient permit so much discourse, it is the minister's first duty, not at once to administer comfort, but by tactful questions and often from slight indications to gather whether he is vacant on religious matters or alive to them, anxious or easy in his mind, resting his hope on the Saviour or on some false foundation. This is delicate work. Sick men cannot think much or long, and in many cases nothing can be elicited that justifies any confident inference at all. Under circumstances so unsatisfactory, it seems to be one's duty, first by brief and plain words to strive to rouse the conscience and spirit to religious needs, and then with the utmost simplicity of speech, mostly in the terms of Scripture or of a familiar hymn verse, to set before the sick man the Gospel call and the Gospel promise. It does not do to assume with a person unknown an adequate knowedge of the Gospel. A clear succinct statement of elementary truth in such a case is always wise. An early repetition

[1] 12[1-13].

of the visit, or several of them, is to be recommended, that one may see if the soul be opening to the light. Supposing no immediate danger to life, it is often well to leave some marked passages of Holy Writ to be thought over in the interval; sometimes an easy form of prayer to be used, either by the sick man or by his attendants in his hearing. But it is always possible, where so little is known, that the stranger is silently resting in penitence on the sure foundation; so that the contrary is not to be assumed in one's manner of addressing him. A warm presentation of God's love and of Christ's atonement in a tone of encouragement and assurance will be equally in place on either alternative.

Every visit to a person who is really ill, of whatever malady, needs to be brief, care being observed on no account to excite or fatigue the patient. One's manner in the sick-room is to be alert and firm, doing and saying at once without hesitation what has to be said or done, yet with quietness and self-possession, showing no trace of flurry or haste. One must speak softly, especially to the sick person, yet not so low as to make hearing at all difficult; and never trouble him with many questions nor force him to talk much. What has to be said to the attendants or relatives had better be said outside the room. The rule is, though there are exceptions, to close with brief prayer in direct petitions, slowly uttered if he be very ill, for the most necessary blessings—as forgiveness, peace of conscience, submission, recovery, or the like,—expressed on his behalf, yet so that the sufferer himself can really appropriate them as his own.

The question is often put: Should the minister be expected to attend infectious cases? I have known instances in which, the sick person being well known for an experienced Christian in no special need of counsel or of comfort beyond what he is receiving from those about him, his family have been pleased to say they would not desire their pastor to expose himself to any risk. Under such exceptional circumstances, a man may use his own discretion and go or not as he deems best. But in every case in which his spiritual services are either needed or wished for, he has no more right to avoid risk than a medical man, and his family also must accept whatever risk there is, just like a doctor's household. It is a part of the conditions of their life. I know that this is not required of the clergy of the Church of England. The sixty-seventh canon of that Church says: "When any person is dangerously sick in any parish, the Minister or Curate, having knowledge thereof, shall resort unto him or her (if the disease be not known or probably suspected to be infectious)." Notwithstanding this excess of caution in the law, there is no reason to suppose that Anglican clergymen show less courage or fidelity to duty in this regard than those of any other communion. Every pastor's true attitude is surely expressed by a Lutheran writer when he bids him take it as a matter of course, an incident of his calling, never raising the question—go or not go, at all.[1] Of course the minister is as much bound as the doctor to minimise the risk by every prudent precaution, and should inform himself what those are. Commonsense will tell him not to visit such cases fasting or fatigued; not to touch the patient, or bend over him so as to inhale his breath; not, if he can help it, to take up his position between the bed and the fireplace; not to make another call or rejoin his family till he has had a walk in fresh air, and so forth. For any more special prophylactics, should they be called for, the medical man will advise him, or the nurse. On the other hand, to betray reluctance or timidity in the discharge of a plain duty must produce a bad impression, for it betrays the feebleness either of his compassion for his fellow-man or of his trust in God.

---

[1] Palmer, *op. cit.* pp. 438–439 : "Gehe ich mit dem einfachen, aber stets gleichen Bewusstsein zu den Kranken, 'das ist mein Beruf,' nehme ich's als eine Sache, die sich ganz von selbst versteht, über die ich also kein Wort verliere, da ich mich gar nicht erst besinne : soll ich oder soll ich nicht ?— dann bin ich auch vor Anstechung am meisten sicher."

3. When any malady has reached a dangerous stage, the pastor's attention is redoubled. The approach of death affects Christian people in various ways. The end may be desired, yet not always in a devout temper; sometimes with impatience at the delay because it means prolongation of suffering. Or it may be feared: either because fresh misgivings have sprung up in the sufferer's mind, doubts as to the reality of his interest in Christ; or from the mere clinging of nature to life, or anxiety for those they leave behind, or a shrinking from the mysterious act of dissolution itself. Some disorders, too, make the spirit dull or irresponsive. In others the patient refuses to admit the thought of danger at all.

To a certain extent the pastor must accommodate his ministrations to such diverse moods. Yet the fundamental remedy for them all, which it is never unsafe to apply, is to counsel an unquestioning committal of both soul and body into the Redeemer's hands, with a humble willingness to await His pleasure, whatever the end may be. Such a readiness for either issue is the only thing that will allay disturbance or the restlessness of uncertainty. It tends to brace and settle the dying man on the safe foundation. The few words which are all that can be spoken, and that at intervals, beside a death-bed, can have but one uniform burden. To hold Christ before the fading eye to the last as the soul's one Hope, and His Cross as the pledge of mercy for every sinner alike, is suitable for persons in any condition of mind. To this in a dying hour must the ripest saint come back. Choice, easy and familiar words out of the Holy Book are the fittest to use. And prayers for the dying, so long as the sick man retains consciousness, must be mere ejaculations such as his feebleness can appropriate. If he be unconscious, then let prayer be made earnestly on his behalf with those around his bed, commending the parting soul to God.

By far the most painful and difficult duty of this sort arises when a minister of religion is suddenly summoned to the death-bed of a person whom he either does not know at all, or suspects to be of an irreligious or evil life. Death-bed repentance is probably infrequent enough. Still, it is not impossible. The servant of the Gospel is bound to persevere to the last in holding out to the sinner both its requirement and its promise. He dare not let the man die without an express warning that if he does not repent he must die unsaved. As little dare he withhold the assurance that, if he will turn to God at his latest hour with confession and contrition, God will be merciful even then for Jesus' sake. At such a moment the pastor has need to have ready upon his tongue the very choicest of those full yet short texts which can be most easily grasped. A quiet slow recital of these, varied only by a broken petition for pardon:—more than that in the article of death it is seldom possible to attempt.[1]

In all these suggestions on the pastoral treatment of persons in danger of death, if not actually moribund, it is assumed that the possibility at least of a fatal termination is frankly faced. Not that the patient must be told he is dying, but that it has been conveyed to him in some gentle way that he is in danger. It puts the spiritual adviser in a difficult position if, as not seldom occurs, objection is raised on medical grounds against the remotest hint of the sort. Relatives or nurses sometimes dread to alarm the patient lest it aggravate his symptoms. Sometimes medical men with more authority forbid it, lest, by weakening his will to live, it may lesson the chance of recovery. For such reasons, a policy of concealment, it may even be of deception, is persisted in to the last.

To disobey doctor and nurse is so strong a step that it should only be taken, if at all, in an extreme case ; that is, only if the minister is practically sure, not merely that the patient is dying, but that he is dying unprepared, and that

---

[1] In Blount's *Directorum Pastorale* (Lond. 1865) will be found some useful remarks on bringing dying sinners to repentance (allowance being made for some High Church expressions).

he does not know it.   It rarely comes to that.   But it does happen not infrequently that a minister has to overbear the professional advice to "keep him quiet" by pressing more or less firmly his opinion that the patient ought to be gently advised of the gravity of his case.   In other cases, he takes it on himself, no objection being offered, to lead the sufferer's mind to the true outlook before him.   Not that in the worst extremity any man can, even if he would, cut off hope from a brother; for to the last we are all in the hand of God to kill or to save alive.   But it is a heavy responsibility, and a most dubious kindness, to let a soul pass into eternity oblivious to its danger and unprepared to meet it.   It may be that the dying man has worldly affairs to settle or family messages of farewell to leave behind.   In any case might he not justly complain of our inhumanity if we persist in concealing from him how soon he may have to stand before his Judge?   Concealment in such a matter is hardly to be distinguished from deception.

I do not think the minister who deals thus faithfully with his patient need be uneasy about the consequences. In a fairly long ministry, after paying some attention to the point, I have never seen harm come of it.   Patients, as a rule, suspect danger where it exists.   Suspicion is more agitating than certainty.   It is often a relief to know the worst.   When the sick man gathers from a few cautious, kindly words, or from expressions used in prayer, that it is feared he may not recover, he will usually put some question that leads to a confirmation of his fear.   The effect is commonly to steady him.   He makes up his mind.   He looks the prospect in the face.   He rallies his moral strength to meet it.   He makes his dispositions.   He gives his mind to spiritual counsel.   He "sets his house in order" to die, as a brave and devout man should.

4. A pastor's ministry of consolation to the bereaved may begin in the death-chamber itself, where, at the prospect of their impending loss, it is often more needful to sustain the relatives by soothing sympathy than to

counsel the departing. At a child's death-bed, or when an adult is long unconscious, there is little else to be done. Yet not much can be done at such a trying moment beyond the support which the mere presence of a minister of religion may afford. It is therefore well to pay an early visit of condolence to the house, if possible before the funeral, chiefly for the purpose of offering comfort to the next-of-kin. At the funeral itself, the religious services being of a public or semi-public character and more or less liturgical in form, not much opportunity occurs for pastoral dealing with individual members of the family. Very shortly after it is over, therefore, a visit, which is not to be a hurried one, is always to be paid to the bereaved home. Where a bread-winner has been taken there is often reason for inquiry into the circumstances of the survivors or their altered family arrangements, with a view to proffer aid as well as consolation. Both advice and assistance may have to be given, in seeking employment for the widow, for example, or a situation for a son, or in finding a new home, or in correspondence with the burial club, or the like. Yet in every case the more spiritual design of the visit must not be dropped out of sight. Comfort continues to be the foremost aim; only that it is now best attained, since all is over, by gathering up the religious lessons of bereavement, directing their thoughts to those abiding fruits which discipline is meant to yield, and to the support which, during the unknown dark days to follow, will have to be sought from our Father's guiding hand and from the sympathy of the Man of Sorrows. Usually it is best to do this quite frankly by arranging a little household service when as many as possible can be present, at which suitable Scriptures are read and enforced, closing with a prayer, in the course of which the circumstances of the family are laid before God with some minuteness.

All this presents no special difficulty; but in the task of comforting individually the next-of-kin, particularly widows and bereaved mothers, the pastor is not seldom in a situation which calls for careful and prudent handling. Excessive or unduly prolonged grief may have, at times, to be repressed, or even to be rebuked where it takes the form of rebellious complaint against the dispensations of Heaven. Sometimes mourners bitterly reproach themselves for remembered faults committed against the departed in his lifetime, or for something omitted, which, had it been done, everything would have been different. One may have to point out the fruitlessness of such remorse, even supposing it to be well founded, and to urge as the only remedy that is left, humble confession, asking pardon of God for every known or suspected error in the past. Better still will it be if unavailing regret for the past can be turned into a penitent resolve to act a gentler or more faithful part towards the survivors.

A worse case is when sorrow is made poignant by a fear that the deceased was not fit to die. When this agonising misgiving haunts the bereaved, they generally try to extract from the clergyman something to confirm their clinging hope that all is now well with their lost friend. Of course, the claims of truth may not be sacrificed even to the charitable wish to speak as well as possible of the dead. One can but say what in the judgment of charity one honestly can, and for the rest, be silent. As our creed does not warrant the idea that prayers can now avail, nothing more is possible but to urge that the departed be left to the unknown mercies of the All-merciful, who will have all men to be saved, with a humble hope that, either in the last hours of life, or by ways unrevealed to us, he may be delivered from the guilt of this mortal life through the merits of Him who is the propitiation for the sins of the whole world. Whenever the pastor fears that, be it from this cause or any other, a mourner—it will commonly be a woman—is giving herself up to a brooding sorrow, the surest remedy is to urge her to active exertion, either for the sake of her own surviving household, or, should that be uncalled for, in the service of some of her suffering sisters worse off than herself.

When he discharges the office of a comforter, the Christian minister needs to make sure that it is Christian comfort he is bringing, not fetched from semi - pagan commonplaces about the "common lot" and so forth, which are current at such seasons. Christ's victory over death, the Fatherly love which sweetens chastisement, the blessedness of the Christian dead, the hope of reunion, the resurrection-glory :—these are the topics drawn from our Christian faith, which alone can solace effectually a broken heart. Visits to bereaved parents in particular, whose children have died young, can be devoted entirely to such sources of consolation and to others peculiar to themselves. Full of peculiar comfort are the baptismal pledge of grace, the Good Shepherd's tender love for His lambs, and the thought that they have been early delivered from the hazards of this world. Care has to be taken not to encourage the notion that it is a child's own innocence, rather than the ransoming blood of Christ, which warrants our belief in its salvation. Some pastors tell of puzzling and unanswerable questions that vex bereaved parents, touching the future life of a child, its growth meanwhile, and the unrecognisable changes that may pass over it. I have never encountered these as a source of disquiet. If they occur, they deserve to be met with sympathy, yet gently relegated to that obscurity which wisely shrouds from mortal vision everything that concerns the world of unseen spirits.

CHAPTER XXVII

THE CARE OF THE YOUNG

THE Christian training of the young is a joint concern of the Home, the School, and the Church. Each of these in succession comes to the aid of the others.

For the first six or seven years of a child's life, the pastor, as representing the Church, can bring his influence to bear only indirectly through the parents; but, though indirect, his influence may be very valuable. It is for the parents to create within their home a Christian atmosphere; to breathe into the young child's opening heart his first thought of God and of the Good Shepherd's love; to train him from tender years to the habit of prayer; to lay deep the foundations of character in reverence, obedience, truthfulness, and the fear of God; and by family prayers and regularity at public worship to set a pious example that shall never be forgotten. Unless the soil be thus tilled with care from the first, a pastor's subsequent sowing of good seed will have a poor prospect of fruitfulness. But parents require to be reminded of their baptismal obligations to those tender members of Christ's flock. Both by sermons in church on family relations and parental duty, which surely might well be more frequent than they are, and in the course of pastoral visitation, the minister can do much to incite fathers and mothers to perform their part. He may even advise them as to the likeliest methods. If he be himself a lover of little children, like his Master, and his leisure allow him to become a familiar guest in their homes, he can easily win such a place in their affections as will in a few years constitute him their trusted spiritual counsellor.

So soon as school age is reached, a minister can begin in addition to operate directly on the boys and girls in his parish or congregation. Less often, indeed, than formerly, through the day-school; for modern legislation has been steadily dissolving the old ties which once subsisted between the parochial clergy and the primary education of the people, till now they seem to be on the eve of disappearance. All the more on that account does every pastor, whether in the National or in the Free Churches of this country, need to watch for and to cultivate every other opportunity for the religious instruction of youth which existing arrangements afford. Of course it is in the first instance for the immature members of his own flock that in his character of pastor each minister is bound to care. His means of access to them for purposes of religious instruction and influence during school years, from seven, say, till fourteen or fifteen, are often less close and effective than is to be desired. Several modern methods for making them more so—some, indeed, of quite recent origin—deserve to be glanced at: a young people's portion in the Lord's Day worship, for instance; children's services; associations for the young, like Bands of Hope, the Boys' Brigade, or Junior Societies of Christian Endeavour; and, above all, the Sunday School.

1. To devote a few minutes during the ordinary morning service of each Lord's Day to the boys and girls present is a well-meant innovation, not possible, of course, where the worship is restricted to a liturgy, but meriting consideration from the leader of a free service. It has of late been pretty widely adopted in one form or another, and approves itself, I understand, to the majority of adult worshippers, being welcomed by parents, and by others not disliked. If, by giving the service greater interest for their children, it is

found to encourage parents to bring them to church and so
to accustom them to a habit of attendance under conditions
less burdensome than formerly—this must be deemed a
distinct recommendation of the change. For there is no
question that a long service, much of which we could not
follow, proved a weariness to many of us in our childhood,
and has sometimes led older lads to forsake the house
of God as soon as they were free to follow their inclination.
Experience alone can show how far this method does
increase the interest of the service to juvenile worshippers;
but at the least it must make our boys and girls feel that
they have a place of their own in the house of God as an
integral part of the congregation; and that is a clear
benefit. The chief drawback urged on the other side is
that by inviting attention to their own part of the worship,
it appears to exonerate young people from any effort to
attend to the rest of it. Fearing this result, some prepare
the juniors to listen and understand what is to follow, by
making their own address a simple rehearsal of the main
thought in the subsequent sermon. In most men's hands
this would be apt to forestall the interest of older hearers.
Others recommend no separate address to the young at all,
but an occasional remark or illustration, adapted to youthful
minds, interjected here and there in the course of the
sermon. That, too, I am afraid, is more than most preachers
could attempt with success. Dr. Blaikie's outlet from the
difficulty is a safer one: to make all one's preaching so
lucid, interesting, and in the best sense popular, that it will
be in the main attractive and intelligible to young as well
as old.[1] Even this, however, is not always attainable;
topics have to be handled which cannot be thus simplified for
juvenile hearers. I think many a minister will conclude
that the drawbacks to the "children's portion" are out-
weighed on the whole by the weekly opportunity, even if
brief, which it gives him for the express instruction of an
important class which it is difficult otherwise to reach.

[1] *Op. cit.* pp. 296-297.

To make as much use as they can of the ten minutes at their disposal—for it is hardly possible to spare more—some prefer to devote the whole time to the address. Where a hymn for the young is included, and perhaps also the Lord's Prayer said by all, so as to make a little service of it, which in itself is surely desirable, no more than five minutes will be left for the sermonette. It is just possible to lodge a single truth or lesson in a young heart in five minutes, and even to make it memorable by one happy illustration or short anecdote; but only if it be very well thought out beforehand. More, of course, cannot be attempted; to do this effectively asks as careful study as a sermon, but is quite as well worth it. The young people are to be addressed as boys and girls (for they resent being called "children"), without preamble, in homely, direct, and impromptu speech; and it is well if the illustration selected be drawn, as a rule, from their own stock of knowledge or field of experience.

2. It is surprising that one so seldom hears of religious services exclusively for the young. Some ministers excuse themselves on the plea that they have not the "gift" of preaching to children. It is a difficult duty, no doubt; and the "gift" is possessed by few. Yet any minister who will practise it early in his ministry may learn how to speak to the youth of his own flock, at least, so as both to interest and benefit them. The difficulty seems to be to find favourable occasions, either on the Lord's Day or on week days, when all the young of the flock, including those at school and older youths, can assemble together for the purpose. Where "Children's Day," as it is called, is observed, such a rally for worship will naturally be a leading feature. Advantage can usually be taken of a Sunday-school anniversary. Such a Christian holiday as Christmas lends itself for the purpose. So does a Harvest Festival or a Flower Service. If advantage be taken of every such opening that offers, it ought to be practicable to gather the young people for separate

worship at least once a quarter, and it would be well-spent time.

At such services the pastor himself should be able to arrange for each occasion a special order of worship, warm and bright, but simple and informal, with the music rehearsed beforehand, and as large a share as possible, recitative or responsive, assigned to the children themselves. If he can hold their attention for a twenty minutes' sermon (not longer), he may by God's blessing leave an abiding imprint on their minds. The amount of actual teaching which can be imparted is probably not great; but that is not his primary object. It is to press upon young hearts the truths of the Gospel as far as they have come to know it, and to make Christ an influential presence in their daily lives. The points to attend to in a sermon to children are not hard to discover: a text brief, arresting, and easy to remember; a single truth, central in religion, but not recondite, lodged firmly in the mind; a few " heads," pithily put and repeated till they cannot be forgotten; abundant illustrations taken from the circle of a child's own life, or, at any rate, appealing to his imagination; and all spoken without notes in a lively conversational tone. Even a few such sermons in the course of the year may prove invaluable for the religious life of a congregation.

3. In these days, when societies of every description are in fashion, even boys' and girls' unions are become common; and although exception might probably be taken on one ground or another against any form yet devised, where they exist the minister will generally be able to turn them to account in his pastoral work.

One of the most widespread groups are Bands of Hope. Their original intention as an outgrowth from the temperance movement in last century is to be preserved; but weekly meetings thrive with difficulty on so narrow a basis, so that they have widened in course of time to embrace other aspects of Christian life and duty as well as temperance, until they often assume, or easily may assume, the general

22

character of religious services conducted with a good deal of freedom. Under this form one can see considerable possibilities lying close to the pastor's hand.

Of a different type is the "Boys' Brigade," started in Glasgow a quarter of a century ago, and now familiar on both sides of the Atlantic. This organisation is recruited from a limited class; but it is a difficult class, and its difficulties have been met with singular skill. Any minister working in the densely-peopled parts of an industrial town, who is puzzled what to do for the bands of undisciplined, ill-taught lads that infest its streets out of working hours, can find no more effective ally. The misgiving aroused at first by an air of "militarism" about these companies has been dispelled by their success in generating in such rough boys habits of discipline, of subordination, and of self-respect. On this foundation their conductors aim at building up a Christian manhood; for which end they invariably hold weekly religious exercises and attach themselves to some Christian Church. In so far as they attain their aim they are doing valuable service, not only to the State, but to the kingdom of God.

What are called "Young People's Societies of Christian Endeavour" (to be spoken of later) have sometimes a junior branch in which boys and girls of school age, say, eight to fifteen or so, are enrolled. Certain features in these unions, particularly the pledge which they require from their members, and the meetings for worship in which the young people themselves are expected to take some small and simple share, many will judge to be better suited for youths of an older growth. The danger of precocity, or even of priggishness, must always be borne in mind, and sedulously guarded against. On the other hand, their main design being as early as possible to train to habits of Christian service, there are certainly humble forms of kindly ministry to others which children may quite well begin to render from a pretty early age, so long as they are superintended by prudent Christians of experience. Before he encourages the formation of these or any similar associations, the minister will, of course, satisfy himself of the wisdom of their arrangements as well as of their general utility.

4. By far the largest contribution which the Churches make, both in Britain and in America, to the religious instruction of boys and girls, is made by the Sunday school. A century and a quarter have elapsed since Robert Raikes of Gloucester began his humble essay at repairing, by a Sunday class, the defective education of a few illiterate and neglected children. During this interval the system has won for itself universal adoption, and enlisted in its service hosts of the most earnest Christians in every English-speaking community. It has also, especially in America, as a fruit of study and pains ungrudgingly spent upon it, undergone immense development. In this country its value as an instrument for training the children of the people in Christian knowledge is steadily rising in proportion as the difficulties which beset religious teaching in the public day-schools of England baffle the efforts of statesmen for their solution. In view of this growing importance of the Sunday school, it is disconcerting to find existing among us a widespread and fairly deep dissatisfaction both with its educational methods and with their results.

It must be recollected that at its origin the Sunday school was a contrivance to meet a religious need. It had to be educational in its method, teaching ignorant children to read their Bible, because they were taught nowhere else, and without a knowledge of the Scriptures their religious need could not be met. But its ultimate aim was not the educational, but the religious one—to reach with the saving truths of the Gospel the souls of children growing up like little heathen in the heart of a Christian land. Things have so far changed since then, that it is no longer requisite to give reading lessons. Nevertheless, it is on essentially similar lines that the Sunday school has proceeded all along and proceeds to-day. The teacher has not hitherto been an educationist, either by profession or by training. He has not set himself as his business to convey to every scholar within the years of school attendance a fairly complete and orderly acquaintance, either with Holy Scripture or with the contents of the Christian creed. If he did, his methods would need to be very different. He is a warm-hearted Christian of the type of Raikes himself, whose aim is to reach and draw to the Saviour the hearts of his pupils, and who is fain to use for this great end a Bible lesson put into his hands.

The question which now occupies friendly critics of the system is not whether conversion and religious and moral training have been too much kept in view. As a Church institute these must be its dominant aims. It can have no other *raison d'être*. But the questions which are asked on many sides are (1) whether its religious results have not been so disappointing as to compel a reconsideration of its methods; and if so (2), how far its imperfect educational appliances may not be responsible for these scanty religious results.

I am afraid the inadequate and disappointing results of Sunday-school work as at present conducted can scarcely be denied. One has long been familiar with the all but universal complaint that senior scholars drift off and are largely lost both to school and Church just at the age when they ought to be professing personal trust in Christ and becoming members in full communion. The number of such members who are drawn annually from the school roll is said to be far too small. Is it equally certain that the method of instruction pursued is to any serious extent responsible for this? That is what a good many observers are nowadays affirming with growing emphasis. They allege that through its poor and desultory or unsystematic style of teaching, the school fails to lodge either in the memory, or in the understanding, or in the hearts, of its scholars a coherent and fairly thorough acquaintance either with the facts or with the truths of revelation. Consequently, so it is said, pupils do not carry away with them

at the close of school attendance what will really hold them
to religion, or keep them loyal to Christian habits of
worship, or mould their conduct on Christian lines. In
this way the admitted deficiency in spiritual results is
accounted for, in good part at least, by faults which they
would fain see reformed in the educational machinery of
our schools.

The changes of method which these critics would like to
see introduced are such as the following: (a) training for
young or prospective teachers in the art of education; (b)
better premises, where classes, larger than at present, could
be taught in rooms by themselves; (c) classification of
scholars according to age and attainments; (d) a scheme of
graded lessons to replace the International Lessons now in
use; and (e) the testing of the teaching by examinations,
not of a few picked pupils as the Sunday-School Union does,
but of entire classes. On all these proposals discussion is
now vigorously going on; although attempts to experiment
upon them have not yet gone quite so far. Obviously they
hang together, and look all in one direction. They aim at
assimilating the methods of Sunday instruction in various
ways to those of the day school. From the point of view
of national education, one may anticipate that, if religious
instruction, driven from the primary school or reduced
there to a minimum, comes to depend much more on Sunday
teaching, then the educational efficiency of that teaching
must acquire as years pass growing importance in the
public eye. But this is not the primary point of view from
which the changes I speak of are urged, or ought to be
urged, inside Church circles. From the traditional point of
view, which remains the Christian one, those methods of
Sunday-school teaching must always approve themselves,
not which lodge most knowledge in the mind, but which win
the pupils in the end for Christ and for His Church. And
the chief obstacle to the changes proposed has arisen from
an apprehension entertained by many of our best teachers,
that their spiritual influence, based on personal ties of

affection between teacher and pupil, would suffer in consequence. Undoubtedly that would be a serious loss; for
hitherto this personal influence based on Christian affection
has been the best feature in all Sunday-school work. To
this problem, therefore, the friends of the institution who
believe in its capabilities are bound to address themselves:
Is it possible materially to reform its methods of teaching
without any sacrifice of its religious value or of the personal
influence of the Christian teacher upon the taught?

The matter is not one to be further discussed here, but
I have referred to it because it seems to me that the
minister's attention should be seriously given to it. No
doubt any extensive reforms lie beyond the power of an
individual pastor. Still, he has something in his power.
He is in a position to encourage a study of the whole
situation by the staff of his own school. He can contribute
to create an intelligent public opinion in Sunday-school
circles. Some changes, too, there are, which, if he and his
teachers are convinced of their wisdom, can be locally
introduced without much difficulty. Indifferent to the
subject he can never be, for in all that concerns growing
boys and girls under his care, the Sunday school ought to
be the right arm of the Church.

The relation of every Sunday school to the congregation
with which it stands connected, ought, in a healthy state of
things, to be as close as possible. It is the Church's own
work—the training for Christ of her own little ones, or of
the children of strangers entrusted to her by their parents.
It is done by her own members in her name. And it ought,
like any other department of Church activity, to be superintended by the minister and the others, if any, who divide
with him pastoral responsibility.

In certain districts of England it is not so. An unhappy
cleft continues to separate the two. Schools are administered
by their teaching staff with hardly a link uniting them to
the congregation, save that they usually occupy church
premises. This unnatural severance is a survival from early

days when schools sprang up through the voluntary enterprise of private Christians, but were looked on askance by
ecclesiastical authorities. Where any minister finds this
independent management in force and jealously conserved,
as it is likely to be, he gains nothing by prematurely forcing
a departure from it. The wiser course is to make the
teachers aware that he respects their autonomy and is only
anxious to co-operate with them to the utmost. By cultivating personal relations with the superintendent, and, if
permitted, meeting the class teachers regularly over the
study of their lessons, he will generally gain their confidence
and have no difficulty in making his influence felt. But
the rule is that a closer relation obtains between school and
church, which, while it leaves a good deal of school business
to the staff, reserves for the local church authority a
sufficient, if vague, right of supervision. The most important
point, then, is that the minister be consulted in the selection
of teachers, above all, of the superintendent. It is rarely
necessary, and, when not necessary, it is undesirable, for
the minister himself to superintend, although he should
frequently be present. If in a very small flock he cannot
find a suitable substitute, he ought at least to be relieved
of clerical and other details. For the most part his influence
will be felt, rather than his hand seen, in the conduct of
school affairs. With its personnel he will keep in close
touch. Of his warm interest in their work and readiness
to render it all the assistance in his power, there ought
never to be any question.

About the age of puberty and for a few years after it,
pastoral care for the youth of the flock ought to be at its
maximum. As they approach that critical stage of life
when adolescence begins, the Sunday school begins to be
left behind as too childish, character develops under a sense
of self-conscious responsibility, action grows independent,
and the passions gain strength. From thirteen to eighteen
or so is the most hazardous period of growth, when grave

risks have to be encountered. Then, if ever, the pastor's eye should be upon a young lad or maiden.

At what time the first movements of the new life normally begin in a baptized child of the Church, no one knows. It may occur at baptism. It may precede the dawn of moral self-consciousness. Christian life may unfold all through childhood with the development of personality and of character. Who knows ? But what by the laws of human growth is likely to happen is, that a crisis is reached in a young Christian's experience, of which the characteristic feature is this, that the inbred unconscious child-faith becomes at length aware of itself. This it does when intellect, conscience, and will are all sufficiently mature to make deliberate and intelligent choice of Christ as Saviour and of subjection to Him as the rule of life. By the wisdom of his dealing with them at this juncture, the pastor may save from wandering and determine for a Christian life the opening manhood and womanhood of those who shall be the very flower and promise of the Church.

But if he defer making close acquaintance with them till they have actually reached or passed the critical period, it will often be too late to commence it then. An age of reserve sets in, even of suspicion. The approaches of one who has till then been a stranger may be sooner repelled than welcomed. The minister's attention ought therefore to be turned to those older scholars still on the school bench who within a year or two more will be ready for his own Bible class. It may be too much to ask a minister to form close ties with the hundreds of outsiders who swell the lists in many schools, having no other link with the Church, yet almost swamping the children of the congregation. With them other helpers may be left to deal. But if he cannot know all, let him at least cultivate the friendship of the children of his own Church members. They are a charge for which he is responsible. They ought by this time to be familiar to him by face and name, through family visits or casual meetings. This acquaintance is now to be improved into a nearer confidence. To invite them to the manse or parsonage, set them small jobs to do about the church, and in every way exhibit a frank interest in them, will more surely and more richly repay his trouble than almost any other duty he can take in hand. If the pastorate had not too much neglected to acquire a personal hold upon the affections of these bigger boys and girls on the eve of adolescence, their transition from the school to the pastor's class would have been, more often than it is, a matter of course.

It is well to make this transition before the scholar's link with the school snaps of itself; to make it on the pastor's own initiative, and to do it in a way which marks its importance as a step upward or makes it somewhat of a compliment. The change ought to be felt as bringing the youth into manlier relations with his pastor, in fact, as his admission to the dignity of a friend. For the same reason it is well when the minister's class meets under another name, and in another place, from the school. Certainly it should be conducted on different lines. Its object never is to cram with more information, even if it be required to systematise the often scrappy knowledge or loose notions about religion which may be all the pupil has acquired at school. Rather it is to educate mind and heart to act for themselves on Gospel truth, so far as known. Often this is best done by setting the members of his class to inquire and reflect, to search the Bible, and to think for themselves. It may also be desirable to knit their ideas into a clearer whole by taking them systematically through the Creed or the Catechism or some easy manual of doctrinal teaching. But what has to be pressed from point to point is the bearing of it all on their own experience—never suffering them to forget that what matters now is not abstract knowledge about God, but through knowledge life in Him.

Wherever a pastor has to deal on these lines with lads or girls of superior education and disciplined intelligence, whom he can really succeed in interesting in his own class for advanced religious education, I question if he wants any other instrument to ripen them for future membership, or need ask for any better means of effective influence over them. In fact, nothing better can be done for adolescents of any class, who, between the age of (say) fifteen and eighteen or over, ought still to be learners. But it is by no means always practicable to secure their attendance. For one reason or another, many young people, just set free from school, cannot be induced to submit to any longer course of instruction. Then it is that a "Society of Christian Endeavour" may be found helpful. Founded in 1881 by Dr. Clark at Portland, United States, these organisations have rapidly sprung up in nearly every evangelical Church. Evidently they offer attractions for young people. Banding together for mutual help in leading a Christian life and for service in connection with the Church, persons of both sexes, whether they already profess themselves servants of Christ or are simply content to place themselves under religious influence, these unions appeal to the love of comradeship and the desire to share actively in common work—both of them powerful motives at that period of life. Primarily they operate on the cultivation of the religious life by daily prayer and Bible-reading, as well as by a weekly devotional meeting at which all in full membership with the society are under promise to take part. Once a month it becomes a meeting for renewal of personal "consecration" to Christ. But they likewise create sundry outlets for youthful zeal by assigning to lesser groups within the society definite forms of Christian usefulness suited to the years or the capacity of the members. "Endeavourers," therefore, if true to their motto—"For Christ and the Church"—are expected by the advocates of this movement to furnish in the near future trained workers, both willing and capable, for every department of religious service. Not to the intellectual side of the growing Christian life of our time, but to its practical side, do these societies profess to minister; and yet it ought not to be impossible in the case of some to link on to their active machinery an easy or alluring method of systematic Bible study, beyond the private perusal of selected chapters.

It is an understood rule that such unions are invariably to be presided over by the minister. It ought to be more than a nominal or honorary presidency. The system not only attracts certain sections of the young, it has possibilities of value. But it is evidently liable to abuse if neglected or abandoned to the unfit or the immature. It may breed a shallow or fussy conceit in the room of growing self-know-ledge and deepening devotion. Possibly a wise minister will find the safest corrective against such evils in the influence exerted over younger members of the society by a few of the older and more experienced ones, whose character has attained a certain maturity.[1]

I suppose opinion will be divided as to the prudence or the propriety of requiring from persons in their teens, who are not yet candidates for Holy Communion, a pledge which, involving as it does a profession of personal reliance upon Christ as Saviour, with a promise of obedience to Him as Lord, cannot be distinguished from the conditions of adult disciplehood. Certainly, so soon as a youthful believer is ripe to take the "endeavourer's" pledge, there is no reason in the world why he should not be at once enrolled in a Confirmation or Communicants' class, with a view to his immediate reception into the full fellowship of the Church.[2]

---

[1] I am not aware that there is any *upper* limit of age for members.

[2] By all candidates for active membership the following card has to be signed : "Relying on the Lord Jesus Christ for salvation, and trusting in God for strength, I promise Him that I will strive to do whatever He would like to have me do. I will pray to Him and read the Bible every day ; I will support my own Church and its services in every way within my power ; and throughout my whole life I will 'endeavour, by His grace, to lead a Christian life. As an Active Member, I promise to be true to all my duties, to be present at, and to take some part, aside from singing, in every meeting, unless hindered by some reason which I can conscientiously give to my Lord and Master, Jesus Christ. If obliged to be absent from the monthly Consecration Meeting, I will, if possible, send an excuse for absence to the Society."—From *Young People's Society of Christian Endeavour : What it is and How it Works*, by Rev. F. E. Clark, D.D.

Both the Endeavour Society and the minister's own class for instruction ought, by the Divine blessing, to yield candidates for Holy Communion. It will always be a conscious aim of the pastor to lead these impressionable lads and maidens into such a definite surrender to Christ as will inspire a desire for the Table of the Lord. For this purpose it is of immense consequence to second other religious agencies by private intercourse. Pastoral influence at that age of self-decision rarely fails to tell. It does so not only by the kindliness and familiarity of the pastor's attitude towards them, but also by direct dealing with them alone on spiritual matters. Not too frequently, yet more than once, he takes occasion to lead the conversation to the subject of personal religion, to elicit, if possible, confidences on their part, and to press home their responsibility not to " receive the grace of God in vain."

The rite which is meant to close this religious crisis in youthful experience is the " first Communion," whether it be preceded by " Confirmation " or by any other form of admission to Christian adulthood. This great step usually comprises two stages. The first is one of instruction. How a little group of professed candidates for Confirmation or for first Communion can best be instructed, is in many Churches left to each minister's discretion. A frequent practice is to concentrate his lessons around the Holy Supper itself—its institution, its foreshadow in the Passover, its doctrinal implicates, its spiritual meaning and practical uses. This has the advantage of not seeming to carry the catechumens back over familiar ground. At the same time everything which is of primary importance in Christian truth can easily find a place under it, if it be desired. The careful explanation of the great sacrament tends to impress the young communicant with the gravity of the step he is taking; and this is valuable, for a first Communion is a critical step which for good or ill can never be retraced. Both in the class and at private interviews everything is to be done to lead the intending participant in the Body and Blood of

the Lord to deeper penitence for sin, to a warmer sense of
Christ's love, to an unreserved dedication to His service, and
to a very tender lively gratitude for what he owes to the
awful Passion of his Saviour.   To know is here not enough;
not enough even to believe.   He is to be led to feel and
to resolve.

There only remains a formal act of reception on the part
of the Church.   The ancient rite of Confirmation retained
in the Church of England follows, of course, its own prescribed order.   Imposition of episcopal hands is really all
that distinguishes it from such a ceremony of admission to
full membership as is usual in other communions.   In them
also the reception ought to be celebrated at a solemn service,
held, when it can be done, in the presence of the congregation.   After an open avowal of their faith and of their
resolution to follow Christ, prayer is to be offered for the
candidates, with invocation upon them of the Holy Spirit, a
brief exhortation to consistent Christian living is to be
addressed to them, and the hand of fellowship to be given.

With their enrolment as adult members, a pastor's care
for the youth of his flock loses its specific quality, and is
merged in that wider ministry to which all the other
members possess a common claim.   Yet in modern days
it has been practically recognised that young men and
women, whether communicants or not, continue for some
time to constitute a group with needs and duties of their
own.   Outside all our Churches, this feeling has given birth
to vast organisations known as "Young Men's" or "Young
Women's Christian Associations."   Within the Churches,
also, young men and women are accustomed to combine
for special objects: for the cultivation of the devout life
in "Fellowship," or Prayer, Meetings; for intellectual
culture in Literary or Debating Societies; sometimes also
for social service, home mission work and kindred forms
of Christian beneficence.   In Scotland each of the two
largest Presbyterian communions has grouped all these

under one organised "Guild," which has its branches distributed over the kingdom in parish or congregation, yet affords the cohesion and strength of a national agency devoted to Christian life and work. Unions of such a character have commonly asked nothing of the minister except his countenance, sympathy, and occasional assistance. But they are full of hope for the future manhood and womanhood of the Church.

Where the young men and women of our time are keenly alive to its intellectual movements, fresh developments may be looked for among pupils of an older growth. One I have lately heard of. Within the last few years, I am told that a number of the junior clergy in Scotland have found in the larger towns a new opening among intelligent young people which promises well. Retaining the old name of a "Bible Class" (after the example of Dr. Alexander Whyte of Edinburgh, with whom the movement originated), it really consists of Sunday lectures delivered in church to audiences of young people at the close of evening service. The subjects range over such heads as the relations of religion with literature, art, and science, the influence of selected authors upon the higher life, and any social or biblical questions that are under discussion. What is noteworthy is that large numbers of persons at an age that may average as high as five and twenty are willing to listen to conversational lectures on such subjects, provided the minister be a scholarly and reading man, who is willing to take pains and to give them of his best. How far the experiment has been repeated in England or in America I am not aware.

CHAPTER XXVIII

CASES OF SPIRITUAL TROUBLE

In the course of his ministry, every pastor meets with persons troubled in mind, who are moved to make him their confidant, in the hope that as God's servant he may be able to bring them relief, or direction, or comfort. Such cases admit of classification. The three groups suggested by Achelis—the suffering, the sinning and the erring[1]— are now usual in German text-books. But the principle of division is too abstract; the cases run into one another. In their features, their circumstances, and their causes, there are never two alike; so that no directory for his guidance is likely to afford the under-physician of sick souls much assistance. It is a department of the *cura animarum* which the Roman Church has found it needful to pursue into much detail, sometimes unpleasant detail, in her text-books for the use of priests in the confessional, but of which Protestant literature has always been shy. Many continental writers indeed, Lutherans especially, discuss the treatment proper for certain marked classes with some fulness;[2] but in most English or American books on pastoral theology little is to be found. Even exact reports of cases met with in actual practice, which might lay the foundation for an inductive study of the subject, hardly

---

[1] *Op. cit.* i. 495.

[2] See, *e.g.*, the treatises of Vinet (posthumous, 1850), Nitzsch (B. iii. 1, 1857), Palmer (1860), Otto (1869), Vilmar (posthumous, 1872), Schweizer (1875), Zezschwitz (1878), Van Oosterzee (German ed. 1879), and Achelis (1890).

exist; the example set by Spencer in his *Pastor's Sketches* having had, so far as I know, few, if any, imitators. The minister's own good sense, sympathy, and spiritual insight must be his best outfit for this work, experience his safest guide, and humble reliance on a wisdom higher than his own his unfailing resource.

One feature there is common to nearly every case of the kind. Unless those who are burdened with such secret loads will be entirely open and without reserve, it is clear that no one can do them much good. In this way a pastor is made the depositary of confidences which, whether they only affect the person making them or others as well, it is needless to say he is bound to hold sacred. No matter whether they refer to the inner experiences of a soul or to the private affairs of a family, he must keep them to himself. Not even in the seclusion of his home may he divulge what has thus been entrusted to his professional honour.[1]

In saying what little I can on a side of pastoral duty so delicate, all I can do is in this closing chapter to give specimens from two or three classes of cases, to show what kind of confidences a minister must be prepared to meet.

I. I shall begin with persons under conviction of sin who are putting the old question: What must I do to be saved?

Every normal instance of this kind a true minister will welcome with solemn thankfulness. One must suppose that numbers of them occur which run their course unobserved by any eye save that of God. Yet in his visiting, or in his class-work, or in connection with the preaching

---

[1] Of course, to tell abroad what reflects injuriously upon character must lay him open to a civil action for slander or defamation. If it be even a criminal act which a penitent has confessed, he is not generally held bound to reveal it unless called upon to give evidence in a court of justice. To the rule of secrecy there is, however, one exception. When it is not a crime committed, but the intention to commit one, of which the pastor is made aware, but from which he cannot dissuade the man, he is bound to disclose the information to the proper authorities, that the perpetration of the crime may be hindered.

of the Gospel, an earnest man, whose ministry is aimed
at soul-winning, may hope to come across them. No joy
is purer or more absorbing than this "joy of harvest."
To him as to his Master it is like meat and drink. He
ought not to need instruction how to deal with them.
Yet if a young minister has any opportunity to take part
in an "inquiry room" at a revival meeting or a successful
"mission," he will be wise to take advantage of it. It will
yield him useful hints. Above all, it will sharpen in his
mind the conviction that he is here in the presence of
a mightier force than his own—a Worker on whose
mysterious sovereign energy everything must depend.

When the inquirer, as will often happen, is one who has
borne a Christian reputation, and in whose past life some
earlier crisis occurred which was taken at the time to be
"conversion," it is better not to let him puzzle himself
over the question whether that previous experience was
genuine or illusory. Counsel him to leave the past with
God, and now to turn to Christ as if for the first time.

In every case it is a mistake to skin over the wound
with premature comfort before the arrow has gone deep
enough. For a radical cure a thorough repentance is
essential. The wise pastor will probe to make sure that
there is more than regret for the past because of its apprehended consequences, and will seek to deepen the sense of
sin's guilt and evil in God's sight. He will urge a full
confession to God of the ungodliness in which the penitent
has been living, with any definite acts or habits of sin of
which conscience accuses him. Then the way of salvation
needs in most cases to be clearly explained; for mere
exhortations to "come to Christ" may mean little, till the
Saviour's expiation and the Divine love of which the Cross
assures us are plainly set forth. This usually calls for the
removal of vague notions as to what is meant by "saving
faith." It has to be urged as an act of personal reliance
on the living Person who has won for us the gift of
forgiveness. When Christ is accepted, His minister will

23

try to make sure that the self-committal to Him is explicit and unreserved, including a deliberate acceptance of the terms of discipleship. Much of the comfort and steadfastness of the after life turns on everything being consciously surrendered from the first which conflicts with loyalty to the commands of Christ as the soul's new Lord. Nor ought the case to be considered closed at this stage; for converts are liable to reaction of feeling and to unlooked for risks and difficulties, such as a tendency to over-confidence in themselves, to intemperate zeal, or to uncharitable judgments upon older believers. They require for some time to be kept in hand, warned of such dangers, and encouraged to confide their new experiences to him who has been to them as a father in the faith.

Abnormal instances of anxiety about one's own salvation also occur, of varied character, but all difficult of treatment.

One of the simplest, not unusual among ill-taught and superstitious people, is when an inquirer will not believe on the naked word of promise, because he is waiting for some sensible token of the Divine favour, a voice, or dream, or bright light, or at least an exceptional access of joyous relief from his anxiety.

More difficult to remedy is the case of one who complains of being beset and hindered in his prayers or quiet meditations on religion by the involuntary intrusion of evil thoughts, sceptical or blasphemous or impure, which he ascribes to assaults of the Evil One. Some bid us look for the cause of this infliction to the evil habits of the past life or to a sinful indulgence still harboured or tolerated, and prescribe a course of moral self-discipline with vigilance and prayer. But this is not always so, for such distressing incursions of evil may be allowed to harass persons of the cleanest life, and in such a case occupation in wholesome labour for others with a simple trust in Him who came to destroy the works of the devil may be the best remedy. No soul need blame itself for sinful thoughts against which it revolts, but suffer them as it would any other infliction.

Again: the sense of sin, instead of yielding to trust in offered mercy, may turn into a settled melancholy that refuses to be comforted, refuses even to pray. This may work out in one of two directions. It may swell into an exaggerated self-accusing, affirming its sins to have been of such exceptional guilt that there can be no forgiveness for them. This often generates a perverted self-importance, for it is quite possible to be proud of being "the chief of sinners." A conscience-twist of this sort is hard to straighten out; but the pride at the root of it must be unsparingly beaten down. We have all to stand before God in one vulgar category of condemned transgressors, if we are to receive the "common salvation."

Or the soul may fall into more grievous despair through the obsession of some fixed idea which shuts out light and hope. The most common sources of this malady have been (1) the doctrine of election, or of man's inability to convert himself, when taken in a fatalistic sense, which paralyses every effort of the will to turn to God in penitence and prayer; and (2) the fear to have committed the "unpardonable sin," forgetting that whatever be the nature of this sin, God cannot have finally withdrawn His grace from any soul that longs for deliverance and recovery. Be the cause what it may, no condition in the range of spiritual pathology is more painful or more obstinate. Dr. Washington Gladden may be correct in thinking that such cases are less numerous than they used to be; yet I should suppose most ministers of experience have met with them. To deal with them requires a combination of sympathy, insight, and firmness of touch. The patient has to be persuaded at the outset that the gravity of his case is appreciated. For this purpose the delusion has to be quietly faced and patiently reasoned down by showing it to be devoid of solid foundation. When that has been sufficiently done, the minister will not allow himself to be pulled back to go over and over again the same dismal story; for it is as bad to humour the trouble as to make light of it. All such patients think their own case quite peculiar. The sufferer's attention needs, therefore, to be diverted from morbid dwelling on what he considers the peculiarity of his own condition. To get him back into the common lot, above all, into the common experience of God's abounding goodness, till he can rest on a hope of mercy open to him as to all men:—this is the road to wholesomer thoughts. Then his will must be plied with incentives to let everything else that is dark or dubious go that he may risk all on Christ and His plain words of promise. Such persons usually refuse to pray for themselves. One should insist on their joining in words of prayer or at all events listening while they are prayed for. But no one need be disappointed if the cure be tedious, and whenever the case proves obstinate it is always well to look for con-current physical causes, for it rarely happens that these are wholly absent. If neurotic weakness or hepatic disorder or the like be suspected, the advice of a sensible doctor should invariably be called in. Obstinate cases are never to be neglected ; for " that way madness lies."

II. Misconduct, secret or open, on the part of members of the Church or of their families, is occasionally brought to the knowledge of the pastor in a way which calls for some action on his part. In every such case the Apostolic direction must, for his own sake as well as theirs, be laid to heart:—" Brethren, even if a man be overtaken in any trespass, ye which are spiritual restore such a one in a spirit of meekness ; looking to thyself lest thou also be tempted." [1]

Any minister who comes into confidential relations with his people may chance to hear confessions which astonish him. Many a life that is full of the best fruits of Christian character is kept irreproachable, and made thus fruitful, only at the cost of a hard inward fight which no onlooker suspects : a fight waged under the eye of Christ against, it may be, constitutional tendencies, it may be, temptations

[1] Gal. 6[1].

that beset from without. Now and again, in an hour of brotherly unreserve, one may be awed by a glimpse into these hidden conflicts in a brother's soul. The better a man knows his own heart, the less will he wonder at it, and the more tender will be the hand with which he tries to lift his tempted brother after a defeat, or to brace him to a fresh struggle.

For one who has been overtaken in an open trespass to come to his pastor with a spontaneous confession of it is, I should think, rare. More often it is left to reach the minister's ears through rumour or confidentially through a relative—it makes a good deal of difference which. Let me speak first of the privileged communications of relatives.

Unhappy homes furnish the pastor with some of his worst difficulties. Manners vary in different ranks of society; and among outspoken working folk, a woman's grumbles about her husband's conduct need not always be taken too seriously. But matters are generally pretty bad in an average middle-class household before one inmate will volunteer a complaint against another—especially before the wife's secret burden becomes too heavy to be longer borne in silence. A heart-broken woman has a claim on the best consolation, counsel, or encouragement to patient endurance which her religious guide can fetch out of God's Word, whether he have any means or not of testing her complaints. She will probably wish her husband spoken to; but if the facts are only known through her own communication, to act upon that private information would be likely to make things much worse. One can but wait until circumstances open up some other source of knowledge or some other opportunity for private dealing with the man. When the trouble has its origin, not wholly in the misconduct of one party, but in domestic misunderstandings where blame is to be presumed on both sides, it is almost never prudent to intervene. Only in an extreme case of conjugal disagreement, with the hope of obviating an open rupture, a minister may consent, on the invitation of both parties, to attempt a reconciliation, or at least an adjustment, just as any other impartial and trusted adviser might be asked to do. But in no case of family strife can one's good offices be hopefully exerted save at the desire, or at any rate with the consent, of both parties to the dispute.

A fairly frequent case arises through the anxiety of parents about the conduct of their children. A father or a mother may confide the trouble to the minister in preference to any other, in the hope that he will have influence where their own remonstrances have proved ineffectual. His action will be made easier if they are willing that the youth be frankly told of their having done so. He can then be approached without reserve, and much will depend on the tact with which the approach is made. To accost him with blunt charges made at second-hand would, of course, be to wound his *amour propre*, and simply throw one's chance away. Nor is that needful; for the gentlest hint will suffice if it be met with candour on his part, as it generally will be when he sees that he is trusted to explain what has given rise to complaint. All his explanations and even excuses are not only to be listened to, they are to be welcomed. Because it is after hearing sympathetically whatever he has to urge in his defence, that he will accept of blame, grave but gentle blame, founded on what he himself admits to be blameworthy. Parents are sometimes apt to press unduly on youthful indiscretions or irregularities. So long as faults have not yet stiffened into habits, and no irretrievable act—say of immorality or of dishonesty—has been committed, it is often wiser to say less about the past than about the future. Should open misconduct have occurred, a severer tone may be necessary. For the difficulty then is to brush aside evasions and extenuations, and to call forth such shame and genuine sorrow as will lead to a frank confession. In any case one may hope to inspire a resolution of amendment. There is always in young bosoms a reserve of manly unspoilt feeling that can be evoked. A young pastor will have an advantage over an old one in deal-

ing with young men. So much so that it is often worth
while for an elderly minister to prepare his own way by
sending some junior friend of the family or of the youth to
talk the matter over. There is a freemasonry among the
young. And, for a similar reason, young women are best
approached, in the first instance at least, by one of their
own sex.

It is pitiable, however, when matters have gone so far.
Better to forestall possible tragedies at the opening of life
by gaining beforehand a friendly hold over young hearts
which will keep them true; and by faithfully warning lads
and maidens, entering upon business or leaving home, of the
risks they are bound to run through doubtful associates or
through the seduction of social pleasure.

Lapses by older members of the Church, either into an
evil habit or into a gross act of sin, come to the minister's
ears, not confidentially as a rule, but by the voice of common fame. Whether they ultimately call on public grounds
for ecclesiastical discipline or not, the pastor has at least a
prior duty to discharge to the individual himself.

We are neither spies upon our people nor censors of
their private manners. We ought neither to be in a hurry to
take up an ill report, nor make any man an offender for a
trifle. There was a time when both in England and in
Scotland the excessive discipline of the Presbyterian clergy,
excessive both in what it counted an offence and in the
severity with which every offence was visited, wrought much
harm. It was not so much that it made Puritan piety
unpopular, as that it evoked in public morals a disastrous
reaction. The present temper of the average man is disposed
unduly to resent clerical censures. It is often difficult for
a conscientious pastor to exert, even in the mildest form, his
legitimate power to rebuke offenders. To have the least
chance, therefore, of doing any good by this function of his
office, a man has need to exercise it with scrupulous
prudence, tact, and brotherly-kindness. It is on the footing
of Christian brotherhood that those "overtaken in a fault"

are to be approached, and the fraternal attitude, not a clerical or professional one, promises the best result. In things indifferent the right of a Christian man's liberty must always be respected. Where brethren may reasonably differ in the view they take of the lawfulness of an act, we are not to judge our neighbour. " Let each man be fully assured in his own mind." [1] This applies to a wide circle of questions, such as amusements, luxuries, social customs, and the like— a wider circle than in the days of our fathers. I do not mean that an earnest minister, whose personal habits are strict, may not upon occasion express his private opinion, or even remonstrate with a member of the Church who seems to be permitting himself a questionable, perhaps a perilous, conformity with the usages of the world. Only he must always recollect, and show that he recollects, that in such matters each Christian is Christ's freeman, not bound to render account of himself to any man's judgment.

Nor will a considerate pastor be in haste to reproach a brother for minor faults unless they are habitual, for from these no one is free. " If any stumbleth not in word, the same is a perfect man." [2] But this does not apply to gross sins of overt act. A single instance, say, of intoxication or of licentiousness, may well justify serious remonstrance. But we must never act on mere suspicion or random gossip nor even on rumour, unless it be persistent and force itself upon us. There is nothing worse than to base an accusation upon a loose report at second-hand, which may be ill-founded, may even be the calumny of an ill-wisher.

As a rule, the pastor goes alone to the person implicated, when he feels it unavoidable to undertake so painful a duty, and never without purging his own motives by secret self-humbling and prayer. Some neglect on his own part may have conduced to this brother's fall. In similar circumstances he himself might have fallen as badly or worse. Has he never been secretly guilty of anything in God's sight as bad? A contrite heart is essential in one whose

[1] Rom. 14[5].   [2] Jas. 3[2].

office calls him to be a reprover of his brethren. Everything will depend on the offender being made to feel that the minister of Christ comes in pure love for his soul, on an errand which gives him pain and is only undertaken under a constraining sense of duty.

Such a visit may be met with denials or excuses. It may be resented. Or there may be a light-hearted admission of a fault the gravity of which is not felt. For any of these alternatives the minister needs to go prepared. A man does not receive rebuke in a right spirit until he is softened, and to soften him, one's own heart must be tender and humble. Even then, nothing one can say will bring a hard proud temper to confession and penitence, unless the Divine Spirit breathe upon the soul. Tones of authority or of rebuke are to be kept till the offender is either penitent enough to receive reproof, or discovers himself so callous that gentle measures are thrown away upon him.

One such case as this in years of ministry is a humbling enough experience for any sensitive pastor. When they occur with frequency, he will ask himself whether they do not indicate a low level of religious life in the Christian community around or in his own congregation. It may be that Church members are slipping into slack and unwatchful ways. They have lost sight of the ethical ideal of Christian behaviour, or they are grown self-righteous and high-minded, having forgotten the warning: "Let him that thinketh he standeth take heed lest he fall." [1] His own teaching may be at fault. It may be his duty to raise the standard of holy living by which his people are measuring themselves, or to speak more plainly from the pulpit for the correction of prevalent faults. The whole tone of spiritual life may need to be improved; and it is for him as overseer of the flock to detect the need and if possible to apply the remedy.

III. Of cases which may call for special treatment, I

[2] 1 Cor. 10[12].

shall name only one class more—those which arise from unsettlement in religious opinion or belief. These also are very varied in their character.

The form of intellectual unsettlement which is probably of most frequent occurrence, and which certainly gives rise to the most serious trouble of mind—is doubt; but it is not the only form of it which a minister may expect to meet. In the present welter of opinion, people are apt to be driven hither and thither " by every wind of doctrine." New ideas work like yeast in minds that are often too ill-regulated or too ill-informed to be capable of a sound judgment upon them; and theories, novel or strange, get afloat which puzzle some and captivate others.

Should a young minister encounter in his pastoral intercourse unfamiliar, or what he deems erroneous, notions of this sort, it may help him to meet them with greater equanimity, to reflect that his primary concern as a pastor is not with the correctness of his people's private opinions. What he has to care for is their wholesome Christian character and spiritual growth in the Divine life—their opinions only in the degree in which these are injuriously affecting their religious welfare. Now, it is true that every morsel of revealed truth, like " every scripture inspired of God," is " profitable," and has some contribution to make, large or small, toward the " completeness " of a " man of God " [1] One can never affirm, therefore, of any teaching in the region of religion or morals that it is certain to be innocuous. At the same time, the harm which a mistaken opinion may work on Christian life varies by infinite degrees. Not every current form of error is deadly ; not every tenet even goes deep enough to do appreciable mischief; and where one might expect it to prove mischievous, it is surprising how much better people can be than their beliefs. The life of God in the soul of man, like lower kinds of life, seems to possess a singular power of appropriating the good and rejecting what is bad. From

[1] Cf. 2 Tim. 3[16, 17].

such truth as each man holds his higher life draws nutriment; the error that mingles with it is often neutralised and rendered harmless. On a multitude of peripheral points even of religious doctrine, consequently, excellent Christians think in opposite ways, without the one being made less excellent by his opinion than the other. On such a subject, for example (to name but a couple of instances) as premillenarianism or the inerrancy of inspired Scripture, the view which a person adopts may be, from the pastoral standpoint, of no practical consequence. Possibly every one may not agree with me, but I think much the same might be said of certain quasi-religious speculations—" cranks " some would term them—which are now and then to be met with among blameless and devout persons : such as the Anglo-Israel theory of the Ten Tribes, or faith healing, or Christian science, or the like. If people lend a hospitable ear to these, yet in such a way that they do not touch their religious devotion to Christ, or trench upon any vital element in Christian faith, or undermine Christian morals at any point—I do not see why they should not be good-humouredly skirmished with when encountered, without occasioning serious alarm to any sensible pastor. If it become necessary to correct any prevalent error, that may be done in public addresses ; but, as a rule, error of every sort is best forestalled or overcome by the intelligent exposition of positive Christian truth in a spirit far removed from polemics.

Cases of doubt or of scepticism, whether in reference to vital doctrines of the faith or to the claims of the Christian religion itself, stand, I think, on a different footing. Doubt is always enfeebling to the spiritual life. With every serious and reverent doubter, therefore, a pastor will show himself patient and painstaking. Each case is best dealt with alone, for each presents features of its own. In each case the minister will do his best to ascertain and sympathise with the state of mind or heart out of which the difficulty has grown. But here also the same test of its practical bearing on the inner life is useful to discriminate between one case of doubt and another. Too much should never be made of minor difficulties. Hesitation about accepting some subordinate article of the orthodox creed, or inability to harmonise with one's religious views the teachings either of biblical or of physical science, is an extremely common state at present; but either the one or the other may be easily detachable from that faith in Jesus Christ by which the soul lives from day to day. If it be so, it ought to be kept in its proper place as a secondary matter. Numbers of men to-day are managing to hold to Christ, and to maintain living relations with Him which they would not for the world surrender, who yet are far from accepting everything that the creeds say, or who keep meanwhile a very open mind on a crowd of problems which they know to be involved in Christianity or in its intellectual implicates.

But it is far from easy for every young inquirer to appraise in this temper of *sang-froid* the bearings of his own doubts. Especially when a youth has been brought up in the unquestioning acceptance of traditional views, all of which he is accustomed to regard as equally certain, so that to doubt the least of them is to imperil, almost impiously, the stability of the whole, it must be with trepidation that he finds his inherited ideas for the first time rudely shaken. The earliest thing to be done may probably be to satisfy him that the case is not so critical as he fears. No quiet or impartial examination of his difficulty may be possible, till he discovers that one can be a very good Christian indeed and yet think on many points quite otherwise from his forefathers. Perhaps the next step will be to suggest that, seeing the "ark" is in no danger, there is no need to hurry to a precipitate settlement of every question that can be started. Wisdom does not lie in embracing with haste, any more than in blindly refusing, every new idea. It is true that an attitude of mental suspense is never agreeable to the dogmatic temper of the young. Yet it is often useful. It may be a moral discipline through which God is making many of us to pass. Truth is valuable, but the love of truth, and the pursuit of it with candour, with reverence, with fidelity to the light we possess, may be even more so. Every doubter is therefore to be encouraged to be patient, retaining an open mind and taking time to inquire and to grow; for a man's theological convictions, to be of much value, are commonly of slow growth. Besides, we are so situated just now that on most matters which occasion difficulty we have reached no finality. New methods of study have invaded the province of religion, and they have not yet had time to work out their final results. That is for all of us the trial of the position—an appointed trial in this generation. The best informed in many fields of study are often the least positive. Just as in every other branch of advancing knowledge, so in biblical scholarship, in theology, in comparative religion, in the history of revelation, investigation may, by bringing fresh evidence to light, within a few years make the conclusions of to-day insecure or untenable. So long as a soul can cling to the person of our Lord and to any inward experience of His power to save which has been gained through trusting Him, it can afford to await with hope whatever growing light the years shall bring.

I do not forget that in some cases there has been no such experience, and therefore no such inward certitude to fall back upon. But those into whose souls the mordant of unbelief has eaten deeper, are less likely to open up their hidden sore to the pastor's eye. Flippant scepticism will not readily expose itself to the faithful rebukes of a clergyman. Still less will that worse state of mind which only airs its scepticism when it is convenient to excuse irregularities of conduct or a scornful rejection of all religion. But how one wishes it were more often possible for a wise minister of Christ to come into intimate relations with that large class of clean-living and sad-hearted men—whether of the professional or of the artisan class—who alienate themselves from the Church because they feel themselves unable to join in those avowals of Christian faith which seem to be implied in acts of worship.   Even when intellectual doubt has advanced so far as to undermine a man's confidence in the whole framework of Christian teaching, there may still be—and with many there is—a basis left of faith in God, sustaining a religious attitude of soul towards all that is sacred and true.   For a doubter of this class there is still one course open : to say little about his doubts, but to keep his life—outer and inner alike—well under the control of those fundamental certainties regarding God and the ethical teaching of Jesus which he can and does hold ; since, if truths at all, they are at least the holiest and most commanding of all truths.   He who can yield allegiance to nothing else can always yield it to the legitimate royalty of the good when he sees it ; and few nowadays refuse to see the good embodied in Jesus of Nazareth.   If right thinking be in some sense a condition of right living, it is still more certain that right living is the path to right thinking.   " If any man willeth to do His will, he shall know of the teaching, whether it be of God, or whether I speak from Myself." [1]   There never was a time when it was more true than now that the value of a man's beliefs for his own religious life is in proportion, not to the number of orthodox statements which he is prepared to endorse, but to the strength of conviction with which he adheres to what he does believe—much or little—and the practical control which he suffers it to exercise over his character and conduct. Nothing but the most tolerant and sympathetic attitude towards sincere and reverent sceptics on the part of ministers of religion, will be likely to retain large numbers of the most thoughtful among us in some attachment to Christ and to the worship of His Church, until they have come either to fight down their doubts or to outlive them.

[1] John 7[17].

INDEX

——◆——

ACHELIS, 54, 131, 308, 313, 322, 351.
"Action Sermon," 158, 214.
Adiaphora, 58.
Agapé, 107.
A'LASCO, 128.
AQUINAS, THOMAS, 156.
ARISTOTLE, 235.
Armenia, 164.
Articles, the XXXIX., 122–124.
AUGUSTINE, ST., 39, 41, 208, 240, 241.

BAIRD, 132.
Bands of Hope, 337.
Baptismal service, 102, 126; order of, 149–154.
Baptist Churches, 151.
BARCLAY's "Apology," 6, 7.
BAUR, 2.
BAUTAIN, 228, 269, 271.
BAXTER's "Reformed Pastor," 49, 54.
BECK, 21, 304.
BEECHER, HENRY WARD, 283, 292.
Benediction, 146, 154.
BEYER, 186.
Bible class, minister's, 345, 350.
Bible-women, 5, 314.
BINGHAM, 89, 136.
BLAIKIE, W. G., 21, 306, 318.
BLOUNT, 328.
Book of Common Prayer. See England, Church of.
BOURDALOUE, 278.
Boys' Brigade, 338.
BRAINERD, 49.
"Brethren," Plymouth, 7, 160.
BROADUS, 243.
BROOKS, PHILLIPS, 190, 230, 255.
BRUCE, 21, 306.
BRYENNIOS, Archbishop, 110.

BURKE, Edmund, 277.
BURNET, Bishop, 21.

Call to ministry, twofold, 30 ff.
  private, 32.
  public, by Church, 36.
CALVIN, 122, 128, 132, 136, 158, 307.
CARLYLE, 281.
CARPZOV, 206.
CARTWRIGHT, 122.
Celibacy of clergy, 51, 66 ff.
Ceremonies in worship, 120 ff.
CHADWICK, 21.
Character, ministerial, 55 ff.
"Charismatic" ministry, 2, 3.
CHAUCER, 232.
Children of minister, 75.
Children's services, 336. See Young, care of.
  "portion" in worship, 334.
CHRYSOSTOM, 277.
Church, Protestant conception of, 11.
"Church Year," 118, 120, 213.
CICERO, 241, 248, 277.
CLARK, Dr. F. E., 346.
Class. See Bible Class.
CLAUDE, JEAN, 206.
CLEMEN, 231.
CLEMENT of Rome, 110.
Communion, Holy. See Lord's Supper.
  seasons, 158–161.
  simultaneous, 161.
Confession, the General, 131.
Confessional, 199, 313.
Confirmation, 348, 349.
COQUEREL, ATHANASE, 86, 234, 259, 269, 277.
Corinthian Church, worship in, 105–107.
Creed, recitation of, 136.

CROSBY, HOWARD, 36.
Cross, use of, in baptism, 121, 152.
Cultus, 88. See Worship.
   theories of, 93.

DEISSMANN, 89.
Delivery. See Sermon.
DEMOSTHENES, 277, 281.
Deportment of minister, 60.
Diction. See Sermon.
Didache, 4, 109, 167.
Directories, 128.
Disciplina arcani, 160.
Discipline, Presbyterian, 359.
Doubt, treatment of, 363–366.

Education of minister, 6, 38, 280.
EHRENFEUCHTER, 93.
Elder. See Presbyter.
Endeavour, Society of Christian, 338.
England, Church of, 10. See also
   Articles, the XXXIX.
   views on ministry, 18.
   on ordination, 40.
   relations with privileged classes,
   80.
   reformation in, 119.
   Prayer Book, 128, 133, 135.
   confession, 132.
   baptism, 150.
   Lord's Supper, 158 ff.
   borrowed sermons, 205.
   preaching in, 276.
   confirmation, 349.
England, Presbyterian Church of,
   129, 132.
Eucharist. See Lord's Supper.
EUSEBIUS, 108, 113.
Evangelistic preaching. See Preaching.
Expository preaching. See Preaching.

FAIRBAIRN, 21, 36, 55, 313.
Family differences, treatment of, 357.
Family of minister, 75.
FÉNELON, 250, 256, 277, 282.
Festivals, 118, 120, 213.
FLETCHER of Madingley, 21.
FORSYTH, Dr., 210, 213.
Friends, Society of, 6.
FROMMANN, 161.
FUHRMANN, 197.
FUNK, 164.

GARVIE, Dr., 210.
Geneva, Book of, 128, 130.

GILLESPIE, GEORGE, 167.
GLADDEN, Dr. WASHINGTON, 355.
GOETHE, 281.
GORE, Bp., 10, 80.
GREGORY THE GREAT, 307.

HAGENBACH, 235.
Hands, imposition of, 39 ff.
HARDWICK, 123.
HARMS, CLAUS, 231.
HARNACK, 164.
HATCH, 4, 37, 39.
"Heads" of Sermon. See Sermon.
HEARD, 319.
Helvetic Confession, 307.
HENRY, PHILIP, 53.
HEUBNER, 197.
HIPPOLYTUS, 239.
Holland, Reformed Church of, 128.
"Holy Week," observance of, 112.
Homily, 200, 208, 239.
HOOKER, RICHARD, 18, 40, 122 f.
HOPPIN, 236, 260.
HORTON, Dr., 229.
Household visits. See Visitation.
HÜFFELL, 8, 231.
Hymn in worship, 143.
HYPERIUS of Marburg, 206.

"Individual" Cup, 168.
Infectious Diseases, visitation of, 325.

JACOBI, 104, 106.
JÜLICHER, 164.
JUSTIN MARTYR, 111, 200.

Kiss in early Church, 108.
KLIEFOTH, 93.
Kneeling at the Eucharist, 162.
KÖSTLIN, 106.

Lapses of members, 359.
LATHAM, 21, 306.
Laying on of hands, 39 ff.
Lay readers, 5.
LEA, 68.
Lectionary, 134.
LIDDON, Canon, 10.
LIGHTFOOT, Bp., 19, 110.
LIGHTFOOT's Journal, 147.
Liturgical *versus* free prayer, 140.
Liturgy, 89, 102, 128.
Lord's Supper—
   institution and early history,
   102–111.
   at Reformation, 118.

Lord's Supper—*continued*.
  in Church of England, 118–121.
  order of service, 155–170.
  first Communion, 347–348.
LUTHER, 117, 118, 119.
Lutheran Churches—
  no priesthood, 10.
  catechisms, 16.
  worship, 117, 132, 147.
  household visitation, 313.

M'CHEYNE, 49.
M'CRIE, Dr., 128, 171.
MACPHERSON, 167.
"Manual acts" in Lord's Supper, 166.
Marriage of clergy, 70.
MARTYN, HENRY, 49.
MATHER, COTTON, 262.
MAURY, Cardinal, 201, 265, 292, 298.
MELANCHTHON, 240.
Methodist Churches, 38.
MILTON, 271.
Minister—
  modern, differs from primitive, 5, 6.
  undue burden on, 23.
  spirit of service, 24 ff., 300.
  call of, 30 ff.
  canonical age, 37.
  devotional life of, 45 ff.
  character of, 51 ff.
  manners of, 57 ff.
  home life of, 66 ff.
  as citizen, 77 ff.
Ministry—
  need for, 7.
  instituted by Christ, 8.
  Protestant theory of, 12, 51.
  source of influence, 14.
  how far a priesthood, 10 ff.
Mixed cup in Lord's Supper, 163.
MOBERLY, Canon, 10, 18.
Montanism, 4.
MOODY, 230.
MOORE, DANIEL, 205.
"Motto" texts, 234.
MULLOIS, Abbé, 281, 294.

NEALE, 163.
NEWBOLT, 21.
NEWMAN, 82, 200.
NITZSCH, 8, 88, 351.

OECOLAMPADIUS, 132.
Offering, the, 144.
Officials in church necessary, 7.

OOSTERZEE, VAN, 37, 323, 351.
Ordination, 32, 37 ff.
ORIGEN, 208, 236, 239.
OTTO, 351.

PALMER, 54, 313, 326, 351.
PARKER, Dr. JOSEPH, 262.
Pastor. See Shepherd.
Pastorate, 300 ff.
  idea and spirit of, 300.
  opposed to officialism, 301.
  responsibility, 302.
Pfarrer, Lutheran, 16.
PHELPS, AUSTEN, 234, 287, 289.
PLINY's Letter, 109.
Politics, 77 ff.
PORTER, 236.
Praise, 107, 109, 112, 131, 133, 143, 146.
Prayer in public worship, 137 ff.
Prayer meeting, 171 ff.
Preacher, preparation of, 282 ff.
  study of Scripture, 285.
  of literature, 287.
  intercourse with men, 289.
  modern conditions, 294.
Preaching—
  what is preaching? 180–187.
  personal and official elements, 182.
  relation to Scripture, 183.
  objects of, 184.
  pastoral preaching, 188–215.
    its matter, 188.
    tone and manner, 188.
    artistic perfection, 190.
    "sensationalism," 191, 296.
    intelligibility, 192.
    tone of assurance, 192.
    predominant note, 193.
    practical aim, 194.
    the "five uses," 197.
    exposition of Scripture, 200.
    rapid output of sermons, 204.
    borrowed sermons, 205.
    diversity in, 206.
    expository lectures, 208 ff.
    comprehensiveness, 210 ff.
    "Church Year," 213.
  evangelistic preaching, 216–227.
    in regular services, 218.
    "mission week," 222.
    characteristics of, 223.
"Preface" to worship, 130.
Presbyter, 1, 22.
Presbyter-bishop, 1, 22, 305.
Priest, how far minister is, 17 ff.

Priesthood, Catholic, 10, 13, 48, 51.
Puritans. See Ceremonies.

Quakers. See Friends.
Quarto-deciman controversy, 112.

RAIKES, ROBERT, 339, 340.
Recreations of minister, 63.
Reformation principles, 115.
Reformed Churches—
    no priesthood in, 10.
    "ministry of the Word," 14, 15.
    catechisms, 16.
    ordination, 37–42.
    marriage of clergy, 67.
    worship, 118.
Roman Catholic Church—
    priesthood, 10, 13, 51, 66.
    worship in, 114, 128.
    the Mass, 155, 158, 163, 166.
    preachers, 189, 199, 213, 292.
ROSCOMMON, E. of, 273.
ROTHE, 161.
RUFINUS, 137.
RUTHERFORD, 49.

Sacramental services, 149 ff.
Salvation Army, 5, 294.
SANDAY, 10.
SCHAFF, 137.
SCHLEIERMACHER, 93, 186.
SCHMIDT, 231.
SCHÜRER, 39.
SCHWEIZER, 44, 54, 62, 70, 95, 351.
Scotland, Church of—
    reform in worship, 118.
    order of service, 128, 131–136.
    baptismal service, 149–154.
    Lord's Supper in, 158–163, 167.
    visitation in, 313.
    excessive discipline, 359.
    Guilds in, 349.
    Bible classes in, 350.
SCOTT, WALTER, 272.
Scottish Book of Common Order, 128, 149, 166, 167.
Scriptures, reading of, 107, 111, 133 ff.
Sermon, 228–281.
    preparing to preach, 228 ff.
    selection of subject, 230.
    text, why from Scripture, 231.
    study of text, 234.
    allegorising, 235.
    plan of sermon, 239 ff.
    rhetoric in pulpit, 239.

Sermon—continued.
    unity of theme, 242.
    of aim, 245.
    of tone, 247.
    parts of sermon, 248 ff.
    introduction, 248.
    theme, 250.
    divisions, 250.
    conclusion, 260.
    diction and delivery, 264 ff.
    writing sermons, 264–267.
    extemporising, 266, 268.
    practising both methods, 269.
    delivering from MS., 275 ff.
    training in elocution, 279.
    "accent of conviction," 281.
Service Books, Reformed, 128, 145.
Service, Order of. See Worship.
SHEDD, Dr., 49, 53, 242, 284, 285.
Shepherd, 22.
Sick, the. See Visitation.
SKEAT, Dr., 53.
Social intercourse, 63.
Social questions and the clergy, 83.
Sophists, 240.
SPENCER's Sketches, 352.
Sponsors in baptism, 153, 154.
SPROTT, Dr., 167, 171.
SPURGEON, 234, 282.
STALKER, Dr., 21.
STEVENSON, LOUIS, 272.
Steward, 22.
STIER, 186.
STIRM, 21.
STORRS, Dr., 269.
STURTEVANT, 207.
Sunday, festival in early Church, 112.
Sunday schools, 339 ff.

Temple services, 102, 105.
Text, choice of, 228. See also Sermon.
THEODORET, 67.
THEOPHYLACT, 67.
THEREMIN, 241.
Transitions in preaching, 257.
TRAVERS, 122.
Trent, canons of, 40.

Unction, 297.
"Unpardonable Sin," 355.

VETTER, 93.
VILLEMAIN, 240.
VILMAR, 55, 351.

Vinet, 21, 36, 53, 61, 231, 242, 248, 256, 351.
Visitation, household, 310–320.
  Lutheran objections, 313.
  difficulties, 314.
  altered methods, 315.
  of sick, 321–329.
  chronic cases, 321.
  serious illness, 323.
  deathbeds, 327.
  of bereaved, 329.
Voltaire, 231.

"Wafer" in Eucharist, 163.
Ware, Henry, 269.
Water used in Eucharist, 164.
Watson, Dr. John, 44, 210.
Watts, Dr., 207.
Webster, Daniel, 259.
Week-day services, 171–179.
  uses of, 173.
  suggestions for, 174.
Weizsäcker, 106.
Westminster Confession, 124.
Westminster Directory, 128, 129, 131, 132, 134, 153, 163.
Whately, 205.

Whitgift, 122.
Whyte, Dr. Alex., 350.
Wife of minister, 72 ff.
Worship, theory of Christian, 88 ff.
  spirituality, 90.
  as intercourse with God, 95.
  in first century, 101 ff.
    in Hebrew Churches, 103.
    in Greek Churches, 105.
  16th century reforms in, 114 ff.
    Lutheran, 117.
    Reformed, 118.
    Anglican, 119.
  order of weekly, 126 ff.
Wright, 167.

Xenophon's Memorabilia, 187.

Young, care of, 333–350.
  in childhood, 333.
  of school age, 334 ff.
  in adolescence, 343 ff.
  communicants' class, 348.

Zahn, 164.
Zezschwitz, 351.
Zürich service book, 132.

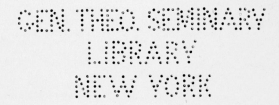

Printed by
MORRISON & GIBB LIMITED,
Edinburgh.

Charles Scribner's Sons'

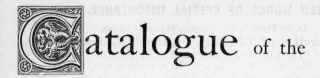 atalogue of the

Publications

of

T. & T. Clark, Edinburgh.

The London SPECTATOR says: 'We may highly commend anything, periodical or other, that comes out from the publishing house of T. & T. CLARK, EDINBURGH.'

MESSRS. CHARLES SCRIBNER'S SONS, SOLE AGENTS IN THE UNITED STATES for the above well-known house, invite the attention of the Trade and the Public to the subjoined List of valuable Books, embracing the widest range of sound and useful Theological and Philosophical Thought and Discussion.

Charles Scribner's Sons,

153, 155, & 157 FIFTH AVENUE, NEW YORK CITY.

LATEST ISSUES.

NEW WORKS OF SPECIAL IMPORTANCE.

In the Press, in One Volume, 8vo, price **$2.00**.

The Authority of Christ. By DAVID W. FORREST, D.D., Author of 'The Christ of History and of Experience.'

While all Christians acknowledge the authority of Christ as final, there is a wide diversity of opinion with reference to what it really covers and the right method of construing it. The purpose of this book is to inquire as to the sphere in which Christ's authority operates, and as to its character within that sphere.

In the Press, in Two Volumes, post 8vo, price **$3.50**.

The Knowledge of God. The Gifford Lectures. By Professor H. M. GWATKIN, D.D., Cambridge.

James: The Brother of Our Lord. By Principal W. PATRICK, D.D., Winnipeg. Post 8vo.   Nett **$3.00**

This volume treats the life of James the Lord's brother with the fulness and thoroughness which its importance demands, and thus makes a contribution to the settlement of some of the most difficult problems belonging to the history of the primitive Church.

The New Reformation: Recent Evangelical Movements in the Roman Catholic Church. By Rev. JOHN A. BAIN. Post 8vo.

Nett **$1.50**

The intensely interesting and important religious movements in Roman Catholic countries at the present time are here described.

Primitive Christian Education. By G. HODGSON, B.A. (T.C.D.), Lecturer on the History of Education, University College, Bristol. Square crown 8vo.   Nett **$1.50**

A work greatly needed by all interested in education; discussing the attitude of the early Christian Church to education.

A Grammar of New Testament Greek. By JAMES HOPE MOULTON, D.Litt. Vol. I. THE PROLEGOMENA. Demy 8vo.

Nett **$3.50**

No other grammar gives an adequate record of those wonderful discoveries of Greek papyri, which within the last few years have altered the entire basis of the study of New Testament Greek.

The Religion and Philosophy of India. The Upanishads. By Professor P. DEUSSEN, University of Kiel. Translated by Professor A. S. GEDEN, M.A. Demy 8vo.   Nett **$3.50**

The Growth of Christian Faith. By Rev. GEORGE FERRIES, D.D., Cluny. Demy 8vo.   Nett **$2.50**

The Gift of Tongues, and other Essays. By DAWSON WALKER, D.D., Durham University. Post 8vo.   Nett **$1.50**

The Christian Doctrine of the Lord's Supper. By Rev. ROBERT M. ADAMSON, M.A., Ardrossan. Square crown 8vo.

Nett **$1.50**

'A scholarly, large minded and trustworthy statement of a great religious and Christian theme.'—*Christian World*.

The Religious Doubts of Common Men: The Duty of the Christian Churches to their Members. By a LAYMAN.

THE SCHOLAR AS PREACHER.

These volumes are carefully chosen. They are chosen because their authors are scholars as well as preachers, for the suggestiveness of their thought, and because they are saturated with the most promising ideas of the present day.

The Eye for Spiritual Things. By H. M. GWATKIN, D.D., Cambridge. Post 8vo. Nett $1.50

Faith and Knowledge. By the Rev. W. R. INGE, D.D., Hertford College, Oxford. Second Ed. Post 8vo. Nett $1.50

'The volume is one which is likely to be especially helpful to preachers, as giving them fresh materials for thought.'—*Guardian.*

'The thought is always lucid and well arranged, and the pages hold the interest with ease. The book is a contribution of value to the storehouse of faith.' —*Watchman.*

Christus in Ecclesia. By the Rev. HASTINGS RASHDALL, D.C.L., New College, Oxford. Now ready, post 8vo. Nett $1.50

'A book which should prove very useful to the inquiring student.'—*Oxford Review.*

Bread and Salt from the Word of God. In Sixteen Sermons. By Professor THEODOR ZAHN, University of Erlangen. Post 8vo. Nett $1.50

'*We fear that Dr. Zahn's reputation as a scholar is not as widespread in England as it should be, although the University of Cambridge has conferred upon him an honorary degree. This is due, no doubt, to our insular backwardness in the acquiring of other languages. . . . The chief reason why we desire to bring the sermons within the reach of English readers, is rather that they may see for themselves how exact and profound learning is compatible with a spirit of childlike reverence and humility, a directness of speech in rebuke of prevalent ungodliness, an ardour of devotion to Christ as the One Master, and to the leading of the Holy Spirit, which are thoroughly in accord with the teaching of the Apostles, and of the Primitive Church.'—From the* TRANSLATOR'S *Preface.*

BY THE REV. ALFRED PLUMMER, D.D.

'*To see what can be done in the way of making the history of the Church attractive reading, to see what can be done in the way of making the reading of Church History thoroughly profitable, read these books.*'—EXPOSITORY TIMES.

English Church History. From the Death of King Henry VII. to the Death of Archbishop Parker. Four Lectures by the Rev. ALFRED PLUMMER, D.D. Crown 8vo. Just Published. Nett $1.00

English Church History. From the Death of Archbishop Parker to the Death of King Charles I. Four Lectures. By the Rev. ALFRED PLUMMER, D.D., late Master of University College, Durham. Crown 8vo. Nett $1.00

'The treatment is succinct, dispassionate, and fair, the style is clear and strong; and this volume will form a useful introduction to the study of the period.'—*London Quarterly Review.*

The Life Everlasting: Studies in the Subject of the Future. By DAVID PURVES, D.D., Belfast. Crown 8vo. Nett $1.50

Prof. MARCUS DODS writes: 'I have read Dr. Purves' "The Life Everlasting" with great satisfaction, and mean to read it a second time. I think he shows great capacity for dealing with doctrinal points. At the present time there is considerable interest— as indeed there always is—in immortality, and I know of no treatment of the subject at once so full and so compact, so well informed and so temperate, sane and convincing.'

The Creation of Matter; or, Material Elements, Evolution, and Creation. By Rev. W. PROFEIT, M.A. Second Edition. Crown 8vo. Nett $1.00

'A storehouse of information, takes cognisance of the most recent discoveries. Packed with thought, but there is no obscurity. A timely and able volume.'—*Methodist Recorder.*

Now ready, in One Volume, demy 8vo, price **$3.00** nett,

Bible Studies. Contributions, chiefly from Papyri and Inscriptions, to the History of the Language, Literature, and Religion of Hellenistic Judaism and Primitive Christianity. By Dr. G. Adolf Deissmann, Professor of Theology in the University of Heidelberg. *Authorised Translation* (incorporating Dr. Deissmann's most recent changes and additions) by Rev. Alex. Grieve, M.A., Ph.D.

Note.—In addition to the supplementary matter specially contributed by the Author, the translation shows considerable alterations in other respects. Not only has the later volume, 'Neue Bibelstudien,' found a place in this edition, but the order of the Articles has, at the Author's request, been completely changed. The Indexes have been combined, and an Index of Scripture Texts has been added. The English translation is therefore virtually a new work.

'In every respect a notable book. . . . As to its value there can be no hesitation about the verdict. . . . Words, syntax, and ideas can all be tested over again by a completely new apparatus of study, the lexicon of the New Testament can be enriched, the grammar re-written, and the theology re-vivified and humanised.'—Dr. J. Rendel Harris in the *Examiner.*

In One large Volume 8vo, price **$4.00** nett,

Justification and Reconciliation. By Albrecht Ritschl. Edited by H. R. Mackintosh, D.Phil., and A. B. Macaulay, M.A.

'Dr. Mackintosh and his coadjutors have earned the gratitude of all theological students in this country. . . . The present translation meets one of the most urgent wants of the hour. Now the great systematic work of Ritschl is open to all.'—Prof. J. Denney, D.D.

Sixth Edition, Revised throughout, in post 8vo.

The Miracles of Unbelief. By Rev. Frank Ballard, M.A., B.Sc., London. Nett **$1.00**

'Written by an expert in science as well as theology, a fair-minded man who faces religious difficulties, not ignores them, and one who knows how to reason out his case like an accomplished advocate, without pressing it like an unscrupulous one. Mr. Ballard has rendered valuable service to the cause of Christian truth, and given us an excellent and useful book, deserving a large circulation.'—Professor W. T. Davison, in the *Methodist Recorder.*

'It is a perfect mine of quotation for men with little time for study, who are called, as modern ministers are, to be not only visitors and workers but also preachers and teachers.'—*Guardian.*

The Relation of the Apostolic Teaching to the Teaching of Christ. By Rev. Robert J. Drummond, D.D. Edinburgh. Second Edition. 8vo. Nett **$3.50**

'No book of its size has taken such a hold of us for many a day. . . . It is a strong book, the book of a scholar and thinker, fearless, yet reverent, new and yet built on a solid foundation of faith and experience.'—*Expository Times.*

Christian Character. By Professor T. B. Kilpatrick, D.D. Crown 8vo. Nett **$1.00**

Contents:—Part I. The Importance of Character—The Sources of Christian Character—Its Culture: Physical and Mental Powers; Moral Powers. Part II. Character and Conduct—The Family—The Work of Life—Social Relations—The State—The Church—Concluding Remarks.

'Throughout the exposition is clear and intelligible, and the book is written in an interesting and attractive style. It forms a valuable contribution to the study of Christian Ethics, and should be in the hands of all who have to do with the moulding of character and the guidance of conduct.'—*Methodist Times.*

The Christ of History and of Experience. By DAVID W. FORREST, D.D. 8vo. Nett $2.00

'The subject has been opened up most admirably in the series of topics which form the subject of the nine chapters. . . . The volume as a whole deserves most serious attention. . . . Many of its discussions, like that of miracles, and the relation of Messiahship and Sonship, are admirable.'—*Biblical World* (Chicago).

The Historical New Testament: Being the Literature of the New Testament arranged in the order of its Literary Growth and according to the Dates of the Documents. A new Translation, Edited, with Prolegomena, Historical Tables, Critical Notes, and an Appendix, by JAMES MOFFATT, B.D. Second Edition, in One large 8vo Vol. Nett $4.50

In the preparation of the Translation the Author has had the valuable assistance of Professor DENNEY, Dr. H. A. A. KENNEDY, Professor MARCUS DODS, Rev. Canon GREGORY SMITH, Professor WALTER LOCK, and the Rev. Ll. M. J. BEBB.

'The most important book on the credentials of Christianity that has appeared in this country for a long time. It is a work of extraordinary learning, labour, and ability.'—*British Weekly.*

The Pauline Epistles. Introductory and Expository Studies. By R. D. SHAW, D.D., Edinburgh. Second Ed. 8vo. Nett $3.50

'A careful and very valuable study of the writings of the great apostle.'—*Interior.*

'Of all the Introductions to St. Paul's Epistles I have read, this is the best.'—*Methodist Times.*

'A thoroughly good and useful book.'—*Guardian.*

'This book is as genuine a surprise as we have had for many a day. Clearly Dr. Shaw is one of the youngest men of whom the Scottish Churches are so proud—steeped in the literature of the subject he has chosen to write upon, and strong enough to handle it with refreshing candour, and yet concerned always and most entirely to reveal the treasures of wisdom and knowledge which the Pauline Epistles contain.'—*Expository Times.*

Hebrew Ideals from the Story of the Patriarchs. By the Rev. JAMES STRACHAN, M.A., London.

PART I. GEN. 12 TO 25. Price $.60. PART II. GEN. 25 TO 50. Price $.60.
₊ The Two Parts can now be had bound in One Volume. Nett $1.00.

'This volume is exactly the thing we wanted. It is one of the freshest and most illuminative books on Genesis we have seen. As a mirror of manners and ideals to make life worthy, it is altogether unique. . . . The book is written in delightful English, piquant and crisp, and the surprises of its style make it easy reading.'—*Critical Review.*

A Primer on Teaching. With Special Reference to Sunday School Work. By JOHN ADAMS, M.A., B.Sc., Professor of Education in the University of London. Nett 20 cents

CONTENTS:—Child Nature—Ideas—Attention and Interest—Class Management—Use of Language—Method in Teaching—The Socratic Method—Questions and Answers—Illustrations.

'Extremely readable and suggestive, clear as the light.'—*Sunday School Chronicle.*

A Dissertation on the Gospel Commentary of S. Ephraem the Syrian. With a Scriptural Index to his Works. By J. HAMLYN HILL, D.D. 8vo. Nett $2.25

The BISHOP of GLOUCESTER and BRISTOL writes: '. . . It is a monument of patient research and intelligent industry, which deserves very hearty recognition.'

The Oldest Code of Laws in the World. The Code of Laws promulgated by HAMMURABI, King of Babylon, B.C. 2285–2242. Translated by C. H. W. JOHNS, M.A., Lecturer on Assyriology, Queens' College, Cambridge. Crown 8vo. Nett 75 cents

'A little book but one of great value.'—*Interior.*

Comparative Religion: Its Genesis and Growth. By the Rev. Louis H. Jordan, B.D., late Special Lecturer on Comparative Religion at the University of Chicago. With Introduction by the Rev. Principal Fairbairn, D.D., Oxford. 8vo. Nett $3.50

*** The Volume contains an exceptionally full and carefully prepared Index ; and also several Coloured Charts giving a Comparative View of the present numerical strength, and of the Territorial Distribution, of the Principal Religions.

'A most excellent and painstaking monograph. Clear in argument, full in information.'—Principal A. M. Fairbairn, D.D.

'Comparative Religion is with us now. Of that there is no longer any doubt. This handsome volume is itself the unmistakable evidence. . . . Mr. Jordan has that spark of life which responds to our more popular conception of genius. His enthusiasm carries him from page to page, down through many notes, and even to the end of model Indexes.'—Expository Times.

By Nile and Euphrates. A Record of Discovery and Adventure. By H. Valentine Geere. Nett $3.50

'Mr. Geere, a member of the staff of the Babylon expedition sent out by the University of Pennsylvania, gives many interesting pictures of life and work while in the pursuit of archæological finds, describes the people and country of the Euphrates and Tigris, and sketches some of the out-of-the-way places in that unfrequented region.'—Bulletin of the American Geographical Society.

'Mr. Geere's volume makes fascinating reading.'—Pall Mall Gazette.

The Religions of Ancient Egypt and Babylonia. The Gifford Lectures on the Ancient Egyptian and Babylonian Conception of the Divine. By A. H. Sayce, M.A., LL.D., Professor of Assyriology, University of Oxford. 8vo. Nett $3.50

'Those who are interested in comparative religion will find this latest work of a distinguished Orientalist most valuable. Sympathetic appreciation and discriminating criticism are in these lectures felicitously joined.'—New York Outlook.

'Extremely interesting. . . . One can have no guide in these complex subjects more learned or more considerate to his readers' difficulties than Professor Sayce. He always writes from the amplest knowledge, and he always writes clearly.'—Spectator.

The Fatherhood of God in Christian Truth and Life. By the Rev. J. Scott Lidgett, M.A. 8vo. Nett $3.00

This book is an attempt to establish the Fatherhood of God as the determining fact of Christian life and the determining principle of Christian Theology. Among the subjects dealt with are : The New Testament Doctrine of the Fatherhood of God. Place in New Testament Theology. The Relation of the Old Testament Doctrine to the Fatherhood of God. The Doctrine in Church History. Validity and Content. Manifestation.

'The work of a devout and vigorous Christian thinker. It is well planned and arranged, and clear in style and diction, more constructive than critical, more expository than controversial in its method.'—Interior.

The Times of Christ. By Lewis A. Muirhead, D.D. With Map. New and Revised Edition. Crown 8vo. Nett 60 cents

'One of the very best of the handbooks for Bible classes—and that is saying a great deal. There is evidence on almost every page of exact and ample scholarship. Yet Dr. Muirhead is never dry ; his chapters are always luminous and readable. This is certain to prove a most useful text-book.'—Sunday School Chronicle.

The Sacraments in the New Testament. By Rev. J. C. Lambert, D.D. 8vo. Nett $3.50

'A real contribution. It is the book to which one can turn for a fresh, careful, truthful, lucid interpretation of the Sacraments.'—Biblical World (Chicago).

'Will, without doubt, come to be regarded as a classic work upon the Sacraments.'—Methodist Times.

Outlines of the Life of Christ. By W. SANDAY, D.D.,
LL.D., Litt.D., Lady Margaret Professor and Canon of Christ
Church, Oxford. Post 8vo.   Nett $1.25

*Although this book is, in the main, a reprint of Dr. Sanday's well-known article, 'Jesus
Christ,' in Dr. Hastings' Bible Dictionary, the Author has worked carefully over the material,
and has broken up the text into Chapters and Sections. An important new Map of Palestine is
added.*

'The most unconventional and illuminating of all extant works of the kind. We
recommend this issue to our readers as the best modern work on the life of our Lord.'—
Methodist Times.

The Spirit and the Incarnation. In the Light of Scripture,
Science, and Practical Need. By the Rev. W. L. WALKER.
Second Edition, Revised and Re-set. Demy 8vo.   Nett $3.00

In a leading article, headed '**A GREAT BOOK,**' in the *British Weekly*, Professor
MARCUS DODS writes : 'It may be questioned whether in recent years there has
appeared, at home or abroad, any theological work more deserving of careful study. He
who intelligently reads it once will inevitably read it again and again.'

The Cross and the Kingdom, as Viewed by Christ Himself and
in the Light of Evolution. By the Rev. W. L. WALKER, Author
of 'The Spirit and the Incarnation.' 8vo.   Nett $3.00

This book is intended as a defence and restatement of the Evangelical doctrine of the
Cross based on the teaching of Christ in the first three Gospels, and on His work as the
Founder of the Kingdom of God.

'We desire to speak with admiration of the good work done in this book. It is
worthy to stand beside his former treatise. Taking both together, they form a magnificent contribution to the theological literature of the age.'—Professor IVERACH in the
Expository Times.

The Ritschlian Theology. Critical and Constructive : An
Exposition and an Estimate. By the Rev. A. E. GARVIE, M.A.
(Oxon.). 8vo.   Nett $3.00

'Mr. Garvie's grasp of the subject is unsurpassed. . . . Nothing could be clearer or,
indeed, more fascinating in theological writing than this.'—*Expository Times.*

'Ritschlian literature is permanently enriched by this publication.'—*British Weekly.*

'The weightiest, warmest, and fairest work in English on its subject.'—Dr. P. T.
FORSYTH in the *Speaker.*

The Trial of Jesus Christ : A Legal Monograph. With Two
Illustrations. By A. TAYLOR INNES, Advocate. Post 8vo.

Nett $1.00

This twofold transaction, the most famous occasion on which two great systems of
law, the Hebrew and the Roman, crossed each other, is described as thus presenting
'probably the most interesting isolated problem in historical jurisprudence.'

'Mr. Innes gives what to most of his readers will be wholly new light and fresh
thoughts . . . This volume is a striking example of the value of the critical examination
of historical problems by an accomplished lawyer.'—*Times.*

The Theology of the Epistle to the Hebrews. With a
Critical Introduction. By Rev. GEORGE MILLIGAN, B.D. In post
8vo.   Nett $2.00

'Any book with the name of Milligan upon it is sure of a ready welcome. . . . We
can unreservedly recommend this volume as a sensible as well as a fertilising study of the
outward features, but especially the inner thought, of this great Epistle.'—*Expository
Times.*

The Christian Salvation. Lectures on the Work of Christ :
Its Appropriation and its Issues. By Prof. J. S. CANDLISH,
D.D. Demy 8vo.   Nett $2.25

'They deal with five great subjects : the Work of Christ, the Doctrine of the Church,
the New Life, the Sacraments, and Eschatology. In each case we have a treatise on the
subject, lucid, connected, and fairly complete.'—*Expository Times.*

The World's Epoch-Makers.

Edited by Oliphant Smeaton, M.A.

NEW SERIES. In Neat Crown 8vo Volumes. Price $1.25 each.

'An excellent series of biographical studies.'—*Athenæum*.

'We advise our readers to keep a watch on this most able series. It promises to be a distinct success. The volumes before us are the most satisfactory books of the sort we have ever read.'—*Methodist Times*.

The following Volumes have now been issued:—

Buddha and Buddhism. By Arthur Lillie.

Luther and the German Reformation. By Principal T. M. Lindsay, D.D.

Wesley and Methodism. By F. J. Snell, M.A.

Cranmer and the English Reformation. By A. D. Innes, M.A.

William Herschel and his Work. By James Sime, M.A.

Francis and Dominic. By Professor J. Herkless, D.D.

Savonarola. By G. M'Hardy, D.D.

Anselm and his Work. By Rev. A. C. Welch, B.D.

Origen and Greek Patristic Theology. By Rev. W. Fairweather, M.A.

Muhammad and his Power. By P. De Lacy Johnstone, M.A. (Oxon.).

The Medici and the Italian Renaissance. By Oliphant Smeaton, M.A., Edinburgh.

Plato. By Professor D. G. Ritchie, M.A., LL.D., University of St. Andrews.

Pascal and the Port Royalists. By Professor W. Clark, LL.D., D.C.L., Trinity College, Toronto.

Euclid. By Emeritus Professor Thomas Smith, D.D., LL.D.

Hegel and Hegelianism. By Professor R. Mackintosh, D.D., Lancashire Independent College, Manchester.

Hume and his Influence on Philosophy and Theology. By Professor J. Orr, D.D., Glasgow.

Rousseau and Naturalism in Life and Thought. By Professor W. H. Hudson, M.A.

Descartes, Spinoza, and the New Philosophy. By Principal J. Iverach, D.D., Aberdeen.

Socrates. By Rev. J. T. Forbes, M.A., Glasgow.

The following have also been arranged for:—

Marcus Aurelius and the Later Stoics. By F. W. Bussell, D.D., Vice-Principal of Brasenose College, Oxford. [*In the Press.*

Augustine and Latin Patristic Theology. By Professor B. B. Warfield, D.D., Princeton.

Scotus Erigena and his Epoch. By Professor R. Latta, Ph.D., D.Sc., University of Aberdeen.

Wyclif and the Lollards. By Rev. J. C. Carrick, B.D.

The Two Bacons and Experimental Science. By Rev. W. J. Couper, M.A.

Lessing and the New Humanism. By Rev. A. P. Davidson, M.A.

Kant and his Philosophical Revolution. By Professor R. M. Wenley, D.Sc., Ph.D., University of Michigan.

Schleiermacher and the Rejuvenescence of Theology. By Professor A. Martin, D.D., New College, Edinburgh.

Newman and his Influence. By C. Sarolea, Ph.D., Litt. Doc., University of Edinburgh.

The Note-Line in the Hebrew Scriptures. Commonly

called PĀSĒQ or PĔSÎQ. By JAMES KENNEDY, D.D., New College,
Edinburgh. Post 8vo.   Nett $1.75

This treatise is the result of a special inquiry, subsidiary to more extensive research into the Hebrew text of the Old Testament. Careful examination led to the conclusion that the line must have been purposely placed beside remarkable readings in the Hebrew Bible. A survey has been made of the entire Scriptures, and the conclusions are now placed before students of the Old Testament as a contribution towards a better understanding of certain phenomena presented in the Massoretic texts.

'Dr. Kennedy, with a delightful avoidance of pedantry, has given an example of the patient, careful, unobtrusive work of which so much must be done before the text of the Old Testament can be satisfactorily restored. If, as seems probable, the "Note-line" does frequently indicate error, it will be a valuable guide to the textual critic.'—*Church Quarterly Review.*

The Gospel according to St. John: An Inquiry into its

Genesis and Historical Value. By Professor H. H. WENDT, D.D.,
Author of 'The Teaching of Jesus.' Demy 8vo.   Nett $2.50

'A searching and discriminative criticism.'—*Speaker.*
'An important contribution to the study of the problems of the Fourth Gospel.'—*Critical Review.*

A Short History of the Westminster Assembly. By the

Rev. W. BEVERIDGE, M.A., of New Deer. Crown 8vo.   Nett $1.00

The Author has worked up this History from original documents, and has had it in preparation for several years. In view of the present crisis of the Churches in Scotland, the book will be found of special interest, as the Author, more particularly in the chapters on the Westminster 'Confession,' has had before him the decision of the House of Lords in the Free Church Appeal Case. Mr. Beveridge is well known as an authority upon the subject of his book.

'A volume full of valuable information and casting much light on the far-reaching questions at present occupying the mind of the Scottish people.'—*Critical Review.*

Apostolic Order and Unity. By ROBERT BRUCE, M.A., D.D.,

Hon. Canon, Durham. Crown 8vo.   Nett $1.00

'As Christian in tone as it is scholarly in its treatment of the subject.'—*Examiner.*

The Testament of Our Lord. Translated into English from

the Syriac, with Introduction and Notes, by JAMES COOPER, D.D.
Professor of Ecclesiastical History in Glasgow University; and
the Right Rev. A. J. MACLEAN, D.D., Bishop of Moray and Ross.
8vo.   Nett $3.00

'Excellently conceived and well executed, and the information given is unique in its way.'—*Living Church.*

'In making the work known, the Editor has done considerable service to the study both of ecclesiastical history and of liturgy. It is a real service, which deserves the gratitude of scholars.'—*Guardian.*

The *Testament* possesses the special interest of being the production of the very period when the great transition in the Church's fortunes, from Imperial persecution to Imperial favour, was leading to the inevitable transformation of her buildings and her services to suit her altered circumstances. . . . The *Testament* reflects this state of things as a mirror. It vibrates, moreover, with the pulsation of the great controversies through which the Church was passing. The volume is thus far more than a mere antiquarian curiosity. It had a message to its own time; it has a message to all time, and very distinctly to the time now present. The *Testament* is also a veritable mine at once of devotional expression and liturgical lore.

The Pentateuch in the Light of To-day. Being a simple Introduction to the Pentateuch on the Lines of the Higher Criticism. By Alfred Holborn, M.A. Second Edition. Crown 8vo.
Nett 75 cents

'Eminently serviceable for a reconstruction of traditional views upon the only ground now tenable for faith in a divine revelation to ancient Israel.'—*Outlook*.

The Words of Jesus. Considered in the Light of Post-Biblical Jewish Writings and the Aramaic Language. By Professor G. Dalman, Leipzig. *Authorised English Translation* by Professor D. M. Kay, St. Andrews. Post 8vo. Nett $2.50

'A very exhaustive study, and deserves attention as an example of searching method and cautious scholarship.'—*Living Church*.

'The most critical and scientific examination of the leading conceptions of the Gospels that has yet appeared.'—Prof. W. Sanday, LL.D.

'He who does not know that Dalman is necessary, does not know much yet about the study of the New Testament in Greek.'—*Expository Times*.

'Absolutely indispensable to the understanding of the New Testament.'—*British Weekly*.

Selections from the Literature of Theism. Some Principal Types of Religious Thought. With Introductory and Explanatory Notes. By Prof. Alfred Caldecott, M.A., D.D., King's College, London, and Prof. H. R. Mackintosh, M.A., D.Phil., Edinburgh. Post 8vo. Nett $2.50

This volume has been prepared with the aim of bringing together within a small compass some of the leading positions in the philosophy of religion. It is agreed on all hands, in our day, that no one, except here and there an original genius, can expect to be in line with twentieth-century thought who dispenses himself from reference to the positions held by great minds. It is by training his mind in their high thoughts that he can expect to win power and insight for himself.

'Will meet a very wide felt want by bringing within the reach of ordinary book-buyers full summaries of the treatises of the great leaders of thought who have written upon Theism.'—*Bibliotheca Sacra*.

'Who would ever have expected so beautiful and delightful a book with such an unpretending and commonplace title? . . . Those are the passages which make Descartes, Spinoza, Martineau, Janet live; and those passages, interpreted as they are interpreted here, make the study of the doctrine of God, even in its philosophical side, alive and practical for all men.'—*Expository Times*.

St. Paul and the Roman Law, and other Studies on the Origin of the Form of Doctrine. By W. E. Ball, LL.D. Post 8vo. Nett $1.50

'Reverent and acute. . . . We have said perhaps enough to show how varied and vital are the subjects of interest touched on in Dr. Ball's essays.'—*Churchman*.

'Dr. Ball has two rare gifts. He is a discoverer and a writer. . . . Every discovery is made known by the same unconscious skill—the touch of nature.'—*Expository Times*.

The Religious Controversies of Scotland. By Rev. Henry F. Henderson, M.A., Dundee. Post 8vo. Nett $1.75

Contents:—Prof. Simson's *Affair*—The Marrow Men—Hume's *Essay on Miracles* —The Playhouse Battle—An Ayrshire *New Light*—The Apocrypha Controversy —Edward Irving—The *Row Heresy*—The Rise of Morisonianism—The *Scotch Sermons*—Robertson Smith and the Higher Criticism—The *Dods-Bruce Case*.

This volume forms the first of a Series entitled 'Religion in Literature and Life.'

'We can remember no book devoted to the topic which Mr. Henderson handles with such ease and power. It has been read by us with genuine enjoyment and appreciation.' —Principal Patrick, D.D.

New Testament Theology; or, Historical Account of the Teaching of Jesus and of Primitive Christianity according to the New Testament Sources. By Professor WILLIBALD BEYSCHLAG, Halle. Authorised Translation. Two Vols. 8vo. Nett $6.00

'Dr. Beyschlag has achieved so large a measure of success as to have furnished one of the best guides to an understanding of the New Testament. . . . These pages teem with suggestions.'—*Methodist Recorder.*

The Teaching of Jesus. By Professor HANS HINRICH WENDT, D.D., Jena. Authorised Translation. Two Vols. 8vo. Nett $5.00

'An admirable translation of the greatest systematic study of the teachings of Jesus thus far produced in Germany.'—*Biblical World* (Chicago).

'No greater contribution to the study of biblical theology has been made in our time. A brilliant and satisfactory exposition of the teaching of Jesus.'—Prof. J. IVERACH, D.D., in the *Expositor.*

Dr. R. F. HORTON refers to Beyschlag's 'New Testament Theology' and Wendt's 'Teaching of Jesus' as 'two invaluable books.'

Old Testament Theology. The Religion of Revelation in its Pre-Christian Stage of Development. By Professor HERMANN SCHULTZ, D.D., Göttingen. Authorised English Translation by Professor J. A. PATERSON, D.D. Two Vols. 8vo. Second Edition. Nett $6.00

'A standard work on this subject may be said to be indispensable to every theologian and minister. The book to get, beyond all doubt, is this one by Schultz, which Messrs. Clark have just given to us in English. It is one of the most interesting and readable books we have had in our hands for a long time.'—Professor A. B. BRUCE, D.D.

The Truth of the Christian Religion. By Prof. KAFTAN, Berlin. Authorised Translation. With Prefatory Note by Professor FLINT, D.D. Two Vols. 8vo. Nett $5.00

'Quite apart from the immediate question of obtaining a knowledge of the Ritschlian theology at first hand, these volumes are welcome. For Kaftan is no imitator, but a fertile and able writer. In the near future his view of theology, its essence and its accidents, will exercise a deep influence in our land.'—*Expository Times.*

History of the Jewish People in the Time of Our Lord. By Prof. EMIL SCHÜRER, D.D., Göttingen. Complete in Five Vols., with exhaustive Index. 8vo. Nett $8.00

'This monumental work by Schürer has made all other histories almost superfluous. In no other account of the period is there to be found such wealth of learning and such admirable arrangement of material.'—*Biblical World* (Chicago).

'Recognised as the standard authority on the subject.'—*Critical Review.*

'Every English commentary has for some years contained references to "Schürer" as the great authority upon such matters. . . . There is no guide to these intricate and difficult times which even approaches him.'—*Record.*

The Ethics of the Old Testament. By W. S. BRUCE, D.D. Crown 8vo. Nett $1.25

'An excellent work. . . . I have found it most interesting and instructive. I hope that the book may have the success which it well deserves.'—Prof. R. FLINT, D.D., LL.D.

The Formation of Christian Character: A Contribution to Individual Christian Ethics. By W. S. BRUCE, D.D. Crown 8vo. Nett $1.50

'A book which combines with a scholarly grasp of the subject a popular gift of interpretation.'—*Examiner.*

'Altogether, this is a spiritually instructive, suggestive, and refreshing book. Ministers of the gospel will find the volume extremely helpful in the presentation of gospel truth in its ethical issues.'—*Interior.*

Lexicon Syriacum. Auctore CAROLO BROCKELMANN. Præfatus est TH. NÖLDEKE. In handsome Roxburghe binding. Nett **$10.50**

' The appearance of a new Syriac Lexicon, designed to meet the wants of students, is an event of considerable importance for the progress of Semitic studies at home and abroad. The work will be welcomed on all hands as fulfilling what has long been the most conspicuous *lacuna* in Semitic bibliography. . . . The publishers have earned, and will certainly receive, the thanks of every Semitic student for thus coming forward to remove what had almost become a scandal to international scholarship, the lack of a student's dictionary of a language so important to the philologist, the historian, and the theologian.'—A. R. S. KENNEDY, D.D. (Professor of Oriental Languages in the University of Edinburgh) in the *Expository Times*.

A Concordance to the Greek Testament. Edited by W. F. MOULTON, D.D. (Editor of the English Edition of *Winer's Grammar*), and Prof. A. S. GEDEN, M.A. In crown 4to (pp. 1040). Nett **$7.00**

It is generally allowed that such a work is much needed in the interests of sacred scholarship. There exists no concordance whatever to the text of the Greek Testament as exhibited in modern critical editions. . . . The present work is a full and complete concordance to the text of the Greek Testament as it is set forth in the editions of WESTCOTT AND HORT, TISCHENDORF (8th), and the English Revisers.

'A Concordance which must displace all others, and which will remain for many a year the trusted companion of the student of the New Testament.'—*Critical Review.*

'I have no hesitation in saying that this work is one of the most important contributions to New Testament study that has been made during the present century. The need of such a work has long been felt by critical students. . . . The typographical execution of the work is beautiful. It will be a boon to all New Testament students, and must supersede all similar works.'—MARVIN R. VINCENT, D.D., Professor of Biblical Literature, Union Theological Seminary, N.Y.

Biblico - Theological Lexicon of New Testament Greek. By Prof. HERMANN CREMER, D.D., Greifswald. Authorised Translation. Demy 4to. Fourth Edition. Nett **$8.00**

This Lexicon deals with words whose meaning in the Classics is modified or changed in Scripture, words which have become the bases and watchwords of Christian theology, tracing their history in their transference from the Classics into the LXX., and from the LXX. into the New Testament, and the gradual deepening and elevation of their meaning till they reach the fulness of New Testament thought.

'Dr. Cremer's work is highly and deservedly esteemed in Germany. It gives with care and thoroughness a complete history, as far as it goes, of each word and phrase that it deals with. . . . Dr. Cremer's explanations are most lucidly set out.'—*Guardian.*

'It is hardly possible to exaggerate the value of this work to the student of the Greek Testament. . . . The translation is accurate and idiomatic, and the additions to the later edition are considerable and important.'—*Church Bells.*

LOTZE'S MICROCOSMUS.

Microcosmus: Concerning Man and His Relation to the World. By HERMANN LOTZE. Translated from the German. In one large Vol. 8vo (1450 pp.). Nett **$5.00**

' The English public have now before them the greatest philosophic work produced in Germany by the generation just past. The translation comes at an opportune time, for the circumstances of English thought, just at the present moment, are peculiarly those with which Lotze attempted to deal when he wrote his "Microcosmus" a quarter of a century ago. . . . Few philosophic books of the century are so attractive both in style and matter.'—*Athenæum.*

' These are indeed two masterly volumes, vigorous in intellectual power, and translated with rare ability. . . . This work will doubtless find a place on the shelves of all the foremost thinkers and students of modern times.'—*Evangelical Magazine.*

Pseudepigrapha: An Account of certain Apocryphal Sacred Writings of the Jews and Early Christians. By Rev. W. J. DEANE, M.A. Post 8vo. Nett **$2.00**

' It is the most complete book on the subject in the English language, and contains the most ample information on these writings. It is indispensable to every scholar who wishes to be acquainted with this class of literature, and should occupy a place in the library of every theologian.'—PATON J. GLOAG, D.D.

Delivery and Development of Christian Doctrine. By Principal R. RAINY, D.D., New College, Edinburgh. 8vo.
Nett $3.00

'We gladly acknowledge the high excellence and the extensive learning which these lectures display. They are able to the last degree, and the author has, in an unusual measure, the power of acute and brilliant generalisation.'—*Literary Churchman.*

BY THE LATE PROF. A. B. DAVIDSON, D.D., LL.D., EDINBURGH.

*'Whatever subject Prof. Davidson touched, there are always two epithets which may be applied to his treatment of it: it is masterly and it is judicial. No one had a better power of penetrating to the heart of a subject, no one was more skilful in the discovery of characteristics of an age, the drift of an argument, the aim of a writer. . . . His mastery of a subject was almost complete.'—*CANON DRIVER.

An Introductory Hebrew Grammar, with Progressive Exercises in Reading and Writing. By the late Professor A. B. DAVIDSON, D.D., LL.D., New College, Edinburgh. Eighteenth Edition. 8vo. Nett $2.50

'A text-book which has gone into its tenth [now eighteenth] edition needs no recommendation here. . . . Certain changes, in the introduction of new examples and the enlargement of some parts where brevity tended to obscurity, will add to the already great merits and widely acknowledged usefulness of the book.'—*Critical Review.*
'The best Hebrew Grammar is that of Professor A. B. Davidson.'—*British Weekly.*

Hebrew Syntax. Third Edition. In demy 8vo. Nett $2.50

'The whole is, it is needless to say, the work of a master; but it is the work of a master who does not shoot over the learners' heads, one who by long experience knows exactly where help is most needed, and how to give it in the simplest and clearest fashion.'—*Methodist Recorder.*

Old Testament Prophecy. Edited by Prof. J. A. PATERSON, D.D. One large 8vo Volume. Nett $3.50

'This must long remain the standard work on Old Testament prophecy.'—Professor MARCUS DODS.

The Called of God. With Biographical Introduction by A. TAYLOR INNES, Esq., Advocate, and Portraits. Post 8vo.
Nett $2.00

'The biographical introduction is admirable. . . . The sermons have thoughts that startle with their depth, they have passages that thrill us with their suppressed emotion.'—*Aberdeen Free Press.*

Waiting upon God. Post 8vo. Nett $2.00

'All through the book we meet with flashes of true insight and almost startling examples of that deep experimental knowledge of the human heart at its worst and its best, which is so characteristic of Davidson's preaching. . . . A striking book.'—*Glasgow Herald.*

The Epistle to the Hebrews. (*Handbook Series.*) Crown 8vo. 75 cents

'For its size and price one of the very best theological handbooks with which I am acquainted—a close grappling with the thought of the Epistle by a singularly strong and candid mind.'—Professor SANDAY in the *Academy.*

The Exile and the Restoration. With Map and Plan. (*Bible Class Primer Series.*) Nett 20 cents

'A remarkable instance of Professor Davidson's gift of compressed lucid statement. . . . It may be safely said that nowhere within anything like the same narrow limits will one get so vivid a view of that period of Old Testament history.'—*Expository Times.*

The Christian Doctrine of Immortality. By Rev. S. D. F. SALMOND, D.D., Principal, and Professor of Systematic Theology, United Free Church College, Aberdeen. New and Cheaper Edition (the Fourth), Revised throughout and Re-set. Post 8vo. Nett $3.00

' It is doubtful whether any book so wide and comprehensive in its scope, so thoughtful and faithful in its statements, so suggestive and quickening in its influence, so valuable in the contribution it makes to our knowledge and our faith respecting the ultimate fact of Immortality.'—*Presbyterian and Reformed Review.*

' This is beyond all doubt the *one* book on the transcendent subject of which it treats. There is none like it — sound, frank, fearless, and yet modest in every page.'—*Methodist Times.*

Life after Death and the Future of the Kingdom of God. By Bishop L. N. DAHLE, Knight of St. Olaf. Authorised Translation from the Norse. 8vo. Nett $2.50

' A work of great ability. . . . He traverses the whole field with the utmost patience, thoroughness, learning, and candour, and, we venture to say, leaves no part of it without helpful illumination.'—Prof. J. ORR, D.D.

Forerunners of Dante: An Account of some of the more Important Visions of a Future Life from the Earliest Times. By MARCUS DODS, M.A., B.A. Crown 8vo. Nett $1.50

This work presents a series of typical visions of Heaven, Purgatory, and Hell, beginning with Babylonian and Egyptian examples and ending in the European literature of the age of Dante, and exhibiting the gradual development of the ideas of punishment and reward in a future state.

' The author has gathered the conceptions of the future life, shown in visions and legends from the earliest dawn of Babylonian and Egyptian literature and the classical period of Greece and Rome down to the invention of St. Patrick's Purgatory and the fiercely dramatic imaginings of Thurcill.'—*New York Churchman.*

Morality and Religion. By JAMES KIDD, D.D. 8vo. Nett $3.50

' We are not acquainted with any other book that has so clearly shown the vital unity between religion and morality. . . . A strong book by a strong man.'—*Methodist Times.*

' It is the work of a master of psychological analysis.'—*Record.*

The Hope of Israel: A Review of the Argument from Prophecy. By Rev. F. H. WOODS, B.D., Oxford. Crown 8vo. Nett $1.25

' It is obvious that the argument from Prophecy must require modification from time to time, as fresh light is continually thrown on exegesis by modern scholarship and criticism. The great advance which has been made in these last of late years has indeed so largely affected it, that in its old form it was already beginning to do more harm than good to the cause of Christian truth.'—*From the Preface.*

Truth and Reality, with special reference to Religion ; or, A Plea for the Special Unity of Life in all its Manifestations. By JOHN SMYTH, M.A., D.Phil. (Edin.). With Introductory Note by Professor R. FLINT, D.D. Crown 8vo. Nett $1.50

' Admirably adapted both as regards content and form—thought and style—to interest and profit not only all philosophical readers, but thoughtful and educated men in general.'—Professor FLINT in his *Introduction.*

The Sinlessness of Jesus. An Evidence for Christianity. By CARL ULLMANN, D.D. Crown 8vo. Nett $1.50

Dean FARRAR, in his *Life of Christ,* says : ' Ullmann has studied the sinlessness of Christ more profoundly, and written upon it more beautifully, than any other theologian.'

WORKS BY PROFESSOR F. GODET, D.D.

(Copyright, by arrangement with the Author.)

For devotional warmth and practical application, Godet is perhaps unsurpassed by any modern commentator amongst foreign Protestants.'—GUARDIAN.

Introduction to the New Testament. The Epistles of St. Paul. By Prof. F. GODET, D.D., Neuchâtel. 8vo (pp. 630).

(In course of publication. Not yet completed in the Original.)

Two Volumes of the English Translation are now ready, viz :—

I. THE EPISTLES OF ST. PAUL. 8vo,   Nett $3.50
II. THE GOSPEL COLLECTION, AND ST. MATTHEW'S GOSPEL. 8vo. Nett $2.25

'Anything that comes from Dr. Godet is sure to receive a cordial welcome, and our familiarity with his eloquent and luminous commentaries prepares us to appreciate very highly a work in which the venerable Swiss thus gathers up the harvest of a lifetime.'— *Critical Review.*

'In every particular it is fully abreast of the times. For the purposes of the hard-working preacher there is no book on St. Paul's Epistles quite equal to this. For the student, it must always lie in a place that his hand can reach. It is delightful reading.' —*Methodist Times.*

Commentary on St. Luke's Gospel. 2 Vols. 8vo. Nett $4.50

'Marked by clearness and good sense, it will be found to possess value and interest as one of the most recent and copious works specially designed to illustrate this Gospel.'—*Guardian.*

Commentary on St. John's Gospel. 3 Vols. 8vo. Nett $6.75

'This Gospel forms one of the battlefields of modern inquiry, and is itself so rich in spiritual truth that it is impossible to examine it too closely ; and we welcome this treatise from the pen of Dr. Godet. We have no more competent exegete, and this new volume shows all the learning and vivacity for which the author is distinguished.'— *Freeman.*

Commentary on St. Paul's Epistle to the Romans. Two Vols. 8vo.   Nett $4.50

'We prefer this commentary to any other we have seen on the subject.'—*British and Foreign Evangelical Review.*

Commentary on St. Paul's First Epistle to the Corinthians. Two Vols. 8vo.   Nett $4.50

'We do not know any better commentary to put into the hands of theological students.'—*Guardian.*

'A perfect masterpiece of theological toil and thought. . . . Scholarly, evangelical, exhaustive, and able.'—*Evangelical Review.*

Defence of the Christian Faith. Crown 8vo. New and Cheaper Edition.   Nett $1.25

'There is trenchant argument and resistless logic in these lectures ; but withal, there is cultured imagination and felicitous eloquence, which carry home the appeals to the heart as well as the head.'—*Sword and Trowel.*

Nature and the Bible : Lectures on the Mosaic History of Creation in its relation to Natural Science. By Dr. FR. H. REUSCH. Authorised Translation. Two Vols. 8vo. Nett $5.00

'Other champions much more competent and learned than myself might have been placed in the field ; I will only name one of the most recent, Dr. Reusch, author of " Nature and the Bible." '—W. E. GLADSTONE.

'We owe to Dr. Reusch, a Catholic theologian, one of the most valuable treatises on the relation of Religion and natural science that has appeared for many years.'— *Literary World.*

BY THE LATE PROFESSOR A. B. BRUCE, D.D.

The Kingdom of God; or, Christ's Teaching according to the Synoptical Gospels. By the late Professor A. B. Bruce, D.D., Glasgow. Sixth Edition. Post 8vo. Nett **$2.00**

'As satisfactory a treatment of the central teachings of Jesus as exists.'—*Biblical World* (Chicago).

'To Dr. Bruce belongs the honour of giving to English-speaking Christians the first really scientific treatment of this transcendent theme. . . . His book is the best monograph on the subject in existence.'—Rev. James Stalker, D.D., in the *British Weekly.*

The Epistle to the Hebrews: The First Apology for Christianity. An Exegetical Study. Second Edition. Post 8vo.
Nett **$2.00**

This book, the fruit of thirty years' study, is a companion volume to Professor Bruce's 'The Kingdom of God,' and 'St. Paul's Conception of Christianity.'

The Training of the Twelve; or, Exposition of Passages in the Gospels exhibiting the Twelve Disciples of Jesus under Discipline for the Apostleship. Fifth Edition. 8vo. Nett **$3.50**

'That minister who has not read "The Training of the Twelve" betrays an indifference to modern thought which is unpardonable.'—President Harper in the *Biblical World.*

'A volume which can never lose its charm either for the preacher or for the ordinary Christian reader.'—*London Quarterly Review.*

The Humiliation of Christ, in its Physical, Ethical, and Official Aspects. Fourth Edition. 8vo. Nett **$3.50**

'These lectures are able and deep-reaching to a degree not often found in the religious literature of the day; withal, they are fresh and suggestive. . . . The learning and the deep and sweet spirituality of this discussion will commend it to many faithful students of the truth as it is in Jesus.'—*Congregationalist.*

BY PROFESSOR JAMES STALKER, D.D.

The Life of Jesus Christ. New Edition, in larger type, and handsomely bound, crown 8vo. Nett **$1.25**

'Even with all our modern works on the exhaustless theme, from Neander to Farrar and Geikie, there is none which occupies the ground of Dr. Stalker's. . . . We question whether any one popular work so impressively and adequately represents Jesus to the mind. . . . It may be despised because it is small, but its light must shine.'—*Christian.*

The Life of St. Paul. Uniform with the 'Life of Christ' in size and price. Nett **$1.25**

'Even to those who know by heart the details of the great apostle's life, this glowing sketch will be a revelation. Written with a fine sympathy for the more tender and personal aspects of his theme, Dr. Stalker has portrayed the outer and the inner life of Paul with a mingled power and beauty which is as rare as it is needed in evangelical writing.'—*Christian.*

*** *Small type Editions of both Volumes in the* 'Bible Class Handbook Series,' *price 45 cents (nett) each.*—See page 35.

The Resurrection of the Dead. By the late Prof. W. Milligan, D.D. Second Edition, crown 8vo. Nett **$1.50**

'In the treatment of such passages as these, Dr. Milligan's thoughtfulness, judgment, and scholarship reach their highest expression. We can but lament that this is the last volume for which we shall be indebted to him.'—*Record.*

The Incarnate Saviour: A Life of Jesus Christ. By W. Robertson Nicoll, LL.D., Editor of 'The Expositor,' 'The British Weekly,' etc. *New and Cheaper Edition.* Crown 8vo. Nett **$1.00**

'It commands my warm sympathy and admiration. I rejoice in the circulation of such a book, which I trust will be the widest possible.'—Canon Liddon.

Messianic Prophecy: Its Origin, Historical Growth, and Relation to New Testament Fulfilment. By Dr. EDWARD RIEHM. New Edition. With an Introduction by the late Prof. A. B. DAVIDSON, D.D. Post 8vo. Nett $2.25

'No work of the same compass could be named that contains so much that is instructive on the nature of prophecy in general, and particularly on the branch of it specially treated in the book.'—Professor A. B. DAVIDSON, D.D.

The Right of Systematic Theology. By Professor B. B. WARFIELD, D.D., Princeton University. With an Introduction by Professor J. ORR, D.D. Crown 8vo. Nett 60 cents

'A powerful blow directed against the attempt to abolish doctrine and creeds and reduce Christianity to mere sentiment. The protest made in this strong essay is most timely. We join Dr. Orr and other Scottish divines in earnestly commending it to the notice of theological readers.'—*Methodist Times.*

Pre-Organic Evolution and the Biblical Idea of God: An Exposition and a Criticism. By Principal L. CHAPMAN, LL.D. Crown 8vo. Nett $1.75

'A volume which will take an important position among Theistic, not to say Christian apologetics, and which, in the present growth of scepticism, we may well be thankful for.'—*Literary Churchman.*

Darwinianism: Workmen and Work. By J. HUTCHISON STIRLING, F.R.C.S., and LL.D. Edinburgh. Post 8vo. Nett $3.00

'Undoubtedly the most trenchant criticism of Darwinianism that has yet appeared. . . . The book is a work of art.'—Professor M'KENDRICK in the *Critical Review.*

Philosophy and Theology, The First Edinburgh University Gifford Lectures. By J. HUTCHISON STIRLING, LL.D. Post 8vo. Nett $3.00

'This volume will make for itself many friends. There is a bracing, stimulating masterfulness about the lectures, which on a careful perusal of them will be found to lead to many rich veins of thought.'—Professor STEWART in the *Critical Review.*

What is Thought? or, the Problem of Philosophy by Way of a General Conclusion so far. By JAS. H. STIRLING, LL.D. Post 8vo. Nett $3.00

'A noble contribution to the philosophy of our time. British philosophy is permanently enriched by Dr. Stirling's remarkable and penetrating piece of work.'—*Critical Review.*

History of the Christian Philosophy of Religion, from the Reformation to Kant. By BERNHARD PÜNJER. Translated by Prof. W. HASTIE, D.D. With a Preface by Prof. FLINT, D.D., LL.D. 8vo. Nett $4.00

'The merits of Pünjer's history are not difficult to discover; on the contrary, they are of the kind which, as the French say, *sautent aux 'yeux.* The language is almost everywhere as plain and easy to apprehend as, considering the nature of the matter conveyed, it could be made. The style is simple, natural, and direct; the only sort of style appropriate to the subject. The amount of information imparted is most extensive, and strictly relevant. Nowhere else will a student get nearly so much knowledge as to what has been thought and written, within the area of Christendom, on the philosophy of religion. He must be an excessively learned man in that department who has nothing to learn from this book.'—*Extract from Preface by Prof. FLINT.*

Handbook of Church History: From the Reformation. By Prof. J. H. KURTZ, D.D. 8vo. Nett **$2.50**

'A work executed with great diligence and care, exhibiting an accurate collection of facts, and succinct though full account of the history and progress of the Church, both external and internal. . . . The work is distinguished for the moderation and charity of its expressions, and for a spirit which is truly Christian.'—*English Churchman.*

The First Epistle of Peter: With Introduction and Commentary. By Prof. R. JOHNSTONE, D.D., Edinburgh. 8vo. Nett **$1.50**

'Dr. Johnstone has done excellent service in publishing this work.'—*Record.*

'Full of thoughtfulness and spiritual power and suggestiveness, and likely to be a valuable book to all Christian teachers.'—*Literary World.*

BY THE LATE PATON J. GLOAG, D.D.

Introduction to the Synoptic Gospels. By the late PATON J. GLOAG, D.D., Edinburgh. 8vo. Nett **$2.25**

'A volume of sterling value; learned, clear, candid, cautious, thoroughly well-considered; it should be a welcome addition to the library of the biblical student.'—*London Quarterly Review.*

Introduction to the Catholic Epistles. 8vo. Nett **$3.50**

'Ought to be eagerly welcomed as a solid contribution to theological literature; it is a work of masterly strength and uncommon merit.'—*Evangelical Magazine.*

Exegetical Studies. Crown 8vo. Nett **$1.50**

'Dr. Gloag handles his subjects very ably, displaying everywhere accurate and extensive scholarship, and a fine appreciation of the lines of thought in those passages with which he deals.'—*Baptist.*

The Messianic Prophecies. Crown 8vo. Nett **$2.25**

'We regard Dr. Gloag's work as a valuable contribution to theological literature. We have not space to give the extended notice which its intrinsic excellence demands, and must content ourselves with cordially recommending it to our readers.'—*Spectator.*

Evening Thoughts. Being Notes of a Threefold Pastorate. Crown 8vo. Nett **$1.50**

'Able, vigorous, and logical, marked by deep and robust thought, and stimulating in the highest degree.'—*Aberdeen Journal.*

Commentary on St. Paul's Epistle to the Ephesians. By Rev. J. MACPHERSON, M.A. 8vo. Nett **$3.00**

'It is an advance, and a great one, on anything we yet possess. . . . The author goes to the root, and neglects nothing that usually comes under the eye of a careful student. . . . Besides all this, the book is a living book. One is conscious of the heart of a man in it, as well as the brains.'—*Methodist Times.*

Christian Dogmatics. By Rev. J. MACPHERSON, M.A., Author of 'Commentary on St. Paul's Epistle to the Ephesians,' etc. Post 8vo. Nett **$3.00**

'Works on systematic theology are so few that we gladly welcome a well-informed and well-written compendium like the present one. . . . The work deserves a wide circulation among readers of theology.'—*Methodist Times.*

BY DR. C. VON ORELLI, BASEL.

The Twelve Minor Prophets. 8vo.   Nett $2.25

'A very valuable and trustworthy compendium of the latest results of critical research, written in a sober and devout spirit.'—*Christian World.*

The Prophecies of Isaiah. 8vo.   Nett $2.25

'The characteristics of this admirable commentary are brevity, separation of the more grammatical from the more expository notes, and general orthodoxy combined with first-rate scholarship.'—*Record.*

The Prophecies of Jeremiah. 8vo.   Nett $2.25

'Will be found a most trustworthy aid to the study of a book that presents many difficult problems.'—*John Bull.*

The Old Testament Prophecy of the Consummation of God's Kingdom. Traced in its Historical Development. 8vo.   Nett $2.25

'Cannot fail to be regarded as a standard work upon the subject of Old Testament prophecy.'—*Sword and Trowel.*

The Apostolic and Post-Apostolic Times. By Prof. G. V. LECHLER, D.D. Third Edition, thoroughly Revised and Re-written. Two Vols. crown 8vo.   Nett $5.00

'It contains a vast amount of historical information, and is replete with judicious remarks. . . . By bringing under the notice of English readers a work so favourably thought of in Germany, the translator has conferred a benefit on Theology.'—*Athenæum.*

THE LATE PROFESSOR FRANZ DELITZSCH, D.D., LEIPZIG.

'Probably no commentator of the age brought so many gifts to the interpretation of the Bible as did Franz Delitzsch. . . . Walking hand in hand with such a guide through the garden of the Lord, one cannot only gather its ripened fruit, but also breathe the fragrance of its flowers and gaze upon their loveliness.—Professor J. F. M'CURDY, Toronto.

A New Commentary on Genesis. By the late Prof. FRANZ DELITZSCH, D.D., Leipzig. Specially Revised by the Author for the English Translation. Two Vols. 8vo.   Nett $4.50

'We congratulate Professor Delitzsch on this new edition. By it, not less than by his other commentaries, he has earned the gratitude of every lover of biblical science, and we shall be surprised if, in the future, many do not acknowledge that they have found in it a welcome help and guide.'—Professor S. R. DRIVER in the *Academy.*

The Prophecies of Isaiah. Translated from the Fourth and Last Edition. *The only Authorised Translation.* With Introduction by Prof. S. R. DRIVER, D.D. Two Vols. 8vo.   Nett $4.50

'Delitzsch's last gift to the Christian Church. . . . In our opinion, those who would enter into the meaning of that Spirit as He spake long ago by Isaiah, words of comfort and hope which have not lost their significance to-day, cannot find a better guide ; one more marked by learning, reverence, and insight, than Franz Delitzsch.'—*Expository Times.*

A System of Biblical Psychology. 8vo.   Nett $2.25

'Still the best book on the whole of the subject.'—Principal CAVE, D.D.

** *For other works by Professor Delitzsch, see 'The Foreign Theological Library,' p. 39.*

Franz Delitzsch : A Memorial Tribute. By Prof. S. I. CURTISS, D.D., Chicago. With a Portrait. Crown 8vo.   Nett $1.00

'A highly interesting little monograph on the personality of the great theologian, and on his work.'—*Spectator.*

BY THE LATE PROFESSOR W. HASTIE, D.D.

The Theology of the Reformed Church in its Fundamental Principles. By the late Professor W. HASTIE, D.D., Glasgow. Crown 8vo. Nett $1.50

'The work so long looked for is now published, and it is to be hoped that it will be widely and kindly received. No intelligent reader of it can fail to find in its pages much information, eloquently stated, regarding both the history and the characteristics of the reformed Theology.'—From Prefatory Note by Prof. R. FLINT, D.D.

'The logical cohesion of the Calvinistic system finds here an excellent expression by an advocate no less skilful than convinced.'—*New York Churchman.*

Outlines of Pastoral Theology for Young Ministers and Students. Crown 8vo. Nett 75 cents

'We have seldom read a book of loftier ideal or more practical value to parish priests than this volume.'—*New York Churchman.*

'How Professor Hastie discovered this book, and how he was drawn to it, how it had to be laid aside, and how it would not lie,—all this is told with thrilling simplicity in the Introduction. We do greatly need a small competent sympathetic guide to the work of the ministry. This is the book we need.'—*Expository Times.*

St. Paul's Conception of Christ; or, The Doctrine of the Second Adam. By Rev. DAVID SOMERVILLE, D.D., Edinburgh. 8vo. Nett $3.00

'The book gives evidence throughout of wide familiarity with recent literature, both exegetical and dogmatic, and manifests in many features a mastery of Pauline thought that makes it very welcome to students of the great apostle.'—*American Journal of Theology.*

Theologia Pectoris: Outlines of Religious Faith and Doctrine, founded on Intuition and Experience. By the Rev. J. M. HODGSON, M.A., D.Sc., D.D., Principal of the Theological Hall of the Congregational Churches of Scotland. In crown 8vo. Nett $1.25

A System of Biblical Theology. By the late W. LINDSAY ALEXANDER, D.D., LL.D. Two Vols. 8vo. Nett $6.00

'Oh that Scotland and Congregationalism had many worthies like Dr. Lindsay Alexander! . . . The ripe man, full of rich experience and heavenly knowledge, will prize each leaf, and give himself a glorious drilling as he masters chapter by chapter.'—Mr. SPURGEON in the *Sword and Trowel.*

The Ancient Faith in Modern Light.

A series of Essays by eminent Congregational and Baptist ministers on some theological questions much discussed in modern days. The subjects include such topics as 'Theism,' 'The Bible,' 'Sin,' 'The Incarnation,' 'The Atonement,' with practical questions such as 'The Church in Modern Society,' 'The Pulpit in relation to Literature,' etc. The Contributors include Dr. GUINNESS ROGERS, Dr. JOSEPH PARKER, Principals VAUGHAN PRYCE, CAVE, and TYMMS, Dr. NEWTH, Rev. W. BROCK, E. MEDLEY, and Dr. SAMUEL G. GREEN, who has edited the work. The object of the book is to vindicate the belief of the Churches in those important topics, and the harmony of that belief with a true philosophy, and its adaptation to the thought of the age. The Volume may therefore be regarded in some sense as a manifesto of modern liberal belief. Nett $3.50

From Apostle to Priest. A Study of Early Church Organisation. By JAMES W. FALCONER, M.A., B.D. In crown 8vo. Nett $1.50

'The story is told with the greatest clearness and convincing force. To any one who wishes a plain accurate account of the growth of the sacerdotal theory of the ministry we confidently recommend this work.'—*London Quarterly Review.*

How to Read the Prophets: Being the Prophecies arranged Chronologically in their Historical Setting, with Explanations, Maps, and Glossary. By BUCHANAN BLAKE, B.D.

PART I. **THE PRE-EXILIAN MINOR PROPHETS (with JOEL).** Second Edition.— PART II. **ISAIAH** (Chaps. i.–xxxix.). Second Edition.—PART III. **JEREMIAH.**— PART IV. **EZEKIEL.**—PART V. **ISAIAH** (Chaps. xl.–lxvi.) and **THE POST-EXILIAN PROPHETS.** (Complete in 5 Vols. crown 8vo.)   Each, Nett $1.00

'It has often been found a difficulty to profit fully from the reading, especially of the smaller prophecies of the Old Testament. To make these prophecies intelligible to the plainest reader, it seems desirable that a chronological arrangement of the prophetic books should be attempted. Alongside of the several prophecies should be placed those portions of the Old Testament historical books which deal with the same period. The aim of these manuals is consequently in this direction: to bring within the reach of the many a clear and succinct presentation of these prophets in their historical environment.'—From the AUTHOR'S INTRODUCTION.

'Mr. Blake seems to have hit upon the right thing, and he has proved himself competent to do it rightly. While these books are the very best introductions to the study of the prophets, even the accomplished scholar will find them indispensable.'— *Expository Times.*

Joseph and Moses the Founders of Israel: Being their Lives as read in the Light of the Oldest Prophetic Writings of the Bible. Crown 8vo.   Nett 1.25

'Mr. Blake hit upon a fresh idea when he wrote his books on "How to Read the Prophets." Nothing has made the prophets so accessible to the average man. He has hit upon a fresh idea again. . . . Have we come to the point as preachers when we desire to make a new start with the Old Testament? This book will enable us to make it.'—*Expository Times.*

'This instructive and always vivid exposition of the narrative.'—*Princeton Theological Review.*

The Voice from the Cross: A Series of Sermons on our Lord's Passion by Eminent Living Preachers of Germany, including Drs. Ahlfeld, Baur, Bayer, Couard, Faber, Frommel, Gerok, Hähnelt, Hansen, Kögel, Luthardt, Mühe, Müllensiefen, Nebe, Quandt, Schrader, Schröter, Stöcker, and Teichmüller. With Biographical Sketches and Portrait of Dr. Kögel. Crown 8vo.

Nett $1.50

'Is certain to be welcomed with devout gratitude by every Evangelical Christian.'— *Christian Leader.*

BY PRINCIPAL A. CAVE, D.D.

An Introduction to Theology: Its Principles, Its Branches, Its Results, and Its Literature. By ALFRED CAVE, D.D., Principal of Hackney College, London. New Edition just published, Revised and largely Re-written. The Bibliography brought up to date. 8vo.   Nett $3.50

'I have just seen your excellent "Introduction to Theology," and feel prompted to thank you for this excellent help to students. I have been lecturing on this subject for forty years, and long wished for some such substitute for Hagenbach (too German to be translated or even reproduced) which I could recommend to my students. . . . It is the best original work on the subject in the English language.'—PHILIP SCHAFF, D.D., LL.D.

The Scriptural Doctrine of Sacrifice and Atonement.
New Edition, Revised throughout. 8vo.   Nett $3.00

'Let readers judge—is this not now the best study of the Atonement in the English language?'—*Expository Times.*

The Bible Doctrine of Man; or, The Anthropology and Psychology of Scripture. By Professor J. LAIDLAW, D.D., Edinburgh. New Edition, Revised and Re-arranged. Post 8vo. Nett $2.25

'The standard work in English on the Anthropology and Psychology of the Bible. . . . A volume worthy of its subject, and likely to hold the first place in it for many days to come.'—*Expository Times.*

Kant, Lotze, and Ritschl. A Critical Examination. By LEONHARD STÄHLIN, Bayreuth. Translated by Principal SIMON, D.D. 8vo. Nett $3.00

'This learned work goes to the very root of the philosophical and metaphysical speculations of recent years.'—*Ecclesiastical Gazette.*

BY THE REV. J. B. HEARD, M.A.

Alexandrian and Carthaginian Theology Contrasted. (Hulsean Lectures.) Crown 8vo. Nett $1.75

'We can heartily recommend these lectures as pursuing a most interesting branch of inquiry in a thoroughly able, scholarly, and instructive way.'—*Scotsman.*

Old and New Theology: A Constructive Critique. Crown 8vo. Nett $1.75

'Progressive theologians, who desire to find "the old in the new, and the new in the old," will be deeply grateful to Mr. Heard for this courageous and able work.'—*Christian World.*

The Tripartite Nature of Man: Spirit, Soul, and Body. Fifth Edition. Crown 8vo. Nett $1.75

'An elaborate, ingenious, and very able book.'—*London Quarterly Review.*

WORKS BY ERNEST NAVILLE.

The Christ. By ERNEST NAVILLE, Corresponding Member of the Institute of France. Crown 8vo. Nett $1.25

'M. Naville is well known as an earnest, faithful, and eloquent defender of the Christian faith, master of a rich French style, and endowed with exquisite tact in adapting his apology to the thoughts and needs of his readers.'—*London Quarterly Review.*

Modern Physics: Studies Historical and Philosophical. Crown 8vo. Nett $1.25

'This work meets, with rare skill, some of the more subtle speculations of prominent writers in our midst.'—*Record.*

The Problem of Evil. Crown 8vo. Nett $1.25

'We give this book our warmest commendation. . . . The brilliant sparkle of the French original is as nearly preserved as could be expected in any version.'—*Literary Churchman.*

Kant's Principles of Politics, including His Essay on Perpetual Peace. A Contribution to Political Science. Edited and Translated by Professor HASTIE, D.D. Crown 8vo. Nett $1.00

Kant's Metaphysic of Ethics. Edited by Professor H. CALDERWOOD, LL.D. Crown 8vo. Fourth Edition. Nett $1.75

'This translation has been accepted by scholars as a real success.'—*Contemporary Review.*

BY PRINCIPAL D. W. SIMON, D.D.

Reconciliation by Incarnation: The Reconciliation of God and Man by the Incarnation of the Divine Word. By Principal D. W. SIMON, D.D., The United College, Bradford. 8vo.

Nett **$2.25**

'A treatise of great value, for its broad philosophical grasp, its subtle spiritual insight, and its apt illustrations. It is a fresh, timely, and independent study of a subject which must ever be to the fore.'—*Baptist Magazine.*

The Bible an Outgrowth of Theocratic Life. Crown 8vo.   Nett **$1.50**

'This book will well repay perusal. It contains a great deal of learning as well as ingenuity, and the style is clear.'—*Guardian.*

BY THE REV. JOHN HUTCHISON, D.D.

Our Lord's Signs in St. John's Gospel: Discussions, chiefly Exegetical and Doctrinal, on the Eight Miracles in the Fourth Gospel. 8vo.   Nett **$2.25**

'A learned, thoughtful, and delicate study of the Miracles of the Fourth Gospel.'—*Bookman.*

Lectures on Paul's Epistle to the Philippians. 8vo.

Nett **$2.25**

'This book has one great merit which separates it from the mass of commentaries and expository lectures—it is not only instructive, but it is also delightfully interesting. . . . The author's moral and spiritual tone is lofty, and these sermons are characterised by a sweet and sunny grace, which cannot but charm and make better those who read them.'—*Literary World.*

Lectures on Paul's Epistles to the Thessalonians. 8vo.   Nett **$3.00**

'The text is at once treated with scholarly ability, and turned to popular and practical account. Such is the character of Dr. Hutchison's work—his exegesis of crucial passages strikes us at once as eminently clear.'—*Baptist.*

Pastoral Theology of the New Testament. By Professor J. T. BECK, D.D., Tübingen. Authorised Translation. Crown 8vo.   Nett **$1.75**

'Thorough knowledge of the Scripture, rigid fidelity to its principles, robust common sense, perfect lucidity of statement and orderliness of arrangement, combined with profound reverence for Christ and fervent love for men, make this by a long way the best exposition of *The Teaching of the New Testament* on all questions relating to the pastoral office and work which we yet possess. . . . Whatever other books are used in our colleges, and studied by our ministers, we believe that Dr. Beck's "Pastoral Theology" will soon be universally regarded as indispensable.'—*Baptist Magazine.*

Outlines of Biblical Psychology. By Professor J. T. BECK, D.D. Crown 8vo.   Nett **$1.25**

'A useful, handy volume, which compresses into small space the results of scholarly and elaborate investigations.'—*Baptist Magazine.*

The Jewish and the Christian Messiah: A Study in the Earliest History of Christianity. By Professor V. H. STANTON, D.D., Cambridge. 8vo.   Nett **$3.00**

'Mr. Stanton's book answers a real want, and will be indispensable to students of the origin of Christianity.'—*Guardian.*

Biblical Essays; or, Exegetical Studies on the Books of Job and Jonah, Ezekiel's Prophecy of Gog and Magog, St. Peter's 'Spirits in Prison,' and the Key to the Apocalypse. By C. H. H. WRIGHT, D.D. Crown 8vo. Nett $1.50

' Solid scholarship, careful and sober criticism, and a style which is pure and lucid.' —*Church Bells.*

BY PROFESSOR C. E. LUTHARDT, D.D., LEIPZIG.

A History of Christian Ethics before the Reformation. Authorised Translation by Professor W. HASTIE, D.D. 8vo. Nett $2.25

' Charmingly written and adequately covers the ground. . . . The ablest and most thorough historical exposition of the subject of Christian Ethics that has been made accessible to English-speaking people.'—*Presbyterian and Reformed Review.*

The Truths of Christianity. Three Vols. Crown 8vo. Each, Nett $1.75

1. THE FUNDAMENTAL TRUTHS OF CHRISTIANITY. Seventh Edition.
2. THE SAVING TRUTHS OF CHRISTIANITY. Fifth Edition.
3. THE MORAL TRUTHS OF CHRISTIANITY. Fourth Edition.

' We do not know any volumes so suitable in these times for young men entering on life, or, let us say, even for the library of a pastor called to deal with such, than the three volumes of this series. We commend the whole of them with the utmost cordial satisfaction. They are altogether quite a specialty in our literature.'—*Weekly Review.*

Commentary on St. John's Gospel. Three Vols. 8vo. Nett $6.75

' Full to overflowing with a ripe theology and a critical science worthy of their great theme.'—*Irish Ecclesiastical Gazette.*

St. John the Author of the Fourth Gospel. Translated, and the Literature enlarged, by Dr. C. R. GREGORY, Leipzig. 8vo. Nett $2.25

' A work of thoroughness and value.'—*Guardian.*

The Church: Its Origin, Its History, and Its Present Position. By Professors LUTHARDT, KAHNIS, and BRÜCKNER. Crown 8vo. Nett $1.50

' A comprehensive review of this sort, done by able hands, is both instructive and suggestive.'—*Record.*

The Kingdom of God, Biblically and Historically considered. By Professor J. S. CANDLISH, D.D., Glasgow. 8vo. Nett $3.00

' Dr. Candlish treats his subject with an admirable combination of scholarly comprehensiveness, historical candour, and regard to the practical demands of mankind.'— *Christian World.*

' As to the ability of this volume there can be no question : it is worthy of the reputation and position of its author.'—*Evangelical Magazine.*

Central Truths and Side Issues. By R. G. BALFOUR, D.D., Edinburgh. Crown 8vo. Nett $1.25

' The book is well worth buying and keeping. The chapter on the Incarnation and Humiliation of the Son of God is admirable in every way—reasonable, liberal, and full of acute and forcible argument.'—*Review of the Churches.*

Ephesians, Philippians, Colossians. By the late Professor J. EADIE, D.D. Three Vols. 8vo. Per Vol. Nett $3.00

The World of Faith and the Everyday World. As displayed in the Footsteps of Abraham. By Pastor OTTO FUNCKE, Post 8vo. Nett $2.00

'A remarkable volume. . . . The plainness and freedom of his speech, the homeliness and force of his illustrations, the general directness and vigour of his method, are such as one does not often meet with. . . . To describe the author in short, we should say that he was a German Spurgeon.'—*Spectator.*

The Footsteps of Christ. Translated from the German A. of CASPERS. Crown 8vo. Nett $2.50

'There is much deeply experimental truth and precious spiritual love in Caspers' book. . . . I own myself much profited by his devout utterances.'—Rev. C. H. SPURGEON.

Gotthold's Emblems; or, Invisible Things understood by Things that are Made. By CHRISTIAN SCRIVER. Crown 8vo. Nett $1.50

'A peculiarly fascinating volume. It is rich in happy and beautiful thoughts, which grow on the root of genuine piety.'—*Witness.*

Sermons for the Christian Year: Advent-Trinity. By Professor ROTHE, Heidelberg. Crown 8vo. Nett $1.25

'The volume is rich in noble thoughts and wholesome lessons.'—*Watchman.*

BY REV. NEWMAN HALL, D.D.

Gethsemane; or, Leaves of Healing from the Garden of Grief. Second Edition. Crown 8vo. Nett $1.25

'A series of meditations, designed for the consolation of the afflicted. Written in the devout spirit and direct style to which we are accustomed in their author, they are admirably adapted to the object they have in view.'—*Critical Review.*

Divine Brotherhood in 'The Man Christ Jesus.' Third Edition. Crown 8vo. Nett $1.25

'This book will receive a cordial welcome from those—and their name is legion—who esteem and admire the venerable author. It is characterised by all his well-known excellences as a writer. It is altogether admirable.'—*Scotsman.*

The Lord's Prayer: A Practical Meditation. 8vo. Nett $1.50

Dr. THEODORE CUYLER writes: 'It is the very book to assist ministers of the gospel in the study of the Model Prayer; it is equally stimulating and quickening to private Christians in their quiet hours of meditation and devotion.'

The Spirit of Power as set forth in the Book of the Acts of the Apostles. By T. ADAMSON, D.D. Second Edition. Fcap. 8vo. Nett 40 cents

Principal MOULE writes: 'It will repay not only reading, but reading again and again. . . . A book of rare and solid value.'

The Gospel of a Risen Saviour. By R. M'CHEYNE EDGAR, D.D., ex-Moderator of the General Assembly, Irish Presbyterian Church. Post 8vo. Nett $2.25

Principal FAIRBAIRN writes:—'Let me thank you for a most instructive and stimulating book. I am struck with its careful workmanship and the way in which it has grouped its material round its central idea. I am sure every evangelical theologian must feel that you have made a most helpful contribution to a great subject.'

An Explanatory Commentary on Esther. With Four Appendices : the Second Targum translated from the Aramaic with Notes, Mithra, the Winged Bulls of Persepolis, and Zoroaster. By Professor P. CASSEL, D.D., Berlin. Authorised Translation. 8vo. Nett $2.25

'No one whose fortune it is to secure this commentary will rise from its study without a new and lively realisation of the life, trials, and triumphs of Esther and Mordecai.'— *Ecclesiastical Gazette.*

Handbook of Biblical Archæology. By Prof. C. F. KEIL, D.D. Two Vols. Authorised Translation. 8vo. Nett $4.50

'This work is the standard scientific treatise on Biblical Archæology. It is a very mine of learning.'—*John Bull.*

Manual of Historico - Critical Introduction to the Canonical Scriptures of the Old Testament. By Professor C. F. KEIL, D.D. Two Vols. 8vo. Nett $4.50

What Think Ye of the Gospels? A Handbook of Gospel Study. By Rev. J. J. HALCOMBE, M.A. 8vo. Nett $1.25

'The author has given the matter much earnest study, and his theory, which can only be thoroughly understood by studying his work, appears to have much in it worthy of commendation.'—*Christian Commonwealth.*

BY PROFESSOR H. EWALD.

Revelation: Its Nature and Record. By Professor H. EWALD, D.D. 8vo. Nett $2.25

'Ewald is one of the most suggestive and helpful writers of this century. This is certainly a noble book, and will be appreciated not less than his other and larger works. . . . There is a rich poetic glow in his writing which gives to it a singular charm.'— *Baptist Magazine.*

Old and New Testament Theology. 8vo. Nett $2.25

'Suggestive on every page, and therefore essential to every student of theology.'— *Record.*

Syntax of the Hebrew Language of the Old Testament. 8vo. Nett $2.25

'The work stands unique as regards a patient investigation of facts, written with a profound analysis of the laws of thought, of which language is the reflection.'—*British Quarterly Review.*

The Church in the Mirror of History: Studies on the Progress of Christianity. By KARL SELL, D.D., Ph.D., Darmstadt, Editor of 'Life and Letters of H.R.H. Princess Alice.' Translated by ELIZABETH STIRLING. Crown 8vo. Nett $1.00

'Eminently thoughtful and instructive lectures.'—*Glasgow Herald.*

Hymns and Thoughts on Religion. By NOVALIS. With a Biographical Sketch and Portrait. Translated and Edited by Professor HASTIE, D.D. Crown 8vo. Nett $1.25

'As a poet, Novalis is no less idealistic than as a philosopher. His poems are breathings of a high, devout soul.'—CARLYLE.

BY THE LATE REV. JAMES MACGREGOR, D.D.

(SOMETIME PROFESSOR OF SYSTEMATIC THEOLOGY, NEW COLLEGE, EDINBURGH.)

Studies in the History of New Testament Apologetics. 8vo.   Nett $2.25

'Dr. Macgregor is a man of vast knowledge and exceptional cleverness; deft in the use of his weapons and always wide awake. His present volume abounds in brilliant passages, clever hits, and decisive argument. . . . The book is lively reading, and carries conviction.'—*British Weekly.*

The Apology of the Christian Religion, Historically regarded with reference to Supernatural Revelation and Redemption. 8vo.   Nett $3.00

'Fresh and original, sustained and powerful, it is an apology of the noblest kind. . . . His book does indeed reach the magnificent claim which its title makes for it.'—*Expository Times.*

The Revelation and the Record: Essays on Matters of Previous Question in the Proof of Christianity. 8vo. Nett $2.25

'The book gives us the thoughts of a strong theologian, who has studied many questions deeply, and is able to hold his own with most opponents.'—*Critical Review.*

Those Three Volumes form Dr. Macgregor's 'Apologetic Series.' Independent works, they yet combine in representation of the view that proof of Christianity (the proof) is constituted by the whole historical appearance of this religion among mankind.

The Life and Writings of Alexander Vinet. By LAURA M. LANE. With Introduction by Dean FARRAR. Post 8vo.
Nett $2.00

'I may say without hesitation that readers will here find a deeply interesting account of a sincere and brilliant thinker. . . . The publication of this book will be a pure gain, if it calls the attention of fresh students to the writings of a theologian so independent as Vinet was, yet so supreme in his allegiance to the majesty of truth.'—Dean FARRAR.

The Work of the Holy Spirit in Man. By Pastor G. TOPHEL, Geneva. Crown 8vo.   Nett $1.00

'These pages are replete with clear, mellow, tender, beautiful, elevating thoughts, eminently instructive to inquiring minds, and such as the devout must delight contemplatively and prayerfully to linger upon.'—*Baptist Magazine.*

Mediæval Missions. By Professor T. SMITH, D.D., Edinburgh. Crown 8vo.   Nett $1.25

'This is a work which will well repay careful study.'—*Watchman.*

The Kingdom of God: A Plan of Study. By F. HERBERT STEAD, M.A. (*Bible-Class Primers.*) Three parts in One Vol.
Nett 50 cents

'It is a plan well worth a trial from every Bible-class teacher.'—*Expository Times.*

A Chronological and Geographical Introduction to the Life of Christ. By C. E. CASPARI. 8vo. $2.25

'The work is handy, and well suited for the use of the student.'—*Guardian.*

The Christian Doctrine of Sin. By Dr. JULIUS MÜLLER. Two Vols. 8vo.   Nett $4.50

The Form of the Christian Temple: Being a Treatise on the Constitution of the New Testament Church. By T. WITHEROW, D.D., LL.D. 8vo.   Nett $1.75

'A model of clear writing, and of satisfactory arrangement.'—*Record.*

Modern Pantheism. Essay on Religious Philosophy. Translated from the French of EMILE SAISSET. Two Vols. 8vo. Nett $4.00

Christmas Eve: A Dialogue on the Celebration of Christmas. By SCHLEIERMACHER. Translated by Professor HASTIE, D.D. Crown 8vo. Nett **75** cents

'A genuine Christmas book, an exquisite prose-poem.'—*Baptist Magazine.*

Studies in the Christian Evidences: Being Apologetics for the Times. By ALEX. MAIR, D.D. Third Edition. Revised and Enlarged. Crown 8vo. Nett $1.75

N.B.—For this book the American Tract Society awarded to the Author the George Wood Gold Medal and Premium, as '*the publication of that year best fitted to promote the glory of Christ as the Son of God and the Saviour of sinners.*'

The Lord's Supper: Its Origin, Nature, and Use. By Rev. J. P. LILLEY, M.A. Crown 8vo. Nett $1.50

'Mr. Lilley supplies us with an excellent and much-needed book. . . . Altogether the volume can be cordially recommended to all who seek clear and reasonable views on the Sacrament.'—Professor MARCUS DODS, D.D., in the *Expositor.*

Words to Young Christians: Addresses to Young Communicants. By G. E. TROUP, M.A. On antique laid paper. Handsomely bound. Crown 8vo. Nett $1.25

'These addresses have a most fascinating charm. Full of literary grace, spiritual insight, and moral elevation.'—*Review of the Churches.*

Homiletic: Lectures on Preaching. By Professor T. CHRISTLIEB, Bonn University, Author of 'Modern Doubt and Christian Belief.' Post 8vo. Nett $2.25

'A new manual of Homiletic was greatly needed. . . . Surely he is a foolish man, and a pithless preacher, who would despise the knowledge which such a master in the art of preaching could impart to him.'—*Expository Times.*

Scenes from the Life of Jesus. By Pastor E. LEHMANN. Crown 8vo. Nett $1.00

'There is in these lectures a tender sympathy, and a spiritual devoutness and simplicity, which gives to them a real charm.'—*Literary World.*

The World of Prayer; or, Prayer in relation to Personal Religion. By Bishop MONRAD. Crown 8vo. Nett $1.25

'One of the richest devotional books that we have read.'—*Prim. Meth. Magazine.*

So Great Salvation. By Rev. G. H. C. MACGREGOR, M.A., London. With Introduction by Principal MOULE. Neatly bound in cloth. Nett **40** cents

'The truth rings from the very first page, and its note is very clear and convincing.'—*Expository Times.*

The Doctrine of Divine Love; or, Outlines of the Moral Theology of the Evangelical Church. By ERNEST SARTORIUS, D.D., Senior Court Preacher at Königsberg. 8vo. Nett $2.25

'An exhaustive treatise, handled with the inevitable copiousness of a favourite subject.'—*Saturday Review.*

Principles of New Testament Quotation. By J. SCOTT, D.D. Crown 8vo. Second Edition.   Nett $1.25

'In terse and well-ordered style the author deals with a subject too little studied and less understood.'—*Record.*

The Free Church of Scotland: Her Origin, Founders, and Testimony. By PETER BAYNE, LL.D. New and Cheaper Edition.
Nett $1.25

'Among the books called forth by the great northern Jubilee, this is by far and away the first. . . . We have seldom read a book with such a glow, with such a lofty, moral, and spiritual fervour.'—*Review of the Churches.*

The Scripture Doctrine of the Church Historically and Exegetically Considered. By D. D. BANNERMAN, D.D. 8vo.
Nett $2.50

'Dr. Bannerman has executed his task with commendable impartiality and thoroughness. His learning is ample, his materials have been carefully sifted and clearly arranged, his reasoning is apt, lucid, and forcible, while he has none of the bitterness which so frequently mars controversial works of this class.'—*Baptist Magazine.*

The Text of Jeremiah; or, A Critical Investigation of the Greek and Hebrew, with the Variations in the LXX. retranslated into the Original and explained. By Prof. G. C. WORKMAN, M.A. With Introduction by Prof. F. DELITZSCH, D.D. Post 8vo. Nett $1.50

'The most painstaking and elaborate illustration of the application of his principles to this end that has yet been given to the world. . . . Scholars will hail it with gratitude, and peruse it with interest.'—*Guardian.*

The Doctrine of the Apocalypse. By Pastor H. GEBHARDT. 8vo.   Nett $2.25

The Doctrine of the Holy Spirit. By the late Prof. GEO. SMEATON, D.D., Edinburgh. 8vo. Second Edition. $3.00

'A valuable monograph. . . . The masterly exposition of doctrine given in these lectures has been augmented in value by the wise references to current needs and common misconceptions.'—*Brit. and For. Evangelical Review.*

System of the Christian Certainty. By Prof. F. H. R. FRANK, Erlangen. 8vo.   Nett $2.25

'No weightier or more valuable theological work has come to us from Germany since the publication of Dr. Dorner's "Christian Doctrine."'—*Literary World.*

Elements of Logic as a Science of Propositions. By E. E. C. JONES, Lecturer in Moral Sciences, Girton College, Cambridge; Joint-Translator and Editor of Lotze's *Microcosmus.* 8vo. Nett $2.00

'We must congratulate Girton College upon the forward movement of which the publication of this work is one of the first steps.'—*Cambridge Review.*

Encyclopædia of Theology. By Professor J. F. RÄBIGER, D.D. Two Vols. 8vo.   Nett $4.50

'Räbiger's Encyclopædia is a book deserving the attentive perusal of every divine. . . . It is at once instructive and suggestive.'—*Athenæum.*

Historical Theology: A Review of the Principal Doctrinal Discussions in the Christian Church since the Apostolic Age. By the late Principal WM. CUNNINGHAM, D.D., Edinburgh. Two Vols. 8vo. Second Edition.   Nett $3.50

The Servant of Jehovah. A Commentary upon Isaiah lii. 13– liii. 12. With Dissertations upon the Authorship of Isaiah xl.– lxvi., etc. By W. URWICK, M.A., Tutor in Hebrew, New College, London. 8vo. Nett $1.25

'A work of great and permanent value.'—*Weekly Review.*

Is Christ Infallible and the Bible True? (Giving the Teaching of Jesus on Holy Scripture, and other burning Questions in Theology and Religious Life.) By Rev. HUGH M'INTOSH, M.A., London. Post 8vo. Nett $3.00

'Such a title is calculated to arrest attention and awaken interest. Nor will any one who reads the book find his attention allowed to flag or his interest to wane, for the points discussed are in themselves most attractive and important, whilst the method of treatment is both vigorous and vivid.'—*Presbyterian.*

BISHOP MARTENSEN'S WORKS.

'The greatest Scandinavian, perhaps the greatest Lutheran, divine of our century.'—EXPOSITOR.

Christian Ethics. Three Vols. 8vo. Each nett $2.25
Volume I. GENERAL ETHICS.—II. INDIVIDUAL ETHICS.—III. SOCIAL ETHICS.

'Dr. Martensen's work on Christian Dogmatics reveals the strength of thought as well as the fine literary grace of its author. . . . His chief ethical writings comprise a system of Christian Ethics, general and special, in three volumes. Each of these volumes has great and singular excellence, and it might be generally felt that in them the author has surpassed his own work on "Christian Dogmatics."'—Principal CAIRNS.

Christian Dogmatics. One Vol. 8vo. Nett $2.25

'The famous "Dogmatics," the eloquent and varied pages of which contain intellectual food for the laity no less than for the clergy. . . . His "Christian Dogmatics" has exercised as wide an influence on Protestant thought as any volume of our century.' —*Expositor.*

Inspiration, and other Lectures. By the late President T. GEORGE ROOKE, B.A., Rawdon College. Edited by TWO OF HIS STUDENTS. One Vol. 8vo. Nett $2.25

'Intrinsically good. . . . The chapters on pastoral work glow with a whole-hearted devotion. The counsels given are excellent.'—*London Quarterly Review.*

The First Epistle of St. John: A Contribution to Biblical Theology. By Professor ERICH HAUPT. 8vo. Nett $2.25

The Atonement and Intercession of Christ. By the late Principal DAVID C. DAVIES, M.A., Trevecca. Edited by D. E. JENKINS, Portmadoc. Crown 8vo. Nett $1.25

'Can hardly fail to be helpful to all who wish to understand what the Bible teaches concerning the most profound and important of all subjects—that of the atonement.'— *American Journal of Theology.*
'It is an able defence and exposition of orthodox doctrine—substitution and propitiation. . . . Full of suggestion and edification.'—*Methodist Times.*

Our Father's Kingdom: Lectures on the Lord's Prayer. By C. B. ROSS, B.D., Lachine, Canada. Crown 8vo. Nett 75 cents

'This is the book to get for clear and simple presentation of the best modern expository work on this all-important section of the Gospels.'—*Expository Times.*

Works of John Calvin. Commentaries. Forty-Five Vols. Tracts on the Reformation. Three Vols. Per Vol. Nett $2.25

THE INSTITUTES. Translation. Two Vols.   Nett $4.50
THE INSTITUTES. Latin. Two Vols. Tholuck's Edition.   Nett $4.50

Beyond the Stars; or, Heaven, its Inhabitants, Occupations, and Life. By President T. Hamilton, D.D., Queen's College, Belfast. Crown 8vo. Fourth Edition.   Nett $1.25

'His writing is solid, he dissipates dreams, but he establishes authorised hopes. . . . This is a book which a believer will enjoy all the more when he draws nearer to those blessed fields "beyond the stars."'—Mr. Spurgeon in *Sword and Trowel.*

Growth of the Spirit of Christianity, to the Dawn of the Lutheran Era. By G. Matheson, D.D., Edinburgh. Two Vols. 8vo.   Nett $6.00

'Fresh, vigorous, learned, and eminently thoughtful.'—*Contemporary Review.*

A Popular Introduction to the History of Christian Doctrine. By Rev. T. G. Crippen. 8vo.   Nett $2.50

'A clear and intelligible account of the course of religions from the earliest times to our own.'—*Freeman.*

The Theology and Theologians of Scotland, chiefly of the 17th and 18th Centuries. By J. Walker, D.D. Crown 8vo.   Nett $1.00

A Critical and Exegetical Commentary on the Book of Psalms. By Prof. J. G. Murphy, LL.D. 8vo. Nett $3.00

The Exiles' Book of Consolation. (Deutero-Isaiah). By Professor Ed. König, D.D., University of Rostock. Crown 8vo.   Nett $1.25

'The appearance of this book is most opportune. . . . The views of Professor König upon the interesting questions he discusses are sure to receive the careful attention of scholars of every shade of critical opinion.'—*Expository Times.*

The Symbolic Parables of the Apocalypse. By Mrs. Stevenson. Crown 8vo.   Nett $1.25

AN IMPORTANT MAGAZINE.

THE EXPOSITORY TIMES.

Editor—Rev. JAMES HASTINGS, M.A., D.D.

THE purpose of *The Expository Times* is to record the results of the best study of the Bible in the present day, in an interesting and practically useful form ; and to stimulate and guide both ministers and laymen towards a fuller, more accurate, more fruitful study of the same inexhaustible precious library.

Published Monthly by T. & T. Clark, price 15 cents. Annual subscription (prepaid), post free, $1.50. *Mailed direct to subscribers from Edinburgh.* Bound Volumes, nett $2.50.

'This excellent journal. . . . There is no more readable magazine dealing with biblical topics.'—President Harper in the *Biblical World.*

'"The Expository Times" is probably the best publication in the English language to keep the student abreast of modern views in the exposition of Scripture.'—*Outlook* (N.Y.).

Send for free sample copy.   Subscriptions received by

CHARLES SCRIBNER'S SONS,
153, 155, and 157 Fifth Avenue, New York City,
SOLE AGENTS FOR THE UNITED STATES.

Handbooks for Bible Classes and Private Students.

Edited by Prof. Marcus Dods, D.D., and Alex. Whyte, D.D.

' I name especially the admirable Handbooks for Bible Classes issued by T. & T. Clark of Edinburgh. They are very cheap, and among them are some books unsurpassed in their kind.' Dr. W. Robertson Nicoll in the *British Weekly.*

' Sound, intelligible, and sometimes brilliantly written handbooks, packed with wisdom and knowledge.'—*Methodist Recorder.*

' These volumes are models of the *multum in parvo* style.'—*Literary World.*

The Prices detailed below are Nett.

COMMENTARIES—

Professor Marcus Dods, D.D. **Genesis.** $.60
Jas. Macgregor, D.D. **Exodus.** 2 Vols. Ea. .60
Principal Douglas, D.D. **Joshua.** .45
Judges. .45
Prof. J. G. Murphy, LL.D. **Chronicles.** .45
Rev. James Aitken, M.A. **Job.** .45
Professor Marcus Dods, D.D. **Haggai, Zechariah, Malachi.** .60
Principal Douglas, D.D. **Obadiah to Zephaniah.** .45

Principal T. M. Lindsay, D.D. **Mark.** $.75
Prin. T. M. Lindsay, D.D. **St. Luke.** 2 Vols.—Vol. I., $.60. Vol. II., .45
Geo. Reith, D.D. **St. John.** 2 Vols. Each .60
Prin. T. M. Lindsay, D.D. **Acts.** 2 Vols. Ea. .45
Principal Brown, D.D. **Romans.** .60
James Macgregor, D.D. **Galatians.** .45
Professor J. S. Candlish, D.D. **Ephesians.** .45
Professor A. B. Davidson, D.D. **Hebrews.** .75
J. P. Lilley, D.D. **The Pastoral Epistles.** .75

GENERAL SUBJECTS—

Prof. James Stalker, D.D.
The Life of Christ. $.45
The Life of St. Paul. .45
(*Large-type Editions, price* $1.50 *each, see p.* 17.)
Alexander Whyte, D.D.
The Shorter Catechism. .75
Professor J. S. Candlish, D.D.
The Christian Sacraments. .45
The Christian Doctrine of God. .45
The Work of the Holy Spirit. .45
The Biblical Doctrine of Sin. .45
Norman L. Walker, D.D.
Scottish Church History. .45
Rev. W. D. Thomson, M.A.
The Christian Miracles and the Conclusions of Science. .60
George Smith, LL.D., F.R.G.S., C.I.E.
History of Christian Missions. .75
Archibald Henderson, D.D.
Palestine: Its Historical Geography. .75
Prin. T. M. Lindsay, D.D. **The Reformation.** .60
Professor Binnie, D.D. **The Church.** .45
Professor T. B. Kilpatrick, D.D.
Butler's Three Sermons on Human Nature. .45
Rev. W. Scrymgeour, M.A.
Lessons on the Life of Christ. .75

Rev. John Macpherson, M.A.
The Sum of Saving Knowledge. $.45
The Confession of Faith. .60
Presbyterianism. .45
President Hamilton, D.D.
History of the Irish Presbyterian Church. .60
A. Taylor Innes, M.A., Advocate.
Church and State. .75
Rev. J. Feather.
The Last of the Prophets—John the Baptist. .60
Rev. W. Fairweather, M.A.
From the Exile to the Advent. .60
Professor J. Laidlaw, D.D.
Foundation Truths of Scripture as to Sin and Salvation. .45
Rev. L. A. Muirhead, B.D.
The Times of Christ. .60
J. P. Lilley, D.D.
The Principles of Protestantism. .75
Rev. J. Strachan.
Hebrew Ideals from the Story of the Patriarchs. 2 Vols. $.60 each; or bound together, $1
David M. Ross, D.D.
The Teaching of Jesus. .60

Edited by Principal Salmond, D.D. Each Nett 20 cents.

BIBLE CLASS PRIMERS.

' An admirable series of *Bible Class Primers.* . . . Each new number is a distinct addition to the cause of intelligent Christianity.'—*Biblical World* (Chicago).

' A most useful series. With such helps as these, to be an inefficient teacher is to be blameworthy.'—Rev. C. H. Spurgeon.

The Covenanters, by J. Beveridge, B.D.—**Eli, Samuel, and Saul,** by C. A. Salmond, D.D.—**Ezekiel,** by Harvie Jellie, B.D.—**Jeremiah,** by J. Robson, D.D.—**History of Egypt,** by Prof. R. G. Murison, B.D.—**The Minor Prophets,** by J. Adams, B.D.—**History of Babylonia and Assyria,** by Prof. Ross G. Murison, M.A.—**The Mosaic Tabernacle,** by J. Adams, B.D.—**The History of the English Bible,** by Burnett Thomson.—**The Exile and the Restoration,** by Prof. A. B. Davidson, LL.D.—**Geography of Palestine,** by S. R. Macphail, D.D.—**Our Lord's Illustrations,** by R. Resker.—**Elijah and Elisha,** by R. G. MacIntyre, B.D.—**The Miracles of our Lord,** by Prof. J. Laidlaw, D.D.—**Christian Conduct; Christian Character:** A Study in New Testament Morality, by T. B. Kilpatrick, D.D.—**The Free Church of Scotland,** by C. G. M'Crie, D.D.—**The Truth of Christianity,** by Prof. J. Iverach. D.D.—**The Making of Israel,** by C. A. Scott, B.D.—**The Sabbath,** by the Editor—**Our Christian Passover,** by C. A. Salmond, D.D. — **The Kingdom of God,** *Three Parts* (*or bound in one vol.,* 45 cents), by F. Herbert Stead, M.A.—**The Parables of our Lord,** by the Editor—**Life of St. John,** by Paton J. Gloag, D.D.—**The Story of Jerusalem,** by H. Callan, M.A.—**Life of Abraham,** by C. A. Scott, B.D.—**Historical Connection between the Old and New Testaments,** by Prof. J. Skinner, D.D.—**Life of Christ,** by the Editor—**The Shorter Catechism,** *Three Parts* (*or bound in one vol.,* 45 cents), by the Editor—**The Period of the Judges,** by Prof. J. Paterson, D.D.—**Outlines of Protestant Missions,** by J. Robson, D.D.—**The Apostle Peter,** by the Editor—**Outlines of Early Church History,** by H. W. Smith, D.D.—**David,** by P. Thomson, M.A.—**Moses,** by Princ. J. Iverach, D.D.—**Paul,** by P. J. Gloag, D.D.—**Solomon,** by R. Winterbotham, LL.D.—**Reformation,** by Prof. Witherow—**Kings of Israel,** by W. Walker, M.A.—**Kings of Judah,** by Prof. Given.—**Joshua and the Conquest,** by Prof. Croskery.

Extra Vols.—**Bible Words and Phrases,** by C. Michie, M.A. 40 cents.—**The Seven Churches of Asia,** by Deborah Alcock. 40 cents.

THE ANTE-NICENE CHRISTIAN LIBRARY.

The Ante-Nicene Christian Library. A Collection of all the
Works of the Fathers of the Christian Church prior to the Council
of Nicæa. Edited by the Rev. Professor ROBERTS, D.D., and
Principal JAMES DONALDSON, LL.D., St. Andrews. In Twenty-four
handsome 8vo Vols.   Per Vol. Nett $2.25

This Series has been received with marked approval by all sections of the Christian
Church in this country and in the United States, as supplying what has long been felt to
be a want, and also on account of the impartiality, learning, and care with which Editors
and Translators have executed a very difficult task.

The following Works are included in the Series :—

Apostolic Fathers, comprising Clement's Epistle to the Corinthians ; Polycarp to the
Ephesians ; Martyrdom of Polycarp ; Epistles of Barnabas ; Epistles of Ignatius (longer and
shorter, and also the Syriac Version) ; Martyrdom of Ignatius : Epistle to Diognetus ; Pastor
of Hermas ; Papias ; Spurious Epistles of Ignatius. One Volume. **Justin Martyr ;
Athenagoras.** One Volume. **Tatian ; Theophilus ; The Clementine
Recognitions.** One Volume. **Clement of Alexandria,** comprising Exhortation
to Heathen ; The Instructor ; and the Miscellanies. Two Volumes. **Hippolytus,**
Volume First ; Refutation of all Heresies, and Fragments from his Commentaries.
Irenæus, Volume First. **Irenæus** (completion) and **Hippolytus** (completion) ;
Fragments of Third Century. One Volume. **Tertullian against Marcion.**
One Volume. **Cyprian :** The Epistles and Treatises ; **Novatian : Minucius Felix.**
Two Volumes. **Origen :** De Principiis ; Letters ; Treatise against Celsus ; and Life of Origen.
Two Volumes. **Tertullian :** To the Martyrs ; Apology ; to the Nations, etc. Three
Volumes. **Methodius : Alexander of Lycopolis ; Peter of Alexandria
Anatolius ; Clement on Virginity ;** and Fragments. One Volume. **Apocry-
phal Gospels, Acts, and Revelations ;** comprising all the very curious Apocryphal
Writings of the first three Centuries. One Volume. **Clementine Homilies :
Apostolical Constitutions.** One Volume. **Arnobius.** One Volume. **Gregory
Thaumaturgus ; Dionysius ; Archelaus ; Syrian Fragments.** One Volume.
Lactantius ; together with the Testaments of the Twelve Patriarchs, and Fragments of
the Second and Third Centuries. Two Volumes. **Early Liturgies and Remaining
Fragments.** One Volume.

ST. AUGUSTINE'S WORKS.

The Works of Aurelius Augustine, Bishop of Hippo.
Edited by MARCUS DODS, D.D. In Fifteen Vols. 8vo.
Per Vol. Nett $2.25

The 'City of God.' Two Volumes.

Writings in connection with the
Donatist Controversy. One Volume.

The Anti-Pelagian Works. Three
Volumes.

Treatises against Faustus the
Manichæan. One Volume.

On the Trinity. One Volume.

Commentary on John. Two Volumes.

The Harmony of the Evangelists,
and the Sermon on the Mount.
One Volume.

'Letters.' Two Volumes.

On Christian Doctrine, Enchiridion,
on Catechising, and on Faith
and the Creed. One Volume.

'Confessions.' With Copious Notes by
Rev. J. G. PILKINGTON.

'For the reproduction of the "City of God" in an admirable English garb we are greatly
indebted to the well-directed enterprise and energy of Messrs. Clark, and to the accuracy and
scholarship of those who have undertaken the laborious task of translation.'—*Christian Observer.*

N.B.—A Selection of Twelve Volumes from either or both of those Series may be
had for $24 nett.

'The ablest grammatical exegete of the age.'—PHILIP SCHAFF, D.D.

MEYER'S COMMENTARY ON THE NEW TESTAMENT.

'Meyer has been long and well known to scholars as one of the very ablest of the German expositors of the New Testament. We are not sure whether we ought not to say that he is unrivalled as an interpreter of the grammatical and historical meaning of the sacred writers. The Publishers have now rendered another seasonable and important service to English students in producing this translation.'—GUARDIAN.

Critical and Exegetical Commentary on the New Testament. By Dr. H. A. W. MEYER. Authorised Translation edited by Professor W. P. DICKSON, D.D. In Twenty handsome 8vo Vols. Per Vol. Nett $2.25

ST. MATTHEW'S GOSPEL, Two Vols.; MARK AND LUKE, Two Vols.; ST. JOHN'S GOSPEL, Two Vols.; ACTS OF THE APOSTLES, Two Vols.; ROMANS, Two Vols.; CORINTHIANS, Two Vols.; GALATIANS, One Vol.; EPHESIANS AND PHILEMON, One Vol.; PHILIPPIANS AND COLOSSIANS, One Vol.; THESSALONIANS, One Vol.; TIMOTHY AND TITUS, One Vol.; HEBREWS, One Vol.; JAMES AND JOHN, One Vol.; PETER AND JUDE, One Vol.

BENGEL'S GNOMON.

'Stands out among the exegetical literature not only of the eighteenth century, but of all centuries, for its masterly terseness and precision, and for its combination of spiritual insight with the best scholarship of his time.'—Professor W. SANDAY, D.D., Oxford.

Gnomon of the New Testament. By JOHN ALBERT BENGEL. Translated into English. With Original Notes, Explanatory and Illustrative. Edited by Rev. A. R. FAUSSET, M.A. The Original Translation, Five large Vols. 8vo. Nett $9.00

STIER'S WORDS OF THE LORD JESUS.

The Words of the Lord Jesus. By Dr. RUDOLPH STIER. Eight Vols. 8vo. Nett $18.00

The Words of the Risen Saviour. 8vo. Nett $2.25

The Words of the Apostles. 8vo. Nett $2.25

'The whole work is a treasury of thoughtful exposition. Its measure of practical and spiritual application, with exegetical criticism, commends it to the use of those whose duty it is to preach as well as to understand the Gospel of Christ.'—*Guardian.*

BY F. W. KRUMMACHER, D.D.

The Suffering Saviour; or, Meditations on the Last Days of the Sufferings of Christ. Cr. 8vo. Eighth Edition. Nett $1.75

David, the King of Israel. A Portrait drawn from Bible History and the Book of Psalms. Cr. 8vo. Second Edition. Nett $1.75

LANGE'S LIFE OF CHRIST.

The Life of the Lord Jesus Christ: A Complete Critical Examination of the Origin, Contents, and Connection of the Gospels. By Prof. J. P. LANGE, D.D., of Bonn. Edited, with additional Notes, by MARCUS DODS, D.D. Four Vols. 8vo. Nett $9.00

'Stands in the front rank of lives of Christ; it first presents the life of Christ as given in the four Gospels together, and then as given by each Gospel separately from its peculiar standpoint.'—Principal A. CAVE, D.D.

SPECIAL OFFER.

TEN VOLUMES for TWENTY DOLLARS.

The Foreign Theological Library.

THIS Series comprises Authorised Translations of the principal Works of the leading Continental Theologians. It is believed that the publication of this 'Library' has had considerable influence upon the progress of theological science in Great Britain and America.

The BISHOP OF GLOUCESTER AND BRISTOL, with regard to Sacred Study, says: 'It may be of some little service to the reader if I mention the long and valuable series of Commentaries on, I believe, every book of the Old Testament, that will be found translated from the German in the comprehensive Foreign Theological Library of Messrs. Clark of Edinburgh. The same Library may be mentioned in reference to the New Testament.'

President W. R. HARPER, of Chicago University, writes: 'THE FOREIGN THEOLOGICAL LIBRARY has exercised a great influence upon the biblical studies in this country and in England. It has introduced to students of the Scriptures some of the best work of German theologians and critics. The forty-five years of publication, at the rate of four volumes yearly, is an achievement to look back upon with pride, and the belief of the Messrs. Clark, that "through the care with which books have been selected, the series has exercised a healthful influence upon the progress of theological science," is amply justified. It is gratifying to learn that they do not propose entirely to give up this special work of publishing such translations, but will discontinue the serial publication, issuing books irregularly, as occasion offers.'

The Series being now completed, Messrs. Clark are desirous of bringing it within the reach of every biblical student, and they have therefore decided to offer any TEN VOLUMES for TWENTY DOLLARS, or a larger number at the same ratio. The published price of each Volume (with one or two exceptions) is $2.25 nett.

A complete list of the Series (173 Vols. in all) will be found on the opposite page, but Messrs. Clark invite special attention to the Standard Works mentioned below :—

History of the Jewish People in the Time of Jesus Christ. By Prof. E. SCHÜRER, D.D., University of Göttingen. Complete in 5 Vols. 8vo. INDEX VOL. 75 cents nett (100 pp. 8vo).

'Recognised as the standard authority on the subject.'—*Critical Review.*
'Every English commentary has for some years contained references to "Schürer" as the great authority upon such matters. . . . There is no guide to these intricate and difficult times which even approaches him.'—*Record.*

Christian Dogmatics, 1 Vol.—**Christian Ethics,** 3 Vols. (GENERAL, INDIVIDUAL, SOCIAL). By H. MARTENSEN, D.D., Bishop of Seeland.

'The greatest Scandinavian, perhaps the greatest Lutheran, divine of our century. The famous "Dogmatics," of which eloquent and varied pages of which contain intellectual food for the laity no less than for the clergy. . . His "Christian Dogmatics" has exercised as wide an influence on Protestant thought as any volume of our century.'—*Expositor.*

Handbook of Biblical Archæology. By Prof. C. F. KEIL. 2 Vols.

'No mere dreary mass of details, but a very luminous, philosophical, and suggestive treatise. Many chapters are not simply invaluable to the student, but have also very direct homiletic usefulness.'—*Literary World.*

The Words of the Lord Jesus, 8 Vols. 8vo (or the 8 Vols. bound in 4). **—The Words of the Risen Saviour.—The Words of the Apostles.** By Dr. RUDOLPH STIER.

'The whole work is a treasury of thoughtful exposition.'—*Guardian.*

Professor Godet's Commentaries on St. Luke, 2 Vols.; **St. John,** 3 Vols. ; and **1st Corinthians,** 2 Vols.

'For devotional warmth and practical application, Godet is perhaps unsurpassed by any modern commentator among foreign Protestants.'—*Guardian.*

Professor Dorner's 'System of Christian Doctrine,' 4 Vols.; and **'Doctrine of the Person of Christ,'** 5 Vols.

Professor Weiss's 'Life of Christ,' 3 Vols.; and **'Biblical Theology,'** 2 Vols.

Clark's Foreign Theological Library.

Octavo, cloth, price $2.25 per Volume, nett. Any Ten Volumes for $20.00 nett.

Baumgarten—The History of the Church in the Apostolic Age. Three vols.
Bleek—Introduction to the New Testament. Two vols.
Cassel's Commentary on Esther. One vol.
Delitzsch—New Commentary on Genesis. Two vols.
—— Commentary on the Psalms. Three vols.
—— Commentary on the Proverbs of Solomon. Two vols.
—— Commentary on Song of Solomon and Ecclesiastes. One vol.
—— Commentary on the Prophecies of Isaiah. Two vols. (Only Translation of the *Fourth*
and *last* Edition.)
—— Commentary on Epistle to the Hebrews. Two vols.
—— A System of Biblical Psychology. One vol.
Dorner—A System of Christian Doctrine. Four vols.
—— History of the Development of the Doctrine of the Person of Christ. Five vols.
Ebrard—Commentary on the Epistles of St. John. One vol.
—— The Gospel History. One vol.
—— Apologetics. Three vols.
Ewald—Revelation: Its Nature and Record. One vol.
—— Old and New Testament Theology. One vol.
Frank's System of Christian Certainty. One vol.
Gebhardt—Doctrine of the Apocalypse. One vol.
Gerlach—The Pentateuch. One vol.
Godet—Commentary on St. Luke's Gospel. Two vols.
—— Commentary on St. John's Gospel. Three vols.
—— Commentary on the Epistle to the Romans. Two vols.
—— Commentary on First Corinthians. Two vols.
Goebel—On the Parables. One vol.
Hagenbach—History of the Reformation. Two vols.
—— History of Christian Doctrines. Three vols.
Harless—A System of Christian Ethics. One vol.
Haupt—Commentary on the First Epistle of St. John. One vol.
Hävernick—General Introduction to the Old Testament. One vol.
Hengstenberg—Christology of the Old Testament. Four vols.
—— Commentary on the Psalms. Three vols.
—— On the Book of Ecclesiastes. Etc. etc. One vol.
—— Commentary on the Gospel of St. John. Two vols.
—— Commentary on Ezekiel. One vol.
—— On the Genuineness of Daniel. One vol.
—— The Kingdom of God under the Old Covenant. Two vols.
Keil—Introduction to the Old Testament. Two vols.
—— Commentary on the Pentateuch. Three vols.
—— Commentary on Joshua, Judges, and Ruth. One vol.
—— Commentary on the Books of Samuel. One vol.
—— Commentary on the Books of Kings. One vol.
—— Commentary on the Books of Chronicles. One vol.
—— Commentary on Ezra, Nehemiah, and Esther. One vol.
—— Commentary on Jeremiah and Lamentations. Two vols.
—— Commentary on Ezekiel. Two vols.
—— Commentary on the Book of Daniel. One vol.
—— Commentary on the Minor Prophets. Two vols.
—— Biblical Archæology. Two vols.
Kurtz—History of the Old Covenant; or, Old Testament Dispensation. Three vols.
Luthardt—Commentary on the Gospel of St. John. Three vols.
—— History of Christian Ethics. One vol.
Martensen—Christian Dogmatics. One vol.
—— Christian Ethics. General—Social—Individual. Three vols.
Müller—The Christian Doctrine of Sin. Two vols.
Oehler—Biblical Theology of the Old Testament. Two vols.
Orelli—Prophecy regarding Consummation of God's Kingdom. One vol.
—— Commentary on Isaiah. One vol.
—— Commentary on Jeremiah. One vol.
—— The Twelve Minor Prophets. One vol.
Philippi—Commentary on Epistle to Romans. Two vols.
Räbiger—Encyclopædia of Theology. Two vols.
Sartorius—The Doctrine of Divine Love. One vol.
Schürer—The Jewish People in the Time of Christ. Five vols. and Index.
Steinmeyer—History of the Passion and Resurrection of our Lord. One vol.
Stier—The Words of the Lord Jesus. Eight vols.
—— The Words of the Risen Saviour, and Commentary on Epistle of St. James. One vol.
—— The Words of the Apostles Expounded. One vol.
Weiss—Biblical Theology of the New Testament. Two vols.
—— The Life of Christ. Three vols.

INDEX

Adams, Prof. J., Primer on Teaching . . . 6
Adamson, Rev. R. M., The Lord's Supper . . 2
Adamson, Dr. T., Spirit of Power . . . 28
Alexander, W. L., Biblical Theology . . . 21
Ancient Faith in Modern Light, The . . . 21
Ante-Nicene Christian Library . . . 36
Augustine, St., Works of . . . 36
Bain, J. A., M.A., New Reformation . . 2
Balfour, Dr. R. G., Central Truths . . 27
Ball, W. E., LL.D., St. Paul and Roman Law . 11
Ballard, Frank, The Miracles of Unbelief . . 5
Bannerman, Dr. D. D., Doctrine of the Church . 32
Barty, J. W., LL.D., Duty of Christian Churches . 2
Bayne, Dr. Peter, Free Church of Scotland . . 32
Beck, Prof., Works by . . . 26
Bengel's Gnomon . . . 37
Beveridge, W., The Westminster Assembly . . 10
Beyschlag, Prof. W., New Testament Theology . 12
Bible Class Handbooks . . . 35
Bible Class Primers . . . 35
Blake, Buchanan, Works by . . . 22
Brockelmann's Syriac Lexicon . . . 13
Bruce, Prof. A. B., Works by . . . 17
Bruce, Canon R., Apostolic Order . . . 10
Bruce, Dr. W. S., Works by . . . 12
Caldecott and Mackintosh, Profs., Theism . . 11
Calvin, John, Works of . . . 34
Candlish, Prof. J. S., Works by . . 8, 27, and 35
Caspari, C. E., Life of Christ . . . 30
Caspers, Footsteps of Christ . . . 28
Cave, Prof., Works by . . . 22
Chapman, Principal C., Pre-Organic Evolution . 18
Christlieb, Prof., Works by . . . 31 and 39
Clark, Prof. W., Pascal . . . 9
Concordance to the Greek Testament . . 13
Cooper-Maclean, The Testament of our Lord . 10
Crawford, J. H., Brotherhood of Man . . 21
Cremer's Greek Lexicon . . . 13
Crippen, T. G., Christian Doctrine . . . 34
Curtiss, Prof., Works by . . . 20
Dahle, Bishop, Life after Death . . . 15
Dalman, G., The Words of Jesus . . . 11
Davidson, Prof. A. B., Works by . . 14 and 35
Davies, Principal, Atonement . . . 33
Deane, W. J., Pseudepigrapha . . . 13
Deissman, Prof. A., Bible Studies . . . 5
Delitzsch, Prof. F., Works by . . 20 and 39
Deussen, Prof. P., Philosophy of the Upanishads . 2
Dictionary of the Bible . . . 4
Dods, Prof. Marcus, Works by . . . 35
Dods, Marcus, Forerunners of Dante . . 15
Döllinger, Ignaz von, Works by . . . 24
Dorner, Dr. I. A., Works by . . 23 and 39
Drummond, Dr. R. J., Apostolic Teaching . . 5
Duff, Prof. D., The Early Church . . . 24
Eadie, Prof. J., Commentaries . . . 27
Ebrard, Prof., Works by . . 23 and 39
Edgar, Dr. R. McC., A Risen Saviour . . 28
Ewald, Prof., Works by . . 29 and 39
Expository Times . . . 34
Fairweather, W., Works by . . 9 and 35
Falconer, J. W., Apostle to Priest . . 21
Ferries, Dr. George, Growth of Christian Faith . 2
Forbes, J. T., Socrates . . . 9
Foreign Theological Library . . 38 and 39
Forrest, Dr. D. W., Works by . . 2 and 6
Funcke, Pastor, World of Faith . . . 28
Garvie, Prof. A. E., The Ritschlian Theology . 8
Geere, H. V., Nile and Euphrates . . . 7
Gloag, Dr. Paton J., Works by . . . 19
Godet, Prof. F., Works by . . 16 and 39
Gotthold's Emblems . . . 28
Gwatkin, Prof., Works by . . 2 and 3
Halcombe, J. J., The Gospels . . . 29
Hall, Newman, Works by . . . 28
Hamilton, President, Beyond the Stars . . 34
Hastie, Prof. W., Works by . . 21, 25, 29, and 35
Hastings, Dr. James, Works by . . 4 and 34
Heard, J. B., Works by . . . 25
Hefele, Bishop, Church Councils . . . 24
Henderson, Dr. Arch., Palestine . . . 35
Henderson, H. F., Religious Controversies . 11
Herkless, Prof., Francis and Dominic . . 9
Hill, Dr. J. H., St. Ephraem . . . 6
Hodgson, G., Primitive Christian Education . 6
Hodgson, Principal, Theologia Pectoris . . 21
Holborn, Rev. A., The Pentateuch . . 11
Hudson, Prof., Rousseau . . . 9
Hutchison, Dr. J., Works by . . . 26
Inge, Dr. W. R., Faith and Knowledge . . 3
Innes, A. D., Cranmer . . . 9
Innes, A. T., Works by . . 8 and 35
Iverach, Princ. J., Works by . . 9 and 35
Johns, C. H. W., The Oldest Code of Laws . 11
Johnston, P. de L., Muhammad . . . 9
Jordan, Louis H., Comparative Religion . . 7
Kaftan, Prof., Truth of the Christian Religion . 12
Kant, Immanuel, Works by . . . 25
Keil, Prof., Biblical Archæology . . 29 and 39
Kennedy, Dr. J., The Note-Line . . . 10

Kidd, Dr. J., Morality and Religion . . 15
Kilpatrick, Prof. T. B., Christian Character . 5
König, Prof. Ed., Exiles' Book of Consolation . 34
Krummacher, Dr. F. W., Works by . . . 37
Laidlaw, Prof. J., Works by . . 25 and 35
Lambert, J. C., The Sacraments . . . 7
Lange, Prof. J. P., Life of Christ . . . 37
Lechler, Prof., Apostolic Times . . . 20
Lehmann, Pastor, Scenes from Life of Jesus . 31
Lidgett, Rev. J. S., The Fatherhood of God . 7
Lilley, Dr. J. P., Works by . . 31 and 35
Lillie, Arthur, Buddha . . . 9
Lindsay, Principal T. M., Works by . . 9 and 35
Lotze, Hermann, Microcosmus . . . 13
Luthardt, Prof., Works by . . 27 and 39
Macgregor, G. H. C., So Great Salvation . 39
Macgregor, Dr. Jas., Works by . . . 31
M'Hardy, Dr. G., Savonarola . . . 30
M'Intosh, Hugh, Is Christ Infallible? . . 9
Mackintosh, Prof. R., Hegel . . . 33
Macpherson, J., Works by . . . 19
Mair, Dr. A., Christian Evidences . . . 9
Martensen, Bishop, Works by . . 33 and 39
Matheson, Dr. G., Growth of the Spirit of Christ-
        tianity . . . 34
Meyer, Commentary on New Testament . . 37
Milligan, Dr. G., Theology of Epistle to the Hebrews 8
Milligan, Prof. W., Resurrection of the Dead . 17
Moffatt, Dr. J., The Historical New Testament . 6
Monrad, Bishop, World of Prayer . . . 31
Moulton-Geden, Concordance to Greek Testament 13
Moulton, Dr. J. H., Grammar of New Testament
        Greek . . . 5
Muirhead, Dr. L. A., Times of Christ . . 7 and 35
Müller, Prof., Doctrine of Sin . . 30 and 39
Naville, Ernest, Works by . . . 25
Nicoll, W. R., LL.D., The Incarnate Saviour . 17
Oehler, Prof., Theology of the Old Testament . 39
Oosterzee, Dr. J. J. van, Works by . . . 24
Orelli, Prof., Works by . . 20 and 39
Orr, Prof. J., David Hume . . . 9
Patrick, Principal W., James . . . 2
Plummer, Dr. A., Works by . . . 3
Profeit, W., The Creation of Matter . . 3
Pünjer, Prof., Philosophy of Religion . . 3
Purves, Dr. D., The Life Everlasting . . 18
Rabiger, Prof., Encyclopædia of Theology . 32 and 39
Rainy, Principal, D.D., Christian Doctrine . 14
Rashdall, Dr. Hastings, Christus in Ecclesia . 3
Reusch, Prof., Nature and the Bible . . 16
Riehm, Dr., Messianic Prophecy . . . 18
Ritchie, Prof. D. G., Plato . . . 9
Ritschl, Albrecht, Justification, etc. . . 5
Rooke, President, Inspiration, etc. . . 5
Ross, Rev. C. B., Our Father's Kingdom . 33
Ross, Dr. D. M., Teaching of Jesus . . 33
Rothe, Prof., Sermons for the Christian Year . 35
Saisset, Emile, Modern Pantheism . . 28
Sanday, Prof. W., Life of Christ . . . 31
Salmond, Principal, Works by . . 15 and 35
Sayce, Prof., Religion of Ancient Egyptians, etc. . 7
Schultz, Prof., Old Testament Theology . . 12
Schürer, Prof., New Testament Times . 12 and 39
Schwartzkopff, Dr. P., Christ's Prophecies . 39
Scott, Dr. J., New Testament Quotation . . 23
Shaw, Dr. R. D., Pauline Epistles . . . 6
Sime, James, Herschel . . . 9
Simon, Principal, Reconciliation by Incarnation . 26
Smeaton, O., The Medici . . . 9
Smith, Dr. G., History of Missions . . 35
Smith, Prof. T., Works by . . 9 and 30
Smyth, Dr. J., Truth and Reality . . . 15
Snell, F. J., Wesley and Methodism . . 9
Somerville, Dr. D., St. Paul's Conception of Christ 21
Stählin, L., Kant, Lotze, and Ritschl . . 25
Stalker, Prof. J., Works by . . 17 and 35
Stanton, Prof. V. H., The Messiah . . 26
Stead, F. H., The Kingdom of God . . . 30
Steinmeyer, Prof., Works by . . 23 and 39
Stier, Dr., Words of the Lord Jesus . . 37 and 39
Stirling, Dr. J. H., Works by . . . 18
Strachan, J., Hebrew Ideals . . . 6
Tophel, G., Work of the Holy Spirit . . 30
Troup, G. E., To Young Christians . . 31
Ullmann, Dr. C., The Sinlessness of Jesus . 15
Vinet, Life of . . . 30
Walker, J. Dawson, Gift of Tongues . . 2
Walker, Dr. J., Scottish Theology . . . 34
Walker, W. L., Works by . . . 34
Warfield, Prof., Right of Systematic Theology . 18
Weiss, Prof. B., Works by . . 23 and 39
Welch, A. C., Anselm . . . 9
Wendt, Prof. H. H., Works by . . 10 and 12
Whyte, Dr. Alex., Shorter Catechism . . 9
Witherow, Dr. T., Works by . . 30 and 35
Woods, F. H., The Hope of Israel . . . 15
Workman, Prof. G. C., Text of Jeremiah . 32
World's Epoch-Makers, The . . . 9
Wright, Dr. C. H., Biblical Essays . . 27
Zahn, Prof. Theodor, Sermons . . . 3

10 +

20 +